CRISIS

Diana Hastings lives in
and two daughters. She
published, including *The Macmillan Guide to Home Nursing*. In her married name, Diana Sale, she is presently employed by West Dorset Health Authority as Acting Chief Nursing Adviser and is also responsible for monitoring the quality of care that patients receive throughout the District. In this capacity she has also published several books for nurses including *Professional Development for Nurses*, *Quality Assurance for Ward Sisters*, to be published in 1989, and as a co-author *Nephrology for Nurses*. She is a registered nurse and nurse teacher, and has been in the nursing profession since 1963, during which time she has worked in many acute hospitals, in the community as a School Nurse, as a Ward Sister on the Dialysis Unit at Guy's Hospital and as a teacher in both basic and post-basic education.

Since 1986 she has been broadcasting regularly with Two Counties Radio, Bournemouth, as their 'Agony Aunt'. It was as a direct result of these broadcasts that this current book was written.

CRISIS POINT

A Survivor's Guide to Living

DIANA HASTINGS
RGN, RCNT

PAPERMAC

First published 1989 by
PAPERMAC
a division of Macmillan Publishers Limited
4 Little Essex Street London WC2R 3LF
and Basingstoke

Associated companies in Auckland, Delhi, Dublin, Gaborone,
Hamburg, Harare, Hong Kong, Johannesburg, Kuala Lumpur,
Lagos, Manzini, Melbourne, Mexico City, Nairobi, New York,
Singapore and Tokyo

British Library Cataloguing in Publication Data
Hastings, Diana
Crisis point.
1.Man.Personal problems.Solutions
I.Title
158'.1

ISBN 0-333-48267-0

Typeset by Wyvern Typesetting Ltd, Bristol
Printed in Hong Kong

To my husband Michael,
and my daughters
Jo and Caroline

Contents

Acknowledgements

I should like to thank all the support groups who introduced me to the people who, so willingly, contributed their experiences to this book. My special thanks to the listeners of 'The Night-Time Show' on Two Counties Radio, Bournemouth, who talked to me during this show and then wrote and told me how they had survived the crises in their lives, which have also been included in this book.

I would also like to thank Alison Simpson, a social worker, who helped with the Child Abuse section; Peter Allanson, from the Department of Health and Social Security, who advised on the Social Security information; my colleagues at West Dorset Health Authority, Mark Jukes, Valerie Myers and Shirley Large for their professional advice; and Ian Carruthers for his enthusiasm and support.

Finally I would like to thank my husband, family and friends Wendy Lees and Hilary Cox for their help and encouragement.

DIANA HASTINGS, RGN, RCNT

Introduction

A crisis is a turning-point. Life for any one of us can be rolling along quite happily and smoothly, then suddenly something happens that shatters and devastates. Margaret Hayworth and her family were the victims of a cruel and devastating crisis. Margaret remembers hearing the remark 'From that moment my life changed' but had not comprehended its meaning until the night a policeman came to the house to tell her that their sixteen-year-old daughter, who had gone out earlier in the evening so full of life, was dead. Life would never be the same again.

When a crisis occurs, you are usually either the victim of the disaster or someone who will be needed to support, comfort and help the people whose lives have been shattered. I have written this book to help people survive and cope with the crises that occur in life. It covers a whole range of catastrophes which may occur at any time during our lives, from fairly minor problems such as a mother whose child has temper tantrums to a serious problem like the sudden death of a loved one.

The book is a series of case-studies and interviews with people who have survived or are still coping with a particular crisis in their lives – how they managed, what help and advice they sought and were given, and what useful advice they would give to help someone else in a similar situation. Following each case-study I have explained some of the advice given in more detail and described alternative sources of help.

When you are faced with a crisis in your life you may well have neither the inclination, nor the time nor the knowledge to discover what resources are available to help you. It is possible, and quite normal, to be so preoccupied and worried that you are unable to think logically and therefore seek the appropriate help.

People who have lived through and survived a crisis may have taken several months or even longer to find effective support. The help that they require is probably already available, but they are unaware of its existence. Help may come in many forms, such as voluntary support groups and associations or even financial help. There is a bewildering amount of information and numerous groups of people only too willing to help, but where are they? Who are they? What can they do to help? To answer these questions I have included a directory of help at the back of the book to make access to assistance so much quicker and easier.

HOW TO USE THIS BOOK

The book is divided into twelve chapters, covering a series of topics which inevitably overlap so you will be referred to other chapters for information. The first half of the book follows the life-cycle from the cradle to the elderly, and many of the problems and crises encountered on the way. The second half of the book takes a look at problems associated with the mentally and physically handicapped of all ages, illnesses both physical and mental, addictions to alcohol and drugs, death and bereavement, working and planning for retirement, and finally the victims of crime and violence. Within the text there is plenty of information and advice about each crisis and suggestions on who to contact for help and support. To find the addresses of the organisations, voluntary and support groups who will help you, and for further information about the groups and financial support, you will be referred to the end of the book where each chapter has its own directory of help. All the information is correct and current at the time of writing.

Many of the people who contributed to this book felt that no one could really understand what they were going through unless they had experienced it for themselves. The people who organise the support groups are people who have survived a similar crisis; they really do know how it feels, and what helped them, and are therefore able to offer good sound practical advice. The experts and the professionals have their part to play, but perhaps they place more emphasis on different aspects of help compared to those people who have lived through the crisis.

I am indebted to, and would like to take this opportunity to thank, all the people who gave me their time, commitment and contributions to this book. They come from all walks of life and have brought with them positive approaches to a variety of crises. Many of them are listeners to The Night-Time Show on Two Counties Radio on which I regularly advise listeners who either write or phone in with their problems on just about any subject that you care to mention.

Some contributors come from the support groups and are people who already devote a great deal of time and energy to helping others through their organisations; while other contributors are friends and colleagues. Without exception their reason for wanting to be involved in this book has been the thought that their experiences, no matter how devastating, might help someone else in trouble. Some of the people in this book have used their real names, while others for a variety of reasons have preferred to remain anonymous or have invented a name for themselves. They are all survivors, and so their thoughts, ideas and solutions are invaluable.

If you are experiencing, or indeed supporting someone else through, any of the problems or crises in this book, I am sure that you will find help and comfort from the experiences of other people who have lived through similar difficult times and survived. Reading about how they coped with a problem may give you new ideas and courage to cope with problems. It is always encouraging to realise that you are not alone, that other people have very similar problems and that there is sound advice at hand. It is very easy to become so overwhelmed by a problem or crisis that you are no longer able to think clearly and logically. Reading about how someone else coped may be all you need to help you sort out a problem. If it worked for them, it may well work for you.

Without exception all the contributors felt that they needed someone to talk to, someone who would really listen. Some turned to the family doctor, others to a special friend or their clergyman. Many found strength in a religious belief, although prior to their life being turned upside down by the catastrophe they had been non-believers; while others preferred to talk to someone from outside the circle of family and friends. Whatever the crisis, it is very important to talk about the problem; bottling up sadness, anxiety, resentment, anger and fear will not help you to survive a crisis. Help is only a phone-call away, and many useful contact-numbers can be found in the directory of help at the end of the book.

I have written this book to help you to survive, or support someone else through, a crisis, no matter what your age or circumstances. By writing and researching this book my faith in human nature has been restored. In a world where we are led to believe that people are self-centred and no longer care for, or about, each other I have discovered that this is not necessarily true. People do care and help each other; it is just a question of finding the right people to help you.

It sounds as though this book will be very sad and depressing, but in a strange way it is the opposite: a positive book describing the lives of people who have survived. One of the contributors, Françoise, describes her crisis as a time when her life was like a dying candle-flame – the flame a tiny flicker, almost snuffed out. As she struggled to overcome her problems, over many months, the flame gradually became stronger. Now the candle burns brightly with a flame that is stronger than it was before the crisis. So many of the contributors felt that, although their lives were shattered and devastated, the experience had made them stronger and more able to cope with life.

The book starts at the beginning of the life-cycle, so Chapter 1 is about pregnancy and childbirth. Each chapter takes a further step through the various stages of life, taking into account some of the most common crises that are likely to occur and looking at ways of surviving each particular crisis.

CHAPTER ONE

Pregnancy, Childbirth and Sub-Fertility

Pregnancy for many women and their partners is a very happy experience, the start of a vitally important and exciting chapter in their lives. They are filled with feelings of great happiness and satisfaction and perhaps, quite naturally, a little anxiety about what will happen in the months to come.

Unfortunately this is not always the case, and for a variety of reasons pregnancy becomes a time of stress and unhappiness.

During your pregnancy you are entitled to certain grants and services which will benefit you and your baby, and you will find the details of these on page 283. To ensure that you have a normal pregnancy and a healthy baby, go and see your doctor as soon as you suspect that you are pregnant. Regular visits to the antenatal clinic are essential so that any potential complications are recognised early, treated and prevented. These visits will also give you an opportunity to ask questions and discuss anything that is worrying you.

You may be suffering from any one of the common problems of pregnancy such as morning sickness, indigestion and heartburn, or emotional problems such as depression. Perhaps you have developed varicose veins or piles, feel faint, have difficulty sleeping, or have developed more serious problems like high blood-pressure or toxaemia. It may be a social problem concerning your partner's attitude to the pregnancy, or perhaps you have a financial problem. Whatever is worrying you, talk it over with the doctors and the midwives, and they will be able to help you. Always be honest with them and tell them exactly how you are feeling.

MISCARRIAGE

Sometimes a pregnancy ends before the baby is able to survive on its own. So many women have written to me to ask for help and advice when they have had a miscarriage because they are overwhelmed by feelings of inadequacy, sorrow, anger and guilt. They are worried that they will not get pregnant again and are frightened that, if they do, they will never be able to carry the baby to full term.

Jenny Wallace wrote and told me how she coped:

> I lost our first baby when I was ten weeks pregnant. I just couldn't believe that it was happening to me: I felt so well and had been so careful about everything. It had never occurred to me that I would lose the baby. It started suddenly; I had this pain, and as I was bleeding we called the doctor and he told me to go to bed at once and that he would come round later. By the time he arrived I had lost the baby. He said that there was nothing that he could have done and it was probably for the best as nature had a way of knowing when things weren't quite right. I just couldn't stop crying and I kept trying to think what I had done to cause it.
>
> My husband and family were wonderful, but it didn't seem to help because I felt that they couldn't know what I was going through. People kept saying things like 'You need to try again', but I was frightened it would happen again and perhaps there would be something wrong with the next one. I needed to talk to someone who really understood. In the end the doctor gave me the phone number of the Miscarriage Association. I phoned them and spoke to a woman who had been through the same thing. It was wonderful; she really understood, and she was able to give me the courage to try again, which we did, and now we have a baby boy.
>
> JENNY WALLACE

After a miscarriage there are sometimes feelings of guilt, just as Jenny described, and you may wonder if either you or your partner did something wrong such as too much activity, too much sex, not enough food or the wrong food. So it is important to understand what does cause a miscarriage and not to jump to conclusions.

Miscarriage is much more common than you would think; about one in every five pregnancies ends in miscarriage, and most commonly within the first three months. There are many possible causes of miscarriage, but it may help to know that the most frequent cause of miscarriage is an abnormality of the developing foetus. This does not mean that there is anything wrong with either parent; it is just that the cells failed to start the proper growth into a baby.

Miscarriages that occur when the pregnancy is at the stage when the placenta (afterbirth) is developing and is taking over some of the hormone production from the mother's ovaries may be due to a hormonal upset. The growing foetus is unable to maintain its placental attachment (the afterbirth) to the wall of the uterus (womb) owing to the hormonal problem.

Miscarriage becomes less common in the second three months of the pregnancy. A rare cause of late miscarriage is a weak (incompetent) cervix which dilates too early, expelling the foetus. This problem can be treated by an operation placing a stitch (Shirodkar suture) around the cervix to keep it closed. It is removed when the baby is ready to be born.

There are many myths and superstitions surrounding miscarriages. One is that a woman is more likely to have a miscarriage during the time of the missed period each month. This is not true. Another is that the mother will miscarry if she gets a sudden fright, is emotionally upset, too active, takes purgatives or quinine; but if you are healthy and your growing baby is normal there is little that will disturb your pregnancy. However, if you are prone to miscarry, then the above factors might precipitate a miscarriage.

Miscarriages occur at a time when you and the father are thrilled and excited about your pregnancy and happily making plans for the expected baby. Suddenly there is no baby, and you need to share this emotional crisis. Talk to each other honestly about how you feel; cry if you want to; if you feel angry, say so; seek help and support from family, friends and your doctor. The chances of you becoming pregnant are just the same as they were before you miscarried, and so are your chances of carrying a baby to term and producing a healthy baby. If you have any doubts about this, talk it over with your family doctor. The best thing you can do is to try again. After a miscarriage you can usually resume sexual relations in four to six weeks.

Make an appointment for you and your partner to see the doctor and:

- Try to find out why you miscarried. Ask your doctor to explain any terminology that you do not understand.
- Ask to see the results of any tests that were carried out, then ask the doctor to explain the results.
- Ask if there are any other tests that could be done.
- Discuss the plans for your next pregnancy, what you should and should not do.
- Find out what signs and symptoms might indicate problems.

Sometimes people need more help and may well benefit from talking to other people who have experienced the same loss; for names and addresses of these organisations, see page 288.

UNWANTED PREGNANCY – ABORTION

Most women experience a mixture of very strong feelings when they find out that they are pregnant, particularly if the pregnancy is unwanted. I talked to Jane Read about the time that she found herself pregnant, single and living in London.

I became pregnant during my first year of training as a student nurse. You would think that a nurse would have more sense than to get caught out. It was stupid really. I just didn't think it would happen to me. I didn't know what to do; I couldn't tell my mum and dad, because I don't know what they would have done. I had only been in London a few months and I wasn't sure how my new friends would take it. I told the man that I had been going with, and he just said I should have been more careful, and hadn't I heard of the Pill. He said I would have to sort myself out, and I never saw him again. I was angry with him for treating me like a piece of dirt and even more angry at myself for being so stupid.

The worst thing was feeling so alone. I used to cry a lot. I couldn't concentrate on my work and I couldn't see any future. I had mucked everything up: my life and my career. I would have to give up my training as I was sure they would sack me. I couldn't go home pregnant and I couldn't afford an abortion.

Looking back on it, I just wasn't thinking straight and I don't know what would have happened if a friend hadn't found me crying and made me tell her what was wrong. She said she would go with me to the doctor and get things sorted out. That evening we went to the surgery, and when I started to talk to the doctor I just seemed to let everything spill out and I cried all over the poor man. He was very understanding and talked to me about what could be done. He told me to go home and think about the alternatives: i.e., having an abortion, or having the baby and then having it adopted or keeping it.

I knew in my heart that I would have to have an abortion, but it was only then that I really thought about the baby I was carrying. That night my friend and I talked it over until the early hours of the morning and the next day we went back to the doctor and I told him that I had decided to have an abortion. He then sent me to see another doctor who was a psychiatrist. I had to wait for two days for the appointment, which seemed like months rather than days. I was scared that he would not agree to the abortion, but he did.

The abortion was arranged for two weeks later at the hospital. By this time I was already nine weeks pregnant and I was being sick in the mornings, and somehow I felt very pregnant and very guilty about what I was planning to do to this poor little baby. The day arrived, and my friend went with me to the hospital. We waited with other women who, I am sure, were there for the same reason. It all seemed so unreal, like a nightmare. I had been told not to have anything to eat or drink, so I was feeling very light-headed and sick. When it was my turn I had a bath, put on a white gown, and was asked to lie on a trolley. I remember thinking that there was no going back now and I would never get myself into a mess like this again. I felt hatred and loathing for the man who had left me to cope with this on my own.

The operation was performed under a general anaesthetic, so I don't remember anything else until I was woken up by a nurse who told me that it was all over. My friend took me home about an hour or so later. I had quite a lot of pain and some bleeding for a few days. In about a week I felt quite well again, but the feelings of sadness and guilt about what I had done to my baby were with me for a long time. I would suddenly burst into tears for no apparent reason. Sometimes I couldn't sleep at night and I would lie awake wondering what my baby would have been like. Had I done the right thing? Would I be punished by not being able to have children when I wanted them? Most of all, I worried about all the lies I had told my parents so that they would never find out.

The thing that really helped me was having someone to talk to. Someone who knew the whole truth and had supported me through the whole business and who was never shocked or made any judgements about what I had done.

JANE READ

Jane came through what was obviously a very difficult time and was helped enormously by the support of a good friend. If you think you are pregnant and you are considering terminating the pregnancy, then you must seek advice quickly. The earlier an abortion is performed, the safer it is.

What to do:

■ If you have used a pregnancy testing kit and the result is positive, go and see your doctor and get the test checked. If you feel that you can't talk to your own doctor, you could contact one of the pregnancy advisory services listed on page 288. The doctor will examine you and

probably send off a urine sample to make certain that you really are
pregnant.
■ Once the pregnancy has been confirmed you need to discuss with the
doctor or the counsellor what you will do about the pregnancy.

The options:

■ To terminate the pregnancy by having a legal abortion.
■ To go through with the pregnancy and have the baby adopted.
■ To go through with the pregnancy and keep the baby.

Ask all the questions you want about the three options. Discuss any
personal and family problems that may influence your decision. What
about the financial implications of keeping the baby – is there any help
available? See page 283. Be prepared to answer some personal questions
about your own feelings or about the man who made you pregnant and
his feelings. Of course, he may be there with you during these discussions. Make sure that you understand what choosing to have an
abortion really means, what will happen, how it will feel, any possible
complications.

If in the end you decide to have a legal abortion, an appointment will
be made in the next couple of days for you to see another doctor, either a
gynaecologist or a psychiatrist. In order to have a legal abortion in the
United Kingdom you have to have seen two doctors who agree to
support your grounds for an abortion.

Once you have been seen by the second doctor the abortion is
arranged, and the waiting-time is usually about one to three weeks.
Before you have the abortion make sure that you have found someone
you trust and can depend on to be with you and help you both during
and after the abortion. It is particularly important after the abortion to
have someone who you can trust to talk to and who will give you much
needed moral support. It will speed your full recovery both emotionally
and physically.

What to do after an abortion:

■ Rest for the remainder of the day.
■ For the next three days avoid any strenuous physical activity.
■ Report to your doctor: vomiting, raised temperature, excessive
  bleeding, a vaginal discharge that smells offensive or severe abdominal
  pain.
■ The blood-flow may increase a little on the third day after the

abortion, with cramps similar to those experienced during a period. If this continues, contact your doctor.

■ Use sanitary towels or pads, and not tampons, for two to three weeks.
■ No douching for two to three weeks.
■ Resume sexual intercourse in two to three weeks. Make sure that you use some form of contraception.
■ Visit your doctor for a check-up within the first week following the abortion.

If you had an abortion within the first twelve weeks of the pregnancy, you will probably be feeling physically fit again in a week; the psychological effects last longer – from three to four weeks, and for some people several months. If you feel that there is no one that you can talk to, contact one of the voluntary services listed on page 288 and talk to someone who wants to listen to what you have to say and to help you if they can.

Jane decided not to have her baby, but many unmarried women become pregnant, keep the baby and manage to bring the child and subsequent children up on their own. Today many women decide that they would like to have a child but have no intention of marrying the father; this is obviously a planned and conscious decision. Other women become pregnant but the man in their life has no intention of sharing parenthood, and they are left on their own to manage.

I was in love with Roger; we had been living together for three years. I wanted our child and I was sure that he would marry me if I became pregnant. So, without telling him, I stopped taking the Pill and became pregnant three months later. I told Roger that I was expecting his baby. I really don't know what sort of response I was expecting, probably that he would be shocked but pleased. He was very cold, physically pushed me away and told me to get rid of it.

I couldn't do that to my baby. Our child was alive. How could he want to kill something that was part of us? He told me that, if I kept the child, he would get out of my life and take no responsibility for it or me. If I got rid of it, then things would be the same as they had always been, just the two of us. We would get married and have children later, but he was not ready for marriage and a family.

I didn't have an abortion, and he left me. I went through the whole pregnancy on my own. There was no one to help me; I had no one to turn to. I gave birth to a very beautiful little boy and I wrote to Roger and told him. I suppose I still hoped that he would want to see his child and, when he did, that he would change his mind and stay with us. He didn't even reply to the letter.

I stayed in hospital for five days. The other mothers were very kind to me, but I felt so terribly alone. Visiting-time was the worst part of my stay in hospital. Proud fathers and grandparents visiting, bringing with them flowers and presents, and I had no one.

When I went back to the flat I found it very difficult at first. But I loved my baby so much that we managed to struggle through. I was still very tired and found that caring for the two of us was difficult, but we managed. I had given up my job, so there was very little money and times were hard. The only money I had was from the maternity allowance and Social Security. The health visitor visited me regularly and became a very good friend. She put me in touch with a group called Gingerbread.

With their help I have managed to build a life for myself and my baby. My advice to anyone who find themselves in a position like this is to contact Gingerbread when you know that you are pregnant and are on your own. They will be your family.

PAT CORBETT

Deciding to go ahead with a pregnancy on your own is something that has to be very carefully thought about. You need sound advice from which you can make the right decisions. If you think that you are pregnant, contact the Pregnancy Advisory Service or a Brook Advisory Centre and talk to someone about your problems, let them help you through your pregnancy and take advice on how to manage after the baby is born. See page 288 for the addresses and more information. In Chapters 4 and 11 there is more about single parents, their problems and help that is available.

GIVING BIRTH THE WAY YOU WANT

Giving birth to your baby the way you want is very important to all prospective mothers and fathers. These days there is a great deal of choice, and many maternity hospitals are using a birth-plan which has been designed to give women more control over labour. In the birth-plan mothers are asked questions about how they would like to give birth, such as squatting, kneeling, in a birthing-chair, in a bath, on a bed. Would she prefer pain-killing drugs, foetal monitoring, an epidural and all the other options that go with this type of birth, or would she prefer a natural birth? The idea is that a written plan will be available and the mother's wishes fully understood when she goes into labour.

When this plan is used well, the midwife will have spent plenty of time explaining all the options to the mother and made clear that the plan can be changed if she changes her mind during the course of her pregnancy, leaving her feeling reassured and happy that she has been involved in the planning of the birth of her child.

Sometimes these birth-plans do not work out so well. One mother told me that she had been handed this list and asked to complete it on her first visit to the hospital. She couldn't understand some of it and was frightened by the idea of having to make decisions about things of which she had no knowledge and which would affect the birth of her child. She left the hospital, went back to her family doctor and asked him to refer her to another hospital, which he did. See also page 351 on how to change your doctor.

Mothers and fathers have strong views not only about how the baby should be born but also about whether to have the baby at home or in hospital. This was the experience of Robert and Susan Ives:

> Our first baby was born in hospital. I had a normal pregnancy and an uneventful delivery. My husband was with me all the time; in fact everything went very well. After the baby was born I was allowed to hold him for a few minutes and he was whisked away so I could rest. During the antenatal classes I had been told that the baby would be left with me to have a cuddle and to put him to the breast. Looking back, I suppose that we should have made a fuss, but we didn't. I saw my baby again several hours later. Although the cots were beside our beds, if the babies made any noise they were removed to the nursery, and my baby always seemed to be crying.

> Breast-feeding was a disaster owing to conflicting advice from the nurses; the fact that my baby was given bottle feeds during the night made me very unhappy. When we got home things started to improve and we all settled down.

> Two years later I got pregnant again, and we decided that we wanted our baby to be born at home. We talked to our doctor about it, and he said that he would not take the responsibility and felt that it was safer for the baby to be born in hospital. We didn't give up; we contacted all the doctors in the area and eventually found a doctor and midwife who were willing to take us on.

> My mother came to stay and looked after Simon, who was two by then. When I went into labour I called the midwife who had looked after me throughout my pregnancy, and she and my husband brought a beautiful little girl into the world. Breast-feeding was easy

and everything was exactly as it should be and so far removed from our experience in the hospital.

ROBERT AND SUSAN IVES

How can you ensure that you are booked into a hospital where having your baby will be a pleasant experience?

- Talk to women who have had their children in the hospital and ask:
Is it a flexible routine or bound by unnecessary rules and regulations?
Are the staff approachable?
Are you allowed to have a bath when you feel like it?
- Visiting:
Are there any restrictions? Can fathers visit any time?
Are your own children allowed to visit at any time? These days no maternity hospital should restrict visits from your own children.
- Is the father allowed to be with you at the birth?
- What happens when you are in labour?
Do you have to stay in bed once you are in labour or are you allowed to walk around? A woman should be allowed to walk around for as long as she wants unless the membranes have ruptured. It encourages the baby's head to engage and it relieves pain.
Does the hospital have and encourage the use of birthing-chairs or stools and baths? Are the staff flexible about the position that you give birth in, such as squatting or kneeling, or do they insist on women lying down?
Can you have pain relief when you want it?
Do the staff make a fuss if you refuse treatments?
How do the staff feel about natural childbirth methods? Will they give pain-killing drugs if you say that you don't want them?
- Will your baby be with you all the time? The answer to this should be 'Yes'.
- Do the staff encourage mothers to breast-feed on demand? Are the staff helpful and sympathetic to mothers trying to breast-feed?
- How soon can you go home after the birth? This could be six hours, forty-eight hours, three days, five days, or a week. You should be able to choose what you do.
You could also ask your doctor if the consultant at the hospital is inclined to induce labour, use forceps, and if many of the mothers have had episiotomies.

Then check out the answers to these questions with the staff at the hospital. The answers to these questions will give some insight into the hospital and help you to make the right choice and avoid the situation that Robert and Susan found themselves in.

If you do want to have your baby at home, you need to think about it and discuss it with your doctor at your first antenatal visit. In the United Kingdom the following women are advised to have their baby in hospital:

- Women having their first baby, as it is impossible to establish whether or not their labour will be straightforward.
- Women having their first baby over the age of thirty-five.
- Women with a history of a previous birth that was difficult or complicated.
- Women who are expecting more than one baby.
- Women with a history of toxaemia, high blood-pressure, kidney, heart or circulatory problems, epilepsy or any other medical condition that might become critical.

There are advantages to having your baby in hospital and advantages to having your baby at home.

In hospital there are doctors and nurses available day and night in case of an emergency. There is a paediatrician to examine your baby and reassure you that all is well. Your anxieties, problems, difficulties and troubles can be shared with other mothers and the nurses, who can also help you to care for your baby, especially if it is your first child.

At home you will be in familiar surroundings with your family, your baby is always near you. You can establish your own routine without worrying about other people. If you have other children, they can be involved with the baby straight away, and of course you will have your own midwife to care for you.

For more information about organisations concerned with women who want to give birth the way they want and those that want to give birth at home, see page 289. If you are having problems getting what you want, I suggest that you contact the relevant association. The addresses and some information about each organisation can be found on page 289.

PREMATURE (SMALL-FOR-DATES) BABIES

For the majority of mothers and fathers the birth of a new baby is a time of joy and happiness; all the family are proud and delighted. The long wait for nine months and the pain are all forgotten. But for some mothers, fathers and families it is the start of a nightmare: the struggle of a little premature baby for survival.

Mary Harding gave birth to twins who were both small for their dates:

It was August, hot and humid, and I had been in hospital for six weeks. The cause: twins. Extra care was needed because twins tend to arrive early. The doctors were right, and although the babies tried to make their way out they were stopped. But at thirty-six and a half weeks, because of a few medical problems, they broke my waters and we waited and waited. Twenty-six hours later, after great difficulty, Anna arrived. She had to be delivered by high forceps and weighed in at four pounds thirteen ounces. The second baby, another girl, arrived thirty minutes later; again, she had to be helped. To begin with, she was breech; then turned and didn't try to come out. First, they tried ventouse suction (a small suction-cup is applied to the baby's head, a vacuum created and the baby delivered by pulling on the cup). This failed. So it was also a high-forceps delivery. Beth weighed five pounds two ounces.

Anna I saw, although didn't hold her before they put her in an incubator, to take her to the special care baby unit (SCBU). Beth I didn't even see or, to make matters worse, hear. All I was told was that it was another girl. She also disappeared to the SCBU.

Once I had been stitched up I was taken back to my bed where until the morning everything was a blur, and I am unable to recall anything except that I must have slept the whole time.

Later that first morning a nurse asked if I had seen the girls. Seen them! No one had even told me how they were. They found a wheelchair and took me to see the girls in the SCBU. I was taken over to the incubators where Anna and Beth lay. Anna seemed quite content, but Beth was very still. Even today I remember the worry and fear that I felt. To make matters worse, none of the nursing staff seemed to help. I know that everything is routine to them and they care for very sick babies all the time, but I was an ordinary mother that didn't understand what was going on and needed support.

I stayed for a while but, apart from looking at them with tubes in their umbilici and their noses, I couldn't hold or touch them. For eight months I had suffered various pregnancy problems and now it was all over, but to what gain? I was apart from my babies; a huge gap seemed to have been formed separating us already.

That first evening my husband came down to see them with me. I know it helped having him there to share the worry. We were told by the nurses that they were pleased with their progress so far.

The next couple of days were spent trailing between bed and SCBU. The third day I was allowed to hold Anna. That was nerve-racking as I also had to try and give her a bottle. The following day I was told that I could 'top and tail' Anna; that means washing her face and changing her nappy. Working through the portholes of an incubator was quite difficult, and trying to remember the techniques that the nurses had told me. As you may imagine, Anna objected strongly, and that worried me.

The next day I was allowed to change Beth and also to hold her. I had a nagging worry because she seemed so quiet, but the nursing staff were not concerned. These activities seemed to take up most of the day. On the fifth day I was allowed to go home, but leaving the girls was dreadful. I cried all the way home. The medical staff suggested that I took the next day off and didn't go into the hospital.

The first day that I went in from home I drove myself because my husband was busy with the harvest. On arrival the girls had the ultraviolet light over them because they were jaundiced. When babies have this treatment their eyes are bandaged so as not to cause eye damage.

Beth, on one of my visits, was crying and very irritable, and I learned that they had performed a lumbar puncture on her [i.e., a small amount of fluid is taken from the spinal column]. The difference from the previous day was very noticeable. Still I was told that there was nothing to worry about – but I did. I went home in tears to my husband with a deep fear in my heart that there was something seriously wrong with her.

By about nine days they were taken out of the incubators and put into cots. A few days later I was asked to stay again in the mother's room. This was to prepare us for life at home. Beth came first into my room to stay with me, and then Anna. Neither of them wanted their feeds; they only took a little. They would settle for a while, then cry again. After forty-eight hours of this we were discharged home with mixed feelings, glad at last to take the girls home to be a complete family, but nervous of the future and whether I was able to cope with two frail babies.

I think that during the whole time with the staff at the SCBU I never once felt that they gave support to the nursing mothers; perhaps it was because they were single themselves and had never been through it.

Home at last. My mother came to stay for the first two weeks. That was a great help, but then she had to go back home and I had to cope alone. The first few weeks were hard work. It seemed an endless job of feeding them. On average it seemed they needed feeding two-to-three-hourly. To try and get the housework done or prepare and cook a meal between seeing to the girls was difficult. When I fed them at six in the morning I then stayed up and tried to catch up on my jobs. Sleep was at a minimum; I would get to bed at about eleven and wake again at one or two in the morning to feed them. These catnaps went on for four months. There were endless nappies to wash and dry, and the next pregnancy I opted for disposables and wished I had done so for the twins. The girls were bathed daily, usually in the mornings, but when on my own with them it was a very noisy affair and at the end of bathing and feeding them I felt totally shattered.

We went to the clinic regularly, and the doctor was always very pleased with their progress, but I was still worried about Beth. She was still very irritable and cried most of the time.

Life went on like this for months. We did survive, but looking back now I do wonder how I did. Having a premature baby causes a great deal of work and worry, and unless you have one hundred per cent support from family, friends and the medical team the road does seem endless. Especially when you are fighting a battle, based only on a mother's instinct, about the health of your child versus the doctor's views.

This time I was correct, and at six months they diagnosed Beth as being mentally and physically handicapped. Although that is another story, at least I was pleased that the battle for the truth was ended.

MARY HARDING

If Mary ever had any doubts about her ability to bring up these two frail babies, surely there is living proof in her two delightful daughters who are now nine years old. Mary will be telling you more about Beth's progress in Chapter 6. Mary experienced some serious problems while she was in hospital, and I would hope that these days the attitude of hospital staff towards mothers and fathers in this situation has improved a great deal.

Prematurity is defined as any baby weighing less than $5\frac{1}{2}$ lb. The most common reason for prematurity is birth before full term; in fact any baby born before thirty-six weeks will usually be premature. Other factors that influence the weight of a baby will be the mother's diet, whether she is a smoker, and sometimes genetic factors or a medical problem affecting the baby. Twins and multiple births are often premature. These days the chances of survival of the premature baby have increased enormously; generally speaking the nearer to term or the larger the baby the better the outlook. The main problem for the small-for-dates baby is the immaturity of the lungs.

These babies need special nursing care until they reach a weight of 5½ lb. After the baby has been born the paediatrician, a doctor specially trained to care for babies and children, will examine the baby, who will probably need to be cared for in an incubator. An incubator is a cot covered with clear solid plastic. Inside the incubator the baby is kept warm at just the right temperature and the oxygen-supply is carefully monitored. Before the baby is taken away, if at all possible the baby is handed to the mother to touch and hold. Feeding for this little baby is also a problem as he or she will not be able to breast-feed; but the best solution is for the mother to express her milk, which is then given to the baby through a small tube. While the baby is being cared for in the special care baby unit the mother and father are encouraged to visit their baby. As soon as possible the staff will encourage them to touch and then hold the baby in the incubator and to become involved in the care; then of course comes the moment when the baby is held and cuddled out of the incubator, and eventually the day when the baby reaches the magic 5½ lb and the proud parents can take him home.

Of course you will get a great deal of support from the staff at the hospital, from other mothers and fathers who have babies in special care, and from your own family. On the other hand, it sometimes helps to talk to someone outside the family and the hospital. There are organisations where you can contact people who have been through the same traumatic experience that you are going through and they are only a phone call away. See page 290.

These days small babies do very well indeed. They may have had a tough start to life, and initially their development is a little different, but by the end of their first year in most cases they are just like any other one-year-old. When you have been through times when you wondered if your baby would survive it must be difficult not to spoil and worry about your child, but most mothers that I have spoken to say that they don't treat them any differently from their other children.

DEATH OF A BABY AT BIRTH

How do a couple feel when their baby dies at birth? How do they ever come to terms with the loss of their baby? What can be done to help a couple and their family through such a distressing time in their lives? These are some of the questions that I put to a young couple from Winchester. Although they wanted to share their experience with other people, they wanted to remain anonymous.

The mother's account of how she felt:
Although the birth had been long and difficult, I still couldn't understand why it had happened. They said her heart had stopped but didn't know why. They took her away, and I never even saw her. I think it would have been better if we had seen her. I know it would have been awful, but I still wonder what she looked like. You see, there is no grave. Nothing. It's as though she didn't exist, but we know she did.

At first I blamed the doctor, but my husband said everything possible had been done and that the doctor and nurses were upset, too. Then I blamed myself. I thought I must have done something wrong. No one wanted to talk to us about it, neither my parents nor his. I don't think they knew what to say. Even some of our friends kept away; I suppose they didn't know what to say.

Things didn't get better over the next few weeks. Everything seemed to be black, and I couldn't see any hope in the future. I didn't want my husband to come near me in case I got pregnant and the baby died. I went to see our doctor, and he suggested tablets to help me, but I didn't want pills. Then he asked if I would like to talk to another mother whose baby had died at birth. At first I said no, I had got enough troubles of my own. Anyway, he gave me the phone number. In the end I did ring her and we met; she came round to my house. It was such a relief to know that I was not alone. She really helped me through those months to come. If I hadn't met her, I think I would have gone mad.

The husband's point of view:
In the hospital and when we were first at home I felt disappointed, guilty and empty. I was there when she was born. I only saw her for a few seconds. She didn't cry, and they rushed her away. I could tell by their faces that something was badly wrong. The thing that is different for me is that I had been given paternity leave to look after my wife and the new baby, and there was no baby. I knew that I should stay at home and look after her but I felt guilty about not being at work. When I did go in to see my boss he didn't know what to say. It was very awkward. So I told him the baby had died and left

it at that. No one really talked about it again.

In the hospital they had been very kind and at home we talked about what had happened. We cried a lot. It was a dreadful time. I did my best to help my wife, but she seemed to be drifting further away from me. She obviously needed more help, which thankfully she got from this very gentle and understanding woman who had lost her baby the same way. Her husband also helped me to come to terms with everything. We needed their help more than we realised. If you have never been through this kind of nightmare, you just can't understand what it is like. I don't think I will ever forget our first baby, but it makes the little boy that we have now very special indeed.

The death of a baby at birth is something that most of us simply cannot imagine; it must all seem so unfair, such a waste of a young life that had only just started. I am sure that the first question you would ask is: Why did this happen? It is important that you ask the doctor and, if he knows the answer, get him to explain until you are sure that you really understand. Sometimes the hospital staff really do not know why a baby died at birth and will suggest that a post-mortem examination is carried out. This may all seem very cruel and unnecessary to you both at the moment, but it may be a good idea to agree and establish what caused the death of your baby. Sometimes it is easier to accept what has happened if there is a concrete reason for it.

Guilt is a very common and understandable feeling. What did I do to cause this? The answer of course is: 'Nothing; it is not your fault.'

One of the saddest aspects of the experience related by the couple from Winchester was that they never saw their baby. These days hospital staff are aware of the need for a mother and father to see and hold their dead baby, so they can then see the baby as a person that they can grieve and mourn in order to come to terms with what has happened. The hospital staff may suggest that the baby is named or christened, and a lot of parents have found this very comforting. In America and in some hospitals in the United Kingdom the parents are given a photograph of the baby.

Parents who have attended a funeral service for their baby have said that it helped them through the grieving process and that there was a place to visit and to remember if and when they wanted to.

The most positive support seems to come from the help offered to bereaved parents from other parents who have experienced the same loss. There are organisations who offer this very valuable service: see page 291. Parents of a baby who died at birth need a great deal of comfort and reassurance that it was not their fault, and someone who has experienced the same loss really understands how they are feeling. Sometimes there are other people who are feeling just as desperate – the grandparents or other children in the family, who are feeling just as sad and distressed; they need help, too: see page 366.

If you are the relative or friend of someone whose baby has been born dead or has died at birth and you want to help, go and see them, be a sympathetic and good listener and give plenty of physical comfort. You may well have difficulty sorting out your own feelings, particularly if you are planning to have a baby, are pregnant or have young children. Think how you would feel if it was you and everyone avoided you because they couldn't face a very distressing situation. It is important to avoid platitudes like 'You must think about your other children; they are alive and need you' or 'You'll soon get over this when you have another baby'. These rather glib statements, although possibly true, don't mean anything to the bereaved parents at the moment. What they need is to grieve for the baby that has died, time to talk it through and, most of all, someone to listen to them and comfort them.

SUB-FERTILITY (INFERTILITY)

These days, with effective contraception, a couple can decide not to have children, but it is a very different matter when a couple who have planned to have a family discover that for some reason they cannot have a child.

> We never really gave it any thought; we just assumed that we would be able to have a baby when we wanted to. When it didn't happen we were shocked as we both came from large families and no one else in our families seemed to have any trouble producing babies, so why us? We both wanted a baby so much we were prepared to have any tests or treatment, in fact do anything that would help us have our own baby.
>
> To start with, we were worried about the tests. Mark felt that if it turned out to be his fault he would be less of a man. When we talked to our doctor he told us all about the tests and about other couples who had the same sort of problems. He said that not being able to have a baby doesn't mean that a man is any less a man or a woman any less womanly and that we needed to tackle this problem as a couple.

The first step was to get some tests done on both of us at a fertility clinic.

MARK AND MARY WILSON

It is surprising to realise that about one in ten couples in the United Kingdom are unable to have babies. It is important to understand that fertility is relative to the couple and not to one individual. There are certain factors that must exist in both the male and the female in order to produce a baby:

- The woman's ovaries must be healthy, regularly and actively producing normal ova (eggs) ready for fertilisation.
- There must be a normal and clear tract down which the fertilised egg can pass, which leads to a healthy uterus (womb) that can maintain the fertilised egg.
- She must have a healthy vagina and cervix through which the sperm can travel to meet and fertilise the egg.
- The man must have fully developed, normal testicles which produce and deliver an adequate number of normal sperm which are regularly deposited in the upper vagina.

Technically a woman is fertile for only a few days in each monthly cycle; these are the days around ovulation. If a woman wants to check that she is ovulating, she could keep a note of her oral temperature at the same time every day for several complete monthly cycles. In the middle of the cycle there should be a rise in the temperature. If this happens, she is ovulating, but this simple test will not tell her anything about whether or not the ovum (egg) actually travels along the fallopian tubes and whether or not it is fertilised and successfully implanted in the uterus (womb).

There is also no way that a man can tell whether or not he is fertile. He may ejaculate normally but he cannot tell just by looking at the ejaculate if it contains the right number of normal sperm.

There are many causes of infertility or sub-fertility, and the first step should be to make an appointment to see the family doctor and talk it over with him. The sooner you seek help the better; you do not have to wait for two years before you talk to someone about the problem. So, if you are worried, talk to your family doctor. If you feel that you can't discuss this with him, write to a doctor at your nearest fertility clinic and explain that you can't talk to your doctor about it but would like an appointment to see someone. These clinics are usually found in large hospitals, and your doctor will know the address and telephone number.

What will happen at the infertility clinic?

At the first visit you will be asked all sorts of questions about your past medical history, general health, sexual activity and social life. Following this the doctor may decide to go ahead and examine you both medically and in particular the genital areas.

This may be followed up with tests such as an analysis of semen. This means that the man will be asked to produce a specimen of semen by masturbating. The same tests would be repeated two or three times over the next few weeks. You may also be asked to have sexual intercourse with your partner at a specified time, after which she will be examined and secretions from the vagina and cervical canal removed, examined and tested to see if the sperm has the ability to penetrate cervical mucus and live in that environment. This is a post-coital (after-intercourse) test.

If there are any problems of impregnation due to impotence, this would be followed up with counselling. If the initial tests indicate too few or even an absence of sperm, there will be further tests to establish the cause. During all these tests it is important for a couple to appreciate that there may be nothing that can be done, and the staff at the clinic will do their best to help them come to terms with the possibility of being childless. If the tests are satisfactory, there are no further tests for the man. The tests may continue for the woman and include:

- Recording the temperature for three to four months: the temperature is usually raised a little at ovulation.
- Taking a biopsy (a small piece) of endometrium (the lining of the womb) about seven days after ovulation. A small instrument is passed into the uterus through the cervix, which is partially dilated, a tiny piece of endometrium is removed and examined under a microscope. Tissue that is formed while progesterone is being produced, after ovulation, is different from that formed before ovulation when oestrogen is being produced or under no hormonal influence. Hormonal levels in blood and urine are also used to establish the hormone levels and whether or not you are ovulating.
- There are also tests designed to show up any blockages in the fallopian tubes. This test is done under a general anaesthetic. A gas or dye which shows up on X-ray is passed into the uterus (womb) and up into the fallopian tubes. If the tubes are open, the dye passes into the surrounding tissue and is safely absorbed.
- The surgeon can look directly at your pelvic organs by making a very small incision at the top of the vagina through which is passed a fibrescope. Through this fibrescope the surgeon can see that every-

thing looks normal, biopsies can be taken and any fine adhesions blocking the tubes can be divided.

You may have to wait for several months for your appointment at an infertility clinic, so you could start by keeping a record of when you ovulate by recording your temperature at the same time each day, to establish when you ovulate, and have intercourse on those days. Try abstaining from sexual intercourse for seven to ten days prior to ovulation; this will increase the number of sperm in the ejaculate. Sometimes it helps simply not to worry about getting pregnant, and you may be more successful; you hear of so many women who start to adopt, or actually adopt, a child and then find themselves pregnant. Worry and anxiety are only going to make things worse.

As you can see, these tests can take a long time and a lot of courage to go through. You will need a lot of support from relatives and friends, but most of all from your doctor. There are also support groups and organisations who can put you in touch with people who have experienced similar problems and are able to help you. See page 290.

When the results of all the tests and investigations are available it may be possible to start an appropriate treatment. Mark Wilson continues:

At the start when we first went to the clinic it was all a bit of a joke: looking at the calendar, taking Mary's temperature, then rushing upstairs to make love. Then the joke began to wear a bit thin and it all became very clinical. Sex to order, so to speak. It seemed to go on for months. In the end the doctor said that both Mary's tubes were blocked. She had an operation, but it didn't work. She became very difficult to talk to, didn't want to go out much. Just sort of went into herself really. I know that we wanted our own kids, but we were still young and had a nice home. We started to look into being able to adopt. They had suggested this at the clinic some time before, but it didn't seem right then.

Mary Wilson:
When I found out that I couldn't have our own baby I felt very guilty. It was my fault, and I knew how much Mark longed for a large happy family. Every time one of our friends got pregnant I felt so jealous and angry. I know they tried to help us at the clinic and suggested that we think about adoption, but I wasn't ready to give up; I still believed it would happen. In my anger I shut Mark out of my life and I think I was lucky not to lose him. In the end I think it was this that made me realise that there was no point in waiting any longer, and anyway we

talked about it and decided to give it a go. It wasn't as easy as we thought it would be and, looking back, we went through some pretty awful moments, but it came right in the end and we adopted Kimberley when she was six months old and now two years later we are hoping to adopt a baby boy – so fingers crossed.

What can be done to help someone who is sub-fertile? There are fertility drugs available, such as Gonadotrophin and Clomiphene. With these drugs ovulation can be achieved in some 75 per cent of women, but about only half of them will become pregnant. Both fertility drugs produce a greater risk of multiple births as they may induce multiple ovulation. There has been a great deal in the newspapers, on the radio and on television about multiple births. We hear that a mother has given birth to six or more tiny little babies, and we all wait and pray that they will survive, and of course some do. Many people have very strong views both for and against the use of these drugs, but for the couple that desperately want children this is their only hope. For more information about coping with a multiple birth, see page 297.

For problems which have caused scarring of the fallopian tubes and the uterus, making the area hostile to the transportation and the implantation of the ovum (egg), the doctor may feel that the woman may be helped by hormone treatment.

Blocked fallopian tubes can sometimes be made patent (clear) with new surgical techniques, and the success of this type of operation really depends on the extent of the adhesions, and your doctor will advise you on what can or cannot be done.

When the cervical mucus is hostile to the sperm, in other words the sperm cannot penetrate the cervix, your doctor may suggest hormone treatment. Again, your doctor will know if this is the appropriate treatment.

ARTIFICIAL INSEMINATION

Artificial insemination involves the insertion of sperm either from a donor or from the husband into the uterus of the wife of an infertile or impotent husband. It can be used if he has had a vasectomy and also if he is a carrier of a hereditary disease which could be passed on to his children. Very rarely it is used because of rare blood-group incompatibilities between the woman and her partner. If one of these is your problem, ask at the infertility clinic that you attend whether this is an option for you. See page 292. If you are considering using an unknown donor, you do need to be really sure about what you are doing as the woman will be carrying a child which is half hers and half that of someone unknown, although her husband is the legal father. This has all sorts of implications, and a man who accepts this as an option will need careful counselling.

The Pregnancy Advisory Service in London explained about artificial insemination by donors:

Artificial insemination has been practised in the United Kingdom for about fifty years, and currently more than 2,500 babies a year are conceived in this way. The semen used can be either freshly produced or frozen. Donors are carefully selected, usually from medical schools and universities. They are examined to make sure that they are in good physical and mental health. They are screened for infections that could be transmitted to the woman and for the presence of hereditary disease. Their blood-groups are determined, and their semen is tested to check that they are fertile and that it can be stored by freezing. All donors are regularly screened for AIDS virus. No donor with the AIDS virus will be used. The service is completely confidential. A donor is selected of the appropriate ethnic and rhesus blood-group for the woman and, as far as possible, will match the woman and her husband for eye and hair colour.

After several counselling interviews and a complete medical examination, including the taking of blood samples, an appointment is made for the first insemination. The insemination itself is painless and simple. It will be done twice a month, usually a day apart, just before and at the time of ovulation, about twelve to fourteen days before your period is due. Insemination is a straightforward procedure. Donor semen is placed at the entrance to the womb (the cervix) by means of a syringe and fine tube. After the insemination you will be asked to rest for half an hour. You can have intercourse after insemination as long as there is no particular reason why it is important not to risk conceiving with your husband or partner's semen, such as a genetic problem.

A pregnancy resulting from artificial insemination donor (AID) should be as normal as any other pregnancy. In any pregnancy, however, there are risks of miscarriage or birth defects and other complications; the chances of these are no more or less in an AID pregnancy.

It is up to you whether you decide to tell your child that conception was by AID. There are differing views about this, but the decision is yours. Your counsellor will be able to help you with this.

AID is not illegal in the United Kingdom and, provided it is carried out with the husband's consent, is not considered to constitute adultery or grounds for divorce. The present legal position is that a child conceived by AID is illegitimate. Strictly speaking, the mother should register the child as 'father unknown', and then arrange adoption by her husband. This is something that you may wish to discuss with the counsellor. You may also wish to consult a solicitor if you have any particular legal concerns: e.g. the child's inheritance rights.

THE PREGNANCY ADVISORY SERVICE, LONDON

IN-VITRO FERTILISATION (TEST-TUBE BABIES)

There is still a lot of work being done on conception outside the uterus (test-tube babies) or in-vitro fertilisation. This system uses the couple's own ovum and sperm. There are only a few specialist organisations in the United Kingdom: see page 292.

What happens is this: the time of ovulation is established and the woman is prepared for a general anaesthetic; meanwhile her husband has to produce a semen specimen to fertilise the eggs that are now ready for recovery. The eggs are removed surgically from the woman and then several eggs are placed together with the sperm and left to incubate. Then one single fertilised ovum (egg) is implanted in the uterus (womb). The egg is inserted via a catheter, a small tube, through the vagina and into the uterus. The woman is then left lying down with the end of the bed tipped up for two hours and then stays in bed until the next day. The hormone levels are monitored very closely for the next few days and until the pregnancy is confirmed. The pregnancy is then monitored very carefully until full term and the baby is born.

SURROGACY

Surrogacy is a woman having a baby for another woman or couple. There is always a great deal of media interest when a woman has a baby for another woman. The idea is that a couple agree a contract with a woman to pay her to have a baby for them, that she will hand it over to them at birth. The surrogate mother and the father simply have sexual intercourse, or the surrogate mother is artificially inseminated with the father's sperm, and she conceives his child. In South Africa recently a grandmother gave birth to triplets for her daughter. The sperm of the father fertilised the egg of the mother as in in-vitro fertilisation (test-tube babies), then the fertilised egg was implanted into the womb of the grandmother who carried the babies to full term for her daughter. This all sounds very straightforward and simple until the mother has to give up her baby. Some women find this part very difficult or even impossible to go through with. If she cannot give up her baby, it is highly likely that the father will start legal proceedings against her, and a battle over the baby begins. On the other hand, when things go right it can be the greatest gift that any one woman can give to another and her husband.

In the United Kingdom there are a great many people who feel that this is wrong and should not be allowed. There are others who say that it has been going on since the time of Abraham, that sisters and friends have been having babies for each other for centuries.

ADOPTION

Childlessness – how it feels, by Penelope Kennedy:

When I was twenty, I had to have surgery to remove dermoid ovarian cysts, so I was always aware that I might have fertility problems. I had trained as a nursery nurse, and have worked as a nanny, looking after other people's children until I could have my own; and, if I thought about it at all, considered that it might happen to others but it couldn't happen to me. After two years of marriage, not becoming pregnant, and feeling increasingly unwell, it was not really a surprise to learn I needed further surgery for adhesions. However, I was still convinced, up to the day of hospitalisation, that I would eventually achieve my ambition.

Imagine, then, my distress, on coming round from the anaesthetic, and feeling terrible, to be visited by the gynaecologist and cheerily told: 'Well, that's the end of your chances of your own cricket eleven.' In other words, my tubes were irreparably damaged and, anyway, I only had one half of one ovary left. Looking back on it, and hearing other similar tales about the insensitivity of doctors, it seems to me they need counselling themselves. On the brighter side, couples faced with the trauma of childlessness have a great deal more available to them in the way of support and help, self-help groups, in the eighties than we did twenty years ago. I lived in a personal slough of despond for months, even years, following this. Although we started the adoption trail pretty quickly after my return home, the emotional scars remained. I took to smoking again, drank too much for my health, and for many years was quite unable to communicate on any level with anyone who was pregnant. I would stare at babies in prams outside shops and could totally sympathise with the state of mind that would consider stealing a baby, even whilst understanding it to be wrong. I also well remember a dinner-party that we had to leave in great distress, after hearing a woman almost boasting of a recent abortion (more of a novelty in those days), as she already had two children and couldn't be bothered with a third. I simply couldn't cope with the idea that she could conceive and dispose so easily whilst I could not.

At this time, the late sixties, there was no shortage of healthy white babies for adoption and, although adoption agencies' lists were beginning to be closed, there was no hesitation in applying to adopt. However, fifteen letters and fifteen negative replies later, we wondered if it was so simple, but after a lot more persistence our application was accepted by one agency and we were approved to adopt. Fifteen months later we were presented with a bonny ten-week-old boy who was all I had dreamed of.

In the 1980s things are very different, as I found when, following a broken marriage and subsequent remarriage, I wanted to increase our family. Knowing that babies were like gold dust, we knew that we had to adapt our needs to those of the many children in care and needing new families. After another assessment of our family and a further wait of eighteen months, we were rewarded with a brother and sister of four and three years old. We were supported throughout by contact with Parent to Parent Information on Adoption Services, a national self-help support and information group for prospective and existing adoptive families.

My childlessness now affects the way I feel about my adopted children's birth-mothers. I have strong positive feelings of love and gratitude for the mother of our eldest (who came to us as a ten-week-old baby), for she decided she was too young to support a child as she was unmarried and felt an adoptive family was the right answer. The next two children were taken into care on a place of safety order following physical abuse and malnourishment. I feel of their mother that she abused the gift she had and deserved to have them taken away. I can rationalise my emotions but accept they come from my continuing cry that 'life's not fair'. No, I know it never can be, but being barren is a hard pill to swallow. I remember lying in my hospital bed, hearing two nurses newly on duty talk of me as 'the fertility case'; I think that was when the full implications sank in. I have to say that right up to my hysterectomy three years ago, despite three children by adoption, I was determined to flout medical history and become the oldest woman to have a first baby, because of the medical progress into my particular problem! However, even I have come to accept that it is not to be. Although I am never able to forget that I am barren, and am still occasionally hurt by thoughtless remarks, adoption has proved a more than adequate substitute. I can't imagine loving birth-children more than I do my adopted children. They are all loving, lovable, irritating, surprising, disappointing, hard work and rewarding, however they come to you.

PENELOPE KENNEDY

It is true that there are perhaps fewer babies that need adopting these days, because of more effective contraception and the introduction of legal abortion. This does not mean that there are no children for adoption; there are in fact many, many children who need loving parents and a good home. These children are perhaps older, or of mixed race, or have a mental or physical handicap; they are not six weeks old and white, but they need homes just as much as any other child. Many agencies confined their work in the past to placing healthy white babies, so if you approach one of these you may be discouraged by their response and be under the impression that there are no children in the United Kingdom to adopt. This is not true; there are over 100,000 children in care, and approximately 20,000 of these could be available for adoption.

If you want to adopt a child, you need to get in touch with either your local authority or a registered adoption agency. You can get a list of agencies and help from one of the organisations listed on page 293. In theory anyone can adopt a child, providing he does not have a serious criminal record. Some agencies make up their own rules: an upper age-limit of thirty-five or forty, a wife who does not work, the number of years you must have been married and no previous marriages that ended in divorce. Try several agencies and you will probably find that the rules change. There will be a great many questions about your life, some of them very personal. If you feel you need help and advice, see page 294.

CHAPTER TWO
Babies and Young Children

The arrival of a baby will bring you enormous pleasure and happiness, and I am sure that every couple spend hours just gazing at their little baby and simply marvelling at the perfect little person that is now their child. Although this is a very exciting time in your life, it also involves a great deal of hard work and sometimes there are problems.

POST-NATAL DEPRESSION

Frances Collier told me how she felt after the birth of her baby:

> After the birth of our first baby everything went wrong. I just couldn't cope, I was hopeless at breast-feeding, the baby cried a lot, and I was terrified that something would happen to him. I went right off my husband, so wouldn't let him near me and blamed him for everything that went wrong and most of the time wished he would just go away and leave me with my baby. I was sure I could cope better without him. I felt very lonely and cried at anything. I didn't tell anyone about this, and the feelings went away about seven months later. It wasn't until I saw a programme on television about post-natal depression that I realised what had happened to me. I wish I had got help, because then the first few months of our baby's life would have been a lot happier.
>
> FRANCES COLLIER

The baby blues are very common and affect about 75 per cent of all women who have babies. They usually occur about three or four days after the baby is born and normally last just one or two days. They often take the form of sudden and unexplained crying, irritability, and there may be feelings of being isolated, alone and uncared for. Post-natal depression is more serious, occurs in about one in ten women and usually begins within a month of the birth of her baby and can last up to about six months. There may be feelings of despondency, tearfulness, tension, a feeling that you can't cope with the baby, fears for your own health and the baby's health. You may also feel irritable, exhausted, or experience pain, poor appetite, difficulty sleeping and a loss of interest in sex.

What can be done to help?

- Although this is not an illness, the family doctor should be consulted; and, if necessary, he may prescribe some antidepressant medicine to help in the short term.
- Contact a self-help group where someone who has been through this experience will happily discuss it with you. See page 295.
- A patient, understanding and caring husband or partner can give reassurance that this is a temporary problem that will soon be over, that it is a common problem which many women feel.
- A husband or partner can help with the care of the baby but most of all help with the household tasks or organise someone else to come in and help.
- A husband or partner can encourage you to get out and resume your social life. Of course a baby needs care and attention, but the mother also needs a life of her own. So organise a responsible babysitter and get out together or, if you are going out to a friend's house, take the baby with you in the carry-cot.

AT HOME WITH A BABY

I don't think that anything really prepares you for that moment when you are at home with your first baby. It doesn't seem to matter how many books you have read [see page 298 for some recommended books], how much advice you have been given or, in my case, how many other people's babies that you have looked after. As a nurse I had looked after dozens of babies, some of whom had been very sick and vulnerable, but at the end of my shift of duty I could hand over the responsibility to someone else. When I was at home with my first child, Joanna, it was total chaos; all my well-laid plans and intentions went out of the window and I simply had to respond to her needs as they arose. I am the sort of person who likes to have a routine, to know what I am doing and where I am going, and it seemed that as soon as we had established a routine Joanna would change hers and we would have to start all over again!

I don't think that I had appreciated just how demanding caring for one small baby was and, although I was well able to manage the physical aspects of looking after her, it was the emotional involvement that made things difficult. If she didn't take her feed or cried a lot, I immediately assumed that there was something seriously wrong and phoned our long-suffering family doctor, who reassured me and helped to sort out the problem that was always something simple.

My husband was a tower of strength and managed to keep calm while I lurched from one crisis to the next. My other source of support was a very good friend who had a baby a few months older than Joanna. She had produced a baby who, like mine, seemed to require very little sleep and a great deal of entertaining. Joanna only slept for a couple of hours after a feed and very rarely settled at night much before ten o'clock; she would then sleep until seven in the morning, which was her only saving grace. So from six in the evening until ten when we were both exhausted she would be wide awake and demanding attention; this went on until she was three years old. When we talked to the doctor about the problem we were told that she was probably very bright and that very intelligent babies needed less sleep. I can assure you that when we were totally exhausted this was of very little comfort. Everyone else seemed to have babies that settled after a feed in the evening and slept through the night, so it was a great relief to have a friend with the same problem.

Then of course there was helpful advice from well-meaning relatives and friends who suggested leaving her to cry herself to sleep. We tried this on several occasions and sat downstairs listening to the screams for hours. This did nothing for our nerves, which ended up shattered, and then we had to calm down a near-hysterical child. In the end we just accepted the fact that she wouldn't settle until about ten in the evening and just enjoyed her company. As she got older she would amuse herself playing happily with her toys as long as she was downstairs with us. Going out in the evening was a problem until we found a wonderful lady in her sixties who adored Joanna and was prepared to play with her until her rather delayed bedtime. If you have a child like this, it is very easy to be affected by remarks made by other people who you feel are criticising the way you are bringing up your child, so just keep telling yourself that babies and children are individuals and some are more individualistic than others. You have to learn to be flexible and not to become defensive when criticised.

DIANA HASTINGS

How to cope with your baby at home

■ Try to remember that being a mother or a father is something that you learn from experience and you will go on learning as your baby grows up into a child, an adolescent and an adult.

■ Ask for help from your spouse or partner, friends and relatives. Share responsibility for the child with your partner.

■ Get to know and talk to people with children that are a little older than yours. They have a lot of experience that will help you to manage.

■ Don't try to do everything in the house; your baby is more important than an immaculate home. Don't start on extra things in the home like decorating or building extensions when your baby is very young. Give yourself time to get used to caring for your baby.

■ Don't move house just after the baby has arrived.

■ When the baby is asleep don't look for household things to do. Allow yourself some time to do the things that you want to do.

■ Don't give up your own interests completely; try to be flexible and rearrange them around your baby.

■ Relax and enjoy your baby; they really do grow up very quickly.

■ Don't listen to old wives' tales. If you are worried, talk to a health professional or your doctor.

BABIES THAT CRY A LOT AND DON'T SLEEP

We have talked a little bit about babies that cry a lot and don't sleep, but how do you cope if your baby cries excessively or is such a poor sleeper that it causes great disruption and concern to the parents and the rest of the family?

Maureen Blackman lives with her husband and children; she told me exactly how she coped with a baby who just cried all the time.

I am the proud mother of a beautiful, energetic, boisterous eighteen-month-old daughter, with mischief written on her face and bright intelligence in her eyes. No one could imagine that this lovely child brought myself and my family to its knees.

Two weeks after a normal birth my daughter started to scream. At first in the evening. Colic, we thought. Then she cried during the night. Within four weeks of birth she was crying all day and all night. It took us longer to rock her to sleep than she actually slept.

She was admitted to hospital at four weeks with 'failure to thrive'; she wasn't feeding well and not gaining weight. They did lots of tests, even a barium meal [this is an X-ray to check the function of the digestive system]. And when they had finished she was not any better. I was patted on the head and told that I was just an anxious mother.

The screaming continued for eight months. I was tired, helpless, and my ears and head ached from the continual noise. My arms and back hurt from carrying her all the time. I could do nearly every household task one-handed, because in the other arm was this red-faced screaming child, who hated me and the world she was in.

Walks in the pram became impossible. People would stare at me when I walked past and ask me if the baby was ill. 'No,' I would reply, 'she's always like this!' How many nights I sat in her room wishing she would shut up and give me some peace. How thin that line is between sanity and insanity. Now I understand why keeping people awake is a good form of torture. There was no time for anyone else in the family, except this hateful creature. We didn't eat properly; good meals were impossible to prepare. My microwave and the tumble drier came into their own. I didn't have time even to hang out the washing during those minutes of peace.

My ten-year-old son spent more and more time away from home, dawdling home from school, playing out late with his friends, pleading every weekend to stay with his grandmother.

My husband was at work all day and when at home spent hours in the shed at the bottom of the garden supposedly mending this or making that! We had no time to love each other any more, and were too tired to love our children. We argued; we cried; we shouted; we hated.

We looked after her in shifts in the evenings. An hour on, an hour off. The off time we spent sitting alone in the garden on a little seat my husband had made. It was a place to get away from the noise and find peace. How funny it must have looked to the neighbours the evening I sat out there when it was pouring with rain. Me with the umbrella up, sitting smoking my evening ciggy with tears dripping off my nose.

I read an article in an old *Family Circle* magazine about Cry-sis [a voluntary self-help organisation: see p.296]. I found the number and rang. I don't think anyone can understand the relief I felt when Yvonne Taylor answered that phone. Oh bliss! Someone who understood, someone who listened. Someone who didn't walk away, patronising me with 'There, there, there, dear'! Someone cared and knew something I could actually do to try and help my daughter. I was sick of people telling me not to do things. Some real advice. Oh wonder of wonders! She sent me Pat Gray's book [*Crying Baby: How to Cope*: see p.296] and the advice in that we took up. Some of it worked, some bits didn't. It didn't really matter. What mattered most to me was the fact that at last I could talk to someone and she understood all my feelings. Then to find out my feelings were not abnormal and I wasn't the only one suffering this kind of torment, and my baby didn't hate me. Yvonne gave me strength; Pat Gray gave me knowledge. We became more relaxed as a family and we loved our daughter for what she was.

Cry-sis gave me the knowledge to cope and courage to carry on, and now I am reaping the benefits and am able to enjoy my beautiful daughter and my wonderful family. We are very close and very proud that with a little help we stuck together and our marriage is stronger for this experience. I now feel that my daughter was hypersensitive to all her surroundings – e.g., light, dark, noise, quiet – and probably allergic to baby milk. No matter what made Hannah the way she was, Cry-sis really helped us cope.

MAUREEN BLACKMAN

Reading Maureen's tale of woe you might be tempted to think that this is a very rare case. In fact one in ten babies cry excessively, and their families need help and support.

The first step is to talk to your doctor or health visitor and establish if there is any physical reason why your baby is crying or not sleeping. There are a lot of myths about crying, and these include that it is healthy for a baby to cry as it exercises his lungs. This is nonsense; babies do not need to cry in order to get air. Another is that the baby who cries a lot is a naughty baby and a good baby is one that does not cry; the answer to this is that babies are not born with the knowledge of what constitutes good or bad behaviour.

Babies usually cry because they are hungry, thirsty or uncomfortable in some way. They may be too hot, too cold, wet, dirty, irritable, sleepy, lonely, frightened or in pain. Crying is a baby's way of telling you what he needs. The sound of a baby crying makes most women feel restless and agitated, and they have difficulty ignoring it. Many mothers can recognise the cry of their own child amongst a crowd of other babies crying. If she is asleep, it will wake her, although her husband or partner may well sleep through it. As the baby and the mother get to know each other, so she is able to recognise the different types of cry: the cry for food, the cry because the baby is uncomfortable, and so on. She knows how to respond to the different cries; but sometimes she listens to others who tell her that she will spoil the baby if she always goes to him when he cries, but this is not true. A mother who responds to her baby makes him feel safe, secure and loved.

But what happens when you do respond to your baby and nothing seems to stop him crying and he won't go to sleep? Then it is a good idea to seek professional advice as there may be a medical reason for the crying. A baby will always pick up his mother's feelings, and if she is agitated and distressed, then the baby is likely to feel the same way. Constant crying will make the mother more tense and agitated; this will make the baby cry even more, and the cycle needs to be broken before she gets to the point where she becomes so tired and agitated that she may well hurt her baby. It is important that any mother in this situation feels that she can talk to a health professional about the problem so that they can help her. These days parents may worry that if they admit these feelings to a health professional their baby will be taken away from them in case they hurt the baby, but professionals are used to dealing with this problem and will give you help and support.

You could also contact a support group, like Maureen did, and talk to someone who has been through this with their own baby. You can do this anonymously if you want to. They will be able to give you constructive advice on what to do and how to cope with the problem and help you establish what the cause might be. But you may feel, just as Maureen Blackman did, that most of all you need someone to talk to who really understands what you and your family are going through. See page 296.

BREAST-FEEDING PROBLEMS

> I really wanted to breast-feed, but the baby just didn't seem to get the hang of it. The nurses kept saying that breast-feeding was the best but didn't really have time to help me get it right.
>
> LYN CASEY

Lyn is by no means alone in her experience; so many mothers have written to me and expressed similar views.

First of all, let's look at why breast-feeding is better for the mother
and the baby. Breast milk is best for your baby because it contains
everything that a baby needs: fat, sugar, minerals and water. It also
contains antibodies that will protect your baby against many infections.
It is free from contamination and is at exactly the right temperature. The
very act of breast-feeding brings the mother in close contact with her
baby, making him feel happy and content. During your pregnancy you
will have stored up extra fat in preparation for breast-feeding, so when
you feed your baby you will burn up this fat and this will help you get
your figure back.

Preparation for breast-feeding starts while you are pregnant, and this
includes washing the breasts daily and gently cleaning the nipple area
and wearing a properly designed support-bra that does not squash the
nipples. If you have flat or inverted nipples, your midwife may suggest
regularly rolling your nipples between finger and thumb or wearing a
breast-shield in order to make the nipples protrude.

Feeding your baby starts when your baby is born, and most hospitals
will let you hold the baby as soon as he is born so you can let him suckle
straight away. He won't feed for long, but being close to you will be
very comforting for him. All babies have an inborn mechanism for
finding the nipple and feeding; if you touch his cheek with your breast,
he will search for the nipple. This is known as rooting. He will then take
the nipple into his mouth and suckle. At first you may well have to help
to ensure that he takes the nipple and the dark-coloured area of skin
surrounding it (the areola) into his mouth. During those first few days
after the birth you may find it more comfortable to lie down on your
side with the baby beside you, his head facing your breast. If you are
comfortable in a sitting position, prop yourself up with a pillow and
hold the baby in your arms, supporting his head.

During the first few days a substance called colostrum is produced,
and this is all he needs at the moment, so put him to the breast for a few
minutes whenever he wakes, which is probably every three hours. The
milk is produced on about the third day. After about ten days he is
usually taking full feeds. Some babies suck rapidly and take all they need
in up to seven minutes, while others suck slowly and need a break to get
up wind. Most babies need a night feed for the first few weeks.

For successful breast-feeding you should:

■ Eat a well-balanced diet. Make sure that you have meat or fish once a
day to supply protein. Eat as much fresh fruit and vegetables as you

can, and one pint of milk as this contains the calcium that your baby needs for strong bones and teeth.

- Drink plenty of fluids. Some mothers feel thirsty when they are breast-feeding, so have a drink near you when you are feeding.
- Avoid medicines such as laxatives unless they have been prescribed by your doctor.
- Don't smoke or drink.
- Sit or lie down comfortably in a calm and peaceful atmosphere.
- Get plenty of rest.

When you first get home you may well feel tired, and you and your baby will have to adjust to a new routine. It is very important at this time that you make sure that you really do relax at each feed. Forget all about the housework or any other problems. If you are tense and worried, your baby will become fretful and breast-feeding difficult.

Your baby is getting enough food if he is a happy and contented baby and gaining about half a pound a week in weight. If he cries a lot and is generally miserable, wakes up two hours after a feed crying and demands two feeds during the night when he usually has one, it may mean that you are producing less milk because you have increased your activity and need more rest and he is demanding more because he is bigger. So the answer is to get more rest if possible and increase the milk-supply by putting him to the breast more frequently. The more he suckles, the more milk you will make; it may take as much as two weeks before your baby is really happy, contented and gaining weight, so don't give up.

Sometimes the nipples become sore, especially in the first few days of feeding. Don't stop feeding; it is better to feed your baby more frequently, and he will not suck so strongly. Also make sure that he is lying comfortably at your breast. He may be sucking more strongly in order to keep the nipple in his mouth. If the soreness continues, seek professional advice.

If your baby refuses to suckle, it may be because he has a cold and is having difficulty feeding and breathing at the same time. So clean his nose and be prepared to take a little more time over his feeds during the next few days. It may be that your breast is pressing on his nose, and you may need to hold it away so that he can feed more easily. If you are still having problems, seek professional advice.

Sometimes he may refuse to feed at one breast, perhaps because it is a slightly different shape or because the milk is flowing more slowly. You can encourage him to feed at this breast by feeding him in the same position on each breast. This is done by simply moving him across without turning him round.

If you are having problems breast-feeding, talk to your health visitor, or you could contact one of the support groups or organisations listed on page 296.

TWINS

Have you ever wondered how you would cope if you had given birth to more than one baby? Mark and Margaret Jukes have twin daughters.

The ultra-sound. Mark:

This was the day of reckoning, the visual picture of what was to be. A time to be apprehensive. I remember many thoughts coming and going in rapid succession, many centred around whether the baby was all right; perhaps the fact that we both work with the mentally handicapped made us more anxious. These were thoughts that most parents have. 'Are twins in your family?' are words that we will never forget, as the probe was exploring Margaret's womb. I was immediately overcome with a feeling of euphoria, pride and pleasurable shock. 'Well there are two here.' The probe constantly surveying and confirming the initial unbelievable diagnosis. Like a disbelieving child I wanted confirmation by insisting on the probe searching and seeing over and over again on the screen those four arms and legs, two heads and bodies separate but yet as one: a highly pleasurable and completely selfish experience to be enjoyed and stored for ever.

The ultra-sound. Margaret:

I approached this with a feeling of apprehension of what we would see, but also excitement of seeing the baby that had grown within me which I couldn't feel or see but only knew was there because of a thickening waistline and feeling sick and tired. During the drive to the hospital a sudden thought hit me. When the radiologist told us there were two, I felt that I had known all along. I felt wonderfully happy and very special. I also had a mental picture of what they looked like. I think that the bonding process, for both of us, started with that first sight of our babies. Fathers should try to be present at the scan, but please remember, dads, to be fully supportive to your partners; don't disappear to the loo as you are waiting to go in as Mark did, while your partner is sitting there with the full bladder that is necessary to carry out the ultra-sound correctly.

Preparation for the birth. Margaret and Mark:
We felt aware, as would-be parents, of the choices parents have in deciding how the birth experiences could be and we had both decided on acquiring the best knowledge and preparation possible. This was achieved by joining the local National Child Birth Trust. These sessions covered thoroughly all that we needed to know about the birth journey on a theoretical level and practical relaxation and breathing techniques, along with valuable information from breast-feeding counsellors, all in all making both mothers and fathers more involved with the prospective birth of their child. The trust also gave us much-needed post-natal support. With twins on the horizon, the pure natural choice for delivery was dependent on any pre-birth complications. Our philosophy was to be very much open and to be guided by the minute. However, we agreed that decisions that we did make would not be put aside purely for any procedural requirements. Our choices would be respected.

Time before birth. Mark:
A programme of days out to places not visited and taking advantage of our independence was important. However, this needs to be well planned before the mother's size becomes a handicap – i.e., the ability to travel distances in comfort – as we discovered later in the pregnancy on our trips around the lanes of Somerset and Avon. We were also conscious of not decorating a nursery or purchasing cots, etc., until the final weeks. Best not to put fate to the test was our view. Three months before the birth we exchanged our saloon car for a large estate car, in anticipation of the increase in size of the family. This was beneficial in the long run as added space was certainly needed. It is amazing how much equipment had to fit into the car when we decided to go out. It is at this time that no end of advice from experienced parents is valuable and can help make you fully aware of how your life will be changed by having one let alone two babies. So our advice is to take full advantage of your freedom while it lasts.

At the hospital. Margaret:
Owing to having lots of rest, I made it to thirty-nine weeks, then on

my weekly antenatal visit I was told that my blood pressure was rising, and was admitted to hospital on Friday, 31 January 1986. The doctor advised that labour should be induced. Later, when Mark came to visit, it was discussed with both of us along with the question of my having an epidural. The doctors were advising this because of my raised blood pressure and as a precaution in case the second twin should get into difficulties and needed to be delivered by caesarian section. Because of this they wanted the delivery to take place in the operating-theatre with a team ready to operate if necessary. This was discussed with us, the doctor and the midwives concerned. We were showed where everything would take place; this was very reassuring, and it was very nice to get to know the people who were going to share the birth with us. We agreed to the induction and the epidural for the medical reasons given and because we wanted two healthy babies.

The birth, Sunday, 2 February 1986. Margaret:
6.30 a.m. and I have had a sedative-induced good night's sleep, probably my last for the foreseeable future. The midwife started the induction. I had a cup of tea, bathed and got ready for Mark to arrive and the birth to commence. I felt full of anticipation and as if it was all happening to someone else. I tried to picture myself holding the two babies but, again, it all seemed unreal.

10.30 a.m. and Mark had arrived with his bag packed ready for a long wait. I was very pleased to see him; this was our birth, and I needed him there. The epidural was inserted and I received an epidural tap which meant that I would have to lie flat for twenty-four hours. A drip was set up in my arm and then my waters were broken to get things moving. As the contractions were very slow I was given a hormone into the intravenous drip. I could feel the sensations of the contractions but not the pain, which was quite nice. After what seemed a very short time to me but in reality was two hours I informed the midwife that I had a very strong desire to push. She asked me not to and, in between contractions, internal examinations showed that my cervix was fully dilated, much to everyone's surprise.

There then seemed to be general chaos around me to get me down to the operating-theatre. All I remember is wanting to push and not being able to; the panting techniques came into their own. Once in the operating-theatre I could push, and it was a wonderful relief. They then gave me more epidural, and I could no longer feel the contractions, so consequently they had to tell me when to push. Which made it seem ineffectual, and as I couldn't sit up, either, this meant that the pushing wasn't strong enough. The midwife and the doctors knew of my desire to do it myself and the fear of an episiotomy, so they let me carry on for as long as it was safe. However, they had to use forceps for both babies, and only a small episiotomy was performed. From the point that they took over it all became unreal again. The midwife was telling me that the head was there and getting Mark to look. Poor Mark had been sat at the back of my head and couldn't speak to me as it made me cry. But I needed him there, to feel his hand on my head.

Then they gave me the first baby – 'It's a girl' – and I started discussing names with Mark. Then eight minutes later the head of the second baby, and another girl. Mark took one baby and the midwife took the other, leaving me to be stitched up. Later I learned that they had had to remove my placenta manually and as I had an epidural there was no need for me to have a general anaesthetic. I was shaking uncontrollably and felt very much out of control of my whole body, but euphorically happy. I was waiting to be taken back upstairs and overheard the doctor talking about how twin placentas develop and whether our twins were identical or not. The midwife showed me the placenta and said that the twins could be identical but she could not be sure. Later through blood tests they discovered that they were not identical.

Then another midwife appeared and said that the second twin was a little underweight and cold and would need to go to the special care baby unit, but I could see her first. I was taken back upstairs and freshened up, then I was given both my babies and put them to the breast to suckle. This was when I knew it was really happening to me, they were my babies, the ones that I had carried for nine months, and I cannot describe all the mixed-up thoughts and emotions that were going around in my head.

Melissa, twin two, went off to special care with Mark. Esther, twin number one, went off with the midwife, and I went to my own room. Mark came back to join me with a very welcome cup of tea and toast. We phoned our parents and both of us welled up with tears of emotion. Mark left me to sleep, which was impossible owing to such powerful emotion. Later Esther was brought back to me and put by my bed, but I had to ring for a nurse whenever she needed anything. Feelings of inadequacy were starting to creep in. Mark returned later that night and visited Melissa, which I couldn't do. He then stayed with me until it was time to go home. I wanted him with me to share all these feelings, and he wanted to be there. Esther went to the nursery for the night. Next day Esther stayed in my room with the nurses changing and washing her. At least I could breast-feed her. I knew that she was mine, and love was growing every time that I held her, but I had another baby to love whom I hadn't held since the birth, and this frightened and saddened me. Could I feel this love for two? In the evening I was allowed up, and my first trip was to the special care baby unit where I saw Melissa. There I held her and tried to breast-feed her, but she didn't suck. All around me were caring but very efficient nurses looking after my baby for me. I was overwhelmed with sadness, guilt, confusion and great feelings of inadequacy. I had to go back to my room. By the next morning I was sobbing everywhere to everyone. I had two babies, and all I could do was to feed one of them and I didn't even know how to start caring for her. The staff were wonderful, understanding and reassuring, showing me all the procedures needed to care completely for Esther. They decided to move me to a three-bedded room for company. My only comfort was that Mark was showing Melissa all the comfort and love that he could by visiting her frequently and letting her know that we were there. I visited her three times that day, but it made me feel so useless. My sanity started to return the next day and I set about caring for both of them the best that I could with the two of them in different places. My determination to breast-feed both of them never wavered and occupied my thoughts positively. I learned the special baby care procedures and always tried to breast-feed Melissa before giving way to the bottle and the naso-gastric tube. I would then go back and express my milk for her and then build up my supplies to feed both of them. Mark was my tower of strength, always helping, reassuring and just listening to me. By day eight I was feeling much more confident as a mother and was so happy when I was able to have Melissa in the ward with me. The euphoria returned when I was able to have my two daughters with me for the first time since they were born and I knew that it was possible to love two babies as strongly as one.

On the tenth day we went home, Melissa was not too happy with breast-feeding and on compliment bottles.

Mark on the hospital and birth:
The night before I prepared sandwiches and a flask, telephoned relatives, keeping them abreast of the situation, and deciding that I would wear my tracksuit and trainers for comfort and to combat the extreme heat of the maternity wards. I was afraid about the amount of

pain that Margaret would be experiencing and that I would not be able to lighten or share this experience.

Travelling to the hospital was unreal. The roads were clear as it was a Sunday morning, but it felt like Christmas morning had as a child full of expectant surprises. I arrived at 10 a.m. and Margaret informed me that things were already happening. We went up to the labour ward where Margaret had the epidural inserted. Things were quite peaceful here, and I recall that the suite overlooked the rooftops of the town. It was at this point that I wished that I had brought a cassette-recorder with me so that we could have listened to some music while things were calm and relaxed.

Panic struck when they realised that Margaret was fully dilated and theatre was imminent. The journey to theatre was via the hospital lift, and I remember thinking how cramped we all were. I began to feel that things were running away, I was losing control. The theatre also felt very small, and I consciously counted twelve people, excluding myself, who were to be witness to the event. This made me feel on the periphery, but also that everything was ready and under control. I was made to feel very much part of the team. I wanted to talk to Margaret and be more helpful but felt inhibited by the distractions and the demands that the midwives were making on her to push under the numbing effects of the epidural. I felt that I offered what words of comfort that I could, sponging her brow and staring at intervals at what was happening and being aware that the doctor was indicating a wish to intervene and at the same time attending to Margaret's wishes to continue to push.

Next I remember being told to look at the baby's head, and the next moment the first baby girl was born. Not as I had seen on TV, all wrinkled, but smooth and pink and silently smiling. I remember thinking how her expression seemed to resemble that of my grandmother. She was named immediately as Esther, and I waited with bated breath hoping that she was all right. Temporary relief as she was examined and found to be perfect. But our second child was still to be born. Eight minutes later a second head appeared and safely delivered. I was given her and asked to carry her down to the nursery to be washed, which I did with pride. On return to the theatre both babies were held by Margaret and she put them to the breast. I felt joy at seeing them sucking and Margaret holding them. Melissa was then taken to special care.

I was aware that special care baby units were for very sick babies, but I was relieved to know that she was only there because she weighed less than five pounds. I was made to feel very welcome and encouraged to become involved in her care. She was in a small room occupied by three other cots and I was shown how to care for her and to carry out assisted feeding through the naso-gastric tube. This tube looks awfully pitiful in a newborn baby. A photo was taken of her as soon as she was brought from theatre, and this was most welcome as I was able to take it to Margaret so that she could keep it on her locker as a constant reminder of her other daughter. I was aware of Margaret's feelings of not being able to have both babies at her bedside, so I provided that link for her, over the following eight days, by caring for Melissa. For me it was a bonding that I will always cherish. Fathers seldom, in these early stages, have such an opportunity to give such practical support to their baby. So changing her nappy, washing and feeding her was for me a feeling of usefulness and being a father in the fullest sense. Later Margaret was able to come and renew her mother's rôle.

Home and the first months. Mark:
The drive home felt strange in that I was a little apprehensive and the enormity of parental responsibility was starting to dawn on me. In the hospital I was not experiencing the impact of twenty-four-hour care as Margaret was. I could go home and still lead my own life. But this was different, and I can vividly recall being overwhelmed and shell-shocked that two babies had managed to change our lives so dramatically. Although I loved Esther and Melissa dearly, to act selfless and unselfish is extremely hard when your lives have been previously self-orientated. The first three months were hard for me, and it took me longer to adjust than it did for Margaret. I didn't want to let her down, so I took on all household chores, cooking and ensuring that Margaret got all that she needed to ensure that she was successful with breast-feeding. However, looking back on these early weeks, it is vital that you have time to spend by yourselves, and this is when you miss having a close family at hand. This also made us buckle down and establish a routine for our babies.

On return to work I had mixed feelings, glad to be back and guilty at leaving Margaret to cope. I knew deep down that she would cope and proud that she was fully committed as a loving mother. On return from work I would set to bathing and changing Esther and Melissa and getting them ready for bed, an activity that I still enjoy today. However, return from work in those early days was disheartening as it also coincided with long crying periods. At one point I was getting quite uptight, thinking that it was me that was causing these episodes and never seeing them happy.

The winter evenings were very long, never having time for ourselves, sometimes until ten and eleven o'clock at night. Margaret would then just want to go to bed, and I would settle down and try and tackle some course work for college. At weekends we would try and go out, but those winter months meant that the preparation to get the twins out was longer than the excursion. You realise the advantages of a summer birth; getting out and about is so vital and is a momentary cure for insanity. On reflection those days of attending to their total needs seemed never-ending, but you cope with it. It really is not that long; it just appears so at the time. For me those first few months were the worst. Gradually independence increases subtly, day after day, and all the hard work is eventually rewarded.

Like all parents we have recorded the progress of our children with photographs and also have a video-recording as from six months. Looking at them brings back many mixed emotions and wonder at how we coped. Looking at the progress of the Walton sextuplets, however, makes me feel humble and a certain sense of relief and I can't begin to imagine how I would have coped.

Margaret:
The first few months were a never-ending round of nappies, feeds, stopping crying, night feeds and all-consuming tiredness for both of us. Mark had two weeks' holiday when I got home and after twenty-four hours appeared shell-shocked by the enormity of the care involved. After three nights the girls went into their own bedroom, as two carry-cots and a double bed in our room made it rather hard to move around and sleep was uneasy with the babies' noises. It took two weeks with a lot of support first from the midwife and then from the National Child Birth Trust to get Melissa off her compliment feed. I must express grateful thanks to the National Child Birth Trust counsellor and for the whole NCBT post-natal support that I received, which was my saviour in those black moments of despair when life seemed full of nothing but crying babies.

The worst day was when Mark went back to work. A feeling of panic arose: there were two of them and only one of me – how would I cope? But like most other situations in life you just have to. I have never had just one baby, so I have nothing to compare, and there were days when I wished I only had one, but which one as I love them both, and couldn't part with either of them. When you start taking them out you are greeted with two common reactions: 'Twins! Oh, how lovely for you' or 'Twins! Oh dear, poor you'. The second one is from mums with babies or toddlers whose memories of those early days are still fresh. But you do feel special again as so many people express so much delight in your babies.

So how did I cope with these two babies? The first is a helpful supportive husband without whom I couldn't have coped. The second was my determination and success at breast-feeding, which was a bonus. It is absolute bliss, with two crying babies, and only you around, to be able within minutes to silence them by breast-feeding. During the first few weeks, when building up my milk-supply and finding it hard going, I'd just think of the number of bottles that are needed for one day that would require sterilising and preparing and how can you feed two babies at once with bottles? In fact the only disadvantage that I could find was that no one can breast-feed for you. Therefore your partner can't take over the night feeds and let you sleep. Luckily, Esther, a very contented and happy baby, slept through the night at three months. Melissa, who was a very demanding baby and who had crying periods every night between six and ten for the first three months, still woke at night until her first birthday.

Another aid to an easier life, and one that I wouldn't have been without, was a home help for three months: no guilty feelings about dust and ironing piling up around you, while you spend most of the day with your feet up breast-feeding or cuddling. To make sure that they both get as much cuddling as a single baby takes up a lot of time. The second: disposable nappies. God bless the person who invented these. As to expense, it worked out that one baby's family allowance covered the cost of nappies for two of them. The automatic washing machine was essential. When the smiles start arriving the hard work seems worth it; when small steps towards independence start happening you know it's getting better and easier. By the end of the first year you look back and think: How did I do it? A friend who also had twins once said: 'As a mother of twins you are statistically one in eighty, when you first hold them you feel like one in a million, but on bad days you think you are the only one.'

The girls are now two. Writing this has made us realise what an emotional time in our lives it was and how much we have changed not only as individuals but as a couple. The first few months put quite a strain on our relationship, tiredness making us very intolerant and also no time to communicate our feelings, no time alone. Total absorption in being good parents and seeing to their demands and needs making us forget our own needs. Now life is back on an even keel, Esther and Melissa are gaining greater independence from us and we are seeing ourselves as Margaret and Mark again, as individuals who share their lives and two wonderful daughters, not just as parents of twins. Margaret, who gave up her career to take up a new one as mother and had never regretted that decision, now can see clearly that soon she can take up her working life again. Mark can now see days ahead of sharing leisure activities with his daughters that we can all enjoy and not tailored days out just to their needs. In fact we can now see ourselves as a family unit respecting all our needs.

Despite all advice and knowledge given before the babies arrived, you are never really prepared for the changes that occur and all the hard work until it happens to you, but once you have got them there is no going back and we wouldn't want to.

MARK AND MARGARET JUKES

If you are expecting twins, Mark and Margaret's experience will be invaluable. You could also contact the National Childbirth Trust and the Twins and Multiple Births Association: see page 296 for the addresses and more information.

TEETHING

A child who is teething dribbles, has his fingers constantly in his mouth and is generally irritable and difficult to live with. Teething does not cause a rise in temperature, bronchitis or a rash; if your child has any of these symptoms, see your doctor. It always worries me when parents put these symptoms down to teething when it could be something more serious. If in doubt, see your doctor.

POTTY TRAINING

My mother-in-law constantly told me how all her children were potty-trained by the time they were nine months old. My child was still wearing nappies at two years and we had had many unsuccessful and very traumatic attempts at potty training. She made me feel that I was a bad mother as I was unable to train my own child.

So much rubbish is talked about this subject by grandmothers, aunts, neighbours and anyone else that you care to mention. Having conscious control over the bladder and bowels is not possible before the age of eighteen months nor is it a sign of intelligence! Potty training is not a problem if it is tackled at the right time.

Bladder and bowel control occur any time from the age of eighteen months; the nerve pathways involved in exerting conscious control over these organs are simply not mature before this age, so anyone who tells you that they never had a dirty nappy after their child was the age of nine months or a year old has quite simply trained themselves to put their child on a potty after feeding and has managed to catch his stool. The normal gastro-colic reflex works like this: if you put food in one end (the stomach), a reflex message goes to the gut and tells it to empty its contents at the other end, which it does.

If you wait until your child is two years old, you will find the process a whole lot easier. There are bound to be occasional accidents, so try to keep calm and not get too upset. Be patient, loving and show consistent understanding.

What to do:

- Go out and buy a strong comfortable potty with a rigid base so that it doesn't tip sideways. You will need one with a splash-guard for a boy. When you go out to buy the potty get your child to help you choose it.
- Keep it in the same place at home, so that he knows where it is. Keep it in a warm room, so he doesn't associate using the potty with feeling cold, and in a room with a washable floor.
- Put him on the potty for a few minutes after meals and once every three to four hours. You will soon be able to estimate how often he needs the potty.
- When he has used the potty get him used to being cleaned and gradually get him to clean himself with soft lavatory paper, then to wash his hands; and don't forget to tell him how well he has done.
- Replace nappies with trainer pants which have towelling linings and a plastic outside with elasticated legs. These are easy to pull up and down, and he will be able to do this for himself.
- When you have succeeded in potty training during the day, then take off his nappies at night. As long as you leave him in nappies he will assume that they are there to be used. Encourage him to use the potty last thing at night before he goes to sleep.

- If possible, start this training in the warm weather so that he can run around with less clothing on, and you will not worry quite so much about accidents that occur in the garden.

Problems:

- Refusal. If you put him on the potty and he simply screams and yells, forget it for now; he is not ready. You will need to try again in a few weeks' time. If he just sits there politely and does nothing, then proceeds to do it all over the floor when you take him off the potty, he is not ready. Try again in a few weeks' time.
- Doesn't use the potty. Don't make an issue about it and don't leave him sitting there for more than ten minutes.
- If a baby has been potted regularly, after every meal, from birth the touch of the potty against his skin will probably cause his bowels to open. This is without any conscious effort on his behalf. When he reaches the age of two his mother may be very upset to find that she has to start all over again in order that her son can achieve conscious control over his bladder and bowels.

Your child is potty-trained when he is able to tell you every time he wants to go to the lavatory and in enough time to avoid accidents and he also knows when he doesn't need to go.

If you let a boy go to the lavatory with his father or a girl with you, they will soon learn how to use the lavatory. We all learn best by imitation but you can make it easier for them by getting a trainer seat, which is a small seat that fits over the lavatory seat.

TEMPER TANTRUMS

When my son was two years old he started having temper tantrums. I had tried everything – giving him a cuddle, smacking him, shouting. Nothing worked, and a friend of mine told me to try and ignore him when it happened. I didn't think it would work, but it was worth a try. One day we were in the greengrocer's and he wanted some grapes. I said 'No', and with that he flung himself on the floor and lay there kicking and screaming. As usual people in the shop started to make remarks like 'He needs a good spanking', 'Spoilt brat', 'His mother should do something about him', and so on. I had heard all this before. This time I ignored both them and my son. So I continued to order my shopping and make myself heard above the screaming, and when I had finished I turned to my son and said, 'I am going home now. Are you coming or staying here?' and walked out of the shop. It worked. He stopped screaming, stood up and followed me out of the shop. Every time he started his tantrums I simply ignored him. It wasn't easy. I still felt embarrassed and uncomfortable, but I managed to hide my feelings and eventually he stopped doing it.

MARY GRANT

What makes a perfectly delightful two-year-old (this sort of behaviour is most common at this age) suddenly become a raging monster? It may be frustration, over-excitement, exhaustion or simply anger. Watch for signs of these situations developing and try to prevent him getting to the stage where a tantrum will occur. If your child is trying to do something that he really can't do, help him to get it right before he becomes so frustrated that he throws a tantrum. If he is becoming over-excited or tired, change the activity to something more restful. If he becomes angry when you try to stop him doing something that he is enjoying because it is tea-time or bed-time, tell him that it will be time to stop in so many minutes' time so that he knows what is going to happen next.

What can you do?

- Try not to over-react when he does have a tantrum. If you start shouting as well, he will feel even more confused, angry and frustrated.
- Keep calm, be firm and try to keep your sense of humour.
- Don't take any notice of what other people think or say, especially if this happens in shops or in someone else's home. You can pick him up and remove him bodily from the audience, then without fussing, making threats or offering bribes just wait for him to stop. When he has calmed down and is back to being his old self, give him a cuddle and reassure him that you still love him but you expect him to control his temper. Later when he has calmed down you can say: 'You were very cross yesterday, weren't you?' This will help him to realise that you do understand.

It really is a question of recognising the signs of an imminent tantrum and, like Mary, finding out what works for you and your child and sticking to it.

These are just some of the problems associated with babies and young children, and of course there are numerous others like nappy rash, cradle cap, coughs and colds, problems weaning your baby on to solids. Perhaps your baby is not talking, crawling, standing, walking or producing teeth exactly at the times stated in the books, or your friend's baby is the same age and seems to be doing much more than yours. Of course it is worrying, but always remember that your child has not read the books, no two babies are exactly alike, and if in doubt always seek professional advice sooner rather than later. Most important of all, enjoy these very special years with your child.

CHAPTER THREE

Schoolchildren and Adolescence

This chapter looks at some of the problems or crises that affect both children from the age of two up to the age of about sixteen and their parents and families.

GOING BACK TO WORK WHEN YOU HAVE A YOUNG BABY

Some women choose to give up their job and stay at home to look after and bring up their children, others choose to go back to work because they need and enjoy the stimulation of a career, while others have to go back to work for financial reasons. When you are expecting your baby it all seems very straightforward and simple: you just find someone to look after your baby and you take up your job again. Once the baby has arrived, feelings and emotions seem to change, and handing your baby over to someone else while you go out to work is not quite as easy as you thought it would be. In the United Kingdom there are statutory rights both before and after the birth of the baby and maternity benefits. See pages 287, 299.

By the time I went on maternity leave before having my baby I was beginning to have doubts about how I would feel when the time came to go back to work. However, it was a long way off, and I thought I would cross that bridge when I came to it. I knew that I had to go back to work as we couldn't survive on John's income.

After the baby was born I was really so happy just being at home with her, and the weeks went by very quickly. Soon it was time to find someone to look after her so that I could go back to work. I went to the library and got a list of the nurseries and crèches nearby, and very soon discovered that unless I was a single mother or in desperate need there was no way that I was going to get a place for my baby. Then I asked the woman at the Social Services to help me find a childminder, as I was beginning to get a bit desperate because I had to go back to work in six weeks' time and I was getting nowhere fast. Anyway, she was very helpful, and we talked about the cost, the number of hours and where I lived and worked.

She gave me the address of three childminders who lived quite near me and told me to go and see them. I went round to the first one, who opened the door with a child under one arm and a cigarette hanging out of her mouth. I didn't even go in. I pushed the pram on up the road; there were tears rolling down my cheeks. There was no way that I could leave my child with someone like that. I went home and told John we would have to cut back and just manage without my money. I knew this was a daft idea, as we couldn't survive on his money. John was really great and said that we ought to see the other childminders as it had been arranged and he would come with me.

The next day we went and saw the other two childminders, and I really liked one of them. She was an older woman who had two children of her own who were fifteen and seventeen years old. She was a very happy, calm and motherly type of person. There was only one other child there, who was a little bit older than my Claire. We visited her several times before I went back to work, and sorted out all the things that were worrying me. Such as how I would manage to go on breast-feeding, etc., and all the little things that Claire liked and was used to.

I can't pretend that it was easy leaving her there all day. In fact it nearly broke my heart. In the beginning I would ring up as many as five or six times a day just to check that she was all right; I must have been very difficult. What kept me going was that Claire seemed very happy and settled in easily; it was I that found it so hard.

It's funny really, but we had more problems when she got to about eighteen months old as some mornings when I left her she would scream the place down. All the way to work I would be really worried and frightened that I was doing the wrong thing and she would end up disturbed or something. I would ring as soon as I got to work and be told that she had stopped crying as soon as I had gone. Later she started to cry and be really difficult when I collected her in the evening, and she would whine and winge until bed-time. I think I was very lucky with my childminder because I could talk to her about all these problems and she had so much experience with young children that she could explain why Claire was behaving like that.

We even managed weaning her on to solids and the potty training between us with very few problems. Claire stayed with her until she went to play school and we still keep in touch; she has become a really good friend.

PAULINE HOWELL

As Pauline has pointed out, it is not always very easy for a mother to hand over the care of her baby or child to someone else. Pauline made a good choice in her childminder, and this is really the key to success. A childminder is someone who is paid to look after children under the age of five in her own home. Childminders must be registered with the local Social Services department, and in order to have registered someone from the department will have checked that:

- There is a safe warm place for the children to play.
- The kitchen and toilet facilities are adequate.
- The childminder is prepared to give all her time to care for the children. She will look after their basic needs, take them for walks, spend time playing with the children.
- There are plenty of suitable toys to play with.
- She is fit and healthy.
- She has previous experience of child care.

Settling your child with the childminder

The following advice could be followed whenever you plan to leave a very young child with someone for the day:
- Visit her with your child several times before you leave your child with her and get him used to the surroundings.
- The first time you leave him make sure that it is only for a short time and gradually increase to the required time as he gets used to it. Always say goodbye, never sneak out while he is not looking, or he will learn not to trust you. Tell him when you will be back, make sure that you are, and he will learn to trust you. If you are going to be late, telephone the childminder and ask her to explain to your child. Even if a child is unable to tell the time it seems that he or she is able to sense when things should happen.
- Make sure he takes his favourite toy with him.
- Leave your work address, telephone number and your family doctor's name, address and telephone number.

- Leave a list of the illnesses and the immunisations that your child has had.
- Food. If you have a baby or a toddler that is still having milk feeds or taking baby foods, you will need to send him with the amount he will need over the day and a bit extra in case some gets spilled or he is hungry.
- Clothes. Make sure that you send enough nappies for the whole day and all the changing equipment, a change of clothes in case of accidents, and his outdoor clothes so that she can take him for a walk.
- Do not take him if he is ill but make sure that you call her and tell her what is happening. This is very important if he has an infectious disease as it will affect the other young children that she cares for.
- He may well cry when you leave him and behave like a monster when you collect him. This is quite normal; he has probably been perfectly all right all day. The childminder will tell you if he has been unhappy or is not settling. If he is really unhappy and the childminder says that he is not settling down, you may have to rethink the situation. Perhaps reduce the amount of time you are away or change childminder. Do not spend ages talking to her when you collect him; he needs to get home, so do you, and your childminder will be busy with the other children and her own family.
- Give him time to settle and get used to being parted from you.
- It is not a good idea to change from one childminder to another unless you have a really good reason for doing so. Continuity and routine are very important to your child. For more information about childminders, see page 299.

Day nurseries are provided for mothers or single parents who have to go out to work. They should take no more than forty to fifty children, divided into small groups and looked after by trained staff. There should be plenty of toys, painting, modelling, climbing, pushing and pulling toys and lots of other things to do. They provide all the care a child needs during the day including a well-balanced diet and facilities so that they can have a rest.

There is usually a long list for places, and priority is given to single parents and mothers in essential services like nursing and teaching. There are also private day nurseries and of course nannies, which are more expensive. See page 299 for more information. Chapter 11 discusses further the problems incurred by working mothers with children of all ages.

STARTING SCHOOL

Whenever your child leaves you for the first time, whether it is to play school, nursery school or full-time education, it is very important to plan ahead and prepare your child for school. The average four-year-old is lively, active, imaginative and well ready for some pre-school education. Play groups are run by playleaders who have undertaken special courses. The children meet together in someone's home, in a hall, in fact anywhere there is space. They provide an opportunity for the child to play with paint, sand, water and many other activities which might be difficult to do at home. A good play group should have lots of toys that fire the imagination, things to climb on, picture-books to look at, clothes for dressing up in, jigsaws and toys which require concentration and effort. Going to a play group gives the child a chance to meet and make new friends and helps him to become more independent and confident without his mother.

Nursery schools are staffed by qualified teachers and assistants holding the National Nursery Examination Board certificate. They may be maintained by the State or be private fee-paying schools. They offer more structured learning than the play groups, including listening to music and stories, starting to read when they are ready to and lots of drawing and painting.

Before he starts either nursery school or full-time education it will help him if you can teach him how to dress and undress himself without help and ensure that he is confident in managing his toilet needs. Most children look forward to starting school, and with a little encouragement from his family he will go to school with the idea that it will be great fun and that school is a happy and enjoyable place where there are lots of interesting things to do.

PROBLEMS AT SCHOOL

Perhaps one of the most common problems for a child and the most worrying for a parent is when he is having learning difficulties and in particular difficulty reading. A child who is having difficulty reading needs extra help and understanding to overcome the problem as this inevitably affects all the other subjects at school. There are several reasons why your child may be having difficulty reading. It could be emotional distress as the result of problems at home or distress caused by problems at school. There may be a physical reason such as poor eyesight or a hearing loss. Another cause is well recognised these days and is called dyslexia.

Dyslexia is a condition where the child is unable to recognise the shape of a word and to link it to the sound of the word. A child who is dyslexic may well have started to speak later than normal, or may be clumsy, have difficulty telling his left from his right or even be ambidextrous or left-handed. He tends to write slowly and hesitantly and leaves very large or small gaps between the letters and writes at an angle. Some letters like 'p' may be written as 'b', and some children write and form their words and even whole sentences back to front, mirror writing. If your child has any of these symptoms, don't immediately jump to the conclusion that he is dyslexic. If he has several of these symptoms, it may mean nothing, but it would be sensible to discuss the problem with his teacher and head teacher. If for any reason they do not seem to think it is a problem, but you are still worried, ask to see an educational psychologist. You can arrange this through your School Medical Officer. You could also get in touch with a specialist organisation: see page 300.

What can you do at home?

Whatever the learning problem, whether it is reading, writing, spelling, mathematics or any other subject, you need to talk to your child's teacher and ask if there is some extra work that you can do with your child to help him to achieve. Whatever you do, remember not to nag and scold when something is done badly; offer constructive criticism and help him get it right, and remember to congratulate him when he does. Offer lots of love and support, stay calm and keep a sense of humour. Do not work at something for too long or he will run out of concentration and enthusiasm. Try to make learning enjoyable; there are plenty of books available in the shops to help you to teach your child: see page 302.

HYPERACTIVE CHILDREN

Some children are naturally very boisterous, lively and busy, but a child who is truly hyperactive is one that is on the go from morning to night to the extent that he leaves his parents exhausted. He is quite incapable of controlling his restlessness or his disruptive and aggressive behaviour, either at home or at school. He is so disobedient or uncontrolled that his parents seek professional advice. A hyperactive child often sleeps for only a few hours and keeps everyone in the family awake for the rest of the night. He has little or no powers of concentration and flits from one activity to the next; he has no sense of fear or danger and becomes aggressive if someone tries to stop him doing something that he wants to do. This obviously leads to constant arguments and battles and upsets everyone in the family. He doesn't make friends very easily or keep his friends for very long because of his aggressive behaviour.

Sometimes the cause is an emotional one and the child is really chronically anxious about life, and he shows this by incessant chatter and movement; he finds it difficult to concentrate and is easily distracted, which may well lead to learning problems at school. Some children react like this if they are bored and there is not enough for them to do. Others are just born restless; they don't seem to want to be still for a moment, don't want to be cuddled, and as they get older seem quite incapable of sitting still for any length of time. In some cases it may be caused by vitamin deficiency or an allergy to certain food additives.

What can be done to help?

- Some children can be helped by vitamin therapy if your doctor thinks that a deficiency is the cause of the problem.
- If a food additive is established to be the cause, a special diet will help.
- A truly hyperactive child will need specialist help, and the first step is to talk to your family doctor. If you have reached the stage where there is so much tension and conflict that there is more unhappiness than relaxed enjoyment with your child, seek professional advice.
- There are also support groups for parents with hyperactive children: see page 303.

BULLYING

Children will demonstrate their anger and aggression by attacking each other, screaming insults and being destructive. Many children go through a stage of biting and hitting other children. Parents can do a lot to put a stop to this kind of aggression at an early stage. If a parent tries to stop this behaviour by hitting the child and showing him what it feels like, it will probably only make him more angry and increase his aggression. It is better to remove him firmly from the scene and find him something else to do. If he tends to dominate children of his own age, try introducing him to older children.

If you find out that your child is a bully, you really do need to look at your own behaviour. Do you bully him? Does someone else in the family bully him? Are you sarcastic when he does something wrong? Perhaps he is using the same tactics on his friends, taunting, teasing and saying hurtful things. Are you consistent in your discipline or do you let him get away with something one minute and shout at him the next? Are there marital problems at home? Perhaps he is taking out his feelings of frustration and anger on someone smaller.

Of course it may be nothing to do with home; he may have got in with a bad crowd at school. If this is the case, you need to sit down and explain to him just what it feels like to be bullied.

He may have a teacher that is bullying him and so he bullies the next person down the pecking order. If this is the case, you need to discuss the problem with the head teacher.

You must tell him that you will not accept bullying, and take away one of his privileges such as his pocket money and say that you expect him to apologise to the victim. This is usually enough to stop the problem, but if it continues you may have to seek professional advice.

What about the victim of the bully? Essentially there are three types of bullying: physical brutality when the child is either hit or hurt physically; mental cruelty including taunting, teasing and mocking; and finally the child that is threatened and made to pay in money, sweets or with his possessions in order to be left alone. The sad thing is that children who are being bullied very rarely tell their parents or anyone else, and this leaves them even more isolated and frightened. Children are often picked on because they are different: taller, smaller, thinner, fatter, wear glasses – in fact anything that makes them look different. You might suspect that your child is being bullied if he has come home looking as though he has been in a fight. You might notice that he has spent all his money and wants to borrow some from you, or you find he is taking it out of your purse, or you notice that some of his possessions are missing. If a normally happy child who likes school becomes withdrawn, unhappy and doesn't want to go to school, check if he is being bullied.

You really do have to tackle this problem; it will not go away. If your child is being bullied, he may be much more unhappy than you realise.

Victims of bullying have been known to commit suicide because of the complete isolation, despair and fear that they feel.

What can you do?

- Talk to your child calmly and quietly. Try not to over-react and become emotional; it will not help him – he has enough to cope with already. This is often very difficult for a parent who feels that his or her child is being threatened.
- A father may well react by threatening to go round and sort out the bully. This is not a good idea and will not stop your child being bullied. In fact it will only make things worse.
- Establish the facts. What has been happening? Who has been doing it? When and where?
- Show him that you care and tell him that you want to know if and when it happens again. Reassure him that he is neither a 'telltale' nor a 'sneak' if he tells you what is going on. Then leave it for a week and you may find that your child will have gained enough confidence and an inner strength from simply finding the courage to talk to you about his problem, and he will sort it out himself.
- If the bullying continues, go and see the head teacher of the school and tell him what has been going on. Schoolteachers have a great deal of experience in dealing with this sort of problem, and if they are not aware that there is bullying in the school they will be very pleased that you have told them. Tell them that you are very concerned about the problem and you expect something to be done about it. State that you are not looking for revenge but simply want the bullying to stop. Work together with the school and your child, and together you will have a much greater chance of solving the problem.
- If the school does nothing about it, you may have to take the problem to the authorities that run the school or even to the police.

STEALING

When a young child of three or four years old takes something that does not belong to him it's because he has no idea about what belongs to him and to someone else. If you have taught him to share his toys, and he does so willingly, he may well see taking someone else's toy home with him as simply sharing. Try not to over-react because you see it as stealing; just get him to return the toy and help him to learn the difference between sharing and stealing. Explain that by taking the toy he will have upset the child that owns it.

There are various reasons why older children steal; they may be encouraged to steal by their friends, so they do so in order to be one of the gang. Some children steal because their parents do, so they see nothing wrong in doing the same thing. It may be they steal because they want something for themselves like tapes, records or a radio. Some children who steal from shops do so purely for the comfort that it gives them when they look at all the goodies that they have stolen and hidden in their bedroom; it makes them feel that they are a more important person because of their possessions.

Some children steal because they find that the danger of being caught is exciting and they enjoy this sensation. A child that finds something and keeps it may well be emulating parents that do the same. As I mentioned before, a child that is being bullied may well steal to pay off the bully, or he may be stealing in order to buy friendship by giving other children presents.

What can you do to prevent your child stealing or stop him if he has already stolen something?

■ Stick by your own code of what is right and wrong, be consistent and make sure that your child understands from a very early age. If your child has taken something that belongs to another child, make him take it back. If he takes something from a shop, take him back there and explain to the shopkeeper that he took it without paying and wants to return it and apologise.

■ Explain to your child why he shouldn't steal, highlight the stress and unhappiness that it causes both for the family of the thief and for the victim.

■ Send your child on errands. Show him that you trust him with money. Help older children to manage money by giving them a clothes allowance.

■ If you find out that your child has stolen something, make it perfectly clear that it goes against everything that you believe in and that you will not tolerate it, but make it very clear that you still love him.

■ Always set a good example yourself. If you find something in the street, take it to the police station and hand it in. If someone in a shop gives you too much change, make sure you point it out and the error is corrected. If your child sees that you are honest, he will copy you. If he sees you stealing, you can hardly blame him for being dishonest.

In Chapter 12 there is more about stealing, burglary and mugging.

TRUANCY

A truant is a child who stays away from school without good reason or without the permission of his parents or teachers. Nearly all children at one time or another stay away from school in order to avoid an examination, a punishment or a particular lesson or activity, and this situation is easily put right with understanding and firmness from his parents to help overcome whatever he is avoiding.

The child that is a persistent truant may avoid going to school for several reasons:

- He may find school boring or really dislike school because he is never successful. If this is happening to your child, try to read the early signs of his feelings and talk to his teacher about the problem. Find out which subjects he is good at and strengthen his success in these; also establish which ones he is having problems with, help him yourself or organise extra help so that he gets some feeling of achievement. The longer the problem is ignored, the worse it will become. It is important for parents to keep in touch with what is going on, and schoolteachers welcome parents who are interested in their child's progress even if it is slow.
- If your child refuses to go to school, it may be because there is something worrying him and you need to find out what it is. It may be something at school that he is trying to avoid. Or it may be something at home that makes him feel that he should be there rather than at school; perhaps someone is or has been unwell, and he feels that he should be at home so that he knows what is going on and in case he is needed.

Whatever the reason, it is important to contact his school and sort out the problem as soon as you can. Sometimes it may be necessary for your child to see an educational psychologist. There is no disgrace in seeing an educational psychologist: he or she is qualified to help children with educational and emotional problems and will be able to help your child.

There are organisations and support groups to help you with these and many other problems that affect the child and his family during his school days. See page 302 for more information.

ADOLESCENCE

The term *adolescence* is used to describe a complex stage of development when physical, mental and emotional changes take place and a child becomes an adult.

A seventeen-year-old boy explains his feelings:

> I am one of the unlucky few who seem to be social misfits. I cannot talk to my parents, and have few friends, and am under great stress myself by keeping feelings to myself. It can be incredibly frustrating when there is no one that you can talk to about love and relationships.

The letter highlights so clearly the feelings of confusion, isolation and frustration felt by young people. These problems can be overcome if the young person and his parents talk and listen to each other. Sometimes this can be very difficult, but it really is up to the parents to make sure that the communication lines are always left open.

Some of the common problems that occur during this period from both the parents' point of view and that of the young person are:

Parents: 'He treats our home like a hotel.'

Adolescence is a time when the young person is trying to become an independent adult, and you need to reassess your attitude towards your child; he is no longer your little baby or little boy. To continue to see him in this light will either lead to outright rebellion on his behalf or he will become increasingly dependent upon you, which will retard his development into an adult. So you need to encourage this independence but at the same time make sure that home is safe, secure, loving and stable even if at times you feel that he treats it like a hotel. He really does need this kind of secure base in order to gain his confidence and independence.

Young people: 'They are always nagging me about my untidy room.'

To you home is really a launching-pad, a place from which you are starting to build your adult life, but try to remember that your family home means something very different to your parents. They have worked hard to build their home and have lived there for many years;

they have seen you grow from a little baby to a young person probably within the same four walls, and it holds many happy memories for them. It will help them if you respect their property and keep the rules about tidiness and cleanliness, particularly in your own room. Do not take money for granted and try to contribute to the home if you can.

Parents: 'He doesn't seem to care about us any more. We are no longer important to him. He won't listen to advice. He is just not interested in what we have to say and he is so moody.'

Relationships between parent and child change; those feelings and emotions of love that were once reserved for you are now transferred to the latest girlfriend or boyfriend. This doesn't mean that he or she no longer loves you, but that the relationship is changing from dependent child to independent adult. This certainly doesn't happen overnight, and there will be times when the young person gets hurt and this in turn will hurt you. It is important to be able to offer sympathy, a willingness to listen and to give practical advice when asked. If the young person doesn't want to take you into his confidence and tell you about a problem, then having offered to listen and help if you can simply drop the subject and respect their wishes. Don't be embarrassed to tell the young person that you still love him and demonstrate your affection.

Any parent who tries to understand everything about the adolescent will have a very hard task indeed, and I seem to remember that part of the business of being a teenager was being misunderstood. There are bound to be times of conflict of opinion, particularly about the time that you expect the young person to come home. Young people need you to be really interested and to listen to what they are saying without putting them down or telling them how to solve the problem. So listen carefully to what the young person is saying and if in doubt check what has been said by repeating it back to them and saying 'Have I got it right?' or 'Do you mean?' It is important to avoid misunderstandings and hasty judgements. Be prepared to negotiate with a bit of give and take on both sides. Young people need help to work out and solve their own problems and not have them solved for them.

Young person: 'They won't let me stay out after eleven, and all my friends are allowed to. They treat me like a child.'

You are changing all the time and probably have days when you feel really good about life and then for no apparent reason you get a day when nothing can snap you out of a bad mood. This is all part of the changes that are occurring in your body, and they are only temporary and do not go on for ever. When you have got one of those bad days, try not to let it lead you to say hurtful things that you do not mean; much better to say 'I'm in a bad mood; best to leave me alone'. If you do end up saying something that you regret, don't be afraid to say sorry and mean it.

If you are having a discussion with your parents, don't lose your temper and storm out of the room as this will only confirm in your parents' minds that you are a naughty child and shouldn't be taken seriously. If they ask you if they can help, don't reply by sulking or refusing to talk to them about it; they are not telepathic and can't help you if you won't let them. If you want to talk to your parents about something that you know is likely to cause conflict and argument, it may be better to have the discussion away from home. If you choose a public place that you will all enjoy, they are much more likely to treat you as an equal, tempers are less likely to fly in public and you are more likely to hold yourself in check and not be tempted to scream 'I hate you' and run out of the room.

Sometimes problems about the time you come in or who you go out with are better discussed with your parents and someone from outside the family. Choose someone whom your parents like and respect and who cares about you enough to help you discuss the problem with your parents. Most parents only make rules about when you should be in by and who you are with because they worry about your safety; they are not trying to spoil your fun. If you tell them where you are going, what time you will be back and who you will be with, they will feel much happier about the whole situation. Don't tell them lies about what you are doing. When they find out it will only make them think that you are still irresponsible.

Don't assume that your parents are stupid just because they don't agree with you. Remember that the only experience worth having is your own, but there is nothing wrong in drawing on other people's experience. So listen carefully to what they have to say before you reject their suggestions. Most parents do remember what it was like to be your age and they want to help you to be happy and successful even if it does seem to you that they are trying to hold you back or stop you doing things just for the sake of it.

Parents: 'He is always comparing us to his friends' parents and making us feel inadequate.'

Adolescence is a time when young people test the values of their parents. They will compare your standards and the way that you live with that of their friends' parents. Stick by what you believe; the very fact that you do this will ensure that the young person feels secure.

Be consistent in your beliefs, standards and views. If you keep changing your ideas, the young person will feel even more confused and unsure. Stand by him or her and remember to give praise when it is due and encouragement when it is needed. Young people just like anyone else need approval and to feel trusted.

It is important to be yourself. Some young people are acutely embarrassed by parents who try to join in and be like them. Whatever the latest trend in teenage fashion, it is better to ignore it on an everyday basis; the more you say how awful he or she looks, the more extreme the look will become. If the young person is going out with you, discuss the problem and come to an agreement over something suitable to wear.

Young people: 'Everything at home is so old-fashioned and boring.'

It is easy for young people to forget that their parents have feelings, too, and one of the things about being an adult is to respect other people's feelings. By saying that your home is tatty, not like your friend's house, or constantly comparing what your parents believe in with that of your friend's parents will only hurt and upset them, and they are really only trying to do their best for you.

Don't be afraid to show your affection to your parents and don't push them away when they are affectionate towards you. There is nothing childish about showing affection for each other.

For some young people these years are very difficult indeed, and the relationship between them and their parents just breaks down completely and they need someone to talk to anonymously; for help and someone to turn to, see page 303.

CULTS

Young people are vulnerable to the people who recruit for the many cults and quasi-religious groups that exist in the United Kingdom. The cult problem is such that many people who have had members of their family rescued from a cult do not want to talk about the problem, especially in a book, just in case the story 'rings a bell' in unwanted quarters. Those parents whose children are safe and sound out of the cult that they joined often do not wish to be reminded of the nightmare. This goes for the children as well, who want to get on with their lives and to forget that they are ex-members.

I spoke to a member of an organisation called FAIR (Family Action Information and Rescue), and they gave me the following advice.

If a member of your family or your child is thinking about or has actually joined a cult, do everything you can to keep in touch with your child, keep on writing and phoning, don't give up. Remember that your child is a product of your love, home environment and heredity, and these influences are hard to eradicate. Try to find out how he or she is responding to cult life. Make sure that your manner is calm and affectionate; this will help to make contact with your child easier.

See if you can find out why he or she joined a cult and what they are seeking. Be sympathetic and understanding in order to re-establish trust between you. You can try to show that these aspirations could be satisfied outside the cult. Do this with great tact and be careful to avoid antagonising and alienating someone who may be fanatically committed to newfound beliefs.

Be informed about the cult. Your local clergy will help you to understand the religious implications of cult teaching. Try to get your child to think and question for himself. Ask what is so special about this particular leader; discuss evidence that psychological techniques can be used to induce conversion and, where appropriate, evidence of political and financial motivation and activity behind the religious 'front'. Ask if he or she is convinced of the honesty of the cult's recruiting and fund-raising methods. Be gentle in your arguing but firm in your beliefs, and adopt the approach that you think will be most effective.

Young people sometimes join cults because of the warmth and acceptance of the group they have joined, and the communal life enables them to escape the problems and difficulties to be faced in the outside world. You may have to look and see if you can think of any reason why this might be the case.

In the end it is up to your child or relative to decide for himself whether or not to join the cult. All you can do is to urge him to complete any training before he joins and to take time to think things over with his family and friends at home before making the final decision.

If your child or relative has actually joined a cult and is allowed to come home and visit you, do all you can to renew their former friendships and memories of the past. Tell them what is going on in the world, especially the good things to counter the propaganda put over by so many cults that the world is satanic. Remind him that there is a lot of goodwill and religious feeling outside the cult.

Don't antagonise any cult leader or member that you meet. Keep the lines of communication open and remember that you too may become taken in by the members of the cult or even your own child or relative. So if you visit the cult take someone along who is strong-minded and able to give you strength.

If you have genuine grounds for concern about your child or relative's medical, psychological, financial or other aspect of his involvement with the cult, write to your local Member of Parliament and ask him to forward the letter to the Home Secretary and, if appropriate, to the Department of Health and Social Security. Keep a written record of events associated with the person's involvement with the group.

- Don't give any financial aid whatsoever to your child or the group.
- If any documents are required by any party, give photocopies and not the originals.
- Don't become intimidated or afraid, or feel ashamed or alone. Your problem is one faced by many families and it affects people from all social, religious and economic backgrounds. Parents can experience strong feelings of failure and guilt when their offspring joins a cult. This is understandable, but do not allow it to prevent you from taking the appropriate action.
- Don't give up; there is always hope. Contact someone who can help you: see page 304.

LEAVING HOME

Leaving home is in some ways like a bereavement; there is a sense of loss of childhood, not just for the young person but also for the parents left behind. Homesickness is probably at its worst about three months after leaving home, when the excitement of the new flat, job, training or university has worn off and the young person longs to go back home. Given time these feelings subside and the new home and life are seen as their real home, but the excitement of going back to visit everyone at the family home is still there. Some young people are so worried by the thought of leaving home that they work themselves up into a state of anger, creating arguments and disruption at home, so that they either storm out of the house and run away or their parents throw them out. This is very sad, because the home has become a battleground and coming back home may be very difficult, if not impossible.

Leaving home should be an exciting time like starting school, with both the young person and his parents feeling a mixture of sadness and pleasure at the thought of an exciting new adult life. Parents can help the young person by encouraging and supporting him in the new way of life and helping him to realise that he will always be welcome home, but do not be rigid in expecting him to return at set times.

The mother of a young person who is leaving home may feel that there is nothing left for her to do, especially if she has stayed at home and looked after the children. She needs to think positively about her own life and what she would like to do: perhaps take up her career again, take some further education or develop a hobby that interests her. It is just like the child that tries to stay away from school because he is worried that his mother is unhappy and lonely at home without him; children and young people need to feel that you are happy with your life so that they can get on with theirs.

When a young person first leaves home he often gets colds, coughs, infections, loses or gains weight, and it is only due to the change in his lifestyle and he is probably under a certain amount of stress until he settles down to his new way of life. It is important for parents to realise that this is what is happening and not put it down to the young person's inability to look after himself.

Of course parents will worry about who the young person will meet. Will he be tempted with drugs? Will he get into trouble? Will something awful happen to him? These feelings are only natural, but if you have brought up your child with love, security and a strong sense of values you can trust him to make the right decisions and he will know that he can always come to you for sound and sensible advice.

Many problems affecting young people are similar to those of an adult, so for problems relating to sex, see Chapter 4; disabled young people, Chapter 6; anxiety and stress, Chapter 8; drug abuse and addictions, Chapter 9; suicide, Chapter 10; getting a job and working, Chapter 11; burglary, mugging and violence, Chapter 12.

CHAPTER FOUR

Adult Relationships

Problems caused by relationships between people must be the source of more stress and worry than anything else in life. Perhaps one of the commonest problems is being unable to form or sustain relationships, resulting in feelings of loneliness and inadequacy.

LONELINESS, INABILITY TO FORM A RELATIONSHIP

I have received many letters from people of all ages telling me that they are lonely, no one finds them attractive and they want to know what they can do to change this. This letter is from a young man with just such a problem.

I am what you might refer to as the male equivalent of an old maid! At thirty-seven I am still single and find it extremely difficult to find a girlfriend. I have only ever had one girlfriend and have never had sexual intercourse with a woman, although I yearn for marital happiness and kids.

I find it very difficult to talk naturally and fluently to most people. I labour at conversation and feel glad when it is all over. By nature I am a loner and I can't seem to stop it and mix with people. Maybe I look bored and fed up in the company of people even when I am trying to enjoy myself. Sometimes I can't relax and open up in company of others, particularly if they are boisterous.

I have given up all hope of ever getting married or giving my mother grandchildren, which she wants. My modest ambition is to get myself a girlfriend. Every unmarried woman I talk to under forty-five is a potential girlfriend. It's awful, isn't it?

I can never seem to sustain friendships. I feel so lonely and isolated sometimes I could cry! I spend most weekends on my own, I regret to say. I think I must be just plain boring.

This young man did not want his name to be mentioned even though he now has a steady girlfriend. He is by no means alone in how he feels; so many people experience the same problem.

The problem probably stems from the fact that some people have difficulty talking to others and therefore forming a lasting relationship. So many people feel that anyone from the opposite sex has to be talked to in a special way and so it takes a conscious effort to talk to them. This really is not true; you talk to a member of the opposite sex in exactly the same way as you would talk to anyone else. Even some people who are very outward-going and confident feel tongue-tied when they are face to face with someone that they find very attractive.

So what this particular young man did was to talk to everybody that he met during the course of the day. Instead of just buying something in a shop and walking out, he struck up a conversation with the person that served him. Several times he made a complete mess of the conversation and left the shop in a hurry, but it didn't matter because he didn't know the person concerned. Gradually he became more confident and actually started to enjoy talking to people of both sexes.

His other problem was that he didn't think that anyone would be interested in him because he was boring and unattractive. Perhaps you feel the same way about yourself. You only have to look around you to see that there are lots of people that have found partners and happiness; many of them are too fat, too thin, very plain, have crooked noses, squinty eyes and could hardly be described as a Joan Collins or a Robert Redford. If it were true that only the beautiful and the handsome found happiness, the majority of us would be out in the cold. What the average person has is 'self-acceptance'; the individual is comfortable with himself. He doesn't go into a pub or to a party thinking: Is anyone going to like me? or Will I succeed? Someone who is filled with self-doubt cannot look outside himself and it is this slightly abstracted, in-turned attitude that makes a person unapproachable. There is something attractive about everyone, so make the best of your looks and then forget about them, go into the social scene and look at the people there. Think about them as people and not as potential girlfriends or boyfriends; that way you have a better chance of widening your social circle, and out of these people you may gradually deepen one particular relationship.

People who lack confidence in themselves because they really believe that they are boring and unattractive often portray this quite unconsciously in their body language. They actively signal 'Keep your distance', although they are consciously thinking the opposite. When someone talks to you turn your whole body towards them, look into someone talks to you turn your whole body towards them, look into their face and smile. You may have been talking to people by looking slightly sideways at them over a raised protective shoulder and avoiding their eyes. If you talk to people like this, they subconsciously interpret your body language and feel that you are giving them the 'cold shoulder'. So next time you talk to someone just note what your body is really saying. If you feel that it would help to talk over your problems, turn to page 304 for telephone numbers of people who are willing to help.

ADOLESCENTS AND SEX

Sex education is vital to any young person, and I believe that it is the responsibility of parents to ensure that their children have a clear understanding long before they start to mature into adults. Every mother should have talked to her daughter about menstruation (periods) long before they are likely to occur. Young girls can start menstruating from as early as eleven years old and sometimes even as early as ten. There can be nothing more frightening for a young girl than suddenly to start menstruating and have no real knowledge of what is happening to her, except what she has learned from her friends. She is likely to assume that she is seriously ill or that she has damaged herself in some way. When a mother talks frankly to her daughter or a father to his son about sex, in the privacy of their home, a very special bond of openness and trust is created, leading to the sort of relationship that welcomes open and honest discussions. The earlier you talk to your children about sex the easier it is; a child of eight or nine will accept the facts for what they are, and you can build on the information as time goes by. Most schools teach sex education, so if your child has already talked to you and understood the basics, then the school will be adding to knowledge that he or she has already acquired.

When you discuss the subject of sex it is important to use the correct terms such as *penis, vagina, erection, sperm, ejaculation, ovum* (egg), so when these terms are used at school he will understand what they mean and feel less embarrassed. It is also important to put sex into context and relate it to love and relationships as well as to a reproductive system; to discuss casual sex and promiscuity and how it affects the way people value themselves. Answer questions honestly, without embarrassment and as well as you can. Later on when the child becomes a young person there are likely to be questions such as:

Can a woman get pregnant every time she makes love? The answer of course is no; she is likely to become pregnant when she ovulates, which is during the middle of her menstrual cycle.

Do you get pregnant if you make love standing up? It doesn't matter how you make love. If you don't use a contraceptive and you are ovulating, then you may become pregnant.

Does masturbation make you go blind or deaf? The answer is no.

Is it unnatural and dirty for a girl or a boy to masturbate? Masturbation is a way of releasing sexual tension, it is a source of sexual pleasure and it is certainly not harmful in any way.

Are teenagers too young to become pregnant? If a girl has started her periods, she can become pregnant.

My friends all say that they have had sex; I feel the odd one out! This is no reason for having casual sex with someone, and it's probably not true anyway. Stress the importance of a loving, caring relationship, the ability to make moral judgements and not the desire to be one of the crowd.

What really happens when a woman gives birth? Young people, both boys and girls, need to know exactly what happens and what words like *caesarean, forceps, umbilical cord, placenta* and *natural childbirth* mean. Answer questions frankly; they need this information.

If you, as a parent, are worried about answering questions because you are afraid that you simply do not know all the answers, I have suggested some books that you could read: see page 305.

The adolescent boy or girl needs to know about contraception. The idea that if you don't talk about sex they won't do it has been proved wrong time and time again. It is much better that they know how to protect themselves from becoming pregnant and from diseases like Acquired Immune Deficiency Syndrome (AIDS): see also page 305. Take time to discuss the different methods of contraception, and there are several: the diaphragm or dutch cap, intra-uterine devices such as the coil or the loop – these will have to be fitted by a doctor; spermicides, which come in the form of foams and jellies, and will require advice on their use and effectiveness; the contraceptive pill – and, again, this requires a doctor who will carry out a physical examination before prescribing a suitable pill; the sheath, condom or french letter, which has received a great deal of publicity recently because it not only prevents pregnancy but also offers some protection against AIDS. To get professional advice and counselling is essential, and I have listed some of the agencies that offer this service on page 305.

The best advice is never to assume that the other person has taken precautions; it is better to be safe than sorry. Some young people carry condoms with them, which you can buy in little, brightly coloured tins so they can be kept clean and intact until they are needed. See page 305. It is important that young people know about contraception even if they never use the knowledge.

END OF A RELATIONSHIP, SEPARATION AND DIVORCE

Angie is chairman of a single parent's support group and helps other single parents to come to terms with, and overcome, some of their problems. Life has not been easy for Angie, and she writes:

My parents divorced when I was ten years old; we stayed with our father who soon remarried. I did not get on with my stepmother, and my father then rejected my affections. My brothers left home. At fifteen I became pregnant, but wouldn't have an abortion. The baby's father did not want the baby. I was determined I would have and keep my baby. I was four months pregnant on my school-leaving date. No one at school knew. My stepmother threw me out of home. I stayed with a family who helped young unmarried mothers. I was desperately lonely there. Jon was born on 8 December 1979 when I was sixteen. My family came to see me and so did the baby's father. His attitude changed when he saw Jon. He asked me to marry him. We lived with his mother for six months. That was hell. We moved to a council flat and got married when Jon was eight months old, I was seventeen and my husband was nineteen. I loved them both very dearly. We were both young, and it was hard work trying to survive.

On 19 October 1981, Jon woke up and was sick. I called the doctor. Jon had purple markings on his body that gradually spread, until he was covered. He died that night from meningococcal septicaemia. He died in hospital; there was nothing that they could do. We both went to pieces. He left me a couple of months later. A year later we got back together for six months and then parted for good. I became very ill during the divorce (I divorced him on the grounds of adultery). I went down to 6½ stone in weight. I didn't want to eat and I smoked fifty cigarettes a day. I felt I had lost everything and had nothing to live for. Our divorce finally came through in September 1984.

The doctors had given me Ativan, anti-depressants and sleeping tablets, but I was determined enough not to rely on them and did not continue to take them.

I found a bedsit to live in and got a job. I was still grieving over Jon's death and felt very alone. I had several men ask to date me, even one proposal of marriage, but I wasn't interested. I worked in a garage as a cashier, my boss harassed me sexually and made life very awkward when I kept refusing his advances.

I once went in desperation to the Samaritans. The lady I spoke to was very nice and calmed me down. I went again to see her, putting on my usual brave cheery face so she thought I'd made a good recovery and asked me to join the Samaritans. I never went back again. Everyone thought I'd got over Jon's death very well, but I cried almost every night for years. I've just got a convincing act that things are OK. What's the point in making others feel miserable?

Most of my friends use me as their 'agony aunt' because they know I'll listen. I listen because I know what it's like not to have anyone to talk to.

One day a man came into the garage and chatted for a while then asked me out. I said 'Yes'. I don't really know why as I was used to saying 'No' as an automatic response. He was really nice; we had a lovely relationship and were thinking of getting a house together. He took a job, long-distance lorry-driving, because the money was good. He was in the middle of a divorce and was renting a place next door to me. He came round one day to say that he was giving up his flat and that he would see me at the weekend. I never saw him again. The following week I discovered I was having his baby.

I spent a long and lonely pregnancy in my little bedsit. I was so scared that something would happen to this baby, too. I stayed in hospital a month before my son was induced, and he was fine. I love Kyle very much, and he has helped me to get over Jon's death.

I see my parents once a week. I was very lonely in the bedsit and got together with others to form the single parent's support group. I find helping others makes me forget my problems.

I had to leave the bedsit when Kyle was a year old. The council won't rehouse me yet. I managed to find a little end-of-terrace to rent. (Very few places accept children.) I have two bedrooms, lounge, kitchen. There is a loo in the garden and a bath on legs in the kitchen. We don't have a bathroom or any hot water. We get a lot of damp and are unable to live here in the really bad weather. It's just too cold, no matter how much heating we have on, but that's only for a few weeks.

When Kyle was fourteen months old we literally bumped into his father in the high street and I told him that Kyle was his. He came to see me twice; he is living with a girl and her three children in his house. He said he wanted to see Kyle regularly and made arrangements. I haven't seen him since. I'm now going through court proceedings for maintenance. He is denying that Kyle is his child; I really didn't think he would do that. He is now thirty-five and I am twenty-four, and quite frankly I have had enough of the bad times. I am determined to start enjoying my life. I very rarely get the chance to go out at night. I've been out once this year, but I don't mind. I'm content to stay at home with Kyle. He will only be young for such a very short time. We get out in the day as much as possible and have one or two good friends that we see once a week. I do most of the organising for the single parent's support group, and this keeps me busy.

I sometimes see my ex-husband. I still love him; maybe one day we'll get back together, but for now we are very good friends and he adores Kyle.

I have been complimented by several people on how well I cope in my situation. Kyle is a happy bright nineteen-month-old child. I make a lot of our clothes. I've renovated bits of old furniture. I make soft toys and have several pen-pals. I do these things in the evenings as that's the time when I sit and think if I am not busy. I know I won't be in this awful house for ever and I know that I won't be this hard up all the time. I have given up smoking, I don't take any drugs and unless I go out at night I don't drink any alcohol.

I still have problems that sometimes get me down a bit, but in general I've pulled through the really bad times. I can honestly say that I am now content most of the time.

ANGIE

Angie has shown how she has managed to overcome so many serious crises and she wanted to be included in this book because she felt that she might be able to help someone who was experiencing similar problems. You really do have to admire her fortitude and courage in the face of such adversity.

A single parent caring for a family on their own inevitably needs help and support. But where do you go to get help? Who will understand?

There are several support groups, and I have listed them on page 307. They offer a range of help and services including:

- A place for both the parent and children to meet and start a new social life to replace the one lost with the loss of a partnership.
- The friendship of other people in the same situation.

■ Help with some of the practical problems like finance, living on one
or no salary and yet trying to meet the same household costs. They
can give help and advice if there is a housing problem. The legal
problems can be complex and confusing, and it certainly helps to get
sound and practical advice, and these support groups are able to do
just that.

■ Practical help with the difficulties of bringing up children. There are
babysitting pools so that the parent can have a night out. Clothes and
toy pools, especially necessary when there is very little money. Help
with learning some skills such as decorating, cooking, electrical
repairs, sewing, carpentry and so on. When one half of a partnership
leaves he or she takes away the skills that were relied on by the other
half.

■ Support by accompanying each other to court, the solicitor's, the
housing department and anywhere else that would help. Whenever a
one-parent family is created, whether through separation, divorce,
bereavement or single parenthood, there is usually a great deal of
emotional stress, making it difficult for the person concerned to think
clearly and make the right decisions. Support groups offer moral and
emotional support and practical advice. They organise day care for
children so that the parent can work. Savings clubs for outings and
holidays.

For further advice on possible financial support, see page 308.

Many people think of the single parent bringing up a family as a
woman, but there are many men managing a home and family on their
own.

> After ten years of what I thought was a happy marriage my wife just
> walked out on me. I was left with three children under ten. I had to
> maintain my job and had a lot of trouble coping with three children. I
> just didn't know where to start. I couldn't cook or manage anything
> in the house. I felt inadequate – but I soon learned, with the help of
> the people at Gingerbread.
>
> MICHAEL ASTON

Divorce is never easy, no matter when it occurs in your life. Jay Allen
explains what happened to her:

> I have been divorced since 1982/1983, having been married for
> twenty-two years. I divorced my husband because of his continued
> association with another woman which had been going on for at least

five years. During that time I did my utmost to save my marriage, but my husband had become a changed person – was no longer the caring father of our two lovely daughters, drank to excess and was a liar.

Initially, I was typing for a company at home but decided that if necessary I would be prepared to earn my own living. I initially had a full-time position, but on one of the reconciliations went part-time. However, finally I was offered a permanent full-time position within the company and took it. I divorced my husband, and we had to share the family home, etc., even though I had two daughters to support (at this time aged fifteen and eighteen). By getting a mortgage I bought my husband's share of the family home and eventually moved to a smaller house. My younger daughter, who was extremely distressed following the divorce, is now married and my elder daughter gets married in July.

I have been through all the anguishes, battles with solicitors, etc., and feeling that I was going from one trauma to another. I was put on Ativan by my doctor (not a good idea, because it took a great deal of effort to kick the habit). I believe it has taken four years to come to terms with things. I do not have a 'man in my life', and it is only recently that I have lost the initial distrust of all men. My advice to people in a similar position is firstly to attempt to become a person in your own right. Not easy, I admit, because at the time of divorce one's confidence is at its lowest.

Although life is not easy financially, and I am sometimes lonely, I am grateful to have two loving daughters, who have been absolutely marvellous, and sincere friends. I enjoy my job as a secretary, and for the first time for years feel proud, if that is the right word, that I am responsible for my own life.

This may sound as though I am one of those people who 'sailed through'. I didn't, and even now there are times when the pain returns. I was on the verge of a mental breakdown, and there was no one to help. I can remember in desperation one day going to the Citizen's Advice Bureau because my solicitor was useless. Finally, I changed my solicitor and decided the matter should be settled as quickly as possible. I would add that I have not seen my husband, nor has he seen our daughters, since the day of the divorce.

JAY ALLEN

A divorcee has many difficult adjustments to make after leaving his or her partner. Jay has described how difficult it was even with the support and love of her daughters and friends. Sometimes this is not the case, and the divorcee becomes an embarrassment to married friends and lacks the support so desperately needed at this time. There are the problems of loneliness, financial difficulties, problems with solicitors over alimony, the children and the house. The stress and the worry are enormous, particularly during the first year, but gradually things will get better. It was very sad that Jay felt that there was no help apart from her daughters and friends; the support groups that are mentioned above would have offered her help and advice as a single parent. Most large towns have social clubs for divorcees where people with similar problems can meet and help each other. See page 308.

It is a mistake to think that a divorce will solve all your problems and with your new-found freedom as a single person that life will be full of fun and excitement. You only have to read the experiences of Angie and Jay to appreciate that it is not easy.

One of the most serious areas of a divorce is the effect on the children. For many children this is a time when they feel that their lives have simply fallen apart, nothing will ever be quite the same again. However much you have suffered at the hands of your partner, your other half is still the mother or father to your children. It is a difficult time for the adults, and sometimes it is forgotten just how difficult it is for the children. They have to go to school and face their friends, and school-friends are not always kind and sympathetic.

They are probably having difficulty understanding why you can't all live together, and they may well blame themselves for what has happened, so it is essential to spend time talking to them and taking their feelings into consideration. The atmosphere created in a home by parents who no longer get along can deeply disturb a child. There doesn't need to be violence or heated arguments, just an atmosphere created by persistent non-cooperation when either parent deliberately doesn't do things that they have been asked to do, or repeatedly does things they have been asked not to do, leaves a child feeling helpless and insecure.

I have talked to lots of children whose parents are divorced, and they tend to agree that they wanted to know what was going on rather than be left out and only guessing what might happen. They needed to know that each parent still loved them and wanted to see them, particularly the one that was leaving. They didn't like it when one parent said unpleasant things about the other, because they still loved them both. They wanted to know where they would be living and with whom, and how often they would see the other parent. It is interesting that most of these children would rather that their parents split up than that the constant rows and unhappy atmosphere at home continued.

If a parent remarries and there are other children in the new home, there are sometimes problems of which the parents are unaware. So often you hear parents in this situation say, 'They all get on so well together'. I can remember someone saying this to me, and I mentioned it to the child, and his perception was very different. He was living with his mother, who had remarried, and he was constantly compared to his stepbrothers and stepsisters because they were brighter and doing better at school. He would have preferred to be with his father, who had not remarried and who accepted him for what he was. So if you are in this situation you need to be sensitive to how your child is really feeling about the new arrangements.

The custody of the children often goes to the mother, but these days it is not unusual for the father to get custody. The judge will take each case on its merits unless you have already decided who should have custody of the children. If the child is over sixteen, he or she can make the decision. Financial arrangements have to be made to support the children, and hopefully this can be done amicably, bearing in mind the parents' individual earnings and the immediate and future needs of any children. If it goes to court, the judge will decide the appropriate amount.

Part of the custodial responsibility is to allow the father, or in some cases the mother, reasonable access to the children. You may not want to meet and see your ex-husband or ex-wife, but your children have every right and probably want to see their mother or father. This often works out as alternate weekends and half the school holidays. Research has shown that it is not a good idea to allow children to have two homes; they need one home as a base and the other as a place to visit.

When families are split like this it is easy to fall into the trap of over-compensating by giving the children gifts and generally spoiling them. They know why you are doing this; it is because you feel guilty and you will soon lose their respect.

If a parent is given custody, then remarries and the children have a stepparent, it may be very difficult for the parent who does not have custody to come to terms with the situation. It will only cause greater conflict and unhappiness if this parent does not accept the situation. It is important that he or she is allowed to see the children as agreed and is not obstructed. If the mother is given custody, whether she remarries or not, the children need to see their father, and the mother should not prevent this. There are still many fathers who lose touch completely with their children after a divorce. See page 309 for information on Families Need Fathers. Sometimes a parent with care of the children resorts to extreme methods to obstruct the access of the other parent even in the face of court orders and agreed arrangements. This is harmful to the children and distressing to the absent parent. Sometimes an absent parent reaches the point of desperation and tries to regain access by removing the children from the care of the other parent.

Both parents have equal rights as well as equal responsibilities, and after a divorce or separation everything should be done to ensure that a child's relationship with both parents is preserved.

SEXUAL PROBLEMS

Many of our attitudes about sex go back to our childhood. How we were treated as a child and what we were or were not told. At the beginning of this chapter I mentioned the importance of accurate and frank sex education given by a loving and caring parent. So many of the myths about sex stem from ignorance and lack of correct information. Someone who has been brought up by parents who were gentle and loving will express sexual feelings in the same way. The child who was brought up expecting to be smacked and handled roughly may, as an adult, express sexual feelings with rough handling and aggression. During childhood sex may be referred to as dirty, or a daughter may be warned by a well-meaning mother that sex will get her into trouble and consequently she may have problems accepting sex within a loving relationship.

Another factor that influences people is lack of privacy. If a young couple are living with parents-in-law with only a thin wall between the bedrooms, they may be unable to relax and enjoy sex for fear of being overheard. Some people feel inhibited when they have young children in the house in case they should come bounding into the room in the middle of it all. If you have financial worries, or are under stress at work or at home, it can affect your sex drive. Although sexual activity occurs below the belt, so much of the enjoyment is actually in the mind, so if you are weighed down with worry and stress you will not relax and enjoy sex.

Sometimes there is a conflict about what is and is not acceptable sex, and these include: any position where the man is not on top, oral sex, anal sex, sex with the lights on, sex with the lights off, sex anywhere but in bed, sex with your clothes on, sex with your clothes off, too frequent sex, masturbation during sex, the use of sex aids, and many others. What you may see as acceptable or unacceptable may vary from that of your partner. It is important to talk about the problem with your partner, but if you feel that you can't talk to him or her discuss it with your doctor or a friend. Once you have talked about the problem you will start to feel better about it. If you don't talk about it, you may well start trying to avoid sex and eventually one of you will become resentful and unhappy.

It is very easy to label a woman frigid when all she needs is a little understanding and help. Any woman who is called frigid will become even more anxious and feel inadequate and useless. Equally a man who is labelled impotent will believe that he is beyond hope, and that is not necessarily the case; with patience and counselling he may well be able to have an erection and control ejaculation.

There is sex counselling and sex therapy available (see page 306), exercises and experimentation that can and do help couples, but if you no longer love your partner or find your partner attractive these are unlikely to be successful.

There are some rare physical reasons why women have sexual problems, and one of these is vaginismus. This is when the muscles of the vagina close down tightly whenever something is inserted into the vagina. This condition can be treated by dilating techniques, and your doctor will be able to advise you about the best course of treatment. Pain on intercourse or dyspareunia can be caused by certain medical conditions which are treatable, and you should consult a doctor. However, the majority of problems are psychological, in the mind, as explained above.

Recently I received a letter from a woman who said that she couldn't achieve an orgasm and asked what she was doing wrong. Women usually take longer to become aroused than men, and it may mean that there is inadequate clitoral stimulation; your partner may well be unaware of your needs and assume that you are getting as much enjoyment as he is, so if this is not the case you need to be more explicit about how you feel. Be a little more directive about what gives you pleasure. The penis and the clitoris are both stimulated by friction; without adequate friction orgasm will simply not happen. Some women prefer the friction to be indirect through the folds of the labia, others direct friction to the clitoris, some achieve orgasm through oral stimulation and for some women a vibrator is the most effective stimulator. There are many women who do not have an orgasm but still enjoy the closeness, romance and warmth shared with their partner during sexual intercourse.

SEX THERAPY

Sometimes a couple are unable to resolve sex problems by themselves. The very fact that the couple have realised and admitted to each other that there is a problem and they need help shows that they have overcome some of their problems already. Sex counselling, sex clinics and sex therapy have all proved to be very successful for many couples whose problems have threatened to ruin their relationship.

This is the story of one young couple.

Before we had children we had a very happy and active sex life, but then I seemed to lose interest in sex. It got so bad that I would feel hatred, disgust and anger when we made love. It did nothing for me any more; it became a chore like the washing or the ironing. I just lay there and hoped that it would all be over quickly. I could feel myself tense up and become totally unresponsive. My husband didn't seem to notice at first, but then he started to say that I was frigid and other hurtful remarks that only seemed to make things worse. We started to have arguments about everything, and I know it all came from the fact that he was frustrated by me and my attitude to sex. I didn't seem to be able to do anything about it and I couldn't talk to him about it. Then he found someone else to have sex with and he took great pleasure in telling me so.

In the end I did talk to someone, and that was our doctor. I didn't go to the doctor to talk about our problems; I went because I was feeling irritable, depressed, and I couldn't sleep at night. He asked me lots of questions including some about our sex life, and I was so relieved to be able to talk to someone that I just told him everything. He suggested that we both went to the sex clinic and, although I thought it was a good idea, I didn't think that my husband would go. So I didn't tell him. One night we had a terrible row because I didn't want sex, and I just blurted out what the doctor had said. I was amazed when he agreed that something had to be done.

On the first visit the counsellor just talked to us about all the problems that we had, including sex, and at the end of the session we had agreed that there was one real problem and we drew up a plan to help us go about putting things right. It was funny really; I thought that I would be really embarrassed about our personal problems, but the counsellor made it all feel so natural and he was very easy to talk to. He said that we both had to agree to give the programme that we had planned a good chance of working by being enthusiastic and willing, and my husband agreed not to see his woman.

After the first visit we were told not to make love; he gave me some exercises to do at home which were to tighten up the sexual muscles. I had to tighten up and then relax the vagina by squeezing my thighs together and then relaxing them. I did this for a week and then we went back to see him. Over the next few weeks we had to discover what pleasure we would get from lying together and just touching, fondling and caressing each other. I had to learn to tell my husband what I enjoyed, and he did the same. It was surprising just how ignorant we both were about what gave us pleasure.

After a few weeks I was able to have an orgasm without actually having intercourse. When it came to us having intercourse again the counsellor suggested that some soft music and a warm room would help me relax. We went home and that night after a candlelit dinner we made love. We had followed his advice and hadn't had intercourse for weeks and when we did it was great. It must have been five or six years since it had been so good for both of us. It has helped us in so many ways to be more open and honest with each other, and not bottle up anger and resentment like we did before.

Both marriage guidance counsellors and doctors can refer people to a sex therapist, or you can go to a Marriage Guidance Council sex therapist. It means that both partners need to attend, and this is usually once a week for about three months. See page 306 for further information.

MARRIAGE GUIDANCE

Marriage guidance counsellors are mainly voluntary but they are trained to help you by listening and encouraging you to talk about your problems with your partner. They are not there to hand out advice or to make judgements. Instead they will help you to gain further insight into your problems so that you can solve them. They will not be shocked by anything that you say nor will they tell anyone else what you have said; everything you say will be confidential. So you will be able to talk freely and openly to someone who is sympathetic and understanding.

The appointments usually last about an hour, and it will take several weeks to gain some insight into your problems and to start working out ways of solving them. Some couples feel that they should be able to sort out their own problems and, if they cannot, then the problem can't be solved. What often happens is that these discussions at home become very heated and things that are said are misunderstood; it often helps to have someone there who can help the discussion along and enable the couple really to listen to what the other person is saying.

HOMOSEXUALS

Many boys and girls pass through a homosexual phase in adolescence. The majority pass from homosexual experimentation to heterosexual feelings. Some of them become very anxious during this stage that they are homosexual and that they will stay that way for ever. They may not want to talk about it. It is important that they understand that this may only be a phase of adolescence. Some of course will be homosexual and go on to form adult relationships. Paul describes his experience:

> I was born and brought up in a small rural community in the north of England, where the word 'gay' is never used to describe a homosexual man – terms of abuse such as 'poof' and 'queer' being far more common.
>
> My parents are good honest people who always doted on me, and were determined that I should have the best of everything. Both my parents, but my mother in particular, were very protective towards me.
>
> I was a shy and sensitive child. I loved books and preferred the company of little girls to little boys – I think because they tended to be less rough. At the age of five or six, it must have been apparent that I was different to the other boys in my class – and I certainly felt different – although I was a happy child. My real unhappiness began when I went to the local comprehensive school, which was several miles away from the village where I lived. I had to catch a school bus with the other children and I found the experience quite traumatic. This was the beginning of adolescence, and my contemporaries had sensed that there was something 'funny' about me. I was a fairly academic child and stuck to my few female friends. However, my peers did not allow me to get on with my life undisturbed. Children seem to have a knack of finding the weakness of their associates. I was called a 'poof' and bullied. From the ages of twelve to eighteen I was

miserable and would find the pressure I faced every day of my life then impossible to bear now. I was continually rejected by the other children because they thought I was 'queer' and I was also beginning to understand that they were right, but having to deny it.

Fortunately I had reasonably supportive teachers who were (I now think) aware of what was going on, and they encouraged me to work hard and get away to college where my life would be more tolerable. My parents were as supportive as they could be – but they insisted that I defend myself by denying that I was a 'poof'. Looking back, I think they were totally out of their depth.

So was I. I didn't know any openly gay people and all I knew of homosexuality was the very negative way my tormentors described it. Nobody was open on the subject, and we certainly didn't learn anything about it at school, or find out that all over the world gay couples were openly living in caring, loving relationships. This sort of knowledge would have helped me to come to terms with myself and – who knows? – I might not have been bullied. My unhappiness continued into the sixth form at school when the others started pairing off with each other. I remained alone with my books, and the growing feeling that I was gay with nobody to confide in.

I did get a place at university and chose to go to London as I knew I would at least be in an anonymous city. This was the beginning of a happier life.

I made friends very easily after the first few terms, though once again my friends were mostly female. I still did not have enough confidence to 'come out', nor did I dare go to any of the gay societies or groups in London. I think really because I had not finally admitted to myself that I was gay.

In the second year, however, I told my two closest friends – both female – that I *was* gay. Neither of them were surprised (this surprised me), both of them were relieved that I had been honest with them (this amazed me), and both knew far more about gay organisations than I did (even though neither of them were gay). They encouraged me, along with other friends, to go out and meet other gay people. I will always be grateful to my friends, and those two in particular, for their total acceptance of my sexuality, their constructive advice and their sense of humour when things went wrong in those first tentative stages. My advice to gay people on the verge of coming out is to find the right friends to talk to about it. This is very important. Coming out is a process of building up confidence to tell more and more people, and the first few reactions should be as positive as possible.

I began to meet other gay men both as friends and lovers. It was an enormously liberating time for me particularly after years of denying my sexuality.

By now, I had qualified as a lawyer, and was also looking for a permanent partner; someone with whom I could share my life. I was working in a firm of City solicitors but worked at a voluntary organisation called Gay Legal Advice one evening a week. I did meet someone there, we got to be friends and then fell in love and now live together. With the support of my friends, and the love and support of my partner, I decided it was time to 'come out' to my parents. I think my parents had suspected that I was gay for several years, but never wanted to acknowledge it. As I mentioned earlier, homosexuality was a dirty word in our village. I was happy and successful – my parents would not be able to reconcile this with being a 'poof'. When I told them on the telephone (too nervous to say it to their face) their initial reaction was one of shock and disbelief. They begged me to reconsider and sought reassurance that I was not 'committed' to this way of life, offering to get me psychiatric help. When I assured them that I definitely was gay, and had been actively so for some years and was now living with my boyfriend, and was proud to be doing so, they were completely distraught. My mother in particular found it impossible to cope with it all. She called me names, said she wished I had never been born and that she would prefer me to be dead. My father coped by pretending that I hadn't said anything. It was a very unhappy time for me. I loved my parents and couldn't lie to them any longer, and it was extremely distressing, particularly after I had screwed up my courage to tell them. After about five or six months, I had not made much progress with my parents. We could only talk about other things, and they would ring me up to cry and curse on the telephone and write unpleasant letters to me and to my boyfriend. In desperation I turned to a voluntary organisation called Parent's Enquiry which is run by parents of gay children who counsel and support parents on the telephone or at local meetings. I would strongly recommend the intervention and support of Parent's Enquiry to any gay child or parent who is having problems like our family. It is a very difficult and disturbing time for everyone. The organisation has helped my parents enormously, particularly as they can see I am still the same son that they have always known, loved and been proud of, and that I still love them. They even mention my boyfriend, and I can now envisage a time when they could meet him or (one day!) come and stay with us in London.

PAUL

Homosexual males may have problems coming to terms with what they are and feel that they must be perverted and try to hide and suppress their true feelings. Some of these men marry and hide behind this so-called respectability while having homosexual relationships with men friends. These days homosexuality is more overt and men quite openly have relationships with other men. With the ever increasing danger of AIDS (Acquired Immune Deficiency Syndrome), which is known to be spread through sex, these men have been advised to stay with one partner, to use a condom and not to indulge in casual sex. See also Chapter 7.

LESBIANS

Lesbians are still seen by society as butch, masculine, over-assertive women. This is not necessarily the case; many very feminine women discover that they are truly lesbian. Sometimes later in their lives they may even be married with children. They have become dissatisfied with their lifestyles and their marriages and feel more comfortable and happier with other women.

Even in the 1980s lesbians are met with a great deal of prejudice and may be afraid to come out into the open and admit that they are lesbians. There are clubs and support groups, which are not always widely advertised; for more information, see page 320.

The parents of a daughter who is a lesbian sometimes have difficulty coming to terms with the situation. This is the experience of a mother who lives in Dorset:

My daughter had a few boyfriends, but they never seemed very important to her. She had a girlfriend that she met at work, and they seemed to do everything together. I never really thought anything of it. They shared a flat and seemed to enjoy being together. I must have been a bit stupid. I never thought that they could be lesbians. It was a friend who told me that the local gossip was busy telling everyone that they were lesbians. I talked to my husband, and he hit the roof; he talked – or, rather, shouted – at her, called her a lot of dirty names and told her to get out and stay out.

He never spoke to her from that day until the day he died of cancer three years later. I used to go round and see them without his knowing. I liked the girl, and it didn't seem to bother me. After he died we made my home into two separate flats. They live upstairs and I live down. I've got bad arthritis and need someone around. We all get on very well, and I don't take any notice of the gossip. I never tell a lie about it; I just look vague as though I don't understand. I expect they all think I am daft.

The addresses and phone numbers for groups that will support and help parents can be found on page 322.

BISEXUALITY

How does a wife react when she discovers that her husband is bisexual?

I felt disgust and revulsion that the man I loved and whose children I had borne could be doing such disgusting things with another man. It would not have been so bad if it had been another woman. Sometimes I felt guilty and wondered if I had not been enough of a real woman so he found excitement with a man.

All these feelings are to be expected, and some expert advice will help to sort them out. The Marriage Guidance Council, whose name has recently been changed to Relate, will help by listening and giving you a chance to talk things through. See page 306.

TRANSVESTISM

Transvestism is the wearing of clothes of the opposite sex. It is little understood by the public, and there is a lack of knowledge among the many families involved and the professionals, the psychologists, psychiatrists, doctors, clergy, police and social workers, all of whom offer help. The unhappiness experienced by the transvestite originates from feelings of loneliness and anxiety about himself and his family. Because transvestites are poorly informed and do not conform to what is regarded as 'normal behaviour' they suffer from feelings of guilt and fear.

They fear discovery, that they may be homosexual, bisexual or transsexual, that the condition may be hereditary or that discovery may lead to ridicule, job loss, divorce, arrest and greater isolation. Transvestism is almost always a male preoccupation; society seems to accept a female dressed in male clothing. Transvestites are usually heterosexual males, who feel compelled to dress as women, whilst not wishing to go so far as wanting a 'sex change'.

John Ferris is a transvestite, and as a result of the efforts of a self-help group, the Beaumont Society (see page 321 for details), has been able to rebuild a shattered life and come to terms with transvestism. He now spends a large proportion of his time as Jean, lecturing to Samaritans and other caring bodies. As Jean he has appeared in several television features and he has written a book on his experiences soon to be published.

I am a transvestite. That's a very short sentence. It took me over fifty years to say it. And saying it changed my life dramatically.

I didn't know I was a transvestite for quite a while. At the age of nine I had a compulsion to wear women's clothes. The best I could do was to borrow my mother's suspender belt, stockings and knickers. Nothing Freudian in that – there was no one else to borrow from. She was a bit bigger than me, though. At that time I didn't even know the facts of life, let alone about being transvestite. What I did have, and all transvestites have, was an enormous sense of guilt, and fear of discovery. In all other respects I was a normal male. Like most transvestites, I was completely heterosexual. I played football, cycled, and my heroes were the drivers of steam locomotives. The only bent I had was a mechanical one.

The compulsion, for that is what a transvestite has, was constant. Transvestites are people who are happy enough with their bodies, but have a compulsion to cross-dress. The trans-sexual, by contrast, is desperately desirous of a physical change of gender. The two compulsions are quite separate and quite different. I joined the Royal Air Force at seventeen, and served nine years. I still had the compulsion, but the opportunity was seldom available. In wartime, you couldn't buy clothes, and the only knickers you could acquire were from a co-operative WAAF. She of course didn't know what she was co-operating in, just imagined you wanted a trophy.

I joined the Colonial Service in Hong Kong. I had married, so the need for secrecy became even greater. By the age of thirty I was completely cross-dressing apart from wig and make-up.

When I left the Service in 1967 I had two teenage children. We settled in England. My job was a travelling one, so I got an opportunity to dress in hotels and in my caravan. But the fear, the guilt, the loneliness, was becoming too much. My marriage broke up. I had ulcers and I suffered from psychosomatic nervous dyspepsia and a hiatus hernia. I was verging on the suicidal. I could not imagine that anyone, knowing what I was, could possibly have anything to do with me. Salvation came unexpectedly. The ulcers perforated, and I was rushed to hospital more dead than alive. When I recovered I was told that I must at all costs avoid stress if I were to enjoy any health at all.

I had heard of the Beaumont Society, which caters for heterosexual transvestites, and I wrote to them. I had a letter from 'Cynthia' suggesting a meal at a restaurant in Windsor. I was apprehensive, but I need not have worried. For the first time I said 'I am a transvestite'. The relief was enormous. I was invited to meet members of the Society the following week at a restaurant in Southampton. There, for the first time, I dressed completely, with other transvestites and their wives. It was wonderful. I progressed from there. I learned the enormous things you need to know as a woman. Cynthia was my mentor. She took me shopping, to museums, and to eating out. I was now Jean. Life was wonderful.

Rapidly I progressed. Cynthia took me with her to give talks, as Jean, to the Samaritans, student bodies, etc. Before long I was going solo. I became very active in the Beaumont Society. Now living alone, I am able to hold monthly socials for members and their wives and partners. I continued my programme of talks, mostly to the Samaritans. For three years running I presented a seminar at the National Conference of Samaritans at York, and this led to further invitations. Then came invitations to appear on television, first with Southern Television on 'Problem Page', the BBC with Kilroy-Silk, with Thames and Sarah Kennedy, and two appearances on Central Television at Birmingham.

For most of my life I lived in loneliness, guilt and fear. To know something about yourself that you have never dared to tell a single living person is to live with a terrible weight on you. Just telling someone lifted that weight. Becoming open meant that I told all my friends and my family. All without exception were most understanding. After the terrible life I had led for so long, the past ten years have been wonderful. I am now physically and mentally whole, and I have more friends than I ever had in my whole life.

I spend most of my time now trying to do for others what Cynthia did for me. If only I had made the effort some twenty years earlier, how different life might have been. . . .

JEAN FERRIS

Jean's moving account shows not only the sadness and guilt but also great courage in displaying his true feelings. There is help and advice available, so if you are feeling lonely and desperate because you are a transvestite contact one of the self-help groups: see page 320.

The wives and families need help and support to understand what has happened to their husband, father, son. Different people cope in different ways. Be positive and don't indulge in self-pity. In time, many people have managed to adjust and share this part of his life. Other people have found that they can tolerate the situation, although they will not involve themselves in his transvestism. Some people find that they are totally unable to accept or understand the situation. Contact a support group and talk to someone who can offer help and advice: see page 320.

TRANS-SEXUALISM

Trans-sexuals have a conviction that their physical anatomy is incompatible with their true gender rôle. A female-to-male trans-sexual would feel she has a man's mind trapped in a female body, and vice versa for a male-to-female trans-sexual. There are probably more male-to-female trans-sexuals. The surgical path for the female-to-male trans-sexual is so arduous that many do not consider having surgery.

Trans-sexuals are generally heterosexual, but they may be homosexual, bisexual or asexual. Their wish is to be accepted totally and irrevocably as the gender they feel themselves to be. They may live and work successfully in their chosen rôle and do so without surgery, which is irreversible. Angela explains:

Briefly, it is a condition whereby an individual feels happier living in the rôle more usually ascribed to the opposite biological sex. The causes are uncertain but probably involve both psychological and physiological factors. It is known to affect far greater numbers of biological males than females, so what follows is derived mainly from my experiences as a member of the former group.

It is impossible to give more than a very brief taste of these experiences in the space available, and I would say that they are just that. Experiences and opinions based upon them. I hope that they may help in a broader understanding of trans-sexualism for the general reader. For those possibly considering a similar course of action, my general advice would be, it should be a last resort, entered upon only after all else fails, and only after seeking professional advice from a specialist clinic.

You will all be familiar with the lurid stories, usually captioned 'Sex-Change', in the tabloid papers. For the most part they are atypical of trans-sexuals. Most of us do not seek publicity; rather, we seek anonymity, to merge into the background as ordinary men or women, and in the majority of cases we succeed.

Dealing with problems:

Probably the greatest worry relates to resolving inner conflict within oneself. Coming to terms with something that is to the outside world unconventional if not incomprehensible. To a family it can seem indefensible, and this leads to a burden of guilt which can be destructive. I know it took me many years to reconcile the fact that I was in no way to blame for the way I am, nor is anyone else. Looking for causes to justify oneself is pointless and negative. It is better to accept it as a fact (or quirk of nature) like left- or right-handedness, because then one's thinking can be more positive and deal with the options arising. Above all, one needs to be true to oneself. If one can't be honest with oneself, what chance is there of honesty to others? Having reconciled with one's own position, if there is close family involved they, too, have to be reconciled to the possibilities. In my case this involved a wife and two children. I had been honest with her from the beginning of our relationship, though it is fair to say I hadn't realised myself the degree of my needs until several years of marriage; despite the openness of our relationship, it was and still is a trauma for her. We are still good friends, and need to be for the sake of our children, but we fundamentally disagree over telling the children. In the end I did tell them and they have coped with the situation very well. My grounds for disclosing it to them was simply that it was better coming from me than from an outsider. They found it easier to deal with the truth than with all the nightmares of their imaginations, and they also knew it was through no fault of theirs that their parents had split up.

So, having reconciled myself and my family to what I was, the next stage was in considering the options and deciding upon a course of action. I was lucky that I was able to pass reasonably well as a woman and had done so on numerous occasions, so I had the option of making the change a more permanent one. I sought the advice of my consultant and we agreed to go ahead, but I insisted it would be at my own pace. The next problem was to demonstrate I could live and support myself and my dependants as a woman. So coming clean with my employers was the next step.

I am fortunate in being in a profession that lends itself to both sexes, so my decision revolved around staying where I was and making the change or disappearing and reappearing elsewhere in my new rôle. I decided on the former and set about telling my bosses. It was an absolute gamble, and I was very lucky; I spoke to the most senior person I knew, who I considered able to cope with being told. He listened bemused but sympathetically; we discussed the more obvious problems, and he agreed to help. The relief was indescribable but, having told him, I had passed the point of no return; it had become official.

In further meetings we decided that only those who needed to know would be told; senior management dropped the bombshell and distributed a handout I had produced explaining the situation and asking for support from the reader, with the back-up of me being available to speak to anyone who felt they needed more information or wanted to speak to me. It was amazing the number of people who took that opportunity and offered their personal support. I was halfway there. Photographs had also been circulated, and several colleagues found they had helped.

On the day of the change-over, I attempted to work normally, but deliberately gave everyone a chance to see me and speak if they wanted. There were several who did, but others who hurried past. Acceptance had to be done at their own pace, but it was interesting that some did not recognise me at all, including my own boss. For the next month or two I was something of a celebrity, and a source of fun for some. It was grin-and-bear-it time and only lasted a matter of weeks. It soon passed, and these days my previous rôle is nearly forgotten.

Two problems that arose out of the blue and were devastating at the time were firstly being found attractive by men who didn't know, and dealing with the press.

ANGELA

Angela has also given me some details on seeking help and some very sound and sensible advice for anyone thinking about having a sex change:

The family doctor: The first person to contact is the family doctor. Explain the situation and ask for referral to a specialist clinic. It is essential to have the support of your own doctor, especially if hormone treatment and surgery are intended. They can also be invaluable in helping to counsel your family.

The Gender Identity Clinic: Several of these now exist, and referral is only accepted from a doctor. They will help to identify the criteria for changing over, and support you through the traumas of doing so. They will not, however, make the decision for you, nor be liable for any consequences that may arise. Their purpose is purely support. Assuming you meet their criteria and are accepted as a patient, then hormone therapy may be offered. Assuming that you are successful in supporting yourself and any dependants, in the new rôle, for a minimum period of one year, possibly longer, and you are seen to be happier in that rôle, then referral may be given for surgery. It is not an obligation upon them and is not certain, no matter how convinced you may be. Depending upon need, these clinics may also be able to offer specialist counselling for partners and children.

Marriage Guidance: Though not specialists in this field, their counsellors may be a source of support in dealing with the marital problems that can arise. The main advantage being that you can ask for help directly.

Friends and family: Probably the greatest asset is a supportive family or friends; they are available at all times. Ask for their help. Most will be only too pleased to help, but remember that it takes time for most people to reconcile the new you with their previous ideas. Give them time to adjust.

Self-help associations for trans-sexuals: They can offer support and advice upon where to get specialist help. They are not a counselling agency but can offer the experiences of others; this can be of great help and comfort. They also publish a handbook full of useful advice. See page 322 for details.

Electrolysis: The only solution for facial and body hair. It can take several hundred hours to remove a beard, and the process is painful and expensive, but without alternative. Go to a properly trained practitioner; your doctor may be able to advise on this.

The road to changing sex is fraught with enormous difficulties and dangers. Many who start the process fail, often through no fault of their own. The consequences can be tragic, to say the least. Support is necessary from friends and relations as well as from professionals. Before starting out upon it, ask yourself the following questions:

■ Is it really what I want?
■ Will I cope with the stress and the trauma?
■ Will I cope with rejection by family, friends and employers? (It can happen!)

■ Do I really appear presentable in my chosen rôle? (Many fail through self-delusion.)
■ Will I be able to support myself and my dependants in the new rôle?
■ Will I be happier?

If the answer is 'No' to any of the above, it may be better to remain as you are. It takes 100 per cent commitment, absolute conviction, a degree of selfishness, thick skin, lots of courage and an element of luck. If in doubt, don't! Before doing anything seek professional advice.

CHAPTER FIVE

The Middle and Later Years

This chapter looks at the middle and later years of life, in this case from the age of fifty onwards. Fifty is a time when people tend to take stock of their lives, assess what they have or have not achieved over the last fifty years. It is sometimes seen as a 'mid-life' crisis, a feeling of being 'over the hill'. You are certainly not finished at fifty; you have got everything to live for if you want to.

THE MENOPAUSE

There are many myths about the suffering caused by the menopause, but there is really no need for this to be the case as you will see when you read how other women have coped. The menopause can occur any time from the age of thirty-five to sixty-five; the average age at which this occurs is fifty. The menopause means the end of monthly periods. It is usually a gradual process lasting over two years or even longer. Just as the young girl took several months or more to develop into a woman with a body that is able to produce a child, so when the reverse happens it takes time. As a woman approaches menopause her ovaries stop producing eggs (ova), and they stop secreting the cyclic supply of oestrogen. At the same time there is a decline in the amount of progesterone produced. Even after the menopause there is still a very small amount of oestrogen produced in the body.

It is these changes in the hormone balance of the body that make a woman infertile and unable to conceive. It is the same hormonal changes that are responsible for some of the uncomfortable physical symptoms that women experience.

This gradual decrease of the release of these hormones begins a few years before menstruation (periods) stops altogether. Many women experience menstrual periods that are scantier, shorter and then farther apart. Some women report that whole periods are missed followed by a very heavy period; others say that the cycles become shorter and the period is heavier than normal; whereas others say that their periods just stopped. Heavy periods can make a woman feel very tired and run-down, and it is advisable to consult a doctor. The passing of clots, bleeding in between periods or after intercourse, and painful periods are not symptoms of the menopause; any change in periods should be discussed with the family doctor just in case it is a symptom of some other medical condition. However, it is also advisable for all women to have regular cervical smear tests; ideally this should be every year, but not all doctors or clinics offer this facility so frequently and it is more likely to be every three years. It is a good idea to keep a diary of your periods once you are over forty.

Hot Flushes or Flashes

Hot flushes or flashes are a very common symptom and can be very distressing, particularly when they disturb sleep.

Rachel Jarvis describes her experience and what her family doctor did to help her.

Suddenly I would become very hot; my face would burn as though I were blushing. It was very embarrassing; I felt as though my face was scarlet, a bit like being a teenager again. It was also very uncomfortable as I would become so hot and sticky that my clothes stuck to me. I could cope during the day, I made sure that I used plenty of deodorant, and even in mid-winter I wore loose light clothing. I would like to have turned off the heating and opened the windows as well, but my family were not too keen on this in mid-winter. It was much worse at night, and I would wake up dripping with sweat and boiling hot. I would throw off the bedclothes in an effort to cool down, leaving my husband cold and shivering. When I had cooled down I was left feeling cold and clammy.

The doctor suggested that I only had a sheet at night and my husband had a duvet. He also said that a cool bath at night and wearing a cotton night-dress would help. I tried all this but still spent most of the night awake while the rest of the family slept peacefully. I needed my sleep as I had a full-time job and a family to look after, and I really couldn't cope if I was exhausted. I didn't want to take any hormone tablets, although I had heard that this sort of treatment was quite successful. I talked to my doctor about the problem, and he suggested that I took a mild sedative at night for a month as the problem would probably only last that long. I did this, and at the end

of the month the hot flushes and night sweats had stopped and there
was no need to continue with the pills.

RACHEL JARVIS

Vaginal Changes

Other changes are those that affect the vagina, and there is thinning,
dryness and soreness. The cells lining the vagina become thin, dried out
and unable to protect themselves against infection; the result may be a
vaginal discharge. This is caused by the drop in the oestrogen level. The
vaginal cells are no longer able to secrete the normal lubricating mucus,
and the result can be that sex becomes uncomfortable or even painful. It
is important that your partner understands what is happening or he may
feel that you no longer want to make love to him for other reasons. A
lubricating jelly, such as KY jelly, which you can buy at the chemist is
often the simple solution to the problem, or talk to your doctor and he
may be able to prescribe a hormone cream or even hormone therapy. Do
not be tempted to use any other type of cream or oil as this may cause
further irritation and lead to infection.

Bone Changes (Osteoporosis)

Osteoporosis is the thinning of the bones, which become weak and
more likely to break. There have been several research studies that have
shown that when the oestrogen levels fall during the menopause bones
are more likely to become thin and weak and therefore prone to
breaking and this is probably the reason for all those aches and pains in
the joints. There is evidence to say that with hormone replacement of
both oestrogen and progesterone this weakening can be stopped, but it
is necessary to continue with the treatment for life. Hormone replacement therapy is given with calcium and vitamin D supplements.

Other experts believe that osteoporosis is related to the overall ageing
process rather than to the levels of oestrogen, and that an adequate
intake of calcium and protein plus adequate exercise is both the
treatment and prevention of this problem.

Mood Changes

Many women say that they experienced moodiness, tearfulness, irritability and depression for no apparent reason. They reported difficulty
remembering names, places and things that needed to be done, problems
making decisions, and that they were more accident prone. These are

not necessarily to do with the menopause but may have more to do with the fact that the woman is going through a mid-life crisis, her children have left home, she feels that they no longer need her. This makes her feel unsure of herself. Her parents and parents-in-law are getting older and probably need some help with their lives. If she has stayed at home to look after her family and has not had a career, she may feel that there is nothing left for her to do and she feels useless and boring.

This should not be the case; it is a question of changing tack and finding other things in life to interest you. This is a time for doing things that you want to do without the responsibilities and restrictions of children. Hormone replacement therapy, anti-depressants and tranquillisers are not going to help these problems, but a talk to your doctor and some advice on how to cope are likely to be of more benefit. If your doctor is unable to help you, talk to a friend who understands how you are feeling and is willing to listen and help, or contact a support group (see page 322), or ask to be referred to a gynaecologist or a special menopause clinic: see page 322.

Headaches

There are many causes of headaches, including migraine, sinusitis, nervous depression, various kinds of medicines, dieting or irregular meals, none of which is necessarily related to the menopause. So it is better to see your doctor if you have headaches so that the cause can be established.

Hormone Replacement Therapy (HRT)

Hormone replacement therapy (HRT) should always be thought about very carefully. Not all women have symptoms that are severe enough to warrant HRT. It involves taking oestrogen and/or progesterone in the form of pills, injections or implants. In the United Kingdom a carefully measured and prescribed combination of oestrogen and progesterone is used to replace the normal combination of hormones produced by the female body during a menstrual cycle. When taken in the form of a pill it is taken for a certain number of days then stopped, which allows the womb to shed its lining every month and causes the periods to start again. There is research evidence to show that the combined use of oestrogen and progesterone does not carry the same risk as the use of oestrogen on its own. There is some evidence that suggests that the prolonged use of oestrogen therapy thickens the womb lining, causing irregular and heavy bleeding and cancer of the womb in some women.

The use of HRT can relieve problems associated with the menopause such as hot flushes or flashes, night sweats, a dry vagina, and stops the further development of existing osteoporosis. A woman may well be advised by her doctor not to have HRT if she has high blood-pressure, a history of thrombosis (blood clots), heart disease, diabetes, chronic liver disease, or is a smoker.

If you feel that this type of treatment would benefit you, discuss it with your family doctor. Ask him to explain all the benefits and the risks involved in this type of therapy so that you can make an informed decision about the treatment. If he is not prepared to treat you with HRT, and you want to pursue the idea, ask to be referred to a gynaecologist or to a menopause clinic: see page 322.

There is plenty of assistance and advice available to help you through the menopause, so there is no need for you to suffer and be unhappy during what must be yet another exciting phase in your life. Just one last word of advice: continue to use contraceptives for two years after your last period if you are under fifty and for one year if you are over fifty. Take advice about contraception from your doctor, a family planning clinic or a pregnancy advisory service (see page 292). The risks associated with the contraceptive pill increase as we get older and particularly in women over forty.

FIFTY YEARS OLD

Reaching the age of fifty is a time that men and women take stock of their lives, what they have or have not achieved. Some people see reaching fifty as having one foot in the grave, a steady decline to a frail old age. Life up until now has probably revolved around a job and a family. Children may be marrying and leaving home, and it's just the two of you again. Sometimes there are unexpected and unwanted changes such as the loss of a job. For more information about redundancy and changing jobs at fifty, see Chapter 11. More employers these days are offering early retirement, but before making a decision it is important to seek some good advice. You need to know how early retirement will affect your occupational pension, if you have one, and your contributory pension. Talk to the personnel manager at work, to your trade union or to an accountant; you are also entitled to ask the Department of Health and Social Security to work out your contributory rights: see page 323.

Suddenly giving up work may well bring with it financial problems such as mortgage repayments, hire purchase agreements still outstanding, and payments must be made. See page 323 for advice on who to contact for sound advice on these issues.

PLANNING FOR RETIREMENT

Planning for a long and happy retirement is more important than many people realise. It is not just a case of stopping work on Friday, moving to a cottage by the sea and living happily ever after. Once retired, and as the years slip by, it is essential to keep busy, keep fit and well, to keep warm in order to enjoy the last years of life. For some people getting old has meant living alone, having financial problems, being lonely and afraid. For others it is living with a daughter or a son. Sometimes this brings great happiness, but for others problems; there may be difficulties when two generations live together under the same roof. What can be done to ease the situation? Who can help? To avoid problems it is sensible to plan for your retirement.

For some people it will be retirement at sixty or sixty-five and a little cottage in the country. Or perhaps you want to retire early at fifty and sail around the world. Whatever your plans, you need to look at the financial implications and possibilities. There are two aspects to financial planning. The first is your pension; it must be able to provide enough income for you to live on, and if you are thinking of retiring early, then you need to have some money saved or invested for the period in between the day that you take early retirement and when you can claim your pension.

Retirement may be seen as a time of great change, a chance to move to somewhere by the sea, or more time together. I live in a country area, and a great many people move down here when they retire; for some it has been a great success and they are very happy, but for others it was a big mistake.

Jack and Kitty live in Bournemouth; they moved from London when Jack retired in 1984.

We had always wanted to retire to Bournemouth; we had spent many very happy family holidays here and felt that we really belonged. We left all our friends and family in London. At first they used to come and visit us and stay for a few days. Then Jack had a stroke and he was in hospital for weeks. He still can't walk properly. I can't drive, and Jack can't now, so we don't get up to London very much, and our friends are in the same sort of state. The family come down here in the summer and at Christmas. We can't afford to move back to London, and sometimes I wish we had stayed put.

It is important to think very carefully about moving house when you retire. The sort of questions that you need to ask yourself are:

- Do we know people in this area and, if not, how will we make friends?
- Is there transport nearby in case we are unable to use a car?
- What will happen if one of us becomes ill or dies?
- How close by are other members of the family that we can rely upon to help if needed?

Family and friends are very important not only during the good times but also when you need someone to lean on and to help you through a crisis.

Time to do what you want to do

When Henry retired he decided that we should spend as much time together as possible. He played golf whenever he had some spare time, but he said that he would give this up so that we could go out and do things together. So in turn I said that I would give up my tennis with my girlfriends. Every morning he would wake up at 7.30 and say: 'Well, what are we going to do today?' There had to be a plan! Everywhere I went he came, too. Shopping was a nightmare; everything that I put in the supermarket trolley he would query, tut at the price and ask if we really needed it and put it back on the shelf. At home he was always under my feet, being helpful, so I was never able to give the house a really good clean through.

After years of being independent I was suddenly expected to have a shadow wherever I went. He nearly drove me to distraction. In the end I suggested that he went off and played golf with his friends and I would resume my weekly game of tennis with my friends. He was happy and so was I; we both had our separate interests, but we also enjoyed being together. Sometimes we just get in the car and explore parts of the country that we have never seen before. We have been on coach trips and taken a couple of 'off-season weekend breaks' in small hotels which were wonderful.

So my advice is to keep up your own interests and hobbies. Don't try to change too much just because you have retired. Let things settle for a while. Enjoy doing all those things that you just didn't have time to do while you were busy working and bringing up a family.

JOYCE FREEMAN

It may well be wonderful to spend more time together when you both retire, but togetherness can be taken to extremes. As Joyce says, don't be tempted to give up the things that you enjoy and do as an individual without your partner. There will be plenty of time to go out and do things together as well as enjoying your own individual hobbies. Planning for a happy retirement also includes what to do with all that new-found free time.

■ Look around you and find out what is going on. Perhaps there is some voluntary work that you would like to do. Contact a Volunteer Bureau: see page 372. There are charities that could do with your help and expertise; ask your doctor, minister, local hospital social worker, Citizen's Advice Bureau or the public library if there is some useful work that you could do.
■ Maybe you have a desire to join a class and learn something new. The library will have details of local classes.
■ Develop new interests. Make a list of all the things that you have wanted to do for years but have never had time to do.
■ Be a 'joiner'. Join in with local events and be prepared to make new friends and really nurture old friendships.
■ Invite people to your home for coffee, lunch or supper. You don't have to spend an enormous amount of money on grand dinner-parties. Keep it simple and informal.
■ See something of the country that you live in by taking day trips or off-season weekends away.

Keeping fit:

■ Exercise. If you play golf, bowls, swim, dance or enjoy gardening or walking, these are excellent ways of keeping fit. If you do not take any exercise at the moment, try to take a short walk at your own pace every day.
■ Diet. Being overweight can be a nuisance as one gets older. It can make you tired as you need more effort to move about. Joints ache because they have to carry extra weight. Breathing may be difficult.

To lose weight cut out some of the starchy foods such as cakes, pastry, sugar, jam, biscuits, cereals and fried foods. Use wholemeal bread instead of white bread, brown rice instead of white rice, and bake potatoes rather than fry them. Eat moderate amounts of protein foods such as meat, eggs, milk, cheese and fish. Eat plenty of green vegetables, carrots, tomatoes and fresh fruit. Avoid chocolate and sweets.

■ Do not smoke, and drink only in moderation.
■ Avoid accidents in the home.

Highly polished floors and rugs look lovely, but you can easily slip on them. Sew or stick foam or rubber under the corners. Tack down the corners of carpets and ensure that stair carpets are not frayed and loose.

Flexes from lamps and televisions can be tripped over, so run them along the wall. Do not put them under heavy furniture or carpets as this may cause a fire.

Electric irons and kettles should be fitted with a thermostat control or cut-out in case you forget to switch them off.

Oil- or gas-heaters should be placed where they cannot be bumped into or tripped over.

Non-slip suction pads or mat in the bath will prevent you from slipping. A hand-rail at the side will help you get in and out of the bath if your knees are stiff.

Make sure that stairways are well lit.

■ If you live on your own, make sure that you have a system to call for help if you should fall. Alarms that you can wear around your neck are a very good idea.

LIVING ON A PENSION

Retirement may mean that there is less money to spend, and when it comes to food it is important to buy the essential foods first. Meat can be expensive, so ask the butcher for cheaper cuts; they are just as nutritious as the more expensive cuts of meat. Dairy foods such as milk, eggs, cheese and yoghurt are good value. It is often better value to buy small eggs rather than large ones. Ask your fish retailer's advice about which fish are in season and cheapest. Buy fruit and vegetables that are in season and really fresh and ripe as there is less waste.

If you are living on your own, it is very tempting to think that you just can't be bothered to cook properly for yourself alone. Good food is just as important for someone on their own as for anyone else. Why don't you ask a friend or neighbour to join you? There must be plenty of people who live near you who would love to join you for a meal and then invite you back to their house. It only needs someone to be brave enough to make the first move.

In the cold winter months it is very important to keep warm. An older person's body is not as efficient at preserving normal body temperature as a younger person's. One of the dangers of cold weather is that you may not know that you are as cold as you really are. If it is too expensive to heat the whole house, or the heating in the bedroom is inadequate, get the bed moved into a warm room downstairs during the really cold weather. Wear lots of layers of clothes, preferably woollen. Wear a hat and gloves indoors; it may seem silly, but it is worth looking a little odd in order to avoid suffering from the cold. At night put on extra clothes as well as night-clothes including bedsocks and a woollen hat. If the bedroom is not used during the day, make sure that it is well heated before going to bed. Warm the bed with an electric blanket or a hot-water bottle. Remember never to use a hot-water bottle at the same time as an electric blanket and to switch off electric blankets before getting into bed.

The room temperature must not fall below 65°F (18°C). Keep a large thermometer in the room and mark off the point below which the room temperature must not fall.

Exclude draughts from windows, doors and floorboards. Cracks can be sealed with newspaper and clingfilm applied to the insides of the window-frames to act as a type of double glazing. Chimneys of old unused fireplaces can be blocked with metal, brick or any other non-flammable material. Be careful not to block up any source of ventilation that is necessary. For advice on grants and services, see page 324.

Eat a nourishing diet and have at least one hot meal a day and regular hot drinks to provide the body with fuel against the cold. If you are living on your own, keep a Thermos flask containing a hot drink by your bed at night and beside your chair during the day. Wrap up warm and get out of the house during the day. If you are unable to get out and about, remember to get up out of your chair at regular intervals and walk about the room.

Security can be a worry, and home security can be improved by fitting good locks to windows and doors. Do not leave windows open after dark. Fit a security chain and a door viewer to your front door so you will be able to see who is calling. Do not open the door to anyone unless you are certain that you know who they are. If you believe that an intruder is trying to break into your home, telephone the police without hesitation. See also Chapter 12.

LIVING WITH AN ELDERLY RELATIVE

Loneliness is perhaps one of the greatest hardships of old age. Being wanted, needed and being important to the family are high priorities for the elderly. Some people prefer to live with their families, but this is not always possible. Moreover, there is no denying that several generations living together can give rise to problems.

Joan's mother was living on her own when she had a stroke. The hospital said that she would not be able to go back to her own home. At first we thought that she would be better off in an old people's home, where someone could look after her. Joan felt guilty about this and wanted to care for her in our home. She didn't need a lot of nursing but she couldn't walk very well and someone had to help her with her meals.

In the end we turned the dining-room into a bedsitter for her, and she came to live with us. It was all right to start with; she was very grateful, and everything seemed to go all right. Then she got demanding; she was always calling Joan to do this or that, never a moment's peace. Then she started to wet the bed, and there were always sheets drying all over the place. Our house was just not big enough.

Joan and I would end up arguing because she spent so much time with her mother. We couldn't even have an argument without her chipping in. The house began to smell of urine, Joan and I were hardly speaking, and in the end we had a blazing row and I went to hit Joan. I stopped myself just in time. I have never done anything like that in my life. Anyway, it meant that we had to do something about the mess we were in. So we went upstairs, so that her mother couldn't hear us talking, and in the end we decided that we would have to find a nursing home for her no matter how much it cost.

We talked to our doctor, and he put us in touch with a local nursing home. We had to wait a while until they would take her, but somehow it was better once the decision had been made.

PETER WILLIAMSON

There are sometimes problems when an elderly person moves in with a son or daughter, because his or her position has changed from being a carer or an equal to that of a dependant and this reversal of rôles is sometimes difficult: it may, for instance, make an elderly relative stubbornly independent or very dependent and constantly demanding attention.

Sometimes the elderly relative may have difficulty accepting that times have changed. Maybe it is the woman in the household that goes out to work, leaving home and caring to her partner. Or maybe that the children have been brought up differently, and it seems to the elderly person that they are allowed to be too independent too soon.

In the case of a grandparent coming to live with the family the authority of the head of the household may be threatened. A strain may be placed on the marriage with the couple feeling that they are never alone and cannot say what they really feel for fear of being overheard just like Peter and Joan Williamson.

Living together like this needs a lot of give and take on both sides if it is going to work. If possible, the elderly relative should have a sitting and sleeping area where she can keep her personal belongings and be independent; this helps everyone concerned to retain a sense of independence.

Nevertheless, elderly people often have a very special relationship with the younger generation and are able to bridge the generation gap. The young may feel that they are able to talk and discuss problems with their grandparent when they cannot talk to a parent.

If the time comes when you feel that you can no longer cope, for whatever reason, you should not feel guilty. In some situations, it is better for professionals or people outside the family to care for your elderly relative, not only for your sake but also for his or hers. This may take the form of short-term care while you take a holiday or moving your relative to a nursing home or sheltered accommodation. For more information, see page 332.

People caring for an elderly relative with senile dementia often find that they are overwhelmed by the stress of caring for their relative. See Chapter 8 for more information.

HELPING AN ELDERLY PERSON TO STAY IN THEIR OWN HOME

The longer you can stay mobile and independent the better. Going to the shops, meeting friends, or expeditions to the cinema, theatre or a social club all help to keep up an active interest in life.

There are many practical aids that may help you to remain independent:

- Dressing can be made easier by replacing zips and buttons with Velcro and giving front fastenings to clothes.
- Shoe-horns, combs and brushes should have long handles, and nail-clippers are easier to manage than scissors.
- Put a stool by the bath to simplify getting in and out, and a non-slip mat in the bath to prevent slipping and falling. Or install a shower; then you can sit on a plastic chair under the shower and wash unaided.
- Hand-rails next to the bath, shower and lavatory are easily fitted.
- Raising the level of the lavatory seat will help you to be more independent.
- Make sure that your bed is at the right height. If you have to drop on to your feet, then the bed is too high. The bed is too low if you have to heave yourself up to a standing position.
- Your ordinary sitting-chair should have a seat that is not too low, about 45–65 centimetres (18–26 inches) off the ground and not too deep so that getting up is easy. It should have a high back and strong arms for pushing on when standing up. If this is a problem, an ejection seat may help; these can be bought from furniture shops or you may see them advertised in the newspapers.

For more information about help for the elderly, see page 333.

Eat a well-balanced diet, keep fit, keep warm, active, busy and enjoy your retirement. The process of ageing begins the day that we are born, and the different stages of our lives should be welcomed with equal enthusiasm. This is not always the case with the later years of life. Some people fear becoming old as though it were something to be ashamed of. Perhaps this is the fault of society today, because we do not value and revere the older generation even though they have so much knowledge and experience that we could benefit from. The elderly are just as much a vital part of society as anyone else.

CHAPTER SIX

The Disabled and the Handicapped

The terms *disabled* or *handicapped* can be applied to people suffering from a very wide range of conditions which prevent them from living their lives as independently as normal. These terms are often used to describe mental handicap which may be hereditary, congenital, the result of brain damage at birth or as the result of an accident. Physical handicaps can also be hereditary, congenital or acquired as the result of illness or accident. They can range from arthritis to total paralysis and include the deaf and the blind.

Over the last few years the media have produced many excellent programmes and articles about the physically and mentally handicapped and have helped people to gain insight and understanding into their problems. Despite all this education, some people still have difficulty accepting both the handicapped person and the family. There seems to be an invisible barrier very similar to the one that is erected when someone dies; other people have difficulty coming to terms with their own feelings and tend to be uncomfortable, embarrassed and simply do not know what to say or do.

In this chapter I have talked to people who have a handicap or a disability and their families to find out how they coped when they discovered that they or a member of their family was disabled. Who did they turn to for help and advice?

MENTAL HANDICAP

Wendy and John Lees have two children, John and James. John, the elder brother, is a chemical engineer. James suffered brain damage at birth, resulting in a floppy weakness of his limbs, difficulty co-ordinating his hands, poor eyesight and slight deafness. The facial bones were damaged, and as he grew older he had difficulty breathing through his nose, sinusitis and asthma, problems chewing food because of the impaired alignment of his upper and lower jaws. He was a slow learner except for reading, which he had no problem with.

James was born in Rhodesia in 1963. When I had our first baby, Johnny, I was advised by the consultant in Malawi that I had a very narrow pelvis and that a caesarian section would be necessary in any other pregnancies. My husband, John, was then transferred to Rhodesia, so we went with him. I had a perfectly normal pregnancy but towards the end I had this recurring nightmare that the baby would be damaged at birth.

The birth was a long and difficult one; the doctor saw no need to perform a caesarian, even though he had received a letter from my consultant in Malawi, and following a forceps delivery a very bruised and battered James was born, face first. Despite this the doctors and the paediatrician felt that our baby was quite normal.

Within a short period of time I noticed that James was unable to bring his arm over to reach his rattle and in fact was going purple in the face with frustration. I discussed it with the doctor, who reassured me, once more, that nothing was wrong.

We came back to England when James was five months old. He was a very placid baby, looked perfectly normal except for a dent in the right side of his head, and slept well. But we were both still worried about his lack of co-ordination. So we took him to our local, Gloucestershire, doctor who told my husband that James would never be normal, never walk, and the best thing that we could do was to put him in a home and forget about him. John didn't tell me exactly what the doctor had said for many years, because he was so upset and outraged. He could not and would not believe what had been said. James looked so normal and was such a happy and placid baby.

We asked that James should be referred to Great Ormond Street children's hospital where they were very helpful and kind. He was then referred to the Wolfson Centre. Here they assessed him several times, the reports were encouraging and the staff supportive and constructive, and eventually, when he was six months old, we were told that he had brain damage. We would advise anyone who is worried about their baby to seek this kind of professional advice.

James had difficulty moving, so I used to put him through a series of exercises such as suspending him, pulling and massaging his limbs and his back, encouraging him to speak. No one had told me to do this; it just seemed the right thing to do, and he responded. Later a doctor confirmed that this was the right thing to do. His brother, Johnny, was marvellous with him and he had endless patience with James, constantly entertaining and encouraging him. Unfortunately James developed asthma when he was eighteen months, which meant that in the winter and on windy days James had to stay indoors. Instead of resenting, his brother was quite happy to keep him company. During this time I felt very angry about what had happened to James. I wanted to hide away from the world, because I hated people staring at him; I suppose I was embarrassed. I was only twenty-three and vulnerable because John was working abroad a great deal. John was always very supportive when at home, and we developed a partnership in managing and coping with James. I had left most of my own family in Rhodesia, and it was not until our adopted sister took me in hand that I really started to live again. She made me become a person in my own right; up until then my whole life had revolved around 'putting James right'.

John also felt anger, not only at the way the birth had been mishandled but also at the doctor who had effectively written James off as no use to anyone. There were times when we wanted to take James back to that doctor and show him just how wrong he had been.

As far as learning to use the potty, dress and feed himself, James had no real difficulties. He was a gentle although sometimes excitable child. His asthma increasingly became more of a problem from the age of two until he was sixteen, when he was able to cope with it himself; otherwise he was a healthy child.

He went to nursery school at five years old. He learned to read quite quickly but had difficulty adding up. The teacher refused to believe that he had a handicap and would smack him and lock him in a cupboard because he wasn't trying hard enough. I only realised this was happening when I went to school for one of James's routine medical check-ups. All the other children came out of his classroom, but there was no sign of James. I asked one of the children where he was, and they said that he was probably locked in the cupboard as that was where the teacher usually put him when he couldn't do his sums. This accounted for why he was sick every morning before going to school. We removed him from that school and refused to send him back, and in time the County found him a place at a marvellous village school.

At the village school James was obviously happy and did very well. At the age of nine he went to special school on the Isle of Wight mainly because of his asthma. Though terribly homesick, he enjoyed school life. It was very traumatic leaving him; he became so very upset, but he soon cheered up when he was back with his friends.

At the age of twelve, his asthma being manageable, we found an excellent day school in Wimborne, and James enjoyed helping and looking after the small children. Sometimes, however, he would come home in tears because someone had made unkind and hurtful remarks. He was and still is very brave about this sort of thing and copes with a lot of this on his own. If I asked him what was wrong, he would simply tell me to go away, and that he would cope on his own. In my heart I knew that someone had said something cruel, I would cry and die inside, but he was always so strong and brave. He was given permission to stay on until he was eighteen, but he had to leave at sixteen to undergo further surgery to his face.

From the age of two James's jaw had started to protrude, and he had some corrective surgery at the age of twelve. By the time he was sixteen it protruded even further and the cheekbones had not formed correctly, causing several problems. The proposed surgery was extensive and involved lifting the whole of his face. The surgeon was excellent, but we as parents were very anxious hearing that only three months before a young boy of sixteen who had a similar operation had died on the operating-table. John and I were very worried about giving our consent. James, however, had stronger views on the subject and said: 'It is not your life, it is mine. I want the operation, so let's just get on with it.' James was in hospital for seven weeks and always remained cheerful. When he was discharged from hospital he continued his education with tutors at home.

We took advice from the Hampshire Careers Office, and at the age of seventeen he went to the Stable Family Trust for eighteen months. After this he joined a Youth Training Scheme where there was one man in particular who picked on him so much that he used to be sick in the mornings before he went to work. He was supposed to be offered a permanent job after twelve months; he stayed eighteen months, and no permanent job materialised.

James then had several assessments at Canterbury Lodge, a hostel run by the Hampshire County Council Social Services, to establish what he could achieve and to help him become as independent as possible.

At the moment James is living away from home and at Canterbury Lodge and enjoys caring for elderly people in a nearby community centre. He has understanding and compassion for the elderly that is rarely seen in one so young. He also has strong religious convictions, which John and I feel has helped him throughout his life. He has changed dramatically since the most recent assessments and is becoming more and more independent and assertive.

We both believe that it is most important to get the best out of your child and to encourage as much independence as possible. James had to conform to a normal world; the handicapped person is in the minority, so the greatest gift you can give them is to see that they are as happy and independent as possible.

WENDY, JOHN AND JAMES LEES

This family have coped so well through both good and bad times and even now James is taking on more responsibility and becoming more independent, which makes his parents very proud of him indeed, although they both say that they still worry about him and have some very anxious moments – particularly when he decides to try something new. Just the other day a member of the church that James attends at home died. Wendy and John were surprised to learn that James had decided he wanted to be at the funeral and managed to get there by taking a series of six buses, then insisted on making his own way back. Wendy was a very proud but slightly nervous mother.

When parents are told that their child is handicapped the news is devastating and very difficult to take in. Feelings of disbelief that this has happened to them are very common. There are feelings of resentfulness and hostility towards the staff at the hospital and guilt, particularly if the disorder is inherited. Some parents feel that they just cannot cope and find themselves totally rejecting the child. All these are quite normal reactions. Fortunately, most parents of children who are born handicapped come to love them and are somehow able to give them the best quality of life possible in the circumstances.

If you are worried that your baby is handicapped, for whatever reason, the first thing to do is to find out if there really is anything wrong and, if so, what the future holds and where to get help. Some handicaps are noticeable at birth, while others become obvious as the child gets older. Sometimes it is just an intuitive feeling that makes the parents believe something is wrong. If you are worried, talk to your family doctor about your fears. Parents of handicapped children often say that their worries were not taken seriously and they were told that they were over-anxious or fussy parents. Early recognition of a handicap often means a better chance of effective treatment. So talk to your doctor and don't be put off, and if necessary ask to see a doctor who specialises in this field of medicine.

I was sure that something was wrong with Beth and was fighting a battle based only on a mother's instinct about the health of our daughter versus the doctors' opinions. This time I was correct; at six months they diagnosed Beth as being mentally and physically handicapped. At last the battle for the truth was over.

MARY HARDING

Mary is by no means alone in her feelings; many other parents of handicapped children have experienced the same battle for the truth. Once the problem has been confirmed, get in touch with the appropriate support group (listed on page 335). Support groups are very helpful, because they can put you in touch with people who have experienced the same problems. Parents of a child with the same handicap as your child can offer sound and sensible practical advice from their own personal experience; they know what you are going through and understand because they have experienced the same feelings. These support groups will also know where you can get special equipment and financial help that will make life easier for you and your child. They are a mine of information and really worth contacting.

I have also listed some useful books that will help you to gain more insight into your child's problem and help you to plan for the future.

Help in the form of physiotherapy, speech therapy, occupational therapy or any other specialised treatment can be organised through your family doctor. Physiotherapists in the United Kingdom are being specially trained to help handicapped children with co-ordination and many other problems. Recently there has been a great deal of media coverage concerning special treatment centres abroad to help handicapped children. Although these centres have a high success rate, it still means enormous cost to the family both financially and emotionally as the family is often split up for months as one parent takes the child away for treatment and the other stays at home with the rest of the children. On page 335 I have listed the hospitals and centres in the United Kingdom that offer a similar service. Here there are highly skilled doctors, nurses, physiotherapists and teachers who have been specially trained to help handicapped children, whether they have been born with a disability or left with a disability following a head injury. They also provide short term care for children with degenerative conditions requiring treatment and those whose families just need a break from the demanding twenty-four-hour care of their handicapped child.

To help your child reach his or her full potential the right education, training and careers advice and employment are essential. The handicapped are people first and handicapped second, so social life, sports and fun, adult relationships, sex and marriage are just as important to them as they are to anyone else. As a parent you may well need some expert advice and help to ensure that your child has a full and happy life, and the best advice that I could find came from the Royal Society for Mentally Handicapped Children and Adults (Mencap) and the Spastics Society. They sent me an enormous amount of extremely helpful information in the form of several booklets. They are easy to read, simply set out and full of constructive and helpful advice covering the following topics:

The early days when you are told that your child is handicapped: what this means, how the family and friends might react and how to cope

How to cope with a young handicapped child

Financial help

Schooling and what happens after school

Training and careers

Sex, relationships and marriage

What will happen when his or her parents are no longer around?

See page 337 for further details and addresses. Training and employment for the handicapped are covered in Chapter 11.

When you write to these organisations briefly outline your child's particular problem, what help and advice you need, and ask for the address and telephone number of your local support group.

GENETIC DISORDERS

The genes in the parents' ova or sperm determine all the physical characteristics in their child. The term 'dominant' refers to a gene which will produce definite characteristics in half the children such as black hair. The 'recessive' means that it will do so only if the child receives two similar genes, one from each parent. For example, two black-haired parents who each pass a recessive gene of blonde hair will produce a blonde-haired child. Characteristics produced by 'recessive' are neutralised by those determined by 'dominant' genes. Some disorders are inherited via the genes. For example, Huntington's Chorea, which is dominantly transmitted and causes mental deficiency and abnormal jerking movements of the arms and legs beyond the control of the individual. It begins between the ages of twenty and forty and progresses slowly. Unfortunately there is no known cure. Anyone with this disease is advised to seek genetic counselling before having children as there is a 50 per cent chance that their children will develop the disease.

Another example is phenylketonuria, which is transmitted by the 'recessive' gene; it is a metabolic disorder which affects approximately one in 10,000–20,000 children. It is due to a deficiency of an enzyme called phenylalanine hydroxylase, which converts amino acid phenylalanine to tyrosine. A deficiency of this enzyme causes an increase in the phenylalanine level, which is toxic and damages the brain leading to mental deficiency. The raised level also causes stunted growth and may cause eczema and convulsions. All newborn babies are tested for phenylketonuria by the Guthrie test, which is performed on a few drops of blood usually taken from the baby's heel. Treatment is by strict dietary restrictions to ensure that the brain is not damaged.

DOWN'S SYNDROME

Genes are sited within the body cells, on chromosomes, and abnormalities of these may produce abnormalities in children. Down's Syndrome, or mongolism, is a congenital disorder present at birth where the child is both physically and mentally handicapped. It is caused by a defect in the genes. In every living cell, genes are carried on tiny anatomical structures called chromosomes. A human being has forty-six chromosomes arranged in twenty-three pairs. The child with Down's Syndrome has one chromosome too many, which is identical to the twenty-first pair.

The most common type of Down's Syndrome occurs in babies born to mothers who are over the age of forty as a result of a fault in the early development of the egg (ovum). The risk of this happening increases as the age of the mother increases. During pregnancy a test can be performed on the amniotic fluid which surrounds the baby (an amniocentesis) which can diagnose Down's Syndrome and, if the test is positive, the mother can have the pregnancy terminated. The other type of Down's Syndrome occurs if there is an abnormality in the genes of either the mother or the father. In this case there is a risk that any children born may have Down's Syndrome.

HAEMOPHILIA

Haemophilia is transmitted on the chromosomes which control the sex of the child. It is a serious blood disease that causes severe recurrent bleeding into any part of the body, commonly into the large joints such as the knees, ankles and elbows – often following only a very slight knock or bump. The bleeding is due to the absence of a major blood-clotting constituent: factor VIII, or the anti-haemophilic factor. The disease is carried on one of the 'X' sex chromosomes by the mother who, if the other 'X' chromosome is normal, will not have a bleeding disorder. The abnormal chromosome is passed to half of her sons or daughters. It is only the sons that develop the bleeding disorder, for as XY's they do not have a normal second 'X' chromosome to over-ride the abnormal. Only half of her sons receive an abnormal 'X' chromosome; the others are entirely normal and are not carriers.

The treatment is to transfuse the anti-haemophilic factor in order to control the bleeding. The disease may be very mild or very severe and life-threatening. There is no known cure for the disease and, because of this, men with haemophilia may be advised not to have children. Their sisters may be carriers and are advised to have genetic counselling before deciding to have children.

Anyone who has a known genetic or chromosomal disease, or think that their parents may have, or a couple who already have a handicapped child as the result of a genetic disorder are advised to receive expert genetic counselling. This will often allay fears, and the couple can then have children without worrying. If the couple are found to have a problem that will be passed on to their children, they will receive help and counselling and may well decide not to have children rather than risk transmitting the disease.

For more information about genetic counselling, see page 341.

DISABILITY AS THE RESULT OF AN ACCIDENT

Spinal Injuries

The lady who has written the next contribution wishes to remain anonymous. She was a normal healthy fit adult until she sustained a spinal injury which left her paralysed.

I sustained a spinal injury while working for the Social Services in 1972. Apart from grieving for one's lost ability, there is poverty and the endless struggle for benefits.

In the early days I was at a loss to know what to do. In the second year I began to attend a day centre, which was a turning-point for me; I met other disabled people and was soon involved in social activities and learned dressmaking, something I had never attempted.

I feel there is not enough help or advice for disabled people. Places of entertainment are mostly inaccessible to disabled people. It would be nice, wouldn't it, if we could take advantage of the shows, etc., that able-bodied people are able to see?

I have a good husband, but if you consider that since 1972 there has been no sex life for us it must be very difficult for him.

No one wants to be disabled, but if we become disabled is there any need for us to be treated as second-class citizens? Life is difficult as it is, but the experience of being patronised makes it a very unhappy situation. We need to be valued, as we have a contribution to make.

For the last three years I have been involved with DIAL (Disablement Information and Advice Lines). It has helped me as it is interesting and good to think we can help each other.

Coming to terms with the sort of disability described above is not only learning to live life with the physical restrictions of a wheelchair but also accepting and adapting mentally to the changes. It is almost impossible for someone who is able-bodied to imagine what sort of effect this would have on one's life. The spinal cord can be damaged by spinal injury, infections and tumours of the spine, blockage of the blood supply to the spinal cord, spina bifida and multiple sclerosis. The spinal cord runs through a chain of bony rings known as the vertebrae. This vertebral column protects the spinal cord, which works like a telephone cable, sending messages of feeling and sensation to the brain which converts them into responses, movement. When the spinal cord is injured, these messages are interrupted or cannot get through at all. Depending on the extent of damage to the spinal cord, a person will be either partially or completely paralysed from the point of the damage downwards.

Paraplegia resulting from a broken back is paralysis from the chest or waist downwards, with little or no movement or feeling in the lower limbs and lower part of the trunk. Tetraplegia, resulting from a broken neck, also affects the arms and hands. Fractures (breaks) or compression of the vertebrae which cause permanent damage to the cord may lead to loss of sensation, movement, bladder and bowel control, as well as affecting sexual function.

Anyone with spinal injury will be cared for in a hospital which specialises in this type of rehabilitation. The staff are highly skilled and will help the injured person to gain his or her full potential. It is often a long and hard process for the person concerned and their family. There are only nine National Health Service spinal units in England and Wales (the one in Northern Ireland, two in Scotland and one in Eire are outside the scope of this service), which means that many people who sustain spinal cord injuries receive treatment at places a long way from home. After a serious injury like this people rely very heavily on the support of their family, who will have to travel long distances at great expense. On page 338 you will find the names and addresses of support groups who have set up relatives' travel funds which will help relieve some of the stress and allow them to be with their injured relative. Support groups also offer other help both physical and emotional: see page 335.

The realisation that you may never walk again is something that is very hard to accept. Feelings of depression, frustration and aggression are all very common and quite normal. It is a way of getting rid of those feelings from within yourself. The staff at the hospital will help you come through this stage. Relatives may well take the brunt of these hostile feelings and will get help and advice from the staff. Skills to help you manage problems such as incontinence, keeping clean, dressing, lifting and moving yourself will be taught by the staff at the hospital.

If you are confined to a wheelchair, your home will need to be adapted to allow you as much independence as possible. Doors may need widening and ramps provided at outside doors instead of steps. The bedroom, living-room and bathroom should be on the ground floor. A shower is preferable to a bath as you can manage a shower on your own or with minimal help. The furniture may need rearranging and the kitchen fittings lowered so that you can reach them. A specially adapted car will help you get out and about. An electric wheelchair will give you greater independence. To get you on and off the lavatory, in and out of bed, the bath or even your car, a hoist in your home will mean that you will need little or no help with lifting and moving. All these practical issues will be discussed and organised by the staff at the hospital. See page 335 for more information.

Apart from the practical issues, you will have been encouraged to participate in various sports during your stay in hospital such as swimming, archery, table tennis and many other sports to strengthen muscles as well as providing the competitive element; it is important to continue this at home. If you had a job prior to being disabled, every effort should be made to get back to work even if it means retraining for something more appropriate.

Social Life

An active social life is just as important now as it was before the accident or injury; you are the same person as you were before, and good friends will still want to be part of your life. The support groups have an important rôle to play here as they will put you in touch with someone in your area with similar problems to your own to help you make the very best of your life. Later on you may well be asked to help someone who has recently become disabled, and the benefit to you of helping others will be enormous. See page 335.

Sexual Problems

Sexual feelings are rarely lost, and there is no reason why anyone should feel that they are not able to enjoy sex. The problems vary from case to case. For example, in the case of a paraplegic woman she may be unable to feel the normal sensations of sexual intercourse, the male paraplegic may be able to sustain an erection but unable to ejaculate. These problems are not all insurmountable; there are specialist counsellors who can help you. See page 335 for more information. Some men who have suffered a spinal injury may have a low sperm count and have difficulty ejaculating. It is important to seek professional advice from a sub-fertility clinic (see Chapter 1), but the support groups may be able to offer some advice or even help by putting you in touch with couples who have overcome these problems. See page 335.

Getting away for a holiday may be a problem and, again, if you contact a support group they may well be able to help you. The Spinal Injuries Association (SIA) has a variety of solutions to the problem. One solution is the provision of narrow boats called *Kingfisher 1* and *2* which have been especially built so that they can be skippered from a wheelchair. They also have mobile homes in France and England. They will also help to assess the suitability of a holiday cottage or hotel to help you select the right place to take your holiday. The assessment is made by people who are wheelchair users who know from firsthand experience, which is reassuring in itself. For more information, see page 343.

Information and help concerning personal injury claims, attendance allowances, care attendants who provide short-term help while your regular carer is away or ill, equipment and many other facilities are available from these groups. For a list of services offered, see page 344.

HANDICAP AS THE RESULT OF ILLNESS

Illnesses such as arthritis, polio, heart disease, strokes, multiple sclerosis and many others can leave a once able-bodied person disabled. There are many support groups, all of whom specialise in a particular problem. I have listed them on page 339.

I was diagnosed as having multiple sclerosis in 1981, at the age of thirty-three. I am happily married and at the time my three children were only six, nine and eleven years old. At first I was shocked when the doctor told me the news. Why me? I had a family to look after and a job that I adored and had to keep as we were unable to survive financially without the extra money. Everything seemed black, no hope for the future. What would happen to my children? I blamed everyone including my parents, the doctors and even God. For a while I could see no point in going on; I was only going to become a burden to my family and everyone else.

Half the time I didn't really listen to what the doctors were saying; all I knew about MS was that I would end up in a wheelchair, a useless lump that was once a person. I must have been impossible to live with, so full of self-pity. During one of my many stays in hospital I met another woman who also had MS, and I listened to what she had to say. She gave me a book to read and answered all my questions frankly and honestly. In the end I discovered that there was far more to the problem than I had realised. It was not the end of the world. I had to fight for myself and my family or go under. I chose to fight.

She suggested that I joined the Multiple Sclerosis Society, which I did; and it may sound corny but it really did help to know that I was not the only one. Other people had learned to live with this problem. They were so positive about life, they offered practical advice and help, but most of all they offered the benefit of experience and how to cope with problems when they arise.

I was lucky. I have had long periods of remission when I feel really well, and then another symptom would appear such as pins and needles in my legs or arms, then there was a numb feeling in my legs and I felt that I was walking on cotton-wool. Another time I had double vision, which I found very distressing. I still managed to keep my job as a secretary, but I have reduced my hours considerably over the years. Sometimes I suddenly get very tired, although I really haven't done very much.

Life over the last few years has not been easy, and who knows what the future holds, so I try to live just one day at a time. My advice to anyone else who has just been told that they have MS is to find out all you can about the disease; ignorance just breeds more fear and resentment. Talk to people who have the disease and who understand how you are feeling. I don't want the whole world to know who I am, so I would rather remain anonymous, but I hope that this contribution will help other sufferers.

Multiple sclerosis is a progressive disease and a condition which affects the central nervous system and attacks the myelin sheath, the insulation protecting the nerve fibres. The nerve impulses are hindered or prevented from reaching their destination, and various parts of the body cease to function properly. This results in disabilities ranging from mild impairments of speech, vision and movement to complete paralysis. It is not infectious or contagious; it is not a mental illness or hereditary. It often affects people between the ages of twenty and forty and can be characterised by a distressing pattern of relapses and remissions. It is this unpredictable nature of the disease that can tear lives apart. At present there is no known cause.

It is a common disease: about 50,000 people in the United Kingdom and 250,000 in the United States are known to have MS. As the MS Society says: 'More than half the people who have MS will never show any obvious signs of handicap and less than one in five will eventually be in a wheelchair. The diagnosis is not always a sentence to a life of disability; it is a warning that you should look at better ways of living and working.'

The MS Society and other support groups which I have listed on page 341 offer a wide range of help and advice, including ways to help yourself, sources of information about MS and sources of help.

STROKES

Strokes are due to disorders of the blood vessels of the brain causing them to become blocked or to rupture. The majority of people who suffer a stroke do so as a result of narrowed arteries, heart disease or high blood pressure. Some people recover from a stroke so completely that you would hardly know that they had had one.

Some strokes are called transient cerebral ischaemic attacks and may only last a few minutes with the person experiencing a weakness or tingling on one side of the body, inability to talk and sometimes there is also dizziness or double vision. Any combination of these may occur. All these come on suddenly and are gone in a few minutes, leaving no disability. One third of the people who have this type of attack never have another, one third go on having transient attacks and one third will have a more serious stroke in the next five years.

Sometimes the person has a slight stroke in which there is a loss of the use of a hand or a leg or speech for a few hours or days. There is no loss of consciousness and there is usually a complete recovery in a week or two. This type is more common in older people and those with high blood pressure.

A major stroke will be followed by disability with a weakness of one side of the body leading to difficulty or an inability to walk. The majority of people do learn to walk again with the aid of a stick or a tripod. During the first month following a stroke the major part of recovery occurs; this improvement continues for half a year and sometimes up to two years following the stroke.

Henry had several small strokes by the time he was fifty-five; he also had blood-pressure problems. In the summer of 1986, at the age of sixty, I found him unconscious on the floor of the bathroom. I called the doctor, who came straight over and arranged for him to go to the hospital in an ambulance. The doctors said that he was very ill and that he might not pull through this time. I stayed with him the first night and most of the next day. The doctor at the hospital said that he couldn't say how long he would be unconscious and that I should go home and get some rest. This went on for several days, and then he started to come round. At first he couldn't speak at all but he seemed to know who I was.

Everyone at the hospital was very kind and they all worked very hard to get him better. He had no movement down one side, and the nurses used to get him out of bed and into a chair by using a hoist. It was at this stage that I began to worry about how I would cope at home. They told me it would be a very long and slow process and they couldn't say if he would ever walk again. There were times when I wondered if it would have been better if he had died, but I couldn't imagine life without him.

Eight weeks later he came home in a wheelchair, he still had this weakness down one side and was unable to walk, although he could stand for a short while. His speech was still slurred, but I could understand what he was saying. The nurses had taught me how to get him in and out of bed. How to help him wash, dress and eat. He had control over his bowels and bladder but sometimes was incontinent, and I learned how to manage all this. I can't say that it was easy. I was not used to this type of thing.

We adapted our home to make life easier by putting a shower in the downstairs toilet. My son-in-law moved Henry's bed into the dining-room and made it into a bed/sitting-room. He also widened the doors downstairs so that we could get the wheelchair in and out of the rooms. I found that the first wheelchair was really too heavy for me to push, so eventually we got an electric one. This also means that I can take him outside to sit in the garden and we can go to the shops and visit friends if we want to. We still have the foldable one which can go in the boot of the car. At first I couldn't get him out of the chair and into the car by myself, but over the last few weeks he seems to be a little stronger and between us we can manage.

At times I feel completely exhausted and wonder how I can go on like this, but then I see a little improvement or he just holds my hand and says 'Thank you' and I know it is all worthwhile. We are lucky because we have a very close family who have been a tower of strength and support. We also have a wonderful family doctor who has helped us to get vital equipment and has also been there to give advice and to listen to our problems. God knows how long Henry will live or whether he will improve any further; we simply live in hope, treasure every precious moment and love him.

VALERIE BRANDON

Henry is so very lucky to have a wife like Valerie who obviously cares for him so well. She has managed with the services offered by her family doctor and the community services. She could also have contacted any of the support groups listed on page 335, who would have given her advice on equipment, adapting the house and financial benefits that she could claim.

When the person who has had a stroke leaves hospital he/she needs plenty of rest but also needs to continue with the therapy that was started in the hospital. Sometimes the staff at the hospital may suggest that he/she returns to continue speech and physical therapy as an outpatient. It is important to encourage the person to do as much as possible for himself, if necessary adapting equipment to make it easier. Consider putting hand-rails in the bathroom and lavatory. You might like to provide a long-handled brush and comb, and to attach a soft nail-brush to the side of the handbasin with suction cups, so he/she can wash unaided. Replacing buttons and zips on clothing with an adhesive fastening such as Velcro makes dressing easier. To make eating unaided easier, place a non-slip mat under the plate and buy a combined knife and fork.

A person who is recovering from a stroke may cry very easily, or become confused, forgetful and withdrawn or even difficult and uncooperative. Support and understanding are needed, but sometimes you may well have to be firm. You need plenty of patience, and so will the person concerned, to adapt to a different way of life.

At times both you and the person recovering from the stroke will feel tired, frustrated and depressed about the slow progress and lack of improvement. Try setting small attainable goals to work to; there is nothing like the sense of achievement, no matter how small, to give everyone concerned a feeling of success and hope.

Getting out and about, keeping up with friends and hobbies is very important for both the carer and the person that has had the stroke. It may seem that the effort concerned to get organised and out of the house is really not worth it, but the contrary is true – it will give you both a great deal of enjoyment.

There are many other handicaps and disabilities; but, whatever the cause and whether the person is a child or an adult, what matters is the quality of life both of the affected person and of the family. For the handicapped person, the need to learn and to experience a sense of achievement is always present, and as an adult the need to feel useful and important. This is often the cause of problems, and the care-giver should seek help from the experts:

- the physiotherapist, for help with mobility, posture, balance and exercises to increase independence;
- the occupational therapist, for help with skills of everyday living, such as feeding, washing and dressing.

Depending on what the handicapped person's individual needs are, it may be necessary to see any of the following:

- a speech therapist
- an audiometrician (hearing)
- an orthoptist (sight)
- a psychologist (emotional problems)
- a social worker (financial problems, housing)
- a dentist (teeth)

Take advantage of these services if they are available. You may well need help with physical and emotional problems related to the disability – self-help groups, voluntary associations, friends and neighbours. Never turn down an offer of help, particularly if it gives you the carer and the rest of the family a chance to take a break and to do something for yourselves.

Some handicaps are so severe that it may mean that the person needs to be cared for in a special home. In some cases when a handicapped person has been looked after at home, the problems become too great for the family to cope adequately and the handicapped person may benefit from the care of professionals. Or it may be that the carer falls ill and is unable to continue caring, or perhaps the family need a holiday. You should not see the need for the handicapped person to move into a temporary or permanent residential home as a failure on your part. Contact the relevant support group or association, or discuss the matter with your family doctor and find the right residential home for the person concerned.

BLINDNESS

For those of us who are fortunate enough to be able to see, it is hard to imagine living in a world of darkness. Some people are born blind and learn to adapt to living in a sighted community, while others born with normal sight lose the ability to see later in life through disease, illness or an accident. Doreen Chaney lost her sight as an adult. She is a very positive person who has managed to adapt to losing her sight.

I was registered blind in November 1979. Until that time my life had been spent as a sighted person, although my right eye had been totally blind from seven years of age.

At this time I was employed by a large American company, as a supervisor in charge of their stores office. My work entailed stock control, recording, distribution and ordering of goods. The keeping of accurate figures and stock levels was carried out with the help of a staff of ten, and information was exchanged from head office by computer printout, with immediate checks by visual display units.

The first sign of a sight problem was with these printouts and VDUs, which became blurred and unclear. As I had been working at very high pressure for about six weeks, in order to clear the full stock-check before going on holiday, I put the trouble down to tiredness. During the holiday, I experienced more problems with straight lines bending, curving and kinking. Driving was impossible, as pieces of the picture seemed to be missing. On my return home, things got worse, and eventually I visited my family doctor and was referred to hospital.

I think that up to the moment my consultant told me nothing could be done for me I had believed it was something small and would be cured by tablets, drops or even a change of spectacles. No one told me what I should expect or what I should do. I had no idea who I should turn to for advice or help.

It was a time of anger, apprehension and frustration. I became frightened and very depressed. I began thinking of the things I was missing. Reading, which had always been one of my greatest pleasures, and recent delights of driving were now gone. There seemed to be no information available giving contact names or addresses, for help or advice. One was confronted by a thick blank wall.

I now became aware of a further change in my life. Friends of long standing, and also some relatives, no longer spoke to me, but at me through my husband. He was questioned on how I felt, coped and what I was doing. It was as if I no longer existed as an individual, able to speak for myself. I now know that this attitude is not exceptional and, indeed, is one normally used to any handicapped person.

Between the time of being told nothing could be done to improve my sight, and my registration, I had been worrying and pestering my local Social Services requesting braille tuition and someone to give me guidance on coping with daily living. None of this could be undertaken until my official registration had been received from the consultant.

Receipt of my BD8 set the wheels in motion, and my fight back to a place in society had begun.

For obvious reasons I cannot name the man who visited me, but I owe him a very great deal. The fact that he, too, was visually handicapped gave me the encouragement and confidence I needed. He taught me braille and arranged mobility training for me. Arrangements and the work entailed to get me on a rehabilitation course were carried out by him.

At the end of the three-month course at the Manor House, Torquay, I was recommended for training as a technical officer for the blind and partially sighted. Those three months were the turning-point and gave me the confidence and independence to go forward living my life to the full.

My training for the TOB certificate was at Headingley Castle in

Leeds, covering seven months. Qualification was gained in November 1981. I was on top of the world, and my worries were in the past ... or were they?

My high expectations were short-lived, and the frustration, depression and fighting were with me again. Despite the fact that I was a fully qualified specialist worker, local authority Social Service departments would not offer employment to a non-car-driver, which effectively ruled out a visually handicapped person. I could not believe what I was experiencing. I applied for any TOB post I saw, regardless of its location, but the same criteria applied everywhere. I felt trapped and beaten.

In January 1982 I heard of an organisation *of*, as opposed to *for*, blind people. After making further enquiries I became a member of the National Federation of the Blind of the United Kingdom. The NFB was, I learned, a pressure group which fought for better conditions, opportunities, standards, and to improve the quality of life for blind and partially sighted people.

Most of the information I had fought for was readily available from the NFB, and anything they didn't know would be found if it were possible. It was by pure chance that I found out that such an organisation existed.

I have come a long way since I first noticed problems with my sight and, looking back, I consider myself to be one of the lucky ones. People ask me if I miss what I had and would it have been better not to have seen at all.

Of course I miss not seeing, but I have my memories. I remember such things as the beauty of a fully blossomed rose; spring flowers emerging from the dew-bedecked ground; pink and white apple blossom making an arbour walk; blue skies, green grass and tall trees, birds in flight, sunrise and sunset, freshly fallen snow on trees and hedges and the spectacular sight of lightning flashing in a thundery sky. I can understand the concept of space, image and reflection and the subtle differences in colour. There are so many wonderful things which a congenitally blind person will never see.

On the reverse side of the coin, I have had to adjust to a way of life which to someone born without sight is the most natural existence. I miss the carefree way of life which sight can give and of not being able to work in the occupation that I desired. I have overcome problems of reading by learning braille and also by listening to talking books. I now have full-time employment as a telephonist.

The bad times, too, are not forgotten. But never allowed to embitter.

My involvement with the National Federation of the Blind has become deeper and I am now the national public relations officer and also chairman of my local branch. In these capacities I am able to pass on not only new information, but to use my own experiences to help others who find themselves in a similar situation.

I know that if I had not persisted in chasing and pestering the local authority I could still be sitting at home waiting for something to happen. I have been lucky and, if this chapter can help in any way, my own frustrations, trauma and disappointments will have been of some help.

I now wait to embark on the next chapter of my life in a blind world. I shall hopefully in the very near future be setting off on guide dog training which at the end of the period will give me even greater independence and confident mobility.

DOREEN CHANEY

As Doreen so clearly points out, anyone who is blind needs information, advice and emotional support, and the National Federation of the Blind of the United Kingdom provides this: see page 344 for their address and the services that they offer.

Like Doreen, many people who are blind said that they needed most help and advice when they initially registered as blind. It was at this time that they needed most explanation of what being registered blind was and what it would mean to them. Many blind people are only too willing to help others, particularly at the time of registration, and their help is available through the support groups listed on page 344.

DEAFNESS

Some people are born into a silent world, but deafness is also something that could happen to any of us at any time in our lives. Link is the British Centre for Deafened People. I wrote to them and asked if they knew of someone who would like to contribute to this book and help others in the same or a similar situation, and they sent me this account from Mrs Walker who lives in Berkshire.

The Link Centre for Deafened People does a wonderful job rehabilitating people who have become deaf in adult life, and priority is given to anyone suddenly deafened or where sudden deafness is anticipated. Priority is also given to those in the working age group, a large number of whom need advice upon their occupation or profession. It is the only organisation which offers residential assistance and includes the family in its programme.

In January 1985 my son became profoundly deaf suddenly after what seemed a short sharp attack of influenza. He was thirty-two years of age, a natural athlete, and had an interesting job as a chartered accountant travelling all over the world. In addition to his deafness he suffered from severe vertigo (balance problem) and tinnitus (noises in the ears). Needless to say, the whole family were deeply shocked. For my husband and me it was like having a small child to look after again. Ian could not go out on his own, because he was so vulnerable in traffic. Communication was extremely difficult, and we realised that lip-reading was the only answer. We wanted so much to help him but didn't know where to start.

One day, as if in answer to my prayers, a complete stranger rang me up and told me about the Link Centre and put me in touch with Rosemary McCall, the director.

The first thing which impressed me when speaking to Rosemary on the phone was her positive approach to the problem of deafness. She realised that Ian badly needed skilled help quickly to help restore his confidence and enrolled him on a two-week course at the end of June. My husband and I were invited to accompany him.

The atmosphere at the Link Centre was friendly and relaxed. Six people (two with total hearing loss and four with some residual hearing) attended the course. Three had their wives with them. Group and individual sessions with visiting therapists were arranged covering topics such as basic human communication, speech-reading, organisations for the deaf, relaxation, speech conservation and tinnitus. Demonstrations were also given of technical equipment available to the deaf, and a personal assessment was performed by a speech therapist.

As communication is the chief problem with deafness the speech-reading classes were a very important part of the programme. Speech-reading has wider implications than lip-reading. The aim of the speech-reader should be to grasp the message as a whole and not attempt to decipher it word by word or even sentence by sentence. My husband and I picked up many useful tips at these classes. We have since passed them on to our family and friends and now, thankfully, we are able to converse with our son without any problems. When we returned home Ian worked very hard at lip-reading with the aid of several books on the subject and a mirror.

A fortnight after getting back from Eastbourne, Ian announced that he was going back to work. This was a big step as he had been at home for six months. He started driving his car again and was delighted to be mobile once more. After another month he flew to Switzerland on business and was soon travelling all over Europe coping with foreign accents and foreign languages.

This year his work took him to Japan and Hong Kong. Whilst in Hong Kong he decided to take a few days' holiday. He went from Hong Kong to Canton on a train (by himself!) and then flew to Peking. He even managed to negotiate part of the Great Wall of China in spite of his vertigo!

We still keep in close touch with the Link Centre and Rosemary McCall. It is a great comfort to know that they are there if we need further help.

I do hope that you can give the Link Centre some publicity for the sake of people like us. If only we had known of this organisation earlier, we should have been spared a lot of worry and heartache. My son became deeply depressed and withdrawn, and I was on the verge of a nervous breakdown. Although Ian was in and out of five different hospitals, we were not told of the help that is available to the deaf. We had plenty of sympathy but we didn't want pity. We needed the kind of help that the Link Centre were able to offer us to enable us to face the future with hope and confidence.

MRS WALKER

This type of positive and practical help is certainly needed by anyone who is deaf, and more information about this organisation and others is on page 343. As Mrs Walker said, sympathy really was not enough; what was needed was someone who really understood the situation.

DEAF AND BLIND

To be deaf and blind is an even greater problem. Can you imagine a dark and silent world without sight or sound? It is almost impossible. You may try with your eyes closed and your ears blocked, but you will still be nowhere near imagining what life is like for a deaf-blind person. For most people, more than 99 per cent of the information that comes into our brain comes from our sight and our hearing. The very limits of our imagination have been defined by what we have seen and heard in the past. But if you can't easily imagine what it is like to be both deaf and blind you can start to understand the extreme isolation into which the deaf-blind people are unwillingly forced.

Jocelyn Brewer gave a speech at a convention for the deaf-blind and wanted it to be reproduced in this book. The topic was 'Smiling Through: The Importance of Friends'.

I am delighted to be participating in our first National United Kingdom Deaf Blind Convention.

When the planning of this convention began, I did not expect to be invited to speak, but somehow somebody roped me in – so here I am, and I hope that you will not all start yawning!

I would like to talk to you about the importance of friends. Whether we are deaf-blind or sighted-hearing we all need friends – but we cannot expect anyone to be a friend unless we are prepared to play our part.

Friendship is always a two-way affair. It is a coming-togetherness-magnetism drawing two people together and through the medium of words – two minds meet. In order to befriend a deaf-blind person, one has to learn how to communicate. Learning the manual alphabet is not as difficult as it looks. Although at first your manual will be slow, it is much better to be slow than to go too fast and get in a muddle. Remember – practice makes perfect. Communication begins with attitude, not works or machinery – you must *want* to communicate.

There are several communication machines which are fine, but all the machines in the world cannot replace human contact. The reaching out of one person to another – the caring – the sensitivity to the needs of another person. Deaf-blind people need friends who are willing to share their eyes and ears with them.

I have learned that one's life becomes happier simply by caring for others. One can only get back out of life what one puts into it. It is rewarding to be able to bring a little happiness into someone else's life.

No one enjoys being deaf-blind, but it is something we just have to live with – and it will not make life any easier if we go around with a face looking like a wet week. But I know from experience that a smile, a cheery word can work wonders. If you have a sense of humour – use it!

A good laugh is one of the best tonics. Smiling is infectious; it draws others closer and makes them want to be friends.

We have here with us our deaf-blind friends and their guides from overseas; and, although our ways of communicating vary, we all smile in the same language. There are times, of course, when one feels that there is nothing one could do to help – but very often all that is needed is someone who will listen and try to understand. Deaf-blind people make good listeners! They can often offer good advice. We want co-operation not dependence.

Our League motto is 'Mutual Aid – Joy in Fellowship'. Deaf-blind people are not helpless – we do not want your sympathy, we want your friendship. We all have problems – we have our different likes and dislikes – we cannot all do the same thing (it would be a very funny thing if we could), but whatever the circumstances we all need friends.

What is a friend? It is someone with whom we can share a laugh, our confidences, our dreams, and someone who is willing to lend a helping hand or offer a sympathetic ear when it is needed. And, more importantly, a friend to a deaf-blind person should always try to let their deaf-blind friend see and hear through their eyes and ears. Deaf-blind people want to be accepted as being no different from anyone else – save that one speaks on the hand instead of speaking with the tongue.

I have learned that it is the sharing and caring for others that makes everything worthwhile.

We hope that many true and lasting friendships will be created during this week.

Wear a smile – all the while. And take others 'smiling through' with you and go forward hand in hand along the road to happiness. There will be bridges – but with a true friend beside you they will be easier to cross.

Thank you for listening – and I hope there have not been too many yawns!

Jocelyn Brewer

The sentiments expressed by Jocelyn are relevant to anyone who has encountered problems and crises in his life, but are even more applicable to the people in this chapter. Really good friends will help you through difficult times, and combine their help with that of a support group and there will be answers to problems that at the moment may seem insurmountable.

CHAPTER SEVEN

Coping with Illness

Illness is the most common of life's crises; it is likely to happen to all of us at some time in our lives. The short-term illnesses, although sometimes very frightening and worrying, are more easily coped with as an end to the problem can be seen. Some of the fears and anxieties can be reduced for both short- and long-term illnesses, and this is essentially the content of this chapter.

SHORT-TERM ILLNESS AT HOME

For an adult the sort of short-term illnesses such as influenza, colds, coughs or even some of the infectious diseases such as mumps, measles and chicken pox are more of an inconvenience than a real problem. It is a question of seeking and taking medical advice. They are short-lived, and the person concerned is soon up and about again. When a baby or a child is ill, even if it is one of the many minor infections that they get, it still can be a very worrying time, and parents are often unsure when they should call the doctor.

A child may just seem a little under par, fretful, or has passed an unusual-looking stool. In this case wait a few hours to see how the situation develops, and this may well clarify your choice. If your child is pale, listless, has no interest in favourite foods or does not want to play, you can be fairly sure that something is wrong. Parents are usually the best judge of how sick their child is as they know what the child is like when he or she is well. On the whole, if your child looks and seems well, it is unlikely that there is anything seriously wrong. However, some symptoms do call for medical attention, and these are:

- persistent or recurring earache
- frequent vomiting (several times an hour over a period of two hours or more)

- frequent diarrhoea (several loose watery stools per hour, for more than two hours)
- diarrhoea and vomiting with a raised temperature and pains in the stomach
- a temperature that is over 39.5°C (103°F)
- difficulty breathing
- a fit or a convulsion (don't leave your child alone until the fit is over)
- a serious injury such as a scald or burn, bleeding that cannot be stopped, an injury to the head or a suspected poisoning
- severe or persistent pain
- rashes with a raised temperature are probably due to one of the infectious diseases such as German measles and chicken pox. It is better to call the doctor and ask his advice: he may prefer to visit the child rather than the child be brought up to the surgery.
- Red spots with mauve patches may be a sign of the onset of meningitis; this may or may not be accompanied by a raised temperature, headache or stiff neck. Get medical help at once.
- If in doubt, telephone your doctor for advice; he would much rather that you contacted him and it was a false alarm than that your child was put at risk.

Call your doctor for babies as above and also if:

- Your baby refuses to feed at all, combined with crying, weakness or unusual quietness and indifference to anything going on.
- Pain. It is difficult to assess when a baby is in pain, but you should be suspicious if your baby cries persistently and cannot be comforted by feeding, nappy-changing or plenty of cuddling and attention. Drawing up of the knees may be an indication of abdominal pain; pulling at an ear or constantly lying on one side may indicate earache.

If your child becomes ill suddenly, and it is out of surgery hours, phone the doctor at the surgery; there will be a recorded message telling you where the doctor can be contacted. Make a note of the symptoms before you call, and calmly tell the doctor what is wrong. Don't panic, and remember to tell him exactly what is wrong with your child. Don't leave anything out. He will need all the information you can give him to help him make the right decision. If you feel that it is a real emergency, and that he should come out and see your child, don't be afraid to tell him so. Be forceful if you need to.

ADMISSION OF A CHILD TO HOSPITAL

You never know when your child may need to be admitted to a hospital in an emergency, so it is a good idea to introduce some discussion on the subject at an early age. One of the best ways to introduce the idea is in play: 'Doctor and Nurse' is a game that children enjoy and they can learn about hospitals at the same time. They can act out the care and treatment, taking on different rôles: the doctor, the nurse and the patient. Never use the doctor or hospital as a threat, or the child may come to see treatment as a punishment.

There are plenty of books about going into hospital, and I have listed these on page 350. These books show pictures of nurses in uniform, doctors in white coats, the beds in a ward area and children in the wards, and they can generally convey the atmosphere of a hospital.

If you know that your child is going into hospital, the staff will show you the children's ward and give you a guided tour. There is often a booklet about hospital life that gives information about what to bring for the child, including suitable toys to bring in, about visiting hours, along with plenty of other useful information. The staff in children's wards are especially skilled in caring for children and will be very aware of the needs of you the parents. As a general rule parents are encouraged to stay with their child, especially if the admission is an emergency. Some children's wards have a special unit where the parent and child can stay, with parents taking over a large share of the day-to-day care.

Helping your child to settle into the ward:

- Take with you a favourite toy or teddy, clearly labelled with your child's name.
- If your child uses a dummy or comfort rag, make sure that this goes to hospital even if you think he or she is a little too old for it. This is not the time to try to break this kind of habit.
- If your child uses special names for various parts of the body, the toilet or anything else, make sure the staff know about the words used.
- Tell the staff about any food allergies or strong food dislikes, and what the normal feeding routine is. If you are weaning your child, make sure that they know exactly how far you have got and what solids are being taken.

- If your child has any fears or worries, tell the staff about them.
- Tell the staff whether your child normally sleeps in a cot or in a bed. If used to sleeping in a bed, he or she is not going to take kindly to being put in a cot.
- If your child is called by a nickname, make sure the staff know the name, so that they can carry on calling him or her by the same name.
- If you are unable to stay in hospital with your child, make sure you send lots of letters, postcards and cards. Encourage your friends and relations to do the same.
- When you leave your child, say when you are coming back and make sure that you are back at that time.
- You can leave your child with something of yours such as a soft scarf; it will be a great comfort to your child.

A child and his or her parents will obviously not enjoy being in hospital, but the experience should not be unpleasant. This is not always the case, as the mother of a child who was then only two years old described to me.

In 1982, at the age of three, Anthony had to be admitted to hospital to have grommetts inserted into both his ears. I was asked to take him into the hospital at eight in the morning, having made sure that he had had nothing to eat or drink from midnight. My husband drove us the twenty miles to the hospital and said he would collect us at six in the evening. The staff took down all Anthony's details and explained what would happen, and I signed the consent form.

A nurse showed us to his cot, then she picked Anthony up and suggested that I left as she would get him ready for the operation. I said that I wanted to stay with him and that I lived twenty miles away, had no transport and could hardly go home. To which she replied that I could spend the day looking round the shops and parents were not supposed to stay.

I said that I was staying with my child and had no intention of leaving. From then on I was totally ignored, and the staff were quite hostile towards me. Everything that was done for my son was carried out in an efficient but matter-of-fact manner. During the entire day I was not offered a chair to sit on, a drink or a bite to eat.

When the operation was over and Anthony recovered enough to go home, the charge nurse came over and told me what to do when we got home and gave me an outpatient's appointment. He then proceeded to tell me in no uncertain terms that my child would not be admitted to his ward again if I insisted on staying and making a nuisance of myself. He would see to it that his rules would be obeyed.

I gathered up Anthony and left the ward in tears. I was tired, frightened and shocked that anyone who was supposed to be in charge of a ward could be such an insensitive bully.

I am sure that I should have done something about all this, but I was frightened that if my child had to go back to the ward the staff would take it out on him.

The woman who wrote this wants to remain anonymous, in case someone from the ward recognises her, as she fears there would be repercussions. This is a sad reflection on the care that children receive in hospital, and I am pleased to say that this is certainly not typical. These days parents are encouraged to stay with their children, and in most cases it positively benefits the child and the ward staff.

If you have a problem like this, the best thing to do is to complain in writing to the hospital, and action will be taken to ensure that practice of this kind does not continue. If you do nothing, the same situation will arise for the next patient or parent. In order to give a good standard of care the hospital authorities need to know when there is a problem so that it can be investigated and corrected. For more details about the complaints procedure, whether it is about a doctor, a nurse or anything to do with the care that you have received, see page 351. There are also details about how to change your family doctor.

A baby admitted to a hospital in an emergency must be one of the most stressful events that any parent can imagine. Patricia Foreshaw explains:

I had been home nearly a week with our little baby daughter after having a caesarean delivery, when she had what I thought at first was a cold, just a bit snuffly. It was a Monday, a nice sunny day, so thinking a little fresh air might help we went for a short walk. Kimberley had not fed very well on the last feed, and I couldn't wake her for the next 2 p.m. feed. By the evening when she was still very sleepy and not wanting her feed I felt something was wrong. Somewhere at the back of my mind I had an idea that babies dehydrated quickly without liquids and that was what was worrying me when I phoned the doctor at about eight that evening. He came round straight away and calmly suggested that he thought Kimberley would be better off spending the night in hospital.

After frantically arranging a babysitter for our three-year-old boy, my husband, Kimberley and I went to Poole Hospital, where they were expecting us. From that moment everything seemed to happen.

X-rays, tests, etc. First, I was told to feed her; then someone else said I shouldn't; then she had a drip attached to her head. It seemed to be a big muddle, and I felt totally bewildered, as though I was going down a long dark tunnel in a dream.

By about 11.30 p.m. my husband had to go home to relieve the babysitter, and I stayed with Kim. I wasn't allowed to be with her, so I couldn't even see what they were doing, except through a glass window from a distance. Eventually they decided to send her to the baby unit at Southampton. I had to phone my husband and try to explain what little I had been told, and we then had a very fast dash through the New Forest in an ambulance with Kim in an incubator. I remember sitting in that ambulance thinking this was a lot of fuss for a cold. Obviously I realised it was something more serious, but nobody had told me anything. I also remember looking at a box of paper towels in the ambulance with the name 'Kimberly' written on them thinking they had spelled it differently, having left the 'e' out.

When we arrived at Southampton everything was laid on and we were whisked up to the baby unit very quickly. Once again I was sat down and Kimberley was taken away and numerous tests were done, but I was told nothing. Eventually the specialist – poor chap had been dragged from his bed at 5 a.m. – came to see me but could still not tell me anything specific. I was given a bed for the rest of the night. My husband came to the hospital in the morning after taking our little boy to nursery school, and we sat around waiting for someone to give us some idea what was wrong. They told us they had done a lumbar puncture, and various other tests, but nothing specific had shown. After two days they were able to tell us that they suspected that Kimberley had meningitis; we had no knowledge of this illness, but they told us that if she survived she would be deaf, blind or mentally retarded. From that moment on I seemed to be living in a bubble; nothing else existed for me apart from the immediate problem of looking after our little boy each evening, arranging for someone to look after him after school each day, and rushing up to the hospital just to look at Kim, as we were unable even to touch her. To this day I cannot travel through the forest without thinking of all the times we drove to Southampton. After about ten days I was able to start feeding her again – I had managed to keep my milk going, and they had been feeding her minute quantities with a bottle once she was well enough to take food by mouth. However, at this point our little boy developed a tummy upset, so I was not allowed to go home to see him in case I brought a germ back with me, so I was hospital-bound as well. Once I was able to hold Kim and feed her I believed she would recover, and after a few more days we were transferred to Poole Hospital again so that I could cope with our little boy and home and get back and forth to feed Kim.

I will never forget the day I brought her home, a week before Christmas. Of course I had done nothing for Christmas, so there was a rush to do all the usual things, then Christmas itself. It was not until everything had died down, when one morning I went into the lounge to draw back the curtains and I started to shake, really shake from head to toe. I sat down thinking this was silly and realised that it was delayed shock. This went on for about a week, on and off. Weeks afterwards I told the health visitor, who had been super throughout, and she really told me off for not getting in touch with her and telling her how I was feeling, but in a funny way I didn't want to tell anyone. I knew what it was and I felt I had to go through it my own way. Kimberley is now a lively nine-year-old with no deficiencies at all, we are pleased to say. So the odd tantrum, whilst dealt with, is secretly forgiven.

PATRICIA FORSHAW

Most of us, just like Patricia and her husband, are distressed at the thought of any child we care for and love suffering a serious accident or illness. It is an experience that, as parents, we hope we shall never have to cope with. Every year many hundreds of parents are confronted with the terrifying reality of their children becoming acutely ill and needing urgent hospital treatment. It can only be described as a frightening and harrowing time, which without adequate support is made even more unbearable.

At the time that Kimberley was so critically ill the only support available would have been from the hospital staff, social workers, the chaplain, her own family doctor, family and friends. When a child is seriously ill in hospital, many parents feel desperate for comfort and support. They are under an enormous emotional strain for days, weeks and sometimes even months. For many reasons they may be unable to rely upon the support and help of close family and friends; if they cannot find support from the hospital staff, parents become isolated, withdrawn, and despairing.

Nursing and medical staff are primarily concerned with the care of the sick child and are hard pressed to find time and the energy to help parents adjust to their child's illness and offer a degree of support. The hospital environment is strange to parents; there is an atmosphere of urgency, the equipment and terminology used are intimidating and alien. Parents are shocked, frightened, and in their anxiety may find it difficult to absorb what the doctors and nurses say to them. Sometimes there are communication problems due to differences in culture, language or social class. Some parents find it difficult to put their feelings into words and are only able to express their fear through anger and hostility. This is very common and often directed at hospital staff, who fully understand the reasons and will do their best to help.

If the staff have not suggested that the chaplain or the social worker may be able to help by simply listening and supporting you, ask to see them. Your child does not have to be dying in order to see the chaplain, nor do you have to be religious; he will just help you through a very difficult and stressful time. The social worker is trained to support and counsel people and may be able to help with some of the financial problems associated with hospitalisation, so ask to see him or her if you think it will help. Since 1985, Parent's Lifeline has been in existence; they are a voluntary group organised by parents and experienced paediatric nursing staff who offer crisis support and counselling to parents of children in intensive care units. They are only a phone call away; for more information, see page 351.

A child who is in hospital, miles away from home, for weeks or even months for specialised treatment is not necessarily critically ill. Being in hospital with your child for weeks on end can be a harrowing experience, and Angela Traskey describes how she survived. Jessica, her daughter had a new bladder created, was on haemodialysis (a kidney machine) and then had a kidney transplant. She tells the story from her point of view.

When Jessica was two and a half years old she started spiking high temperatures. We took her to the doctor, who assured us it was a virus. This would last a few days, go away and come back again in a few weeks. This went on for a long time, and each time we were told it was only a virus. When she was about three years old Peter, my husband, and I noticed that when we put her on her potty at night her urine smelt odd. We wondered if there was anything wrong with her kidneys and then put the idea aside. The next time she had a high temperature we took her to the doctor, and he said that it was a virus; when we mentioned that the urine smelt odd we were told that this didn't mean anything and so we went away again.

The time sequence I forget, but it can't have been long after that that one afternoon when she was having her rest I heard her screaming. I rushed upstairs to find her sitting on her pot holding on to her side and her little legs pummelling on the floor in absolute agony. I called the doctor, she was rushed into hospital that evening and within an hour we were told that there was something wrong with her kidneys. The next day a specialist from Southampton came to see her and we were told that her ureters needed reimplanting, she had reflux and her kidneys had been damaged. She also had a duplex (double) kidney on one side.

At Southampton General the ureter was reimplanted and the top part of the kidney removed. The next year we went back and she had the ureter on the other side reimplanted. She was permanently on antibiotics at that time, so I don't remember her having any more urine infections. She was seen regularly for years; we were never told anything very much about her kidney function, just that she was all right and to come back in three months.

In 1981 we were in America staying with Peter's relatives when she got a really bad urine infection. Fortunately Southampton Hospital had given us the name of a specialist at Johns Hopkins Hospital. She was admitted there as an emergency, and that was when we were told for the first time that she would need a kidney transplant, also that her bladder was in a very bad state. We couldn't take it in about the bladder. We just didn't know what to think. The staff there were wonderful; they spent so much time talking to us, they wrote everything down in a letter to the consultant in Southampton and gave us a copy of the letter. I was terrified. For the first time we knew exactly where we stood and what was going to happen. When we got home we were back to the old routine of no one discussing the problem. It was not that we were told not to take seriously what had been said in the States; it was simply ignored. We were not allowed to discuss it any more even though we had all this information written down.

Over the next few years Jessica was admitted several times and treated for urine infections, but we were never really told that it was leading up to anything, so I think we put out of our minds what had been said in America. Just after Christmas in 1983, Jessica was admitted because of yet another urine infection, and the consultant from Southampton said that the trouble was her bladder, so we asked: 'Why can't you give her a new one?' To which he replied that he would if he could but it was not possible.

In the summer of 1984, following a routine check-up at Dorchester Hospital, we received a phone call to say that Jessica's kidneys were in a very bad way and her creatinine was very high. This was the first time that we had heard about creatinine, although I am sure that they mentioned it in America but we simply had not taken it in. Measurement of the creatinine level is a test which indicates kidney function: the higher the creatinine, the worse the function of the kidney. They also said that she needed to go to another hospital for specialist treatment and would we prefer to go to Guy's Hospital in London or Exeter in Devon. We live in Dorset, so neither are very nearby; we chose Guy's Hospital, which is three hours away from home.

Jessica was admitted to Guy's for tests, and we were absolutely blasted with information. They were so kind about it and knew that we hadn't been getting enough information, and each of them said that we were free to ask them about anything that we liked. Three different people told us about her needing a transplant; they told us very gently, and I think that they wanted to be sure that it had sunk in so they told us in three different ways. The nursing sisters spent time with us, getting to know us, getting our confidence. One of the things that was said was that if only you had been sent here years ago we could have prepared you for all of this so much better.

Jessica needed a transplant, and they hoped that they would get a kidney before she needed dialysis. So they put a fistula in her arm, which is drawing an artery to a vein and joining them together to make a large enough vein to put the needles in for dialysis. The blood is taken from one needle, pumped through the artificial kidney where the dialysis takes place, then the blood is returned through the other needle. In the mean time she must see the urologist about her bladder. Having seen the urologist, I was told that her bladder was very bad and that there was no way that she could have a transplant with a bladder that was in such a bad state. There would be no point in giving her a new kidney as it would be destroyed by the infection from the bladder. I thought: This is the end of the world; they are telling me that there is nothing that can be done. But they then said that they had a consultant at Guy's who was able to perform a very special operation and make a new bladder. In August 1984 he came to see us, and I recorded everything he said on tape because I was worried that I wouldn't remember our conversation and be unable to tell my husband what the plan was. The recording is awful because you can hear Jessica screaming with her head under the pillow because she just didn't want to hear another word. He explained that he would make a new bladder out of part of her bowel.

In November 1984 she had the operation, which was probably the most traumatic operation of all, far more so than the kidney transplant. She was in great pain and was in hospital for a month, during which time she learned how to catheterise herself in order to empty her bladder. The nurses really came into their own; two of them would concentrate on her, winning her confidence and helping her.

We went home, but she wasn't well and just after Christmas she became very ill and we went back up to Guy's. They said that she would have to go on dialysis. When they told me I just ran out of the ward. I don't know why I took it so badly. I just sat in the chapel and sobbed. I thought it was horrific, even though at that point I hadn't really thought what it would entail: that we would have to live in London. It was just the fact that she would have to go on the machine. She started her dialysis in February 1986 and went through hell because of her fear of needles. It was always ghastly, the lead-up to dialysis, because she was so petrified of needles. She gradually got used to it, and they taught her to set up her own machine. It was a great psychological help because she enjoyed doing it. The needle business became better as time went on. She dialysed three times a week, so we stayed up in London all week, came back at the weekends. We stayed with friends, which was not easy; they said we were not being a nuisance, but you felt that you were. Then we were lent a flat for three months, so at least we were independent. The hospital didn't offer us accommodation, probably because they knew that we had somewhere to go. They do have a flat where people can stay. Financially, the train fares were all paid for out of a charity. If we had had to rent somewhere, I think the hospital would have helped financially.

Jessica was dialysed from February until August, and in the end it became a routine. We got to know a lot of people through the local church, Holy Trinity, Brompton. They even arranged for her to go to a school on the Tuesday and Thursday when she was not on dialysis, and provided her with a uniform; we didn't have to pay for anything. I am sure that they would do the same for other people, too. On Wednesdays, while Jessica was on dialysis, I walked to the church in Bishopsgate and met a young man who would listen to my problems; he was such a comfort. During this time I met so many people who were kind and helpful. I have a strong faith and I do pray; I couldn't have coped without it. Jessica feels the same and she has seen lots of answers to prayer both for herself and for me.

In August 1986, Jessica had gone on holiday to Kent with other children from the dialysis unit, Simon our son was away, Peter and I had just returned from a few days in France and we had a phone call to say that they had a kidney for Jessica. It was the most amazing thing. We were just hysterical – it was the most awful shock. They said that Jessica was already on her way to London. We arrived at about one o'clock in the morning. She was so excited; there were four transplants being done at the same time. The place was alive with excitement because all these transplants were being done for the children who had been waiting so long and who were very special to the staff. We were all carried along as if in a dream. They were all transplanted that evening.

The time after is very worrying because you are waiting for the kidney to work. Some do and some don't. Jessica's kidney didn't work straight away. However, it eventually started to work, and she was discharged to the hospital flat because she had to go to the hospital for a check-up every day. Then she had a series of urinary-tract infections and she had to be readmitted. On 9 September a very sad thing happened. The little boy who had the matching kidney to Jessica's died. Neither of us had been near to the death of a child in any way before; it was just heart-breaking. The staff were wonderful. Professor Chantler, who had been on duty and caring for this little boy all night, came and saw Jessica in the morning to explain what had happened to this little boy and to reassure her that it didn't mean it would happen to her, even though they had had kidneys from the same donor.

She was in and out of hospital for several weeks, during which time we heard that another boy on dialysis had died and we both started to get in a state. At that time there was a doctor from New Zealand, and he took Jessica in his arms; they cried together, he comforted her, and told her that she wasn't going to die. It was so beautiful to see him do that; he was so loving. In the end they discovered that she had a virus which would go on for months but accounted for her feeling so low. They sent me home because they thought that I needed a complete break. I hated leaving Jessica, but by now I had been in and out of that hospital for a year.

You get very close to the other mothers because they are really the only ones who understand how you are hurting, because they are hurting in the same way. The nurses are very supportive but they are not hurting, they are not frightened. There are also plenty of mums to be avoided, in particular the ones that think they know everything and spout off about this, that and the other. You have to learn to be patient and kind and help the other mums, even though you are hurting. There are times when you blow up, sometimes at a nurse. They handle it very well. I always apologise, and they understand.

Sometimes the nurses will come up and hold you, and that is what you crave: someone to put their arms around you and comfort you. I know the nurses just don't have the time. Other mothers will comfort you, but sometimes you want a nurse to because she is in authority and knows more; you want her to say that everything will be all right. That's all you want to hear all the time.

Time went by and then another child that Jessica knew died, and this was just the end. I told Jessica that I couldn't stay with her that day; I felt awful about it, but I knew that I had to get to a Bible-study group. When I arrived I just couldn't stop weeping. One of them called my husband; he came up to London, drove me home, and then went back up to Guy's to stay with Jessica. I wouldn't have trusted anyone else to stay with Jessica. At home, I went to the doctor, and he gave me some sleeping pills and I went to stay with some friends on their farm. All I needed was peace, calm and to be cared for. I was supposed to stay at home for two weeks but within a week I felt so much better and Peter and Jessica came home for the weekend.

On 1 November 1986, Jessica was allowed to go home. There were still the twice-weekly routine visits to Guy's and a few urine infections. Last year there were one or two problems with a few short stays in hospital, but since June 1987 she has had no infections.

There have been lots of ups and downs, dreaded visits to the hospital and anxious waits for the results of tests. We try to put it out of our minds, and you can do this very successfully until the time for another check-up draws near.

My advice to anyone in the same position is to make sure that you are told everything. You can't deal with something unless you know all about it. At Guy's they certainly tell you everything, in fact more than you can take in. They prefer you to write things down or tape the conversation. We used to keep a journal of the results of tests and the questions that we wanted to ask. I am a very anxious person anyway and I know that some of the other mothers were able to cope far better. Everyone copes in their own way, but you do need support. You just couldn't do it on your own. I think that we do need a support group where mothers can meet once a week with one of the doctors to discuss our fears and worries. We did meet with a psychologist and a social worker, which I didn't like at all because it developed into a group therapy session. What you need is comfort and reassurance that you are doing all right.

ANGELA TRASKEY

Jessica really does not remember very much about her time in hospital, and it is obviously better that she doesn't.

There is something that blocks it all out and I really can't remember. I feel really well now and owe it all to the person that gave me the kidney and the staff who cared for me so patiently.

JESSICA TRASKEY

Transplantation is an emotive and always topical subject. By pure coincidence, and long before I knew Angela and Jessica, I was a sister on the haemodialysis unit at Guy's Hospital and have seen the progress of both dialysis and transplantation develop from an experimental and sometimes hazardous method of treatment to an effective and acceptable treatment for those patients whose kidneys have ceased to function. Without this type of treatment these people would inevitably die. No one is saying that dialysis and transplantation are something to be taken lightly; as you can see by Angela's account of their experience, it is sometimes a long and exhausting trail to recovery – especially when the patient has to be cared for so far away from home, family and friends.

Every day people die through accident or illness, and their kidneys and other organs could save the lives of those who wait for a transplant, but their organs go unused. Some people are afraid that, if they carry a donor card, in the event of an accident or illness the staff caring for them will be more concerned with the fact that their organs could be used to help someone else than with doing everything possible to save their life. This is not true; the staff will always concentrate all their efforts on the patient in their charge and will only consider them as a potential donor if there is nothing more that can be done and death is inevitable. By carrying a donor card it not only ensures that the doctor caring for you is aware of your wishes but also means that your relatives will already know your feelings on the subject and are more likely to give their permission for your organs to be used for transplantation. At a time of great sadness at the loss of a loved one, many grieving relatives have said that it has helped them to know that their loss has not been in vain but has helped someone else who was desperately ill. For more information, see page 356.

The months that both Angela and Jessica spent in hospital were made bearable by the support of the church, friends, family, and the staff at the hospital. Not everyone feels that God will help and support them; in fact sometimes it is quite the opposite – they feel let down and angry because this has happened to them. There are support groups, voluntary services and financial help available: see page 356.

ADMISSION OF AN ADULT TO HOSPITAL

If you are admitted to a hospital as an adult, you should be well informed about any care or treatment that you are likely to receive and have been involved in the decisions that were made. Some people prefer not to know the 'whys' and 'wherefores' about their treatment, and of course that is entirely their decision. If you are interested in your care and want to be involved, you will need information about your condition.

Sometimes it is difficult to remember all your symptoms and problems. When you are anxious or nervous it is easy to forget all the questions that you wanted to ask, so write them down on a piece of paper and take it with you when you see the doctor. If you don't understand what has been said, ask the doctor to explain again, more slowly and simply. If you don't feel confident, ask someone to come along and support you. Don't leave the consulting-room, or allow the doctor to go, or consent to treatment until you have fully understood what has been said.

David had been waiting to go in for an operation on his hip for two years and when he was eventually admitted he was relieved but not altogether satisfied with the treatment that he received.

I was told to arrive at the hospital at ten in the morning and my operation was to be the next day. When I arrived I was told that there wasn't a bed and that I would have to wait until the doctors had done their ward rounds. They also had to discharge the patient who was occupying my bed at the time. At twelve-thirty I was still waiting in a corridor on a very uncomfortable chair outside the ward. I explained to the nurse that I was very uncomfortable and needed either to stretch out on a bed or sit on a more comfortable chair. She explained that the bed was still occupied and at the moment there were no armchairs available and that they were still waiting for the doctor.

I could see into the ward and there was a man sitting beside his bed fully dressed, so I couldn't understand why I was not allowed to use the bed. Just before one o'clock a young doctor arrived and said that he needed to examine me, and with that the man in the ward was moved, the bed stripped and I was hurried to the bedside, told to undress and get into bed quickly so that the doctor could examine me.

He told me that I would have the operation in the morning; it was all routine and that there was nothing to worry about. It might have been routine to him but it wasn't to me, and I wanted my questions answered before I signed the consent form. He said he hadn't got time at the moment and rushed away saying he would be back later. 'Later' was six that evening when he told me very briefly what would happen. I still didn't understand but thought I had better sign the form in case they decided that I was being a nuisance and sent me home again. I was still worried, so I asked one of the nurses what would happen and how I would feel after the operation. She explained it all to me and the next day I had my hip replacement and it was a great success. I can get about now and feel years younger.

I am going back soon to have my other hip done, and this time I intend to get my questions answered even if I do know most of the answers.

DAVID MILES

David is quite right: he should not have signed the consent form for the operation until he knew exactly what he was signing. Hospitals are busy places, and sometimes patients feel that they shouldn't bother the staff with their questions. If you experience problems while in a hospital, talk to the ward sister and see what she can do to help. Don't just sit there worrying and saying nothing. David followed up his unsatisfactory stay in hospital with a letter of complaint and received an assurance from the hospital that the admission procedure would be improved. Complaints procedure: see page 351.

Be part of the discussions about your care. If a doctor suggests an operation or a course of treatment, ask about the effect it will have on you. Will it be painful? If so, what will be done to control the pain? Is there an alternative? What are the advantages or disadvantages of alternative treatments? How long will you be in hospital? When will you be able to go back to work? You need to know what is going to happen to you in order to make the right decisions.

On local radio recently I did a phone-in programme on the Health Service, and a lady phoned in to talk about her experience. She was admitted into a hospital for a dilatation and curettage (D and C). (This is when the cervix is dilated and the womb lining is scraped with an instrument called a curette.) She was told that she would only be in hospital for a couple of days. So she arranged for someone to look after her children, her husband took some time off work and she told the people that she worked for that she would be back at work in about three or four days.

She went into hospital the next day. There were several other women having similar operations, and the nurses were busy getting them ready to go to theatre. No one seemed to be doing anything for her, so she asked a nurse when they would help her get ready. To her surprise she was told that she would be going to have her operation the next day because she was in for a hysterectomy. This is a fairly major operation in which the womb is removed, the stay in hospital is about five days and most people are off work for about three months at least. She was a little shocked, to say the least, and asked to see the doctor, who felt that she must have misunderstood when he told her about the operation at her outpatient appointment!

In this case the lady concerned was able to take the change in plans in her stride and went ahead with the operation, but someone else might have reacted very differently. Which only goes to highlight how important it is to be absolutely sure about what is said to you and to ask the doctor or nurse to explain until you are really sure what is going to happen to you.

A CHILD WITH A CHRONIC ILLNESS

Mary Harding explains how she copes with three children and a husband who all have asthma.

Asthma is caused by several things, an allergy to either inhalants such as pollen, moulds, dust, animal hair or foods such as eggs, milk, fish or chocolate. It can occur when there is a chest infection, there are psychological influences, and it can be inherited, especially when it commences in childhood.

I have learned a tremendous amount about asthma since I married ten and a half years ago. I married a man who had been an asthmatic since he was four years old and still suffers from it now. In fact two days prior to our wedding he had an attack, but we did manage to get to the altar on time.

I also have three children. My youngest daughter, now aged seven and a half, has had asthma since she was three years old. As a young child she did suffer a great deal. My other girls are twins aged nine. They started to develop asthma at the age of six, a month between each other.

To help anyone who has a child or adult that suffers from asthma I have listed below a few things that I found helped me to cope with this very worrying and sometimes frightening problem. It is so easy to panic when you see the person concerned finding difficulty breathing. You feel so helpless; it seems there is so little that you can do. But don't panic. You must remain calm and positive. It is much easier for them to improve if they are not smothered by you. Treat them with love and care but literally give them breathing-space.

A typical asthmatic, at whatever age, hates other people to know that they suffer with asthma. At last I have got my own family to realise that they must not keep it hidden and that people really do not take any notice if you have to take a puff on your inhaler in a crowded place. It is better to use the inhaler early than to wait until you are alone; by then you may be very tight-chested and the drugs will not work so effectively.

Doctors will prescribe different drugs to asthmatics depending on the doctor or the patient. Gradually you find the ones that suit you the best. Here I will also add it is better to take certain drugs early rather than wait: 'I'll see how I feel in an hour's time.' By then you could be so tight-chested that the drugs will not be able to get down to the lungs to work as needed.

Life has to carry on, and in our family, with it being hereditary on both sides, I guess we will have to cope for many years to come. Because of this you must plan to lead as normal a life as possible, whatever they wish to do – don't stop them from doing it. All forms of sport are excellent therapy. Don't be put off or put them off because of their asthma. As quoted by one famous physician: 'The way to treat asthma is not to get it.' In other words, prevention is better than the cure.

If you find that certain foods are the cause, don't eat them. If the pollen in spring and summer causes troubles, try to keep away from these areas as much as possible. Two of my family suffer a great deal from reactions to pollen and especially from harvest dust, and as my husband is a corn farmer it is very difficult to keep away. So we take precautions. If he needs to be near the combine harvester or the corn-drier he wears a space-age air-flow helmet. On the other hand, I do keep my daughters away as much as possible from the direct dust, but if we are near to this type of dust they wear a mask. They all like to go and help their daddy, so rather than say 'No' it is 'Yes, but wear a mask'. They also have the irritable eye and nose problem, all due to allergic responses again. We use certain drugs, which do help, although if we can relieve the symptoms without the drugs I prefer to do so. Hence cats, rabbits and horses are not allowed at home, and they are forbidden to play with their friends' pets because they know the results if they do. When they are tempted to have a quick cuddle with the farm cat, their eyes tell me the story – all blown up, runny and very itchy.

Last of all a little about the psychological side. They do worry about themselves, and it is frightening for them not to be able to breathe. The situation is made worse because of the worry. My seven-year-old daughter said just a few months ago: 'Oh, Mummy, will I ever get better? Will I ever stop getting asthma?' I found it hard to answer her question. I don't know the answer, but while she and the others get asthma we will stick together, talk through the problems with each other, and we will get by.

Life has to go on, and we will not be beaten by the fact that four out of five of us are asthmatics. With a great deal of understanding, love and care, and long walks that I take alone with my Irish Wolfhound, we shall survive.

MARY HARDING

Understanding the problems associated with asthma, eliminating the causes as much as possible, taking medication that has been prescribed and coping calmly when an attack occurs is very sound and sensible advice. The other key factor is attitude: Mary Harding's positive approach to the problem obviously helps her family to adopt a similar attitude, giving them the ability to cope with asthma. Her no-nonsense approach is refreshing, and her family will only benefit from being encouraged just to get on with life and not being wrapped up in cotton-wool. For more information and the addresses of support organisations, see page 352.

DIABETES

The British Diabetic Association told me about a five-year-old girl who was just about to start school when she was diagnosed as a diabetic, her name Ceri Darby. For Ceri and her parents, Pam and Michael, the diagnosis was quite a shock: 'It came out of the blue. I suppose, to a large extent, we were dropped in the deep end – all parents are. And we were confronted with a double set of problems: coping ourselves and helping the school to cope.'

Within a week of Ceri's diagnosis, Michael and Pam had received the special school pack published by the BDA. Designed to help both parents and schools to understand the needs and treatment of a diabetic child, the school pack proved to be a great help to the Darbys. They handed out the relevant sections of the pack to Ceri's teachers, all of whom now know about Ceri's condition and how to deal with it. The school cook is involved as well: she and the Darbys discuss menus for the week's school dinners.

Avidly reading everything they could find on the subject of diabetes, Pam and Michael found the British Diabetic Association to be a welcome source of information and support: 'The BDA back-up is wonderful. I think they've been great,' says Pam. 'We look forward to getting *Balance*, and I think *Countdown* is brilliant.'

Balance is the BDA magazine; it is published every two months, it keeps readers in touch with the latest medical care and new treatments, diets and recipe ideas. *Countdown* now helps the school cook to calculate Ceri's dietary requirements. And it is not just staff members who have learned about diabetes since Ceri joined the school: a BDA youth officer gave the children a talk, so that they, too, now have some understanding of their classmate's condition.

In February, Pam, Michael and Ceri took part in a BDA family weekend held in London. Ceri's elder sister, six-year-old Kim, went with them, explaining: 'I think it's important I learn about diabetes so I can help you with Ceri.'

'We wanted to learn as much as we could about diabetes and also talk to other parents about how they coped and adjusted.' Both Michael and Pam felt that the weekend provided them with just those opportunities. 'What it did was to reinforce what we'd learned and to make us more confident. It also made us realise that we were coping quite well.'

The weekend gave parents a chance to discuss their concerns in a relaxed forum amongst people who understood their feelings. 'We've had to try, as much as possible, not to let Ceri see how worried we've been. But talking to other parents you can see the worry in their faces. I think most people's fear isn't about the condition itself, but what you have to do – the things you have to subject your children to; and I think that quite often, if you're not careful, your own fear – about injections, for example – can rub off on the child.'

There was a chance to ask questions and learn from other parents' experiences: 'I liked listening to the people with teenage children – hearing about their problems. From Ceri's point of view I think it was great for her to meet other children who have diabetes. She loved it! And it's still going through her mind; just yesterday she said to me: "What was the name of the little boy I met at the weekend?" '

The weekend also provided a welcome break for overworked parents:

'We didn't see much of the kids during the day – they were entertained while we were being talked to. That was marvellous. They wore the helpers out – literally! It was a great weekend; I'd recommend it to anybody,' says Pam.

Within a month of her diagnosis, Ceri was already injecting herself and she has recently started doing her own blood tests. 'Diabetes has brought out the good things that I didn't know were in her, like her strength of character, and she's coping well; but every now and then she'll just say "Why?", "What's gone wrong?" and "Will it go away?" '

Diabetes affects over a million people in the United Kingdom and there are over 30 million diagnosed diabetics in the world. It can strike anyone at any age, many of them children, and it is on the increase. Its cause is the failure of the pancreas to produce insulin. The reason is still being investigated; it may be partly due to a genetic defect, and in children viruses may play a part. Before 1921 the majority of diabetics died in a coma, but with the discovery of insulin in 1921 by Frederick Banting and Charles Best in Toronto, Canada, an effective treatment was established.

The treatment for 30 per cent of people with diabetes – mostly young adults and children – is insulin injections and a special diet. For the middle-aged and elderly the treatment may well be tablets and diet. The tablets stimulate the production of insulin and help storage of excess glucose. For the overweight middle-aged and elderly diet alone may be the treatment.

If it is not controlled, it can kill, and cause complications such as blindness, heart disease, kidney damage and gangrene. There are some special points on health care for all diabetics:

■ The doctor and the hospital staff will help to calculate the correct diet. Meals should be frequent and regular, taken at the same time each day to help stabilise the level of sugar in the bloodstream. If you are injecting insulin, a meal should follow within half an hour of each injection.

■ If you are injecting insulin, ensure that at least one other member of your family is also taught the technique by the hospital staff. Vary the sites of injection to avoid problems of infection and to keep the skin supple and prevent scarring. Possible sites include the arms, thighs, buttocks and abdomen.

■ If you have been prescribed tablets, make sure that you take them at the correct time in the right dosage.

■ Test blood for sugar and urine for glucose and acetone as regularly as advised by your doctor.

- Visit your doctor as regularly as he thinks is necessary.
- Get your eyes checked regularly as diabetes can cause sight problems. The optician will tell you how often you should visit.
- See a chiropodist regularly as your feet will need special attention. This is because a diabetic's circulation tends to be poor and any sore spot may become infected. The chiropodist will tell you how regularly you should make an appointment.
- Always carry a card or wear an identity bracelet stating that you are a diabetic.
- Carry glucose tablets or sweets in case you go hypoglycaemic (the blood sugar drops too low). This may happen after a missed meal, unusually strenuous activity or an accidental overdose of insulin.
- Make sure your family and friends know what will happen and what to do if you go hypoglycaemic.
  If you are conscious and able to swallow, they should give you glucose tablets, sugar lumps, a piece of chocolate or a sugary drink.
  If you are unconscious, they should turn you on your side in the recovery position and call for medical help urgently. They should not attempt to get you to swallow anything.
- If you are a car driver, tell the licensing authority and your insurance company that you are a diabetic.

There is plenty of help and support available. For more information, see page 355. I have also listed the support groups for other chronic illnesses on page 352.

CANCER

Cancer is a word that frightens everyone; it is seen as a death sentence – nothing can be done. This is not always the case. Rosemary Mundy has given me her account of how she fought and won the battle against cancer.

I found I had cancer quite by accident! For a couple of days I had had a very slight stiff neck which had started on Wednesday, and as it was still there on the Friday plus there was a slight swelling at the base of my throat I decided to phone my doctor to see if there was an appointment free as I didn't consider it to be any sort of emergency. Fortunately he had had a cancellation and gave me an appointment at 4.30 p.m. that day.

My GP has known me for a long time, and I quite expected some comic comment about my stiff neck; instead of which he seemed to take it extremely seriously and made an immediate appointment for me to see a surgeon on the Saturday morning (this, by the way, was the only time I paid as my GP said if I could afford to pay for this initial appointment it would be to my benefit as he wanted to get me seen very quickly but would not comment further).

I went home extremely worried as obviously he suspected something. The following day, as arranged, I saw the specialist, who hinted at very serious things but did not put into actual words what the problem was. On Monday I was at the hospital for X-rays, etc.; in hospital by the Thursday for a biopsy, the result of which was eventually passed to Professor Hamblin at Boscombe Hospital who then told me that I had what they termed a T-cell Lymphoma which had reached my bone marrow and also affected my lung. They were extremely surprised that it had gone so far as I did not appear to have any symptoms. I was subjected to further tests including the injection of a dye into my feet which enabled an X-ray of the lymph system to be carried out. I saw the funny side of this as when I was awaiting the biopsy I had a small arrow painted on my neck – so they knew which side to cut, I suppose – and with the dye injection a small X cut on the top of each foot. I decided I was a guided tour for Dracula!

After these tests were completed I then saw Professor Hamblin, who explained that after a great deal of research they were unable to find any recognised treatment for the type of Lymphoma I was suffering from and that he regretted the very drastic treatment that I would have to undergo – which of course they could not guarantee would work. I still felt in a state of shock as everything had happened so fast. I had not been feeling ill and couldn't believe what was happening to me. Professor Hamblin was marvellous and explained exactly how the chemotherapy I was to undergo worked, and basically it is a course of drugs which kill not only the cancer cells but also the 'good' cells – which is why you feel so ill – but as the cells regrow the 'good' cells renew far more quickly than the cancer cells and eventually, it is hoped, the affected cells would cease to regroup completely. My course of treatment would be over six months, with one treatment per month.

It was at this stage that I made some decisions, one of which was to ask the doctors to explain every course of treatment and not keep any secrets from me – and I found that as time went on this helped a great deal, and all the people who treated me were always completely honest. My second decision was that my son who was twelve at the time should not be told how ill I was: he was booked to go on the school cruise, and I did not want that spoilt. And, thirdly, and perhaps in some ways the most important, that I was going to get better. I still felt it was all a mistake anyway and that the treatment could not be as bad as people said.

As I was divorced – although my son still saw his father – I had to explain to him that I was going to have some medical treatment but that it was to make me better. It was at this stage that I asked him if he would like to stay with his father during the hospital period or stay at his grandmother's. He said he would like to stay with his grand-mother. My mother was marvellous whilst I was waiting to go into hospital for my first course of treatment, and indeed right the way through my illness. But basically – not being a demonstrative person – I kept a lot of my feelings to myself and I did wish at times there was someone to put their arms round me and just say 'Don't worry – everything will be all right', but I managed, and some of my friends were marvellous.

Eventually the time arrived for me to commence treatment. I was warned my hair might fall out and that I would feel a bit sick! Boy, was the latter an understatement. I was given the first course of drugs and spent the following two days being violently sick; they tried the antisickness tablets and injections, but they had absolutely no effect. Another two days and I felt fine; in fact I was allowed home for the weekend. I decided that this chemotherapy treatment was an absolute doddle.

I returned to hospital on the Monday, and on Tuesday received my second course of drugs. Again, the dreadful sickness, but this time it didn't stop and my mouth became very ulcerated. As well as sickness I suffered from diarrhoea, then constipation, and my hair started to come out in handfuls! I started to run extremely high temperatures – there was thick snow outside, and the nurses were removing my blankets to try and cool me down!

I really felt at a low and used to lock myself in the bathroom and have a good cry then go back to bed as though I didn't have a care in the world – at a shuffle as I was too weak to go very fast. A very dear friend brought me a stretch towelling turban which I wore as being an extremely vain creature I hated anyone seeing me without hair. I was losing weight and went down to 6½ stone from just under 8 stone. I was fighting a losing battle. I couldn't eat much as my mouth and throat were badly ulcerated, and when I did eat I was sick. The hospital tried their best and mixed up a liquid food solution which I drank and immediately threw up and then they came up with an orange type which tasted very nice but you can imagine the acid content when it was in contact with the ulcers in my mouth and throat. However, eventually a week before Christmas they allowed me to come home. I had been in hospital for just over six weeks.

My next course of treatment was due just after Christmas, but they agreed to delay until New Year. So I went home – half-dead but determined to enjoy Christmas. I spent the next couple of weeks getting my strength back and bought myself a wig, which I felt extremely self-conscious in but was assured it looked fine. I then made a horrifying discovery: my hair had gone, but now my eyebrows and eyelashes followed suit. I really did feel peculiar and, being fairly dark, I had never had to draw in eyebrows before. I can tell you it took ages before I got them reasonably even so that I didn't look continually surprised.

It was now time to return to hospital for my second course of treatment – they decided to give me six treatments in all. The first course in hospital was to check the dosage; they decided to reduce the amounts for future courses as they felt the first course was a bit strong.

My routine for the next six months went like this. I would arrive at the hospital on Tuesday morning at 10.30 and a blood test would be made. After this had been checked I would then be attached to a drip for the three drugs to be injected one after the other. This was not always easy, especially as, as time went on, all my veins had collapsed and by the time the doctor had drawn some blood it took eight attempts at one time then another vein had to be found for the drugs. I would then return home early in the afternoon, and by about 5.30 p.m. I would start to feel ill and go to bed, and vomiting usually started about 10 p.m. This lasted about forty-eight hours, and I would start to feel a little better on Friday and over the weekend. On Tuesday I would return to hospital for another blood test and would begin to feel ill about lunch-time on that day, and from then on for another week at least I would become more and more ill. At this stage I was told by the hospital that if ever I felt too ill I should contact them and they would arrange immediate admittance. I decided there and then that no matter how ill I became I would not be re-admitted and, although on occasions both my mother and son pleaded with me to go into hospital, I never did. During my monthly treatments I was also taking twenty-eight tablets a day for three weeks, and although the pills were sugar-coated they made my chest, as I swallowed, feel raw, rather like a severe case of prolonged intense heartburn.

During all my treatment I continued to work when I could. It usually consisted of two days one week, then a break for a fortnight, then another couple of days and so on; and on many occasions even the effort of walking up the road to the office left me exhausted, but I was determined to keep going.

People told me that as the treatment progressed I wouldn't feel so ill, but this didn't happen. Each one seemed to bring another side-effect to contend with. It was at this time that I sometimes regretted being on my own. I had my mother, who was a great help, but I felt I couldn't unburden to her as she was so worried about the whole illness and I felt it was bad enough my son seeing me so ill at times without trying to tell him what I was feeling.

I tried to look forward to the few days at the end of every month just before the start of the next course of treatment when I felt a little bit more like a normal human being.

It was at these times when I was really down that I tried to make myself look to the future – how nice it would be just to walk up the road without being exhausted and to have my own hair back again! It didn't always work, and I would have a little cry on my own and feel sorry for myself and wonder: Why me? Strangely enough, I never thought of giving up. I dreaded going to the hospital, and once the drugs had been given I couldn't wait to get safely home, but I never thought of not going.

The comment made by Bob Champion that the 'treatment is worse than the disease' is very true.

Most of my trips to the hospital were made with me appearing cheerful and on top of the world so that the nurses wouldn't think me a coward, and by play-acting in this way I seemed to get through. The one occasion when I did break down was when it was decided that I needed a blood transfusion. I went to the ward at 8.30 a.m. and was to receive two containers of blood plus my drugs. The ward closed at 4.30 p.m. and I eventually had my drugs injected at 5.00 p.m. The reason for this length of time was that my veins were so small they had to keep changing the transfusion needles. But that is the only time the hospital saw me so down. In fact on one occasion I was actually given a lecture by the doctor. As usual I was trying to lead a more or less normal life on my 'good days' and complaining when I couldn't do all the things I wanted to, and he informed me that they had never ever told me that I would be able to lead a completely normal life during the treatment period and that I must accept the limitations it imposed and not overdo things. I did listen to what he said, but I don't honestly feel I followed his advice.

I am now fully recovered, and on my last visit for my six-monthly check-up was told that I could consider myself cured!

I would say to anyone who is faced with this treatment: Accept it but don't ever give in to it. At times you will feel so dreadful you wonder if it is worth it. It is! If you are given six treatments, as I was, look at it this way: after the first one there are only five more, and so on.

When you lose your hair it really isn't the end of the world. A wig does have its advantages as your hair always looks immaculate through rain and shine – and when else could you wash your wig before you go to bed and put it on in the morning and have a perfect hairdo right away? I still think I have the best-ever excuse for being late for work: one morning I couldn't find my wig and after searching high and low remembered I had put it in the airing-cupboard to dry! Good thing I had such an understanding boss.

ROSEMARY MUNDY

It takes great courage and determination to fight for your life as Rosemary did. Rosemary was lucky; the treatment worked. Others are not so fortunate, and I have discussed the problems of living with a disease that can't be cured in Chapter 10.

Cancer Link is an organisation founded in 1982 by a group of people with personal and professional experience of cancer. It grew out of a perception that there was not enough support available for people affected by cancer. It provides an information service about all aspects of cancer. The nurses in the Information Service offer support and information, and help clarify the user's options, enabling them to make informed decisions. It helps people with cancer, their friends and families. The Group Support Service acts as a resource to cancer support, including a list of all the support and self-help groups throughout the country. They also help people to set up new groups. See page 353 for more information.

About one in three people in the United Kingdom will get cancer at some time in their lives. Many people think that cancer is a disease that has emerged in the twentieth century, but it has always been around; but, because it is largely a disease of ageing, as we live longer more people are likely to die from it. It has also come to the fore because many of the diseases that caused our ancestors to die have been eliminated or are now controllable: for example, tuberculosis and diabetes.

Today doctors have made great advances in the treatment of cancer; early diagnosis and treatment can prevent some cancers from becoming fatal. The growth of some forms of cancer can be slowed down and stopped with treatment; but the cancer cells stay in the body, so doctors are unable to guarantee that the cancer will not return. It is this fear and uncertainty that can be so difficult to come to terms with.

'Cancer' is a word used to describe a group of illnesses that arise from an abnormality of one or more cells in our body. The body is made up of millions of cells which are constantly dying and being replaced by new healthy cells. Sometimes these cells multiply in an uncontrolled way and a tumour or growth forms. Tumours are not all cancerous; some are called 'benign' or 'innocent', do not spread to other parts of the body and can usually be removed surgically and successfully. Other tumours are malignant or cancerous, and these will grow and invade the tissues surrounding them. Sometimes some of the cancer cells travel into the bloodstream where they are transported to other parts of the body; these are secondary cancers or metastases. The treatment of a tumour varies considerably because they all grow at different rates, in different body tissue, and respond to a variety of treatments. So it is possible that two people with cancers of the same origin may receive different treatments.

It is important to remember that these days many cancers can be cured. However, the early detection and treatment of cancer is vital. So take note of the early-warning signs listed below and if in doubt seek medical advice.

See your doctor as soon as you can if any one of the following signs or symptoms appears:

- any sore, especially a sore with raised edges on the face, that does not heal quickly
- any unusual bleeding or discharge from any natural body opening
- any painless lump, especially on the soft tissue such as the breast, lips, tongue
- any persistent indigestion or unexplained weight-loss
- any persistent hoarseness or cough or difficulty in swallowing
- any unexplained changes in normal bowel habits
- any mole that enlarges, becomes irregular in shape, bleeds or itches

(From the American Cancer Association)

The Treatment of Cancer

Before it can be said that someone definitely has cancer, a biopsy is needed: a small piece of tissue is taken from the affected area and examined under the microscope. If the tissue is cancerous, a decision is made about the necessary treatment.

Cancer can be treated in different ways, which will vary according to the type of cancer, the extent of the disease and other factors. Treatments include surgery, special medicines (chemotherapy), X-ray treatment (radiotherapy), or a combination of these. There are less conventional treatments such as homeopathy, diets and so on; if you want to try these, discuss it with your doctor.

Surgery was the first effective treatment for cancer and is still often the first line of attack. Chemotherapy and radiotherapy are often given on an outpatient basis. Not everyone experiences severe side-effects to these treatments, but you should ask your doctor what they are likely to be in your case, and what will be done to help you if they occur. For example, if you are likely to lose your hair, it is a good idea to get a wig that really suits you before your hair starts to fall out.

Discuss all the options with your family doctor and/or the hospital doctor. Don't be afraid to ask if you do not understand something that has been said. If you want to know exactly what is going on, ask the doctor; the chances are if you don't ask he will assume that you do not want to know and is likely to withhold information. Some people prefer to be told everything at once, while others would rather be told in stages, so make your feelings known and clearly understood. If you feel that you are not getting the service that you want from your family doctor, change doctors: see page 351. If you feel that you would like a second opinion or to be referred to another hospital doctor, make sure you have considered the implications of cost and travel if it means attending another hospital. Then ask your doctor tactfully to refer you to another specialist or, if you already have one in mind, to the specific specialist by name. Talk it over with your family or friends. There are also organisations that will help you with these decisions: see page 353.

ACQUIRED IMMUNE DEFICIENCY SYNDROME (AIDS)

Some illnesses are described as 'socially unacceptable': the sort of disease that is not talked about, such as the sexually transmitted diseases and in particular Acquired Immune Deficiency Syndrome (AIDS). Val Myers is a nurse with special responsibility for counselling and helping people with AIDS, and she has contributed Alan's story.

*

I am twenty-six years old and have just been through the worst six weeks of my life. I have not seen my family since I left home at the age of sixteen. I have had a variety of jobs since I left the Army. Following the break-up of a long-term relationship I have tended to move around the South-West taking casual labouring jobs and living in bed-and-breakfast lodgings.

A couple of months ago I went to the doctor because I still felt so weak and had lost weight after a bout of flu. The doctor seemed unconcerned and thought I might have anaemia. He took a number of blood samples for testing and explained that one was for HIV antibodies. This didn't worry me as I didn't think that I had been at risk.

When I went back for the results he calmly told me I was HIV positive. He probably said a lot more, but I was so stunned I don't remember anything else.

That first week I walked around in a haze and couldn't sleep at nights. Thinking over and over again: Why me? I had never had a relationship with another man, or injected drugs, and wasn't exactly promiscuous with women.

Suddenly this became unimportant; it was too late to worry how I had become infected. Now all I could think of were my shattered dreams of settling down, getting married and having children. I became more and more depressed and withdrawn, thinking of a lonely horrible death. Suicide seemed the only logical answer.

I eventually confided in a workmate, who shared my lodgings, but I wasn't prepared for his shocked reaction. He must have quickly told everyone at the lodgings because after breakfast they smashed the crockery that I had used in the sink. The landlady then asked me to leave and asked for money to replace the bedding I had used because she had to burn it. Later that day I was given my cards from work without explanation.

I started walking, and two days later arrived at a religious community. I related my sad tale to the priest, but this time I didn't get the same reaction. He let me talk for hours and then put me in touch with the local AIDS counsellor. She gave me literature to read and answered all the questions that had been going over and over in my mind.

I began to realise that being HIV positive meant that I had been exposed to the virus and had antibodies in my blood. I was infected, but this did not necessarily mean that I would get AIDS and die. Only about 10 per cent of HIV positive people go on to develop

AIDS in the first two years, and after seven years some people remain fit and healthy.

We talked about how important it was to help my immune system by getting a balanced diet, with extra vitamins and protein, by cutting down on excessive alcohol and tobacco, by relaxing and getting plenty of fresh air and sleep.

I discovered that I had a future and to a large extent it was in my own hands. I can still have a loving relationship, but there are certain precautions that I must take to safeguard others. It will be hard to change my habits, but now I have everything to live for.

I have learned, the hard way, to be very selective about whom I tell. I have told my doctor, who has prescribed a high-calorie supplement to stop me losing weight. I know he will not let me die a lonely painful death.

I am working again and living in lodgings, but I have told no one there because I now know that they are not in danger of being infected by HIV from normal social contact. It would only cause unnecessary fear. If I feel lonely or depressed, I can talk to my counsellor or priest. There are other help-lines that I can contact, even at night, such as the Samaritans or the national AIDS help-line, but right now I have a positive future.

ALAN

AIDS is a very serious disease caused by a virus that attacks the body's natural defence system. The virus is called Human Immunodeficiency Virus (HIV). At the time of writing there is no known cure. Not everyone who has been infected by the virus has developed AIDS, but anyone who has the virus can pass it on to others.

AIDS is transmitted by sexual intercourse with an infected person, both heterosexual and homosexual; this is the main method of spread of the disease. The only way to reduce the risk is to reduce the number of sexual partners, and to adopt safe sexual practices, and always use a condom when having sex with someone you cannot be certain does not have the virus. It is also transmitted from an infected mother to her baby, so women who are HIV positive are advised against becoming pregnant, or can be offered an abortion if they do become pregnant. HIV is transmitted between drug addicts who inject; they should give up the habit, or never share their needles or other equipment. HIV when present in blood and blood products has, in the past, resulted in recipients of blood transfusion and haemophiliacs being infected with the virus. Everyone in high-risk groups is now asked not to donate, and since 1985 all blood in the United Kingdom has been screened, so the risk is now extremely remote.

HIV cannot be caught from normal social contact, ordinary school activities, touching or shaking hands, hugging or 'dry' kissing, swimming-pools, saliva or tears. HIV cannot be caught by sharing or using objects used by an infected person such as cups, glasses, cutlery, food, drink, towels, toilet seats or door handles.

If you think you may be infected, go to your family doctor for advice about having a blood test. Or you could go to a clinic for sexually transmitted diseases for confidential advice and a blood test. If you have the virus, they will let you know and give you help and support. See page 352 for more information.

CHAPTER EIGHT

Mental Illness

Mental or emotional illnesses are common, but only very rarely are they so severe that the person needs treatment in hospital. Prejudice is based on fear, and many of us are afraid of the idea of mental illness or of someone who is mentally ill. This is because we do not understand mental illness and so try to protect ourselves from it.

There are two broad groups of mental illness: the neuroses and the psychoses. Neurotic illnesses are an exaggeration of the way that people usually respond to stress. The problems in a person's life become so large that they interfere with their normal lifestyle and he or she becomes unable to cope with them. There may be periods of depression or anxiety, occurring in people whose personalities make them less able to cope with stress, and whose problems temporarily overwhelm them. Although their feelings become disturbed, they are still able to reason, and are aware of their problems and difficulties.

Less common are the psychotic illnesses, such as schizophrenia and manic depressive psychosis, in which a person's thoughts become so disordered that he or she loses touch with reality, and thinks and behaves in a bizarre way. Someone with a very severe psychotic illness is still able to experience times when he or she is able to think and reason normally. In these cases drugs are needed to treat the psychotic illness, and a period of hospital treatment is often necessary.

The mentally handicapped and the mentally ill are often seen as the same; they are not. Mentally handicapped people are usually born with this handicap or it is acquired through illness or accident. People are mentally handicapped because their brain is unable to develop as quickly as, or work as well as, other people's. It is a permanent condition. However, they can be encouraged and helped to overcome their handicap. Someone with a mental illness becomes ill when he can no longer cope with his problems. Mental illness is a temporary condition which can be treated, although it may well return. One person in six will be affected by mental illness at some time in their life. One person in every hundred is born mentally handicapped. In Chapters 2 and 6 there is more information about the mentally handicapped.

NEUROTIC ILLNESSES, ANXIETY, PHOBIAS, OBSESSIONS AND COMPULSIONS

Every day most of us experience some degree of anxiety: being late for work, getting something done on time. ... There is a reason for the anxiety, and once you have got to work or the task has been done the anxiety subsides. Someone who suffers from general anxiety feels anxious regardless of the situation. The symptoms vary from a feeling of being tense and worried to an anxiety attack which suddenly overwhelms the person with fear for no apparent reason, experiencing symptoms which include nausea, palpitations, an increased heart rate, chest pain, dizziness, faintness, intense sweating, difficulty breathing, choking, weakness in the legs, shaking, restricted vision or hearing, and feelings of unreality, impending insanity or death. These symptoms can become totally debilitating for some people. Although sufferers usually manage to face what they fear, they find it very difficult, sometimes impossible. They may be excessively anxious about family health and the future. Depression can be a very important concealed cause of anxiety. The depressed person is likely to lack energy and as a result become anxious, and his problems grow out of all proportion. Some people resort to alcohol, barbiturates, tranquillisers and other medications, which then complicate the problem as they easily become dependent upon them. There seems to be no warning of an anxiety attack; it often occurs in a crowded place, and the person becomes terrified of losing control in front of other people. This problem may lead to a condition called agoraphobia, because the only place that the person feels safe is in his own home.

The first time that I had an anxiety attack was about two months after my husband had been made redundant. I was shopping in the supermarket and suddenly became very shaky; my heart was pounding in my head, there was sweat pouring off my body, so much so that my hands, hair and body were wet. It was like a nightmare – all the blood seemed to drain out of my body, leaving me so weak that I thought I was going to collapse and die. I could see people looking at me and I couldn't move. I knew that I had to get out of the supermarket and into the fresh air. Once outside I began to feel a little better. I managed to get home where I broke down and cried. At first I thought that I must have some sort of illness and so I went to bed and felt better the next day.

Over the next few months this happened on several occasions, the attacks became more frequent and in the end I simply stayed at home, I could not go out as I was sure that these attacks would occur. I had become a prisoner in my own home. My husband suggested that I went to the doctor, but I was afraid to go to the surgery; in the end I called the doctor, and he came to see me at home. He said that they were anxiety attacks brought on by the stress and worry of John's redundancy and that I had become an agoraphobic. He gave me a mild sedative for a month and asked me to try and go out with my husband for a few minutes each day, extending the time by a few minutes until I was able to walk down to and into the shops without an anxiety attack occurring. He also taught me some relaxation exercises and said he would see me again in two weeks' time and that I could call him at any time if I wanted advice or simply to talk to someone outside the family. It was with his support and help that I managed to get over this problem.

It wasn't easy; the first few steps to the gate outside our house, which is only a few feet away from the front door, were terrifying, but my husband was so gentle and encouraging that I managed to get there and back. I felt awful but was determined to beat this problem. The next day I tried making all sorts of excuses in order to avoid going out, but John was firm but kind and insisted that we walked a little further, which we did. To start with I could feel the attacks starting, but John would tell me that I was doing very well, that I would be all right, he was with me and would help me. After four weeks we were able to walk down to the shops; we even went into a large shop and managed some shopping.

When I saw the doctor he said that he was very pleased with my progress and he would reduce the dosage of the sedatives. We were to continue our daily outings and the relaxation exercises. Eight weeks later came the biggest step of all: I was to go out on my own. We started the whole programme again: the first day I walked to the gate and back, then five minutes down the road and back, gradually increasing the time until I was able to go shopping on my own. I know this all sounds so silly, and a lot of people thought that I should just pull myself together and get on with life, but I was just unable to do so. At times it was very difficult, and John was very firm but gentle; he encouraged and helped me to overcome this problem.

Three months later I was able to go out on my own and I was no longer taking the sedatives. I still do the relaxation exercises but I now feel in control of myself.

The advice that I would give to anyone in the same position is to get help as soon as you can. You can conquer this problem; it takes time, determination, and you need the support of someone who really cares about you.

MANDY JOYCE

Agoraphobia is a common phobia, some 100,000 people in the United Kingdom suffer from some degree of agoraphobia. The word *phobia* means 'fear'. Everyone experiences fear or is frightened by something; it may be associated with having a surgical operation, the fear of the outcome, what will happen. This is not a phobia but a natural anxiety. It only becomes a phobia when there is real and persistent terror associated with a situation that is apparently harmless.

The word *phobia* comes from the Greek word *phobos* meaning a 'dread' or 'horror'. Phobias are very common, and there is research which indicates that more women than men suffer from this problem. Many people are afraid of heights, snakes, spiders, birds, mice and cats. Although these fears are very real and frightening, they are not disabling, as they do not interfere with the person's everyday life. The fear is avoided, and by doing so their lives are not affected. Having a phobia is very different from being afraid: a person who is phobic will experience a panic attack when confronted with the spider, cat or bird. They will then restrict their lives in order to avoid the object of their phobia; this leads to the phobia becoming stronger, and a vicious circle develops which is very hard to break. People with phobias know that their fear is irrational, but they cannot control it and often try to keep it a secret because they feel so foolish.

There are some phobias that are really disabling, affecting the person's everyday life. Some people have such a fear of cancer that their minds are totally preoccupied with the belief that they have cancer, even though the doctors have told them that they do not. I have nursed several people who have been convinced that they have cancer when there has been nothing wrong with them, and this fear seems totally to obscure their reasoning. I have listened to the doctors explain that they do not have cancer, showing them their X-rays and the results of tests, but the patient refuses to believe it. People like this probably need psychiatric help to treat a possible psychiatric disorder.

Claustrophobia is a morbid fear of small enclosed spaces, and agoraphobia a morbid fear of public places. Agoraphobia is very disabling, and it may well have an element of claustrophobia within it. The agoraphobic finds it difficult or impossible to go into a crowded or public place, lifts, public transport or anywhere that is not close to home or where escape or immediate access to help is not available. An agoraphobic may well ensure that they do not go out alone, that there is always someone with them. Any of the above activities may bring on a panic attack, and the symptoms include palpitations, nausea, chest pains, difficulty breathing, dizziness, vertigo, feeling 'unreal', 'jelly legs', intense sweating, faintness, restricted vision or hearing, and feelings of impending insanity or death. Because of these symptoms the agoraphobic will avoid any situation that is likely to trigger off the fear. Many agoraphobics have spent years trapped in their own home.

Social phobia is an irrational fear of being the centre of attention and behaving in an embarrassing or humiliating way. The symptoms are similar to those mentioned above and also include worry and tension when the sufferer is faced with entering any social situation which may include speaking, eating or drinking in public, using a public lavatory, or doing anything while being watched by someone else. Just as with the other phobias, the sufferer is well aware that his or her fear is irrational and that it greatly exceeds being self-conscious.

An obsessive or compulsive disorder is a phobia-like condition in which there are frequent repetitive rituals and actions which the person develops in order to attempt to contain the anxiety which is crippling his life. Someone under stress may become obsessed with the idea of getting an infection from germs. They believe that the only way to avoid this is by ensuring that they are really clean, so they spend all their waking hours washing themselves over and over again and cleaning the house.

About 4 million people in the United Kingdom suffer from the disorders described above. Dr Lewis Hodgson started a voluntary organisation called Action on Phobias. This is a recently formed charity whose purpose is to help all those suffering from a phobia or general anxiety difficulties to overcome their problem. Dr Hodgson has established local self-help groups around the country, organised a link-line which offers mutual support and advice based on shared experience, educated members of the public and the caring professions about the nature of phobias and provided a self-help training programme for use at home. He says that by learning to overcome anxiety in the company of fellow-sufferers the phobic receives support and encouragement from people who truly understand the nature of the problem. He goes on to say that you can learn to control the distressing mental and physical symptoms of acute anxiety. The best person to help you overcome the anxiety or phobia is a clinical psychologist. Ask your family doctor for a referral to the psychology department at your local hospital. If you would sooner work on the problem for yourself, Action on Phobias has a number of cassette training programmes developed to help people suffering from either general anxiety or specific phobias. See page 357 for details.

You could also try the technique described by Mandy Joyce: ask your family doctor if he will help you to overcome your phobia or anxiety. Some people have successfully used hypnotherapy as a method of treatment, which you could also discuss with your doctor.

DEPRESSION

Everyone has the occasional period of gloom. Sometimes there is a reason, such as after a bereavement, when it is quite natural to feel depressed for quite some time. Most people manage to cope with life normally despite the fact that they are feeling great sadness, and gradually their mood lightens and life gets back to normal again. Others react to a difficult or stressful time quite differently; their depression does not lift, but persists and deepens until it disrupts their ability to lead a normal life. It is at this point that they are said to be suffering from the mental illness depression.

Some people develop a depressive illness not as a reaction to stress but for no apparent reason. Depression is also quite common after a viral infection such as glandular fever; it may also develop as the result of hormonal changes which follow childbirth (see page 32). Depressive illness is also common among the elderly, but people seem to be particularly vulnerable during the stressful years of late adolescence, middle age and post-retirement.

No matter what the cause or the reason, people with depression experience feelings of deep unhappiness and regret, tearfulness, loss of enjoyment of life, difficulty making decisions and loss of concentration, lack of interest in work or home life, absent-mindedness, feelings of guilt, failure and pessimism about the future. In a small minority of cases the depression becomes severe. The person withdraws into himself, losing touch with everyday life. He sometimes becomes confused and acts in unpredictable ways. He may well complain of an overpowering sense of tiredness. There may be feelings of guilt and self-criticism leading to feeling and believing that he is worthless and hopeless. Time seems to stand still, there is no hope for the future, little point in going on, so suicide may seem the only option.

Colin suffered from depression for several months. He describes what it was like.

*

I have a successful career and a happy marriage, two lovely children who are happy and healthy. I enjoy my work, although it is sometimes stressful, am reasonably successful and work hard. So with all this it was difficult to accept that I was suffering from depression.

I started to lose my self-confidence, I became indecisive and had difficulty making decisions that before had been easy. I couldn't remember people's names, I became incapable of initiating anything. I was convinced that people at work and my family were all conspiring against me.

Elizabeth, my wife, tells me that I spent hours sitting in a chair staring into space, totally wrapped up in myself. Nothing made me laugh, I just slipped into a deep dark well. I can remember sitting there doing nothing and I seemed to be drowning in myself. Everything was black. I was so tired that I wanted to sleep for ever, but when I did sleep I had the most dreadful bad dreams and nightmares.

COLIN HARGREAVES

Most people who experience a mild depression probably need someone to talk to. But as symptoms become more severe and begin to interfere with concentration, sleeping and eating habits and work-performance other forms of help may be required.

If the depressed state of mind is not just a temporary problem, and talking to friends and family have not helped, it is advisable to contact the family doctor. The family doctor knows the individual concerned and will be able to prescribe medication and refer to other professionals if necessary. Many doctors have a counselling service attached to their practice or, if not, they will know where this sort of service can be obtained.

Psychiatrists, psychologists, psychotherapists and counsellors are all professionally trained and are concerned with assessing and treating emotional and psychological disorders. It is by these professionals that someone with depression may well be treated when the family doctor has decided that the depression is not responding to his treatment, or that the person concerned needs more time to talk than he can realistically provide. Other services associated with care in the community for people with depression can be found on page 357.

The most common treatment for depression is by medication. The drugs used may be minor or major tranquillisers, sleeping pills and anti-depressants. Alternative medicine such as acupuncture, osteopathy, chiropractice, homeopathy and herbalism are also ways of returning the body, and therefore the mind, to a state of calm or natural order through techniques designed to regulate faulty energies, metabolism and posture.

There are also relaxation techniques for preventing or alleviating stresses in our lives such as autogenic training, biofeedback, meditation and yoga, all of which can have beneficial effects. However, it is important to remember that these methods are aimed at maintaining health and not at treating severe psychological disorders, even though they may well be used in combination with conventional treatment. There are also self-help groups, which are listed on page 358. These groups recommend a combination of professional help and mutual self-help.

SCHIZOPHRENIA

The term *schizophrenia* is applied to a group of mental disorders with a wide range of symptoms the most significant of which are delusions, which are a false unshakeable belief which is out of keeping with the person's educational, cultural and social background. Hearing voices, or auditory hallucinations, is a common symptom. He may hear voices which are not there, or ones that are expressing his own thoughts, or commenting on his actions or arguing with each other; and passive experiences, which are experiences which feel as though they were being made outside the person concerned – he feels that thoughts, mood, emotion and volition are being controlled. Schizophrenia tends to run in families; the cause is unknown, though a schizophrenic-like illness may be induced by some drugs such as the amphetamines and LSD, by epilepsy or by sleep deprivation.

Schizophrenia usually appears for the first time in late adolescence or early adulthood. Although it is a life-long condition, it is episodic, with attacks usually triggered off by emotional stress. These acute episodes are treated in hospital, but the rest of the time he or she may be able to lead a relatively normal life. Some chronic schizophrenics eventually need long-term institutional care because they can no longer cope alone.

Even between acute attacks the schizophrenic is a very vulnerable person, and likely to become emotionally withdrawn and have further problems if put under stress. This can put an enormous strain on the people he is living with, who will need support and advice not only from the medical profession but also from people who understand the situation because they are coping with it themselves. See page 359 for addresses of support groups and other sources of help.

ANOREXIA NERVOSA

This is an eating disorder which is most common amongst teenage girls but can also affect other age groups and males. In a recent article Professor Bryan Lask and his colleagues in the Department of Psychological Medicine at the Hospital for Sick Children, Great Ormond Street, London, report that a growing number of pre-teenage children are being diagnosed with this condition. Some of their patients were only eight years old and may well have developed the condition a year prior to diagnosis. The loss of body weight ranged between 25 per cent and 40 per cent, which can be low enough to cause the death of the child.

Sufferers tend to have a distorted picture of their own 'body image'; they see themselves as being fat when in fact they are of normal weight or even underweight. It can also be a wish to regress to childhood and a desire to avoid adult responsibilities. Sometimes these children or young people come from families where there are some problems and difficulties and anorexia develops in response to them. The increasing commercial pressure to be thin may play some part in the development of this condition, but anorexia is probably caused by a combination of very complex psychological and social factors.

An anorexic usually refuses to eat fattening foods such as carbohydrates, sweets and fats. Periods of eating may be interspersed with binges, and guilt feelings arising as a result of this. They are often very devious and go to great lengths to hide food and make it appear that they have eaten it. They may also make themselves vomit if they feel that they have over-eaten. This is a very serious condition and may well lead to the death of the sufferer.

If you notice that your child is losing weight, whatever her age, then take her to the doctor and ask if it is anorexia. Unexplained weight-loss should always be investigated and never ignored. If it is anorexia, be prepared to be fully involved in the treatment. Even the treatment is not fully understood, but will be based on increasing the person's weight by ensuring that food is eaten and retained and also possibly psychiatric help. For the address of an organisation that will help, see page 359.

BULIMIA NERVOSA (BINGE EATING)

This is associated with extreme anorexic binge-eating and with people who have never been grossly overweight but who have a history of dieting and failing on an endless cycle, and who discover that if they vomit they can actually eat and not gain weight.

Bulimia sufferers can sometimes be recognised by the smell of vomit. Constant vomiting can lead to tooth erosion and lack of potassium in the blood, which can cause extreme tiredness, tingling fingers and symptoms similar to a heart attack. If the potassium levels are not corrected, the person may die.

People suffering from bulimia need help. See page 359 for the address of an organisation which specialises in research and the treatment of this problem.

STRESS

A moderate amount of stress is actually good for us because it improves the way that we perform, makes us more efficient, increases productivity, and many of us thrive on it. When stress goes beyond a certain level, we become over-stressed and everything seems to fall apart, and this can lead to physical and mental illness. So it is important to understand what causes stress and how to cope with it.

The body responds to stress physically and emotionally. The brain sends messages to the adrenal glands, which are situated on top of each kidney. This causes the glands to pump out a hormone called adrenalin. Adrenalin has several effects on the body. It causes the blood vessels to constrict (become smaller) in the skin and the internal organs. This is to ensure that there is plenty of blood available for the muscles of the body, so preparing the body to run. The heart beats faster, so that the rate at which blood is pumped around the body is increased, so that the body is ready for action.

The breathing rate is increased in order to provide the body with more oxygen to ensure that the muscles are able to work efficiently. The pupils of the eyes enlarge to ensure clear vision. The blood sugar rises to give extra energy. So in effect the body has prepared to run or to fight in the presence of danger. Unfortunately most of the stressful situations that we face today cannot be resolved by fighting or physically running away.

The emotional response to stress is very individual and influenced by the way that we have been brought up, our sex, cultural background, heredity and environment. It is acceptable for a woman to cry, or an Italian man to cry and shout, but an Englishman keeps a stiff upper lip and holds back the tears and emotions.

In a stressful situation the body is both physically and emotionally primed to cope with stress, but as there is no reason to run or physically fight the body remains tense and ready for action that simply does not come. The increased tension produces more stress and a vicious circle develops.

Stress can be caused by so many different events, some short-term, some long-term. If you are stuck in a traffic jam, late for an appointment, you can literally feel your body's reaction to stress. Your heart pounds away in your chest, your breathing gets faster, your muscles tremble and shake; you may even feel nauseated. You deal with the stress at the time perhaps by drumming your fingers on the steering-wheel, uttering a few well-chosen words, going over in your mind your explanation for being late. When the traffic finally gets going you probably drive too fast, get to your appointment and the stressful feelings subside.

Long-term stress is caused by events in our lives over which we seem to have very little control. Unemployment, moving house, divorce, difficult working conditions, illness in the family, death of someone close to you, financial problems, starting or finishing school or college, retirement, holidays and many other situations which can cause varying degrees of stress.

The result of long-term stress can manifest itself in physical illness such as migraine, skin conditions such as eczema and psoriasis, and gastric problems such as spastic colon, dyspepsia and duodenal ulcers. Doctors feel that high blood pressure, heart disease, peptic ulcers, arthritis, asthma and diabetes may be linked to stress and that a person under stress is more susceptible to infections and illness.

The following symptoms may be a sign that you are under stress: headaches, problems sleeping, chest pains, palpitations, stomach pains, diarrhoea, constipation, menstrual disorders, pins and needles in hands and feet, dry mouth, twitching eyelids, skin rashes, compulsive eating, unexplained muscle aches and pains, sweating palms or cold hands. It is advisable to see your doctor if you have any of these symptoms and you feel that you are under stress.

Ways of Coping with Stress

There are ways of helping yourself cope with stress. The first is learning to relax; this neutralises the effects of stress on the body. Learn and practise how to control your muscles used for breathing. The idea is to breathe from your abdomen rather than high up in your chest. Lie flat on the floor with your knees raised, place one hand on the upper part of your chest and the other on the top of your abdomen. Breathe in. You should feel the abdomen rise at the start of the breath and not the top part of your chest. Practise breathing in and out until there is very little movement in the upper part of your chest and plenty in the abdominal area. Pause for a while and breathe in and out naturally. Practise this as often as you can, breathing slowly and evenly from your abdomen.

Relaxation is another method of overcoming stress. Put on your favourite soft music, turn down the lights. Lie down on a comfortable bed or sofa, a soft cushion behind your head and a warm cover over you. Close your eyes and slowly say over and over again 'Relax, relax, relax'. Then concentrate on each part of your body, starting with your toes, then feet, ankles, knees, then up to your back, abdomen, neck, face and forehead. Make each part feel relaxed, loose and weightless. While you are doing this, slow down your breathing to about half your normal rate and take deep breaths in through your nose and out through your mouth. After ten minutes of complete relaxation you will find yourself calmed and refreshed.

Alternatively you could learn to meditate or take up yoga. Some people cope with stress by dissociating themselves from the cause of the stress by putting it out of their mind. Some find this easy, while others are unable to dissociate themselves. Try to ignore the problem for as long as possible. The longer you manage to keep calm the more time your body has to lessen the effects of stress. This may well help you to approach the problem and cope with it in a calm rational manner, instead of becoming agitated and irrational.

Working off the stress through a physical activity that you enjoy is an effective way of counteracting stress and usually leaves you feeling more relaxed and rational about your problems. If you do not take regular exercise, are overweight or have medical problems, consult your doctor first and ask about the sort and frequency of exercise that you should take.

Having fun and enjoying yourself is another way of combating stress. In fact anything that you enjoy is a way of relaxing, and you will notice that while you are enjoying yourself and afterwards you feel better able to cope with your problems.

Sometimes it helps to talk to someone with whom you have no personal connection; they may just listen, and once you have talked about a problem it may not seem so insurmountable. You could talk to your family doctor, a clergyman or the Samaritans (see page 360). Sometimes they can put problems into perspective. Family and friends will be sympathetic and probably very happy to give advice but will see you as part of a family or circle of friends whereas someone outside that circle will see you as an individual.

You could also look at the way that you manage your time. Stress is often caused by the mismanagement of time, getting behind with work or household chores. It is important to assign priorities to your tasks, do the most important things first. It may help to write down all your activities, the relevance of the activities to sorting out the problem, and the result when they are achieved. You only need to do this for a few days and you may well be very surprised at the amount of time wasted on non-essential activities and how much was put to useful purpose.

It is important to recognise your own limitations, and take on only what you can realistically achieve in the time allowed. Set yourself a realistic goal and you will gain an enormous sense of achievement and lessen your stress when you reach that goal. Setting goals too high and failing to achieve will only increase your stress.

Some stressful situations can be coped with by withdrawing from the situation. Sometimes this can create great difficulties: for example, if someone at work is causing your stress to the extent that it is affecting your health, a change of job may be the only solution. But you would have to weigh up the consequences of such an action very carefully before making a decision.

To help you deal with stress it might be helpful to write down and analyse the problem. First, define the problem clearly. Then write down all the options in order to solve the problem. Then select just two or three of the most realistic solutions. Choose one of these and develop an action plan by writing down each step that is necessary to reach the solution. Set a realistic time-limit to each step and follow the timetable.

A combination of these techniques will lessen your stress, but you may also feel that a visit to your doctor and a discussion about your problems may help as well. Many people feel that their family doctor is only available and interested in helping people with physical illnesses, but this is not the case; they are only too willing to help with problems associated with stress and in so doing prevent physical problems occurring.

SENILE DEMENTIA

One in four people over the age of seventy-five suffers from some degree of dementia; it is a growing problem as the number of elderly people increases all the time.

Dementia is a condition in which there is a progressive deterioration in the brain function, especially in memory and intellect. It is a speeding-up of the normal ageing process whereby a certain number of brain cells die each day. Someone suffering from dementia reaches a point where there are not enough healthy cells to sustain normal mental activity. If they are over sixty-five, the condition is called senile dementia.

People suffering from dementia are forgetful, particularly of recent events. They become confused and lack judgement, especially in new situations or environments. This is why it is best to help them to stay in their own familiar homes for as long as possible. They slow down, both mentally and physically, and lose interest in the world around them. As the condition progresses, they find it increasingly difficult to express themselves. In the later stages of the condition there is severe decay of intellect and emotions. They will probably not know who they are or who is with them. Their personality changes, social and table manners deteriorate and often personal hygiene is neglected. In the final stages they may become unstable, alternating between behaviour that is uninhibited and apathy and even aggression. These symptoms can also be shown by people suffering from Alzheimer's disease, which is dementia occurring in people under the age of sixty.

My mother had always been a very independent and outgoing sort of person. Even after my father died she insisted on staying in the family home; she went out and met new people and really started her life again. She was always a very gentle, loving and happy person. In the summer of 1986 she came to stay with us for a couple of weeks, and it was at this point that I realised that something was wrong. She was very forgetful and seemed a little confused about time. At first I thought that at the age of seventy-three it was hardly surprising, but things became progressively worse. One night I was woken by the sound of someone downstairs in the kitchen. There she was in the middle of the night cooking. She told me that it was two o'clock, she was hungry and if I wasn't going to cook lunch, then she would. It was two in the morning, and she really believed that it was lunch-time. I made a joke of it, we solemnly sat down and ate the food that she had prepared, she realised what she had done and we laughed about it. Both my husband and I decided that it would be better if she stayed with us and did not return to her own home for the moment.

As time went on she became more disorientated, and several times she was unable to find the lavatory and unfortunately had the occasional accident, which was very embarrassing for both of us. These occasional accidents became more frequent. Sometimes she didn't know who I was, and I found this very distressing. In the end I took her up to see the doctor, who said that she was suffering from senile dementia, that it was a progressive condition and that there was no known treatment or cure.

So we struggled on. Things went from bad to worse. There would be days when she would be on the go all day, poking about in cupboards and walking up and down stairs. One of her most irritating habits was asking the same question over and over again. I would answer the question, and two minutes later she would ask again. Sometimes I would go into the kitchen and smell gas: she had turned it on and forgotten what she had done. She would light matches and then drop them on the carpet. I was constantly afraid that she would burn the house down or initiate some other dreadful accident. It was like looking after a two-year-old.

I was nearly at the end of my tether. Our doctor was really of no help at all; in his opinion we would just have to cope. A great friend of mine came round one day and witnessed one of Mother's worst days. She was standing in the sitting-room removing all her clothes and tucking each item of clothing behind the furniture, in drawers and cupboards. She was horrified and suggested that I contact the local psychiatric hospital, which I did, and they sent round the community psychiatric nurse.

She explained what I could do to help matters. First, the family and I had to be very patient; losing our tempers and shouting would only make things worse. Try to recognise the aspects of her personality that were still intact, and help her to maintain these. Establish a daily routine with special high spots such as meals, a favourite television programme, a walk after lunch. Provide memory aids such as a large clock and a calendar, to remind her of the date, time and year, and to reinforce this in conversation as often as we could. To write signs in large print and put them on the doors of the kitchen, sitting-room, dining-room, bedrooms, bathroom and lavatory, so that she would be reminded of where she was. To make sure that she carried identification with her at all times. Remind her to go to the lavatory every two or three hours. Not to treat her like a child. When she was particularly confused to respond to the confusion and disorientation with facts, not to go along with the delusions as this would only reinforce them. To get out the old photograph-album and talk about people in them that she would remember.

She also suggested that I should get some help in the house to give me more time to cope with my mother and she would talk to our doctor and the staff at the hospital and see if my mother could be admitted for a week or so to give us all a breathing-space when we felt that we needed it.

I cannot describe the relief that I felt having talked to the nurse and being given something definite to do to help my mother. We did as she suggested, and life improved; the nurse was a regular visitor to our home and a tower of strength.

My mother had regular assessments at the hospital and eventually the time came when we really couldn't cope any longer; my mother had bouts of aggression, she didn't know who anyone was and would then withdraw into herself. She also began to wander, and we would have difficulty finding her. At this stage she was admitted to the hospital and she is still there. But I and my family feel no guilt because we were able to do what we could for her for as long as possible.

This family prefer to remain anonymous, but they felt that their experience would help other people to cope in the same situation. The positive advice that they were given by the psychiatric nurse and the hospital was good sound practical advice and well worth putting into action if you are caring for someone at home who is confused or demented. Caring for someone who is demented brings great personal sadness for the carers who have known and loved their relative for many years and now, at times, have difficulty recognising them as the same person. Perhaps one of the worst features of this condition is the inability to maintain a conversation with them. The carers need support and help, and I have listed the sources of both financial and continuing support on page 362.

Sometimes problems, like the ones that I have discussed in this chapter, become so overpowering that the people concerned can see no way out of the predicament that they are in and the only solution that they can see is to commit suicide. Death seems a sweeter option than continuing the struggle of life, and I have discussed this in Chapter 10.

CHAPTER NINE

Addiction to Drugs, Alcohol and Tobacco

Addiction is a term used to describe a compulsion to continue taking a substance as a result of its repeated administration. The substance is taken to avoid the physical discomfort of withdrawal symptoms. All addictive drugs are potentially dangerous and are those which produce a pleasurable mental state. Alcohol, heroin, morphine, barbiturates, amphetamines, cannabis, LSD and the inhalation of solvents are all potentially addictive. Once they are taken regularly a tolerance is developed, the body gets used to the drug and needs more to produce the same effect. If the supply is not available, the user feels physically ill or mentally very low.

YOUNG PEOPLE AND DRUGS

Young people may start to take drugs simply because a friend, or someone they know, offers it to them and they accept. Perhaps they do so in order to be accepted amongst a circle of friends, or just out of curiosity. For some young people it is a way to escape and remove discomfort or anxiety, perhaps about school work or problems at home, and depending on how they feel the first time they take the drug they may carry on if they enjoyed the experience or if it seemed to block out other worries and problems. Others may take on a new identity under the influence of a drug that turns a shy person into the life and soul of the party. Sometimes it is a way to escape boredom, something new, exciting, dangerous, and they know that their parents and other adults will disapprove. Most children and young people say 'No' but a minority say 'Yes'; a few of them will only use the drug a few times, and the remainder will experiment with drugs and go on to become regular users or addicts.

Many parents worry that their teenage children will get involved in taking drugs and need to know what the signs of drug-taking might be:

- sudden changes in mood, cheerful and alert one moment and sullen and moody the next
- unexpected irritability or aggression
- loss of appetite
- loss of interest in hobbies, sport, school work or friends
- bouts of drowsiness or sleeplessness
- telling lies or furtive behaviour
- money or belongings disappearing
- unusual smells, stains or marks on the body or clothes, or around the house
- unusual powders, tablets, capsules, scorched tinfoil or (more rarely nowadays) needles or syringes

Many of these signs could and may well be just the normal signs of growing up, and parents should be careful not to jump to conclusions.

If you think that your child is taking drugs of any sort or description, try not to over-react. First, establish the facts. Talk to your husband or wife, the teachers at his school and even your family doctor. Talk to the young person and discuss any worries or problems; show him that you care and want to support and help him all you can.

> Bob had always been a very hard-working and happy boy. He had done well at school and managed to get into a university to read economics. All seemed to go very well at first; he missed his home and friends, but was enjoying life at a university and came home for the holidays. When he came back for the long summer holiday he looked very pale and tired, and we both assumed that he had been working and playing hard. He was very cheerful at times and then he would become very moody and lock himself in his bedroom for hours on end.
>
> The last weekend of the holidays he invited a friend to stay who was also at the university, so I decided to give his room a really good clean. While I was clearing up his room I discovered some charred pieces of foil under his bed. I had heard that people smoked rather than injected heroin, and became anxious and worried that he was taking drugs. When my husband came home from work I told him; he was really angry, and there was a dreadful family argument with the friend witnessing the whole thing. They both said that lots of their friends were using drugs and they could stop any time they

wanted to. Then they packed their bags and left.

I don't think that we handled it very well, and in retrospect it would have been better to have waited until Bob was on his own and discussed the matter calmly.

My husband contacted the Dean at the university, told him the whole story and asked his advice. He arranged for Bob to see the doctor. A few days later the doctor contacted us and suggested that we all meet to discuss the problem. Bob was worried and frightened; he agreed to come home and attend a clinic locally where they would help him come off the drugs. The specialist at the clinic prescribed medication to help him come off the heroin, and Bob made regular visits to the clinic to talk about his feelings and problems. They helped him to avoid getting into a situation where he would take drugs again.

There were times when we knew that he had managed to get hold of the drug and taken it, but we all approached the situation calmly and took each day as it came. Our main concern was that it would start all over again when he went back to university and was amongst his friends who were still using drugs. The doctor at the university was extremely helpful and supportive and continued his treatment. A year has gone by since Bob last smoked heroin; it has been difficult for everyone, and we can only hope that he will not take drugs again.

This family wish to remain anonymous as Bob is still at university and they managed to keep the whole episode secret from the rest of their family and friends.

There are other dangers associated with drug-taking besides addiction or dependence on the drug. Under the influence of the drug the person is likely to take risks and become involved in an accident either on the road or in any other potentially dangerous situation. It is very easy for the user to take an overdose of the drug which may lead to unconsciousness or even death.

The drugs that are used are legally controlled drugs; they come under the Misuse of Drugs Act and are normally only obtainable through a doctor who prescribes them for specific medical problems in a dose carefully calculated to solve the problem without doing the patient any harm. When these drugs are sold illegally by people with no knowledge of the correct use or dosage of the drug, the user is in great danger from the potentially harmful effects of the drug. There are people who sell drugs for profit but never use them, there are those who buy more than is needed for their personal use who then share out the remainder, and there is the addict who sells drugs to support his own habit. These people encourage others to use drugs by making the taking of the drug sound attractive and exciting, they tend not to mention some of the unpleasant side-effects that these drugs can have on the unsuspecting user.

The Amphetamines

The amphetamines, known as 'uppers', are stimulants; they can be taken by mouth, dissolved in water and injected, or even smoked, but the powder form is more usually sniffed. They stimulate the central nervous system. The effect of this drug is to make the user feel wide awake and full of life; it lasts about three or four hours but, as the drug wears off, leaves a feeling of depression and great tiredness, so the user takes another one to get back on to the high. This will eventually lead to physical and mental exhaustion and possibly nervous collapse, also an increase in irritability, aggression and intolerance. Amphetamines will eventually create a psychological dependence; they are addictive.

The Barbiturates

The barbiturates, known as 'downers', are normally prescribed as a sedative and, just like alcohol, depress the normal function of the brain. They come in powder form and are commonly sold in capsules and generally taken by mouth, but can be injected. The effect of this drug will appeal to the user who wants temporarily to block out the world and all its problems. They tend to make the user less inhibited; they become talkative, excited, irritable, and even tremble. The speech becomes slurred; there is unsteadiness with difficulty standing up, followed by drowsiness, confusion and, if an overdose has been taken, unconsciousness leading to coma and even death.

It is very easy to take an accidental overdose of barbiturates because the difference between a normal dose and an overdose is very small. When drugs are bought from an illegal source there is no way of being sure what the exact strength of the tablet is; they all look very similar, but there is a great difference in the potency of the tablets. If alcohol is mixed with a barbiturate, the two substances interact and increase each other's potency, which can lead to an overdose. If these drugs are taken over a long period of time, they can cause psychological and physical dependence; they are addictive.

Cannabis

Cannabis comes from *Cannabis sativa*, a bushy plant which is easily cultivated. The active ingredients are concentrated in the tops of the plant. Hashish, or 'hash', the commonest form in the United Kingdom, is the resin scraped from the plant and compressed into blocks. Herbal cannabis, known in the United States of America as marijuana, is a less strong preparation of the dried plant material. The strongest of all is cannabis oil, a liquid prepared from the resin. In the United Kingdom the preparation is usually rolled up into a cigarette and smoked; often combined with tobacco, it can also be smoked in a pipe, brewed into a drink or put in food. It has a complex action upon the brain, with the properties of both a hallucinogen and a sedative, making the user feel relaxed, confident, and having a mild hallucinating effect. The use of cannabis can precipitate mental and nervous breakdown in people in anxiety states.

It is illegal to cultivate, produce, supply or possess the drug, except in accordance with a Home Office licence issued only for research or other special purposes. It is also an offence to allow premises to be used for producing, supplying or smoking cannabis.

Lysergic Acid Diethylamide (LSD)

LSD is a synthetic white powder. The minute amounts required by the user to hallucinate are usually mixed with other substances and formed into tablets or capsules, to be taken by mouth. The drug may also be absorbed on paper, or gelatine sheets, or sugar cubes. The strength of all these preparations is uncertain. It is a hallucinogen, and a 'trip' begins about half an hour or an hour after taking the drug, peaks after two to six hours and fades out after twelve hours, depending on the dose. The effects of the drug depend on the mood of the user, where he is and who he is with. It makes the user hallucinate, sometimes with intensified colours and visual and auditory distortions such as distortion of space and distance. A few people have walked out of windows because they believed that they could fly. Bad 'trips' or unpleasant reactions may include depression, dizziness, disorientation and sometimes panic. These are more likely if the user is unstable, anxious or depressed, or in hostile or unsuitable surroundings.

It is one of the most powerful drugs known to man. It is sold in tablet form as microdots which have been made in illegal drug factories, so it is virtually impossible to establish the exact strength of each tablet.

The psychological state induced by LSD is so unusual that there is a risk of developing various psychotic states from its use.

The Narcotics

These drugs are derived from the opium poppy. Opium is the dried 'milk' of the poppy and contains morphine and codeine, both effective painkillers. From morphine it is not difficult to produce heroin, in pure form a white powder over twice as potent as morphine. These opiates are used medically as painkillers, cough suppressants and anti-diarrhoea treatments. There are also some synthetic opiates which are manufactured and used as painkillers; these include pethidine, dipipanone (Diconal), dextropropoxyphene (Distalgesic) and methadone (Physeptone), the drug usually prescribed for opiate addiction.

These drugs in powder form can be swallowed, or dissolved in water and injected, and heroin can be sniffed up the nose like cocaine, or smoked ('chasing the dragon'). As with other drugs, injecting into a vein maximises the effects. Over a period of time tolerance to the drug develops and the dose has to be increased in order to reach the euphoric state that the user craves. Overdose can occur when the user takes his usual dose after a break from the drug and the tolerance has faded.

Sudden withdrawal of the drug leads to flu-like symptoms; the effects start eight to twenty-four hours after the last dose of heroin and include aches, tremors, sweating, yawning, irritability, anxiety, running eyes and nose, restlessness, diarrhoea and vomiting, limb pains and stomach cramp. These generally disappear in seven to ten days, but a feeling of weakness and loss of well-being lasts for several months. Psychological dependence on the drug is much stronger.

Dangers in General

As you can see from the detailed information about drugs, they all have some very unpleasant side-effects. These include confusion and frightening hallucinations, unbalanced emotions or more serious mental disorders. The first-time heroin-user may vomit, and regular users can become constipated; girls may miss their periods, and more serious mental and physical deterioration may follow. Injecting can cause infection leading to sores, abscesses, jaundice, blood poisoning, hepatitis B and AIDS.

What to Do if Someone Has Overdosed

Someone who has taken an overdose will be drowsy or unconscious.

- Make sure he gets plenty of fresh air.
- Turn him on his side. Stay with the person in case he vomits. If he vomits while unconscious and lying on his back, he will inhale the vomit and stop breathing.
- The recovery position: Lie the person on his side with the left knee and arm bent, and the head turned to the left. Do not place a pillow or any other support under the head. If the person has already vomited, clear the vomit from his mouth.
- Telephone for a doctor or an ambulance straight away.
- Take with you to the hospital any powders, tablets, capsules or anything that you think may have been used to take the drug. This will help the doctor establish what has been taken.

As with most things in life, prevention is better than cure. In order to avoid a serious drug problem in your family bear the following in mind:

- Youngsters may turn to drugs if they see the adults at home are dependent on legal drugs like tobacco and alcohol.
- If you are using tranquillisers, keep them locked away and explain to your children why they are necessary and that your doctor has carefully worked out the dose to help you with a specific medical problem.
- Talk to your partner about how you would react if you discovered that one of your children was taking drugs. If there is a drug problem in your area, discuss it with other parents or the teachers at school.
- Make time to talk to your children about drugs, their hopes and fears for the future, sex and anything else that they want to talk over. Help to give them the sort of confidence that grows in the knowledge that you care and will willingly help them with any problem that comes along. Young people who have a good open relationship with their parents are less likely to need drugs.
- Talk to your partner and work out whether or not it is a good idea to bring up the subject of drugs and how to go about it.
- If your child has already taken drugs and enjoyed the experience, try not to dwell on the horrors of drug-taking, because he will not be convinced and it will make anything else you say appear less believable.
- Don't be over-suspicious of your children. This would be unfair and could push them into drug-taking instead of away from it.

For more information on how to get help locally, or to get in touch with other parents who can offer support and advice, see page 362.

Glue- and Solvent-Sniffing

Solvent-sniffing is often referred to as glue-sniffing. The fact that you can get high from sniffing glue was first discovered in the 1950s in the United States and has become quite common in the United Kingdom as well. Some organic (carbon-based) substances produce similar effects to alcohol or anaesthetics when the vapours are inhaled. A number have applications as solvents including glues, paints, nail-varnish removers, dry-cleaning fluids, de-greasing compounds and so on. Others are used as propellent gases, in aerosols and fire extinguishers, or as fuels, petrol, cigarette-lighter fuel. Sometimes sniffers increase the effect by concentrating the vapour by excluding the air – for example, by sniffing from inside a plastic bag placed over the head.

The effects of sniffing solvents are light-headedness, giddiness, confusion and drowsiness. People have been known to hallucinate and see things that are not there. These hallucinations may be funny, ugly, beautiful or frightening. Solvent-sniffing may also lead to headaches, sickness and, if too much is inhaled, unconsciousness. The effects usually last for about half an hour.

The methods of sniffing vary, and I have refrained from describing them in detail to avoid unnecessary spread of information:

- inhaled directly from the container
- sniffed from small plastic or paper bag held over the nose and mouth
- cloth or handkerchief saturated with the substance and then held over the face
- use of large polythene bag put over the head
- aerosols sprayed directly into the nose or mouth. This is particularly dangerous and sometimes results in death.

Sniffing is mainly a group activity taking place away from adults in secret places or open ground like a playing-field. Glue-sniffing is not addictive, but some people who sniff regularly feel that they cannot do without it; but once they have given it up they feel no physical urge to return to the habit. However, the psychological need to get high may continue and lead to experimentation with other drugs.

Glue-sniffing itself does not kill, but people have died in accidents that have happened during or after the sniffing, asphyxiation or suffocation from inhaling vomit, also from the plastic bag held over the head.

Most deaths associated with sniffing are due to falls or accidents caused by confusion and lack of co-ordination on behalf of the user. Aerosols containing fluorocarbons should on no account be inhaled as sudden death has occurred after inhalation. Fluorocarbon is a liquefied gas present in most aerosols; when sprayed into the nose and mouth the whole substance is inhaled and not just the fumes from the solvent. This could coat the inside of the lungs, causing suffocation.

Early Detection: Warning Signs

A child in a caring environment is less likely to get involved in glue- or solvent-sniffing. Early detection depends on knowing the person well enough to notice important clues:

- He or she has become moody.
- He or she is truanting from school.
- He or she is listless, has a loss of appetite.
- He or she is spending long periods alone in the bedroom or elsewhere.
- There has been a decline in school work and loss of energy.
- He or she is asking for extra money, taking loose change or money from your purse or wallet.

In addition to the above list: he or she is pale and generally tired, there is a chemical smell on the breath, stains on clothing, a sudden interest in adhesives, fuels, nail-varnish removers and other solvents, and he or she possesses a collection of paper, plastic or crisp bags; there is a change in personality, unusual spots or rashes around the nose and mouth, mental confusion, slurred speech, loss of co-ordination and drunken-like behaviour.

If you discover someone who has been sniffing and is unconscious or ill:

- Don't panic or run away.
- Remove any harmful substances and send for medical help immediately.
- Open any doors and windows to let in as much fresh air as possible.
- Check the breathing, clear the airway and apply artificial respiration if the person is not breathing.
- When breathing place him on his side, so that if he vomits it is not inhaled. Lay him face down with left knee and arm bent, and head turned to the left. Do not place a pillow or any other support under the head. If the person has already vomited, clear the vomit from his mouth.
- Remain with the person and check the breathing continuously until medical help arrives.

■ Ensure that any evidence of the glue or solvent that has been inhaled is sent with the person to the hospital.

For names and addresses of organisations and people who are willing to help, see page 362.

ALCOHOL

Alcoholic drinks chiefly consist of water and ethyl alcohol, or ethanol, produced by the fermentation of fruits, vegetables or grain. Beer is about one part alcohol to twenty parts water, wine is about twice to four times as strong, and spirits consist of almost half alcohol and the rest water.

Alcohol is absorbed into the bloodstream and has an effect within five or ten minutes, and the effect lasts up to several hours depending on the amount taken. If someone gets to bed at midnight with a blood alcohol level of about 200 milligrams (six pints of beer), and then drives to work at 7 a.m. the next morning, he would still have a blood alcohol level well over the legal limit of 80 milligrams. Because just a few drinks impair physical and mental functions, the most likely cause of injury is from falling or from driving a car badly. There is a very remote chance of death from an overdose or from choking on vomit while unconscious. Alcohol is one of the drugs most likely to be combined with another, and when combined with barbiturates is particularly dangerous.

Physical and psychological dependence can occur and may be severe. Excessive use over a number of years could lead to liver disease, ulcers, heart and circulatory disorders and brain damage. Sudden withdrawal from heavy drinking produces sweating, anxiety and trembling, and can cause delirium and convulsions (fits).

Excessive drinking can harm relationships with family and friends and can affect the person's whole social behaviour. Eventually the person with a drink problem can become so dependent on alcohol physically and/or psychologically that he can be called an alcoholic.

Alcoholism has no respect for age: children at school, young people, adults and the over-seventies are all liable to become alcoholics.

I started drinking when I was at school, and I really enjoyed the taste and the feeling of happiness that it gave me. I trained as a secretary and managed to get a job in a very busy and successful business company. By this time I was drinking at lunch-time and in the evenings at home and socially.

The work at the office was piling up. I had been given a lot more responsibility, and I would take a drink to get me through some of the difficult times. I kept a bottle in the office for emergencies, but the emergencies became more frequent. In the morning I would have a drink before leaving for work. I realised that I was drinking too much and tried to stop, but I became ill and had to stay off work, and the only thing that stopped me shaking and feeling so ill was a drink.

What really brought the whole thing to a head was a very firm warning from my boss that if my work did not improve I could look for another job. I burst into tears and ran out of his office and straight to the bottle in the bottom drawer of my desk. I was standing there with the bottle in my mouth and in walked my boss. He told me that he suspected that I had a drink problem and said he would help me if I would join Alcoholics Anonymous, which I did. I had no choice.

I went to my first meeting. Everyone was very kind; they listened to what I had to say about myself, and Sarah, my sponsor, said I was to phone her if I felt like taking a drink. It wasn't easy. I went to many meetings, tried to follow their suggestions, had many lapses, but now I feel at last that I may be winning. I thank God for the programme and the true friendship and support that I received from AA.

My name is Carol and I am an alcoholic.

Alcoholism is a fatal illness for which there is no known medical cure, and many of its victims are forced to wage a losing battle, not only against the ravages of the illness, but also against the ignorance of society which largely refuses to regard the alcoholic as a sick person.

To many people the word 'alcoholic' means someone who is perverse and weak-willed. 'Why on earth doesn't he control his drinking?' they ask.

Those of us who are alcoholics, and who have tried to control our drinking know just how impossible a task that is. This is because alcoholism is an illness.

While we stay away from drink, we function much like other people. But if we take any alcohol whatsoever into our systems something happens both physically and mentally which makes it difficult or impossible for us to stop.

Alcoholism is a progressive illness often of gradual onset. No alcoholic starts as a down-and-out. It is our drinking and the behaviour which accompanies it that in time may lose us our homes, families and jobs. Accidents, gaol sentences, hospital admissions, suicides and murders are frequently linked to alcoholic drinking. We know because we are alcoholics.

We know what it is like to give up drink, and then wait in agony for the off-licence or pub to open.

We know what it is like to spend money that we cannot afford; to be driven to steal; to hide drink in half a dozen places round the house; to wake up not knowing where we have been or what we have done, or knowing only too well.

We, too, have felt those terrible feelings of loneliness, despair, depression, remorse and self-hatred that this illness brings.

Through coming to the fellowship of Alcoholics Anonymous we found out how to stop drinking, and how to stay stopped. Furthermore we have discovered that life without alcohol is not only bearable but positively enjoyable. We were able to start to get better as soon as we stopped fighting the idea that we were alcoholics.

(Taken from *Who Me?* by Alcoholics Anonymous)

If you think that you are an alcoholic, contact Alcoholics Anonymous; their address and the addresses of other organisations that can help are on page 364. The only requirement for AA membership is a desire to stop drinking.

TOBACCO

Tobacco is the dried leaves of a plant that grows in many parts of the world. Most tobacco is sold in the form of cigarettes. Cigars are made from stronger, darker tobacco rolled up in tobacco leaves, and this stronger tobacco can also be smoked in pipes.

Cigarette smoke consists of droplets of tar, nicotine, carbon monoxide and other gases. How much of the nicotine and these other substances is absorbed through the lungs depends on how much smoke is actually inhaled. Nicotine is a stimulant, and smokers can use smoking to maintain performance when they are tired. However, smoking is also used to alleviate stress and anxiety.

The more a person smokes, the more likely he is to develop heart disease, blood clots, heart attacks, chest infections, bronchitis, strokes, circulatory problems, lung cancer, cancer of the throat and mouth, and ulcers. There is also recent evidence that suggests that children and other people living with a smoker inhale the smoke and become passive smokers, thereby at risk from developing the same problems as the smoker.

Tobacco contributes to 100,000 premature deaths in the United Kingdom every year. Women who smoke during pregnancy tend to have smaller babies, and there is a high incidence of losing the baby before and after birth.

Someone who stops smoking is likely to feel restless, irritable, depressed, and crave a cigarette. The first three days of withdrawal are the worst, but even after ten years or more some ex-smokers experience a desire for a cigarette. Many smokers have given up, and then after a week, a month, even a year they return to the habit. Some feel that they have conquered the habit and just one cigarette won't hurt, and it is straight back to square one, and they are smoking again.

How to stop smoking:

■ Tell your family and friends that you are going to give up smoking and you will need their support.
■ Develop a plan that suits you:
Plan 1. Decide two or three weeks in advance that you are going to give up smoking on a specific date. In the mean time cut down on your smoking, and on the date you have set yourself stop.
Plan 2. Some people find it easier to give up smoking when they are on holiday away from the stresses and everyday situations that encourage them to smoke.
Plan 3. When you give up smoking change your daily habits, go for a walk instead of smoking. Change your eating habits; most smokers enjoy a cigarette after a meal or a snack. Make a conscious effort not to smoke after a meal and cut out the snacks and drinks that you usually associate with smoking. Travel in non-smoking compartments; eat in the no-smoking areas of restaurants; if you can, spend the first few days with people who do not smoke and, if possible, try to persuade someone to give up smoking with you. Wash all the curtains, the chair covers, your clothes and anything else that smells of smoke.

To cut down on cigarettes, cut out the first cigarette of the day, then the second and so on. Each day try to put off having a cigarette for a little longer each time, until you are down to one cigarette; then cut that one out.

There are chewing gums that will help, but some people become addicted to the gum and have difficulty giving that up. Hypnotherapy works for some people, as do acupuncture and herbal remedies. There are tablets that make cigarettes taste revolting, and dummy cigarettes, but there is no miracle cure; the only way to stop is to be really determined and want to stop. If you want to stop smoking and feel that you need help, see page 365 for more information.

TRANQUILLISERS

Tranquillisers and sedatives are prescribed to help people cope with anxiety, loneliness, grief, frustration with children, isolation and difficulty in sleeping. In the past people managed to live through and cope with these moods, but today people are often given tranquillisers as though there was something wrong with experiencing these feelings.

Tranquillisers are also prescribed when there is crisis in our lives, when someone dies, when someone has been raped or been the victim of domestic violence, or when people are going through a difficult time such as divorce or a separation from their partner, or if you are unemployed or are stressed by your job or faced with some of the problems associated with getting older.

Doctors may even prescribe a tranquilliser for problems such as premenstrual tension or anxiety prior to an operation. Of course there is a place for short-term use of tranquillisers, when the doctor prescribes a short course and says: 'Come back and see me and we will talk about the problem and see how you are getting on.' Most doctors these days take this approach and no longer give patients repeat prescriptions without seeing them. Tranquillisers are only effective for a short time to help someone over a few of the worst days following a bereavement or some catastrophe in our lives. If tranquillisers are prescribed without the doctor spending time talking to the patient and finding out what the problem is and then the prescription is repeated for months or even years, the problem is simply tranquillised; it doesn't go away, and the patient becomes dependent upon them.

I had been taking tranquillisers and antidepressants for eighteen years. One drug was prescribed for me originally when I was in my thirties; I felt ill but had nothing physically wrong. Over the years I was given other drugs in ever-increasing doses. I spent a lot of time in hospitals and nursing homes, sometimes having ECT – electro-convulsive therapy. It was never suggested that I reduced the drugs prescribed.

I was not the only one to suffer in this nightmare. My husband and children could hardly cope with the situation. I left the job that I enjoyed. My children got married and left home. My husband became addicted to alcohol. Finally we decided to separate because neither of us could continue to support the other.

I moved into the country and built up a new life, with the help of my son and daughter. All this time I was having monthly repeat prescriptions. I asked my doctor if I could stop taking them as I felt dreadful anyway. Was it possible that I would feel better without them? He told me bluntly that I would not survive if I didn't take them, and he would not be responsible for me. He offered no help at all and didn't even know of a group who might help.

My daughter, who had supported me throughout, was as upset as I was. She rang Capital Radio to ask for advice and they told her of Tranx and she took me there that same afternoon.

That day in January 1986 was the most important day to me for eighteen years. A Tranx counsellor, who had herself stopped taking tranquillisers, told me I was addicted to these drugs. It would be possible for me to stop, too. My relief was intense. Here was the living proof that it could be done.

I registered as a client and was given a chart with instructions on how to reduce the drugs gradually over many months. I was warned that I would probably have withdrawal symptoms, but I would be supported by counsellors all the way. I could phone whenever I wanted, come to group meetings and have individual sessions. I went there every week for a long time. I often felt like giving up as I certainly went through hell. The counsellors explained to my children what was happening, so that they felt supported, too. My recovery became a family affair, masterminded by Tranx. I took my last pill on 11 May 1987. Things have not been easy, but I could still be taking tranquillisers! I am now working part-time on the telephones at Tranx speaking to and helping other clients.

JILL WORRALL

Jill had become dependent on the tranquillising drugs, but how do you know if you are dependent on your drugs? If any of the following statements applies to you, you are dependent on your pills:

- You have been taking sleeping pills or tranquillisers for a long time.
- You have asked your doctor to increase your dose.
- You are taking doses that are larger than recommended.
- You are getting extra pills from different doctors.
- You always make sure that you have an adequate supply of pills.
- You always carry your pills with you just in case you need them.
- You have taken one or two extra pills when you knew that you had to face a stressful situation.
- The drug is interfering with your life, causing difficulties in family relationships, in your social life or at work.
- You have tried unsuccessfully to cut down your dose or to stop taking your pills altogether.

Addiction to or dependency on tranquillisers is not just an emotional dependency but also a physical one. Someone is said to be physically dependent on a drug when it has produced biological changes which are enough to cause withdrawal symptoms when the drug is discontinued.

Tranquillisers taken over a long period of time will leave the body dependent on them, as with any other addictive drug. These drugs are taken up by the body through the bloodstream and concentrated in the brain. Here they react biochemically with the brain tissue in special sites in the brain. Here they act on the natural substances that we have in our bodies which control our level of anxiety, tension and calmness. These drugs in effect dampen down the activity in the brain by increasing the natural calming substances and stopping the natural arousing substances.

Anyone who has had a pre-medication before an operation will have experienced the short-term effects of this type of drug. When used for this purpose they are beneficial, leaving the person feeling calm and relaxed before an operation.

In the long term these drugs seem to turn off the brain's own control mechanisms and it becomes difficult to function without them. If this goes on for months or years, the brain becomes so dampened down that the mechanism for controlling anxiety and tension no longer functions.

When you stop taking the drugs there can be an enormous amount of excitability of the nervous system, which in turn affects nearly every system in the body, causing the symptoms of withdrawal. These include nausea, anxiety, difficulty sleeping, muscle aches and pains. Some people experience withdrawal symptoms while they are taking tranquillisers because the body has become tolerant to the drugs and now requires a larger dose to control the original symptoms.

Withdrawal symptoms can last for many months, because the drug stays in the tissues of the body and is gradually released in small amounts even after you have stopped taking the pills.

How to come off tranquillisers:

- Go and see your doctor and tell him that you want to come off your pills. He may well suggest slow withdrawal and gradually reduce the number of pills that you take until you no longer need them.
- You could also contact a support group like Jill Worrall, and they will work with you and with your doctor, or on your own with your doctor's knowledge that you are stopping your pills. For more information, see page 365.
- Some people prefer the quick way and just stop taking their drugs, and if you choose to do this, then you will need the help of your doctor, and may even need to be in hospital or in a drug dependency unit.

Dos and Don'ts while you are coming off the tranquillisers: advice from Tranx. Tranquilliser Recovery and New Existence is a registered charity founded by Joan Jerome, who herself was a long-term addict. In 1982, as a result of her own addiction, she became aware of how little help there was available for people suffering withdrawal symptoms from minor tranquillisers or sleeping pills.

Do keep busy, persevere, join a support group and talk to people who have successfully come off their drugs and those that are still trying. Listen to relaxing music, take exercise, go gently through the day and remember: 'It's the drug, not me.' Remember you are the most important person in recovery; record the good moments you have had to look back on. See it through, accept the withdrawal symptoms for what they are. Think of others worse off than yourself and remember: you will get better like Jill Worrall and many others who are living proof that it is possible.

Don't get more tablets from your doctor than you need to gradually reduce, don't take any other medicines to help you through if it can be avoided and don't substitute alcohol for pills. Don't sit around doing nothing or lie in bed all day. Don't pressurise yourself. Don't rehearse and analyse symptoms to yourself. Don't expect it to be easy or compare yourself or your progress with others'. If possible, don't: drive, despair, give up, be frightened, panic about panic attacks, feel guilty or ashamed or expect others to understand – if they haven't been through it, they won't.

Tranx and other support groups also provide tapes that you can listen to and help you to relax. See page 365 for more information.

CHAPTER TEN

Dying – the Last Chapter of Life

Death and the dying are subjects that many people feel uncomfortable talking and even thinking about. The very words bring out feelings of insecurity and fear of the unknown. Today most health professionals feel that anyone dying is best cared for in the familiar and loving environment of their own home and in some cases in the final stages in a hospice. A hospice is a special hospital where the staff are highly trained specialists in the care of the dying. The care here concentrates on providing the dying with mental and physical comfort and on enabling death with as much dignity and happiness as possible. The emphasis is on giving the dying person, and their loved ones, time to talk and express their feelings to people who are able to help by meeting their spiritual needs, who can help dispel their fears and control any pain, all within a homely atmosphere which encourages friends and family to be involved.

Caring for someone who is dying may arouse feelings of fear that you may not be able to cope with the care involved, or will be unable to manage the person's pain and other symptoms competently, and in the end that you will be left on your own. There is no need to feel like this; there is help and advice available in the form of both your family doctor, other health professionals and support groups. See page 365 for the addresses and telephone numbers of support groups and contact them as soon as you know that a loved one or yourself is dying. You will be able to talk to people who have experienced caring for someone who is dying, so they will be able to offer good, sound, practical advice and will be very willing to listen to what you have to say about your fears and anxieties.

On hearing that you or a loved one is dying, it is common to experience a particular sequence of emotions. Not everyone goes through all these stages, nor are they necessarily in this order. The sequence starts with feelings of denial, of not allowing yourself to admit the reality of what is happening: 'This is not true; it is not happening to me.' This can produce anger, rage and hostility. These feelings may well be taken out on those around at the time, such as doctors or the hospital staff. Parents of a dying child may even become aggressive towards other members of the family or the professionals caring for their child.

The next stage involves trying to put off the inevitable by bargaining with God or fate, in order that life may be extended. This is often followed by a state of depression. The dying person may be preparing to accept the loss of everything and everyone that he or she loves, the family preparing to lose someone that they love. A great sense of sadness may make them withdraw into themselves, preferring not to talk about feelings yet needing reassurance that people around understand.

Eventually there comes the stage of acceptance. The anger and depression have passed. There is a desire to sort out practical details, such as writing a will. Although perhaps seeming calmer, this does not mean that the dying person has given up the fight against death. The family start to come to terms with the inevitable separation.

The most common fear of a person who is dying, and the people that are caring for him, is that any pain will not be well controlled and that he will suffer. The first step is to reassure the person that he is not expected to put up with pain, encourage the person to say when there is pain, how severe it is and the effect that any painkilling medications are really having. He should not feel that he is being cowardly or ungrateful if he says that the medication is not working and that he is still in pain. Any medication for pain should be given regularly, and it is important to check the effect of the medication about thirty minutes after the dose and again thirty minutes before the next dose is due. If the pain recurs between dosage of medication or is ineffective, discuss the problem with your family doctor. If he seems unhelpful or unable to control the pain, ask to be referred to a hospice and they will assess the pain and prescribe the correct medicine in the correct amount. Painkillers should always be taken regularly. Don't wait until the pain becomes severe, and then take the medication; the aim is to be pain-free.

Many people are frightened that they will become addicted to the painkillers, particularly drugs like morphine, but research has shown that this is not the case when they are taken to control pain. Some of the stronger medicines do have side-effects such as drowsiness, nausea or light-headedness, but these usually go within twenty-four to forty-eight hours. If they have not, contact your doctor; there is usually an alternative that is suitable. There are also health professionals who are expert in pain control, so contact them: see page 366 for the address.

Some of the physical problems such as constipation, diarrhoea, incontinence, infections and problems sleeping can be alleviated, so seek advice from your doctor or health professional. Never feel that they are too busy and you don't like to bother them; they can only help if you are open and honest with them and talk about any problems.

If you or the person who is dying feels the need for spiritual help, even if you are not a regular churchgoer, contact the local clergy who will offer spiritual help, comfort and support. It is important to talk about the future with the family in order to get things sorted out and to say everything that you feel should be said. Allow yourselves time to express fears and anxieties, listen carefully to what is being said and try not to avoid the truth.

My husband became ill very suddenly in September 1987, when he was only forty-five. He was rushed into hospital and had an emergency abdominal operation. Afterwards the doctor told him that he had cancer and there was nothing that they could do to help him. My husband asked the doctor how long he had to live and was told it was only a matter of days or weeks at the most. So he said that he wanted to come home. He came home by ambulance the next day. We sat up all night talking about our life together and my future alone with the children, who were twelve and fifteen. He got out and went through the wills, all the insurance policies, found his birth certificate, our marriage certificate and anything else that he felt that I would need after his death. We talked about the children and how I would cope. In the morning our family doctor called round to see us and asked what sort of night John had had. When we told him that we had been up all night sorting everything out he seemed surprised.

I felt very shell-shocked, and close to tears if not actually crying most of the time, but my husband was so strong and positive that I was carried along by him. Two days later he became unconscious and died, in my arms, at home, peacefully with all his family beside him. After his death I was able to grieve with my children knowing that everything had been sorted out and settled. We were all filled with a great sense of sadness, but I think what helped us most was that we had talked about his death and said so many important things to each other which gave us the strength to carry on with life. If he had stayed in hospital, he probably would have lived a little longer but I would have been left with an awful lot of things to settle, and so much unsaid that I really don't think that I would have been capable of going on without him.

Anonymous

John's untimely death was perhaps unusually sudden, but his decision to go home and sort out life for his family before his death was a very brave and unselfish one. It might have been easier for him to have stayed in hospital and left the rest to his wife, but on the other hand he was able to spend those last few very precious days with his family in the comfort of his own home.

When someone dies there are certain formalities that have to be attended to: registering the death, the funeral and so on. For help with these and other problems associated with the death of a loved one, see page 366.

SUDDEN DEATH

Coping with sudden unexpected death is very difficult, perhaps because there is no time to adjust; one minute the person you love is very much alive and the next he is dead. There has been no time to express feelings of love or to say goodbye.

Pamela Beavan lives in Poole and she describes the sudden death of her dearly loved husband some fourteen years ago, which, as she says, could have been yesterday.

It began on 22 September 1973, our son Stuart's wedding day. A lovely time was had by all, although for some reason I felt a sense of foreboding. Don't ask me why; I don't know, although when a friend asked me my answer was 'I think I am going to be ill'. But it wasn't me! After the weekend away the newlyweds came to stay with us, as they were saving up for the deposit on their home.

Wednesday came and my husband went off to play squash, which was a regular thing. All this time I still had this feeling of impending danger; that's not really the right word, but the feeling is difficult to describe. That afternoon my husband, who was 6 foot 2 inches tall, healthy and a sports fanatic, had a massive heart attack. At 6.30 p.m. a police car screamed to a stop outside our house. My son raced to the door, tears streaming down his face, shouting: 'Dad's dead.' I didn't believe it, didn't want to know. I felt if I closed my eyes when I opened them he would be there. But no, all that was there was the lead weight on my chest which was there through the identification, autopsy, inquest, funeral and for months after. I must have gone round like a zombie for the first few days, cannot even remember changing my clothes or washing – what an admission! We were living in Stafford at this time owing to my husband's employment as branch manager for a finance house. I thought: Right, let's get busy, sell the house and get back home.

Then wallop! The house was mine, bought and paid for, but – and this is the most important point I wish to make, as hopefully it can save so many others the heartache – there was no will, and no life insurance. Silly, isn't it, how one takes all these things for granted? After three trips to the solicitor's and waiting six months, I moved house. By now I could look round a little more rationally, not quite so bitter. I got myself a job, which was a must as my widow's pension at the age of forty-one was £3.75 a week, so I said to myself: 'Get on with it.' It was tough, but now at fifty-six I look back and think of all the wasted years. I still get lonely and at times ask myself: Why him, a dear good man, but then he will never grow old to me?

But I cannot stress too strongly the importance of making a will and having life insurance, as what money there is at the time soon dwindles away.

It was a very difficult period of my life, and if it had not been for the love and support of my two children, Theresa and Stuart, I don't think that I could have coped. Remembering, too, that they also had lost the father that they loved and a very good friend, something which can never be replaced.

PAMELA BEAVAN

Pamela is a survivor, and with the help and love of her two children she has built a new life for herself. It is hard enough coming to terms with the death of someone that you love without the added burden of the problems that Pamela describes. Seek legal advice and get a will drawn up. Alternatively, you can get a pre-printed form from a stationers and write your own will.

DEATH OF A CHILD

Margaret Hayworth is a contact person for the Compassionate Friends, an organisation which helps bereaved parents and offers friendship and understanding. Margaret's experience is one that probably every parent dreads. As our children grow up and start to lead their own lives, there comes a time when parents have to let go, allowing them to go out on their own at night, usually with strict instructions to return by a certain time. Night after night anxious parents wait for the sound of the key in the front door and the safe return of their child. When their child is late they start to imagine the worst – perhaps there has been an accident? For Margaret these fears and worries became reality.

I had heard the phrase 'From that moment my life changed' but had not comprehended its meaning until the night a policeman came to our house to tell us that our sixteen-year-old daughter, who had gone out earlier in the evening so full of life, was dead.

Immediately it was as though I was a member of an audience watching a play unfold and yet I was a personality in the situation being depicted. A few days later I can remember thinking and congratulating myself on how well I was coping – little realising at the time I was numbed by shock. The anaesthetising shock gradually wore off, exposing the realities of grief, but the feeling of being apart from the world with the business of daily living accomplished as if on automatic pilot continued for well over a year.

Normal grief reactions are identified as sadness (usually manifested by crying), anger, guilt, anxiety and fear, loneliness, fatigue, confusion, preoccupations with thoughts of the loved one, sleep and appetite disturbances, absent-mindedness, social withdrawal and restless activity. These may be accompanied by the physical sensations of tightness in the chest or throat, hollowness in the stomach, breathlessness, dry mouth and lack of energy. All who are bereaved experience these feelings, but they vary in intensity and duration according to the age of the deceased, relationship with the loved one and the mode of death. The death of a child is acknowledged by all experts on bereavement as causing the most emotional anguish of all deaths. A child is part of ourselves, and the thought that one's child will die before oneself is very rarely considered a possibility in the Western world. 'I feel as though part of me has been amputated' is a frequent comment.

I experienced all the grief reactions, some more intensely than others. Grief has no rhyme or reason. I found that I would never know when I would feel devastated. It washed over me rather like a tide advancing and receding, but without a tide's regularity. Events or meeting people that I expected to devastate me seldom did (although I would feel upset). In retrospect I think it was because I had started to prepare myself mentally. It was usually the unexpected small poignant event that devastated, but more often than not there was no identifiable trigger to the hours of intense grief that threatened to overwhelm, when life seemed so bleak with no hope for a better feeling or future. The individual grief reactions which affected me most particularly were of going crazy, aloneness, vulner-ability and fatigue. Fatigue and the length of time it lasts is grossly underestimated. As shock wore off, so my mind became obsessed by Janet, pictures of her life constantly going round over and over again in my mind to the exclusion of everything else. The feeling of going crazy was intense. The most frightening emotion, though, was the one of aloneness. Despite having other family and friends around I had never before felt so alone. The realisation that in the final analysis I was alone, that in no way could I have prevented the death, nor had I any control over how long before or by what means the rest of my family might die, made me feel increasingly vulnerable and helpless. For a long time I had the constant fear that they would not return home when we were separated, with panic sweeping through me if they were only a few minutes late. I learned life's paradox that we are very much on our own, that we can only survive by our own efforts, and yet how much we need caring compassionate friends to give support and help in times of crisis.

The Compassionate Friends is an organisation of bereaved parents that support other bereaved parents. To talk to others on an individual basis or within a group setting, to exchange letters and to read the quarterly newsletter is a source of great help and comfort. To communicate with people who really do understand the emotions being experienced and the problems arising within a family unit cannot be underestimated and needs to be more widely recognised by the bereaved and non-bereaved alike. Each member within the family is having their own particular all-consuming difficulties with grief, so usually each one is incapable of helping the others with many sub-sequent misunderstandings. In the great majority of cases the belief that a child's death brings the family closer together is erroneous. Fifty per cent of marriages break up after the death of a child.

For the resolution of grief it is so essential that feelings are expressed, experienced and worked through for however long it takes. (An average of two years is quoted, but this varies considerably according to circumstances.) To have contact with others who are at different stages of grief and those who are looking back from a distance of some years gives hope and encouragement to the newly bereaved.

Tragically, many on becoming bereaved have no idea that what they are feeling is normal, and they, with their relatives and friends, think the routine of home life should have resumed its usual course within a few months. Life, though, can never return to the previous normality. The painful experiences of myself and watching them within other loved family members altered us as people. Our values changed; we matured. More than ever we realised people count, and money and material possessions have no importance above basic needs. It spurred me to thinking and reading about life and death and to forming my views on the reasons for my life, Janet's death and world events. Forming a philosophy for the meaning of existence is an essential ingredient in the resolution of grief. It puts a person's circumstances into context for the rest of their lives, making it more meaningful and contented. Whatever is believed is personal. The explanation which each individual feels comfortable with is the correct one for them, whether based on religious belief or not. I can genuinely say now, seven years after the event, how grateful I am for the life and the death of my daughter. This does not mean that I do not have times when I shed some tears for 'what might have been' or have a deep longing to see her and talk to her. These feelings are especially aroused at Christmas and special family events. I expect them to be with me for the rest of my life, because love does not cease with death. I have found that love has increased in depth and developed with the passing of time, thus enriching my life.

MARGARET HAYWORTH

Although the death of a child in our Western society is relatively unusual, over 15,000 children and young people die every year in Great Britain. So there are many parents faced with the loss of a child, their lives cut short by accident, illness or some other cause – leaving unfulfilled their dreams and aspirations.

Many people find it difficult to comfort grieving parents, though increasingly the caring professions are becoming concerned to help families cope with their loss. Immediately after the death of a child the parents are often surrounded by relatives and friends. However, as time goes by, they seem to be around less frequently, perhaps because of the intensity of feelings involved and/or the pressure of other responsibilities. The parents are left feeling abandoned and depressed. It is very difficult for others to understand just how long it takes the parents to go through the grieving process to eventual readjustment. Parents and families need to feel free to release pent-up anxieties, feelings of guilt, anger, hopelessness, and to talk to understanding and compassionate friends. The address and more details about the Compassionate Friends are on page 291.

The death of a baby at birth is discussed in detail in Chapter 1, but the grieving for that lost baby is no less than for the loss of any other child. Cot death, or sudden infant death syndrome, is the sudden, unexpected and unexplained death of a baby usually between the ages of four weeks and six months.

Jonathon was our second child; his sister Elizabeth was two years old when he was born. I had a very uneventful pregnancy and an easy birth. Jonathon was born a healthy happy baby. I breast-fed him for a few weeks and then he went on to a bottle as I didn't seem to have enough milk.

When he was six weeks old he was having a feed at ten o'clock at night and then would sleep through the night until six o'clock in the morning. When he was three months old I put him to bed as usual, looked in on him before I went to bed and he was sleeping soundly. The next morning I woke at 7.30 and was surprised that he had not woken us up earlier. I went into his room and he was lying in his cot, but he was a strange blue colour and felt cold. I screamed for my husband, who came running into the room. I was sure he was dead, but I couldn't believe that he was. I picked him up and cradled him in my arms; he looked so peaceful I couldn't believe that this little body was lifeless. My husband called the doctor, who came round immediately and confirmed that he was dead and arranged for him to be taken to the hospital. Later a policeman came and asked all sorts of questions about how the feeds had been mixed, had he had a cold and so many other questions. I somehow felt it must have been my fault.

The doctor told us that Jonathon had died as a result of a cot death. The next few weeks were a blur, but somehow we managed to get through the post-mortem examination and the funeral, but I really can't remember very much about it. I kept going over and over in my mind what could I have done to have caused this – I must have done something wrong. I felt that the neighbours were saying that I had killed my baby. I know it is irrational now, but at the time I was sure that was what they were thinking. None of them were supportive in any way. In fact in the end we moved house to start our lives again. It was a health visitor who suggested that we contact the Friends of the Foundation for the Study of Infant Deaths. Here we talked to other parents whose babies had died unexpectedly and they offered us friendship and support.

We now have another child, a baby boy who is nearly a year old, but I still feel anxious if he does not wake in the mornings. Ever since he was born we have had a baby alarm in his room, so I can hear him breathing, which is very reassuring. I am still rather over-protective towards both the new baby and Elizabeth, but I suppose that is only natural.

MRS E. BARTLETTE

The feelings of guilt expressed by Mrs Bartlette are felt by many parents whose child has died for no apparent reason. The cause of a cot death is unknown, although many theories have been put forward and there is a great deal of research being done at the moment. Cot deaths are tragic events, and at the moment there seems to be no method of prevention. Parents need expert advice and support to help them to adjust to their loss. See page 367 for the address of the Foundation for the Study of Infant Deaths.

Parents who have to try to rebuild their shattered lives after the loss of a child need friends and family who will support them for a long time after the death of their child. The Compassionate Friends have drawn up a list of Dos and Don'ts to help people who know bereaved parents.

Do:

- Let your concern and caring show.
- Be available to listen, run errands, help with the children or whatever else seems needed at the time.
- Say you are sorry about what happened to their child and about their pain.
- Allow them to express as much grief as they are feeling at the moment and are willing to share.
- Encourage them to be patient with themselves and not to expect too much.
- Allow them to talk about the child they have lost as much and as often as they want to.
- Talk about the special qualities of that child.
- Give extra attention to brothers and sisters (they are hurt and confused and in need of attention which their parents may not be able to give at this time).
- Reassure them they did everything they could, and tell them of everything true and positive about the care given to their child.

Don't:

- Avoid them because you are uncomfortable (being avoided by friends adds pain to an already intolerably painful experience).
- Say you know how they feel (have you lost a child?).
- Tell them what they should feel or do – like saying 'You ought to be feeling better now' or 'You must pull yourself together'.
- Change the subject when they mention the dead child.

- Avoid mentioning the child's name because you are scared to remind them of their pain (they won't have forgotten it).
- Try to find something positive about death (e.g., closer ties with the rest of the family, a moral lesson).
- Suggest they have another child (it wouldn't replace the one they've lost).
- Say it's good they've still got other children (children are not interchangeable).
- Make any comments which in any way suggest that the care given to their child at home, in hospital or wherever was inadequate (parents are plagued by feelings of doubt and guilt without any help from their family and friends).
- Let your own sense of helplessness keep you from reaching out to a bereaved parent.

BEREAVEMENT

For most people the most natural way of expressing grief is to cry, but some people find themselves unable to do so. This is often the case when someone has managed to put on a brave face while caring for a loved one through a long or serious illness and now that it is all over is unable to let go. Men are particularly inclined to keep 'a stiff upper lip' and are inhibited about showing their emotions.

It is a physiological fact that women live longer than men, and therefore the majority of bereaved are female. Many are more able to cope if the death of either partner has been discussed and plans made to help the remaining partner. As described earlier in this chapter by Pamela, the effects of sudden unexpected death of a husband and father are devastating but if there had been a will and life-insurance cover it would have been a little less difficult after the initial trauma.

CASE-STUDY: HUSBAND CARING FOR A WIFE WHO WAS TERMINALLY ILL AND HOW HE COPED AFTER HER DEATH

My wife and I had been happily married for twenty-three years, and our two children were twenty-one and nineteen. The elder, David, was in the Army, and our daughter had just started at university, when my wife was diagnosed as having cancer. Unfortunately she had not discovered a lump in her breast until it was too late. She was only forty-six years old, and I can't describe how I felt when we were told that she would die and that there was really nothing that could be done to save her; they would remove the lump and could only hope to make her comfortable.

The day that I brought her home from hospital I could not believe that the doctors were right, because she looked so well. We talked over the whole business and decided that we would carry on our normal lives for as long as we could, but when the time came I would get time off work and stay at home and care for her. We both felt that it was unfair to expect our daughter to come home and care for her mother, although that is exactly what she wanted to do. I had never been domesticated in any way; my wife had looked after me from the day that we had married. I couldn't boil an egg, work the washing machine, the vacuum cleaner or anything; in fact I was pretty useless. When either the children or I had been ill she had cared for us, so I had never looked after anyone who was sick.

They followed up the lumpectomy with a course of radiotherapy. This made her very sick, but between us we managed to work out what she could eat, and she really coped very well with the side-effects and had plenty of rest. Over the next few months she seemed to be fairly well, although she became very tired easily. Then she started to complain of pains in her back, and the doctor said that the cancer had spread into her spine and suggested another course of radiotherapy to reduce the pain in her back. This time it made her very weak and sick, and I had to stay home and care for her. I learned to prepare small special meals, which I did with great care. Because I was no expert, they took rather a long time to cook, and I have to admit to feeling irritated and disappointed when she would either refuse the meal altogether or pick at it then leave it.

When she was physically sick I would stay with her and care for her, but it wasn't easy as it made me feel so ill. I felt very inadequate, because I was unable to overcome these feelings and cope better. I felt that I should be able to care for her, but it wasn't easy and it didn't come naturally to me. This went on for the duration of the radio-therapy, which did seem to reduce the pain and afterwards she seemed to be a little better. Gradually she became stronger again, and I was able to go back to work. In the morning I would get her up and prepare our breakfast, help her dress and leave her a cold meal for lunch. In the evening I would prepare the supper and help her up the stairs to bed. I did find this very tiring, but we managed and gradually it became a routine that seemed to work quite well.

Then she seemed to get worse; the pain had returned, and she was losing weight fast. I was no longer able to bring her downstairs, because it hurt her when I lifted her up in my arms. So I would gently lift her into a comfortable chair by the window in our bedroom so that she could see the garden. The doctor was marvellous and provided a variety of medicines to help the pain until we seemed to get the right one that controlled it. He suggested that she went into a hospice, but we all felt that she was better off at home. I would look after her with the help of our children, when they came home, and a wonderful nurse from the Macmillan Nursing Service who advised and helped us to care for my wife. It was made very clear to me that I would find it very hard work and sometimes distressing caring for my wife, but we had decided that it was the best thing for everyone.

It was extremely hard work, and sometimes I found it very difficult to care for her, but I loved her so much that I was prepared to do anything to help her. Over the next few weeks she became very thin indeed; she was so light that I could lift her out of bed by myself with ease, but it caused her so much pain that the nurse suggested that she would be better left in bed. This meant that I had to change her position every two hours to prevent her from getting pressure sores. I hated to see her in pain; it made me feel so pathetically inadequate, but the nurse was very good at getting the medications just right so that the pain was controlled. She was fully conscious and able to talk to us. There were times when I wished that she would die so that her suffering would stop, but a selfish part of me wanted her to live, to stay with me. How would I be able to cope without her?

During the last few days she slept a great deal, and I had to do everything for her. Sometimes she would have an accident in the bed, and I would have to clean her up just like a baby. The nurse was there as much as she could be and gently prepared the whole family for the inevitable outcome. Judith eventually died peacefully as the children and I sat by her bed and held her hand. I had cared for her for nearly a year. When she died I was so confused; I felt relief that she no longer suffered but an emptiness and longing for her to be with me still. I was still a fairly young man in my late forties. It all seemed so unfair. Why Judith?

My children came home a few days before she died and were obviously shocked and saddened when they saw their mother, a small shadow of the person that had brought them into the world and cared for them. I resented their interference in her care; this was my wife, and it was my responsibility to look after her to the end. After Judith's death the children stayed with me until after the funeral; then I asked them to go. They had to get on with their lives, and I had to get on with mine. It would have been very easy to have asked one of them to stay, but that was not what Judith and I had agreed. I had to go back to work and pick up the threads of my life. I thought it would be difficult, but I never realised how hard it would be in reality.

For weeks I was unable to concentrate properly. I went to work like a zombie, went through the motions of doing my job. Looking back I must have made some appalling mistakes and bad decisions. At home I would wander from room to room; I have no idea why. The silence was awful, the house so empty. I really had little or no reason to go on living. When I closed my eyes I could see Judith, but not as I had known her for all those healthy years but as the wasted sick woman that I had cared for. I wasn't eating or sleeping and was drinking far too much, and I was fortunate enough to have a very good friend who spent a great deal of time with me and he suggested that I saw the doctor. Our doctor was very kind and understanding and suggested that I contact the Compassionate Friends, which I did, and with their help I have managed to get my life back into some sort of order. Life was never the same again. Judith was my special love, the mother of our children. When she first became ill we were able to talk about the future. She knew she was dying and wanted me to be happy after she had gone and to find someone to take her place. At the time I agreed, but in my heart I felt that I would never find anyone to make me happy again.

Eventually, some five years later, I met a woman called Sarah and we are now married. I don't feel guilty or that I have betrayed Judith; in fact it just seemed to be what Judith wanted. Sarah never knew Judith, but she respects her memory and we talk about her quite naturally. My children are both married and are very fond of Sarah.

I am sure that caring for Judith helped me to accept her death. I believed that I had done all that I could to help her through her untimely death. My advice to anyone else in this dreadful situation is to be open with each other, to discuss all the options and to agree to do what they as a couple feel is right for them. Life is never the same again, but somehow you learn to accept a different life, one without the person that you loved so much.

SIMON JAMIESON

Simon's account of how he cared for his wife is very moving and typical of many husbands who dedicate themselves to the care of their wives. It is interesting to note that many wives who know that they are dying often say to their husband that the greatest compliment that he could pay to her is to marry again as it would mean that he couldn't manage without a wife like her. For details of the Compassionate Friends and the Macmillan Nursing Service, see page 365.

Whatever the cause of death, whether expected or unexpected, the expression of grief is a very personal, individual and necessary process. There are several stages of bereavement which can be recognised by the way that people react after a loved one has died. At first there is a numbness as described by the people in this chapter. They manage to get through the post-mortem, if one is required, then the funeral and family gathering as though it was not really happening to them but to someone else. It all seems unreal; very often the reality of the death of a loved one does not penetrate completely. Particularly in the case of the death of a loved one after many years of marriage, and the widow or widower is likely to live life as though the partner were still alive – for example, by continuing to cook and shop for two. This denial can continue for days or even months; it is not abnormal in any way but simply a stage through which this particular individual has to work.

For others the numb feeling immediately after the death may be followed by depression; there is a huge void in their life and the future seems to hold little or no hope for the grieving relative. Sometimes there are feelings of anger and a need to blame somebody else for the death of the loved one. Perhaps the doctor or the hospital is blamed and accused of inadequate or incompetent care. Sometimes the blame is placed on a relative or a friend because, in the eyes of the grieving relative, his failure to do something may have led to the death.

Another feeling during this stage is guilt: 'If only I had. . . .' Sometimes when the person has died after a long illness at home the carer feels that he should have done more, or the carer had spoken sharply to him before he died, or was not with him when he died. All these feelings are quite natural and need to be talked through until the bereaved person is able to accept that it was not his fault. These feelings of guilt and emptiness can so easily lead to depression if there is a lack of support and help. Depression and anxiety may well become apparent in a physical form by producing physical illnesses such as colitis, diver-ticulitis, gastritis and problems such as difficulty sleeping, lack of appetite, an inability to concentrate, agitation and tearfulness. Sometimes there may be psychological problems and even a desire to end his own life by committing suicide. Some people turn to alcohol, tranquillisers and drugs to blot out the sadness and depression.

As time goes on, an interest in life is reawakened; perhaps new interests are developed and, although life will never be the same, it does go on. This stage is known as acceptance; it is a very gradual stage and may take many years before the person is able to make plans for his future and adapt to a new way of life. There are still bound to be moments of great sadness – sometimes, as Margaret said, 'for no apparent reason and at the most unexpected times'. Christmas and other family occasions are inevitably going to reawaken memories, and the person will indeed need a great deal of comfort and support at these times.

When a child experiences the loss of a parent, a brother, a sister, or someone close, he or she may feel frightened, insecure and worried that other people in his or her world may also die. Sometimes a child has a deep-seated fear that it was something that he did that caused the death, so it was his fault. A child in this situation needs a great deal of love and affection, much more than normal. The child needs to be physically and mentally drawn closer to the family and given a chance to express anxieties and fears. When one of the family dies and the adults are feeling an enormous sense of loss and emptiness a child can, quite unintentionally, be left out, perhaps in order to spare his feelings. The reality is that this makes the situation worse.

A child's perception of death changes with age and experience. Under the age of four death may be seen by a child as being asleep for a long time, a reversible state, a temporary separation from someone that the child loves. This fear of being parted from someone loved leaves a great sense of insecurity. If it is the child that is dying, this may be one of his greatest fears. From the ages of five to nine the child may see death as something that really does happen; there is a certain curiosity about death and what happens to the body. If the child is dying, death may be seen as a punishment for something that he has done wrong. In the event of the death of someone close to the child he may feel that he has done something so very wrong that the death was a punishment for his wrongdoing. By eleven a child begins to perceive death on an adult level, as something final, and the inevitability that everyone will die at some point.

Children tend to express grief in their behaviour, by acting out feelings and emotions. They may become withdrawn, aggressive, panic, become anxious, display fear, regression and physical signs of grief. It may be months or even years before a child displays signs of the full impact of a death in the family.

Coming to terms with the death of a child will inevitably take a very long time. One of the reasons for this is not only the grieving for the loss of a very precious life but also the loss of what might have been, the child's future, and for parents the loss of part of themselves. The loss is no less when a child is stillborn or dies at birth; the parents, other children and grandparents all need to grieve for the loss of the baby. See also Chapter 1.

COPING WITH BEREAVEMENT

When someone dies friends and relatives are often very supportive initially but tend to underestimate the time it takes to grieve. They also tend to avoid talking about the person who has died, in case it upsets the bereaved.

Widows and Widowers

If your partner dies and you have no family at home, you may find it easier to stay with a relative or a friend in the very early days after the death, or you may prefer someone to come and stay with you in your own home. In general the recently bereaved gain great comfort from their own home and a regular routine, even if it does seem quiet and strange at first. Sometimes well-meaning relatives or friends try to persuade the bereaved person to take a long holiday or move house. However, it may be better to leave these decisions until a later date when decisions about the future can be taken more rationally. Often decisions made at this time will be irrational, confused by the shock of the loss of a loved one.

Support from friends and relatives is very important, but sometimes there is such an overwhelming feeling of apathy that you may not be able actively to seek support, but you do need to talk to someone about how you are feeling. Relatives may well be trying to overcome their own sense of loss and grief and feel unable to support you as well. There are self-help support groups which really are very beneficial. They offer time to share feelings and problems, can help with practical matters, offer a bereavement counselling service and can really understand how you are feeling because they have been widowed as well. See page 366 for more information.

Expect to feel emotionally confused. Allow yourself time to go through the stages of numbness, denial, grief, depression and even anger. Don't expect everything to get back to normal within a few weeks. Give yourself time. Don't turn away friends and relatives. Try to encourage their support; accept invitations to go away and stay with them for short periods if you feel it will help. In time try to develop some new interests, rekindle old interests and hobbies, get out of the house and into the community. All this will help you to become active and prevent depression.

Many people say that a strong faith and support from their church helped them through a very sad time in their lives.

Sometimes medical help is necessary if there is depression or physical illness; then the family doctor should be consulted. Contact a support group; they will help you. Don't be afraid to talk about your feelings and the loved one that has died. There is no need to forget someone who has died; they were and still are a very important part of your life.

The Loss of a Child

On page 366 there is information on how anyone can help parents whose child has died: what to do and not do. Try to remember that when a child dies his memory lives on. Don't be afraid to talk about your child, share stories of events and occasions, the crushed dreams and hopes. At first this will be very painful, but eventually sharing good memories will help you all. Encourage brothers, sisters and other members of the family, friends and neighbours to express their feelings and to talk about the child. Maybe they don't know what to say, so help them to help you.

Give your faith a chance to grow; even if you are not particularly religious, support from the church and prayer may well help you more than you once believed. Recognise and believe that the way you are reacting to the death of your child is normal, you are not going mad. It is normal to feel weak, helpless, powerless and confused. If you have a good day when you feel all right, don't feel guilty about it.

Get in touch with a support group and share your grief with other people who have also experienced the death of a child. Some of these people will be at different stages in their grief and will give you support and hope for the future.

You need time to enjoy yourself, to divert your mind in the midst of grief, so accept the invitation to go out to dinner, take a holiday, take up a new hobby or a sport and don't feel guilty if you find that you are enjoying yourself. Some people have found that taking a job, or doing voluntary work and generally not spending too much time at home, has helped them in their grief. It may help to keep a diary and to write down each day exactly how you feel. Later when you read this you will be surprised just how much progress you have made.

A Child and the Loss of a Parent or Sibling

Make sure that the school is aware of the death of the sibling or parent so that they can help, too. This is particularly important in a large school where a chance remark by a teacher who doesn't know what has happened may be very hurtful. The child may well react by behaving in a variety of ways including withdrawal, aggression, panic, anxiety, anger, guilt, fear, regression, and the school should be aware that this might happen. It is important that a child is able to express feelings, to cry, be sad or angry both at home and at school.

Teachers and friends at school are the bereaved child's second family, and it sometimes helps if the school can plant a tree or create some other kind of memorial to the dead person so that other children and teachers can acknowledge and share the grief and help the child through a very difficult time in his or her life.

Children need time to express their feelings, to talk about any feelings of guilt and their thoughts about death and the person that has died. They need even more love and attention at the moment than normal; they need to know that they are loved and it was not their fault in any way. They need time and to be encouraged to talk about the person that has died, the good times that they had together. Keep photographs and special mementoes around the house. Don't be tempted to hide them away in case it should upset the child; it is important to keep the memory alive.

How to Cope with Special Occasions

Probably the most difficult occasion for anyone who is bereaved is Christmas-time. Everyone seems to be busy preparing for a happy family occasion, and the bereaved person is only too aware of the huge void in his life. If you are planning Christmas and have been recently bereaved or someone is going to be with you who has been bereaved, then talk about any plans, try to establish what should be done for the best. Some people prefer to stay at home and maintain the usual Christmas tradition, while others would prefer to do something completely different, perhaps taking a holiday abroad. If the death has been in your family, don't be afraid to make changes. You could open presents on Christmas Eve instead of on Christmas Day, have your family meal at a different time, or go to a friend for the day, attend a different church service.

If it was a child that died, some parents gain comfort from donating the money that they would have spent on their child to a favourite charity. If you have other children, you could put up the stockings as usual, or in a different place, or put up a stocking for the dead child and put in a note with special thoughts from yourself and the other members of the family so that they can be shared and read, giving everyone a chance to express their feelings.

Some parents decide to do something special to remember their absent child, such as burning a special candle or buying a special plant for the family as a living memorial to the child.

Don't be afraid to say how you feel and what you would like to change or not change. Do whatever makes you feel most comfortable.

WHAT TO DO WHEN SOMEONE DIES

This may well vary depending on where you live and the circumstances of the death, but in general there are some basic guidelines:

- If the person has died at home, contact your family doctor who will certify the death and give you a certificate. If the dead person was not receiving medical treatment from a doctor prior to the death, there may be a post-mortem to establish the cause of the death. The doctor will also tell you how to register the death. If any organs are to be donated, tell your doctor about these wishes and he will organise all this.
- If the death occurs in hospital, the doctor will certify the death and the ward staff will tell you how to register the death. If there is to be a post-mortem, they will organise this. If any organs are to be donated, make sure that the hospital staff are aware of these wishes.
- Contact any relatives and tell them what has happened. Ask for support if you feel you need it.
- Contact your local clergyman.
- After death the body will be put flat and the arms crossed across the chest and the eyes closed. In hospital the staff will do all this and the body will be taken to the chapel of rest or the mortuary. The funeral directors will collect the body from the hospital. If the death occurs at home, contact the funeral directors and they will fulfil the family's wishes. They will also help you to decide where the body will wait until the funeral, the starting-point, time and place of the funeral, whether there will be a funeral service, where the dead person is to be buried or cremated, whether you want flowers or donations to a named charity.

- Contact your solicitor and anyone else that is important in sorting out any problems such as an accountant or business partner.

These steps have to be taken immediately, and it will help you if a relative or a close friend is with you to help or even to do these things for you.

- Later the death will have to be registered at the register office.
- You will need to establish if there is a will and who the executor is.
- If there is no will, letters of administration must be obtained.
- You may need legal advice to sort out taxes, financial problems, any life-insurance cover and what will happen to any property, in particular your home.
- You will need to return the passport, driving licence, membership cards, credit cards and so on.
- Eventually you may feel that you want to sort out and dispose of some of your loved one's belongings. This is a very stressful chore, and it is advisable to get someone to help you when you feel that you want or indeed need to.
- Contact a support group if you feel that they can help you. See page 366 for the addresses and for advice on financial help.

As you can see by this list, many problems have to be sorted out following the death of a loved one, so it is much better for the people left behind if these questions are raised and discussed before someone dies.

SUICIDE

People are driven to take their own life for a variety of reasons and at any stage in life from the desperate young person to the elderly person who sees no reason for living. Françoise, through a series of circumstances, decided to take her own life and was unsuccessful. She has described to me her feelings and how she has survived.

In my case I didn't plan to take my own life; it just happened. It was a very quick thing. I was in so much mental pain at that time in my life that I couldn't see the end of the tunnel. I just couldn't cope. I had had enough. I took a lot of dangerous pills that had been prescribed for me by my doctor because of all the problems in my life. I swallowed these pills with a large amount of alcohol. Looking back, I don't think that doctors should give people with problems like mine so many pills at a time. The combination of the pills and the alcohol was certainly enough to kill me. I knew exactly what I was doing. I wasn't going to live the rest of my life on doctor's pills and visiting psychiatrists. If I had had more understanding from my doctor, I don't think I would have done it. The doctors really don't have enough time for people like me.

I was found by my husband, and taken to the Charing Cross Hospital. I knew that my husband would be coming round to the flat later that night but I thought that I would have been dead by then. I became unconscious very quickly. He must have found me and arranged to get me to the hospital. However, I do remember the staff at the hospital putting a large tube down my throat which was very painful and extremely unpleasant and then having a stomach washout. Apparently I was on a life-support machine for twenty-four hours; I was in some kind of coma. I remember a nurse coming and shaking me to wake me up; she was wonderful, so very kind. I was very lucky she understood and wanted to keep my husband away as she appreciated the torment that I was in. I can remember that I couldn't see her properly when she approached me; it was as though she was filtered, but I could hear her voice quite clearly. I tried to kill myself because of the problems in my life that had accumulated until I had what I can only describe as a major breakdown and suicide seemed the only solution. It happened because I no longer had any control and could no longer bear the mental pain.

In hospital they did nothing to help me. I was in a big hospital in London miles away from my home; there was no one to visit, no one came to smile at me, to hold my hand and show some affection. On top of this there was no room for me on a female ward, so I was on a male ward. They moved me after two days into a small room; they took away all my clothes, and I felt as though I was in a prison. Psychiatric help was offered, but I didn't need it now; I was not mentally ill. I was more normal after my suicide attempt than before. My system had broken down before, and looking back I think it was all brought to a head, but it has taken me years to recover. I was and still am very pleased that I did not succeed in killing myself.

When I came home my recovery was very slow and progressive, occurring over many years. I needed an enormous amount of affection and understanding; you really need someone to help you. But basically you have to do the work yourself.

The person who helped me most was our local clergyman. It all happened by accident really; I am not Church of England and had never been to his church, but one day he happened to call on me at home. He used to tour around the village and just drop in on people. It was not difficult to see that I was under stress, because I had tears in my eyes all the time. I was trying to disguise my distress and we were walking around the garden, and then he asked after my husband and I just literally burst into tears. I just told him everything. He listened as I emptied out everything that was hurting me. After that he visited me frequently. He never preached religion or the word of God to me, and never told me to go to church. He helped me with myself to regain my confidence. He used to make me laugh and brought out all the good in me, making me realise the sort of person that I was. He helped me to get rid of some of the bad things; he worked very hard to get me back on the right road again.

I felt an enormous sense of relief that I could talk to him; he absorbed some of the pain. I needed someone to take away some of the pain and, because he was not related to me or even knew me very well I felt I could talk to and trust him. He was very gentle and understanding. He used to make me laugh, and that was the best medicine. You have to be very careful who you talk to; you learn to be selective, because you are very vulnerable and people tend to take advantage of you.

I went to see a psychiatrist, but it didn't help me. My local doctor was very good; he gave me tablets to calm me during the day. I carried on with my life and I think I coped fairly well – caring for my son, my husband changing jobs, moving house – but I am the sort of person who makes things happen. At times I was so anxious that I was shaking, my heart beating fast; I had difficulty breathing and a tight painful feeling in my stomach. It was real panic, and I felt totally drained.

I knew that something had to be done about all this, so I went to a specialist and he explained that there was nothing physically wrong with me but that I was under stress. It has taken me five years to get to where I am now. Anyone experiencing problems like mine should not expect things to improve overnight; it takes a long time, but it will depend on the amount of support and the surroundings that you have. I was very much alone; if you have a family around, it might be easier.

I have never thought of taking my life again and I never would; the whole experience was just so horrific. Part of the convalescence is a feeling that you are in touch with the world again; you grow up and recognise yourself as a person. Then you start to believe in yourself, no longer being pushed around by other people; you become stronger. It also helps to help other people with all sorts of problems; your experience can be used to benefit others.

The worst thing you can say to anyone in this state is 'Pull yourself together'. Because you just can't; words are very hurtful. When you are depressed and overwhelmed with problems, hurtful words go round and round in your head. I felt as if I had been demolished by a bulldozer and I have had to put all the pieces back together.

FRANÇOISE

Françoise's suicide attempt was fortunately unsuccessful, and like so many other people who decide to take their own life she did not really want to die; it is more a case of they can't go on living with all the problems and unhappiness in their lives. What they need most of all is someone whom they can really trust and talk to, to try to sort out problems that appear so overwhelming. Not everyone is lucky enough to find that special person to help, but you could always call the Samaritans and talk to someone there who will listen to you and try to help without making judgements. See page 367 for more information.

Often people are successful in their attempt to commit suicide. A bright intelligent young man of only sixteen was successful in his suicide, and his parents, who wish to remain anonymous, explain what happened and how they felt.

Our son had been a very happy child but during his adolescence had become withdrawn and was prone to bouts of severe depression. He was having difficulty at school and seemed unable to talk about his problems. The family doctor treated the whole thing as 'Just a phase he was going through; he would grow out of it'. We never felt that he took it very seriously.

Our son hanged himself when he was sixteen, and we still believe that really he did not want to die. We have both blamed ourselves and wondered if we did all we could to help him; perhaps there was something that we should have done to prevent this destructive end to his life. These questions will never be answered, and we can only hope that in time the pain will lessen.

ANONYMOUS

Every year over 200,000 people in the United Kingdom try to kill themselves. Many of these people don't want to die; they simply do not want to go on living with things the way they are. But 4,000 of these people do kill themselves. Suicide is one of the ten main causes of death, and the second most common cause of death amongst young people under the age of twenty-five. Most people who attempt suicide are not mentally ill, but are desperate and lonely. Many of them have problems that they feel they are unable to talk through with friends, family, the doctor or even a clergyman. The Samaritans are friends to people who are feeling desperate, lonely or suicidal. They are all volunteers and come from every age, background and walk of life.

The Samaritans are there to listen to you when it seems that there is no one else that cares or wants to listen. They will listen and try to help you sort things out. But they won't tell you what to do, and they won't tell anyone about what you have said unless you want them to. In fact you need not even tell them your name. You can talk to them on the telephone, write, or meet a volunteer face to face. See page 367 for more information. The Compassionate Friends will also support families bereaved as the result of a child's suicide: see page 366. Official statistics and studies indicate that those people who are most likely successfully to commit suicide are:

- those with psychiatric illness, depression, alcoholism, other addictions, early dementia or organic brain syndrome;
- those who are suffering stress from life due to bereavement, separation, moving house, loss of a job or incapacitating physical illness;
- where there is a family or previous history of depression and alcoholism – those who have attempted suicide before;
- those who display symptoms such as suicidal thoughts, ideas of guilt and unworthiness, lethargy and social maladjustment, hopelessness, agitation and restlessness;
- personal aspects: people over the age of forty, immigrants, the widowed, divorced, separated, unemployed, recently retired or socially isolated.

The rôle of the family doctor is clearly vital as the majority of suicide attempts are made by people taking medication prescribed by their doctor. One study of 100 suicides in 1974 found that 40 per cent had visited their family doctor in the week before they died and over 70 per cent in the previous three months. It is important for friends and members of the family to take suicide threats seriously and seek help from either the family doctor or someone like the Samaritans.

Suicide attempts in adolescence are more common in girls, and the most common form is taking an overdose of drugs such as aspirin. The word 'attempt' should not be taken to mean a failed suicide but, rather, an expression of deep feelings and difficulties which the person is unable to express directly. It is quite likely in these cases that both the young person and the family will need help and support in the form of family therapy. Ask your doctor for advice and for more information.

CHAPTER ELEVEN

Work

Deciding on a career needs to be undertaken very carefully by the young person concerned and planned in conjunction with school and parents. Young people these days are only too aware of the difficulties of obtaining employment, and parents become anxious that their child will not be able to find employment and will become disillusioned with life.

> My parents told me not to worry about getting a job until I left school. I tried to talk to them about my worries because I knew that so many of my friends had not been able to get a job and they have nothing to do and no money. The school told me that I had to pass exams and get qualifications, but I was not very good at school work.
>
> When I left school at sixteen I couldn't get a job and I am still unemployed, so I was right, but it hasn't done me much good.
>
> MARK BOLT

Mark is certainly not alone; so many young people are in exactly the same situation. Unfortunately his parents were wrong. Decisions and plans about the future should have been made long before he left school.

The young person is the one who should make the final decision about the sort of career that he or she would like to follow. Parents can help by discussing what the young person is interested in. Together draw up a list of his or her strengths and weaknesses. Try to establish what they would like to achieve. Start by asking these questions: What is he or she good at? Would he or she like to work with their hands, indoors, in an office, outside, with people or on their own? Write down the answers to these questions in two columns, the first column containing likes and strengths, the second dislikes and weaknesses. Start to draw up a picture of preferences and abilities.

The next stage is to investigate what jobs are available in your area. This can be done by visiting the local job centre and asking for advice or scanning the local paper. Next establish what these jobs involve, talk to people who are already undertaking this kind of employment and find out how much they enjoy or dislike the job. If this type of employment appeals to the young person, the next step is to find out what kind of qualifications are required. If it involves training, how long will the training last? Investigate the working conditions. How far will the young person have to travel to work? How will he or she get there? How much holiday is allowed per year? What hours will be worked? What is the pay? Are there any benefits? What are the promotion prospects?

Young people who have an idea of what they would like to do and the qualifications required are much more likely to make an effort to gain qualifications if they can see a reason for doing so. Parents can also help by encouraging the young person to get some experience of the working world by helping him or her to get some work in the school holidays. It is important that parents look closely at their own values. How important is work to them? Young people are bound to be influenced by their parents' and friends' attitudes. Simply talk about the world of work, the jobs that are difficult to find, the ones that have a high stress level, the ones that involve travel, the professions, the risky jobs, the job opportunities for women, the exciting ones, the jobs that offer security, the jobs that offer prospects of promotion and all aspects of as many jobs as you can find out about. Inside experience is always valuable, so friends and relations should be encouraged to talk about their job experiences.

The school also plays a very large part in the young person's future. It is important to discuss career hopes and plans with the teachers; gaining the right qualifications for a specific career is very important. Parents need to find out exactly which subjects are being studied and which jobs or careers does this exclude. Talk to the teachers and the careers adviser and find out if your child is likely to be successful in the examinations required for a chosen career. If not, what can be done to help or what career would be more suitable? There is no point in setting unachievable and unrealistic career goals.

MAKING AN APPLICATION FOR A JOB OR A CAREER

If the job looks attractive or a career decision is made, discuss it with the young person and establish that it is the sort of thing that the young person would like to do; then find out how to apply, to whom and when.

The next step is for the young person to write to the prospective employer for an application form. The letter should start 'Dear Mr So-

and-so' and end 'Yours sincerely'. If you do not know the name of the person, then begin 'Dear sir' and sign it 'Yours faithfully'. Sign your name with your usual signature and then print your name in capital letters under your signature. Write it in your very best handwriting, ensure the spelling is correct. Include details of where you saw the advertisement and ask for an application form. This letter is the first impression that a prospective employer will form of you, so it is very important that you give a good impression. If you then put in an application form, this letter will be filed with it and referred to when your application arrives.

COMPLETING AN APPLICATION FORM

So many young people fail to get an interview for employment because their application is badly or incorrectly completed. If you, the parent, are not sure how to complete an application form, suggest that the young person takes it to school and asks the English teacher for advice. The important points to remember about completing an application form are:

- Photocopy the original form and practise on the copy. Make sure that all the details fit in the spaces provided and that the information is in the correct space.
- Answer the questions truthfully; there is no point saying that you have more qualifications than you have as they will ask for proof of the qualifications, and will not accept that the certificates were all burned in a fire or the dog chewed them!
- If you can get someone to type in the answers to questions, this will look far more impressive than a handwritten application. It will also give the impression that you have taken time and trouble over the presentation and are serious in your application. If your application is handwritten, make sure it is very neat and clear.
- Read the instructions carefully before completing the application form. For example: 'Complete this application form in capital letters in black ink or in type.' Not a good start if you write in long hand in blue ink. Some will specify the colour of the ink used, so that the application form can be photocopied. If your application form arrives and you obviously have not read the instructions, there is little chance that you will be offered an interview.

- Make sure that there are no spelling mistakes. When you have written it out in rough, on the copy, read it through and get someone to check it before you copy it carefully on to the original application form.
- Some application forms ask you to write any further remarks or comments. Do not leave this blank; this is your opportunity to sell yourself on paper. Tell them why you would be good at the job. Don't repeat information that is already in the application form, but add anything else you feel will demonstrate that you are the right person for this job.
- If they ask for 'referees', choose people you have known for at least two years, who will give you a good reference and have some standing in the community. Always write and ask the people concerned if you may give their name as a reference and tell them something about the job that you have applied for.
- Make a note of the closing date and be sure that your application arrives in good time.

If on application the young person is unsuccessful, you may need to go back to the original questions and reassess the situation together.

PREPARING FOR THE INTERVIEW

Parents can help a great deal in preparation for the interview. From early childhood encourage the young person to mix and talk to adults; this builds confidence and helps them to conduct conversations with adults that are not relatives. Encourage the young person to talk to adults on the telephone. Teach him or her how to introduce himself to strangers. Practise asking suitable questions about the job for which he has applied. When the interviewer says 'Is there anything that you would like to ask me?' there is nothing worse than a negative reply, so plan and rehearse a few suitable questions. If the young person is still at school, the staff will be able to give some practice at interviewing skills; if not, you can have a few practice runs at home.

Practise showing interest and enthusiasm by looking alert, smiling at the interviewer, sitting upright and forward in the chair and not slouching or sinking into the chair. Look at the interviewer when being spoken to and when answering questions. Help the young person to present his or her good points without bragging or showing off. Help the young person to develop the ability to listen and concentrate on what is being said and to answer clearly and concisely.

Presentation is very important, so looking smart and well groomed is essential, but don't force the young person to wear something that is uncomfortable or out of character. Make sure that all the travel arrangements are well planned so that the young person arrives at the right place at the correct time. Ensure that all the necessary documents such as examination certificates, birth certificate and anything else that is relevant are collected together in good time prior to the interview. Plenty of encouragement towards positive thinking during the days leading up to the interview and reassurance are very important. This is particularly important these days with so many young people applying for the same job, and there is a greater chance that they may not be successful, so reassure the young person that if they are not successful this time it is very good experience for the next interview.

THE UNEMPLOYED YOUNG PERSON

These days there is a strong possibility that a great many young people will be unemployed, and this can give rise to problems at home. Parents are naturally anxious that the young person is wasting his life but really through no fault of his own.

My son had been unemployed and for three years, ever since he had left school. At first he applied for lots of jobs but was unsuccessful and he seemed to give up. At nineteen he was still unemployed and at home. He used to get up in the morning just before lunch-time, did nothing to help in the house, either argued with the rest of the family or sulked in his room. He was in with a bad crowd and eventually got into trouble with the police. My husband threatened to throw him out of our home. He was put on probation. This was probably the shock that he needed to bring him to his senses.

Over the years we had tried to get him interested in one of these training schemes but when we suggested it we were told that it was 'a government con to get people to work for nothing'. When the probation officer suggested it . . . well, that thankfully was a different matter. He went on a course and learned all about motor mechanics. He had always been interested in motor bikes and cars. Eventually a garage took him on, for very little pay, but it was a start. I suppose he was one of the lucky ones; he learned a trade and now has a job.

My advice, for what it is worth, to anyone with a son or daughter in this situation is to get help and advice from someone outside the family, if your child won't listen to you.

HELEN SPENCER

There are a variety of training schemes available for young people: see page 368 for more information. Young people who seem unable to find employment need to reassess their strengths and weaknesses and make sure that they are looking for employment in suitable areas. They may have received poor career advice at an earlier stage and are now in need of some further help. See page 368 for more information.

Unemployment means plenty of time and very little money and, as Helen points out, this leads to problems with young people floating about with nothing to do; but this doesn't necessarily mean that they are willing to help around the house and make themselves useful. However, it is important to help the young person to keep his self-respect, to prevent him from becoming bitter and depressed. Signs of problems are when the young person says that he feels worthless and of no importance. He spends more and more time locked in the bedroom alone, stays in bed for most of the day, is bored and only interested in watching television; there may be a loss of appetite, excessive drinking of alcohol or even drug-taking. In the event of problems like this it is important to seek help from outside the family; a talk with your family doctor would be a good place to start.

To help the young person through a time of unemployment parents might try encouraging him to take a short course at the local college or a training scheme or to develop a hobby. It is surprising how many hobbies become full-time employment. Keep on the lookout for part-time work or temporary employment just for work experience. See page 312 for how this affects unemployment benefits. Encourage the young person to join a sports club, or to keep fit at home, to join any club activity that he enjoys, to keep in contact with friends whether they are in employment or not, to continue to look for a job and not to give up. Reinforce and reassure the young person that he is not a failure; the lack of a job is not his fault but a sign of the times.

ADULTS WORKING

Women who work are almost certainly under the same pressures as men; in fact married women and single parents are likely to be under

greater strain than married men. Married women and single parents have
all the problems of home and work to balance and contend with. Single
parents both male and female and working women have to survive in the
world of work and caring for the family. They start the day by getting
children up, dressed and fed; then have to get to work, cope with all the
stresses and responsibilities of the working day, make sure that children
are collected in time, taken home, fed, entertained, homework
supervised and finally put to bed. Then there is the housework, the
washing and cooking. Extras include children's hobbies and outside-
the-home activities, time spent listening to tales about school, having
time for discussions and listening to problems and worries. There may
also be other family responsibilities of ageing parents. The married
woman also has to support and care for her husband.

WORKING MOTHERS

Many married women work because they have to and not necessarily
because they want to. These days only a few single salaries are enough to
support a family, so the woman goes out to work to provide the second
salary. Other career women, perhaps in middle management or in jobs
where they compete with men, are under the same stresses as their male
colleagues, but sometimes the stresses are greater. A woman doctor puts
her point of view.

When I was a medical student in the seventies I was very much in the
minority. I felt that I was tolerated by some of my colleagues, while
others openly admitted to thinking that giving a woman a valuable
place in a medical school was a waste of resources as I would
inevitably get married, have babies and leave the profession.
Throughout my career I have always had to work hard and prove to
my male colleagues, nurses and patients that I am good at my job.

I did get married, to another doctor, and worked throughout my
pregnancy and until four weeks before the birth of our first baby. I
went back to work six weeks later. I could have stayed at home with
my baby, but I knew that if I took this time out I would be overtaken
by my male colleagues and have difficulty getting back into the
profession. I had worked hard to become a doctor and intended to
climb the professional ladder, so inevitably there were sacrifices to be
made. I met a great deal of prejudice from senior doctors and younger

colleagues who believed that women should stay at home with their children.

I am now a senior registrar at a London teaching hospital and intend to become a consultant. I have two very happy and well-balanced children who have come to no harm because their mother has a career.

Working mothers are often criticised for having children and then employing someone else to care for them while they go out to work. Most working mothers already have feelings of guilt about leaving their children, and this only reinforces their fears and worries about the effect of their actions upon their children. Many working mothers feel guilty that they are falling short of being the perfect mother and wife. The other side of this guilt problem is that her family responsibilities will mean that there may be a shortfall in the way that she does her job. What working mothers need to remember is that they bring back to the home their experiences of the working world, and as a result are more interesting and often make more time for their family than if they were with them all day.

Many women work to raise the standard of living for their family, while others go back to work because they are bored and lonely at home. Today women with young children manage to combine work and a young family, many of them taking part-time jobs. This is particularly true of women who have completed a training and have an intellectual need that is not met at home, where they become bored and even angry and resentful. In Great Britain there are about 6 million women who go out to work, and about half of them are married.

In order for the wife and mother to work successfully she needs the support and encouragement of her partner. The most important issue to sort out is the safe and adequate care of the children. For some families with relatives living nearby, the choice may well be that one of the family care for the child while she is at work. The most important point is that the mother trusts the relative to care for her child. This is often a very satisfactory arrangement as the child is cared for by the extended family who love him as one of their own. Another option is to share the care of your children with a friend. You look after her child while she goes out to work, and in return she will look after yours. Times when children are ill, or you have to change the hours that you work, or you are unavoidably detained at work, can put a strain on a friendship and cause problems.

Other women prefer to put the care of their children on a more business-like footing where relatives and friends are not involved;

careful selection of a childminder who is paid to care for your child is a solution. See Chapter 3 for more information. Selecting a childminder has to be done very carefully as the wrong person could have a detrimental effect on your child.

Another alternative is a nanny, someone who is professionally trained to care for babies and children. Nannies can be quite expensive. They will live in your home or some of them will come to your home on a daily basis. If you are thinking of having a nanny who lives in, you will need to provide suitable living accommodation and be prepared to treat her as one of the family. The advantage of employing a nanny who lives with you is that she is always there and is able to establish a close relationship with your child. When your child starts school she will be able to take and collect him or her and relieve you of the worry of being back in time to collect your child. If the child is unwell, you will be able to leave him or her in the capable hands of someone that you trust in the comfort of your own home. To find a nanny look in the national newspapers and certain magazines or contact an agency. See page 299 for more details.

Mother's helps and *au pairs* are another alternative; many are very good indeed, although professionally untrained. Careful selection of the right person is very important. For details of where to get this kind of help, see page 300. You could advertise in the newspaper for a mother's help and then interview the candidates bearing in mind that you are looking for someone who is caring, loving, kind and has the best interests of your child at heart – someone who will care for your child, who will be an interesting and stimulating person and most of all who is completely trustworthy. Make sure that you ask for references and follow them up before making your selection.

For the under-fives there are day nurseries which offer a good standard of care as they have to comply with government guidelines. They are usually open every day of the week and for longer hours than school hours. Some day nurseries will take babies from three months old, and others are for children from two to five years old. There are also private day nurseries which are run by private individuals, and the charges can be quite high. Workplace day nurseries are provided by the company for its employees. The charges are usually subsidised. Voluntary and community day nurseries encourage the parents who use the care to be involved in managing the day nursery; charges are usually relatively low. See page 299 for more information about day nurseries.

The woman who goes out to work may feel that in order to be successful in her career she will need to put a great deal of energy into ensuring success at work and meeting the needs of her children.

Sometimes this leaves very little for her husband or partner. This is by no means intentional; she wants to be a loving, caring and good wife or partner to him, but in some cases has difficulty living up to his expectations of what a wife should be, which leads to feelings of guilt. This of course depends on the attitude of the man in her life.

Inevitably meals will be late and may be out of a tin or the freezer. The house will not be quite as clean and tidy as it was when she was at home all day, even if someone does come in and do the cleaning. Buttons don't get sewn on shirts, socks are not always mended, the ironing tends to pile up. But there is no reason why everyone in the family shouldn't lend a hand with the household chores. Children, as soon as they are capable, are usually very willing to lend a hand, and partners are perfectly capable as well.

Planning is a very important part of the life of the working mother – making a list of all the things that should be done, on a daily, weekly and monthly basis. Things written down are more likely to be remembered and attended to. It also relieves the overwhelming feeling of too much to do if you can see what you have achieved when items are crossed off the list. Plan the whole day and work through the tasks that have to be done. Rushing about in the morning, leaving in a hurry with all the breakfast things stacked in the kitchen sink, is a bad start to the day as those dishes will look even more sordid when you return in the evening. The same principle applies at the end of the day. Give yourself some time to think about what you will wear in the morning, lay it out all ready. Try to allow yourself some time to relax before going to bed. Ensure that you get adequate rest; if you become over-tired, every day will become more difficult.

Time for yourself and your family is essential. Make time for pleasure, sport and exercise and you will find that you are better able to cope with any stress. Shopping is a problem if you are working all week and unable to get to the shops, so do a large weekly shop making sure that you have enough supplies for the family for the whole week. Keep up a stock of basic items such as toothpaste, soap, washing powder, cleaning materials and so on.

Make appointments for the whole family to see the dentist and hairdresser at the same time. You obviously cannot plan for the unexpected visit to the doctor, but other appointments can usually be arranged so that the whole family can be seen on the same day.

Children of twelve years and under should not be left in the house alone. For older children who return home before you, with no friendly neighbour to look after them, here are some guidelines to ensure their safety:

- Tell your child that he or she must go straight home and telephone you at work as soon as he or she gets in.
- Leave a spare key with a neighbour in case the child loses his or her own key.
- No cooking until you get home. Leave a cold snack for them and a friendly note.
- No friends to come round to the house until you are home.
- Suggest that he or she gets on with homework and that you will look at it as soon as you get home. Make sure that you remember to do so. If there is no homework, he or she could work on a hobby. It is important to show an interest in whatever activity has been done.
- Leave the phone number of the doctor, and an emergency number to call if there are any problems.

School holidays can be a problem if you are unable to take enough holiday to cover the entire period. Well in advance, find someone who will be able to look after the children. There may be a responsible student at your local college who would like to earn some extra money. Make sure that you check references and are completely satisfied that they are trustworthy.

There are organised camps: see page 307 for more information. There are also organisations that will help if you are a single parent: see page 369.

SINGLE PARENTS

In Chapter 4 I have also discussed the problems associated with being a single parent, whether by choice or because your partner has died or you are divorced or separated. Working and caring for a family on your own, whether you are the father or the mother, generates many of the problems that I have discussed above, and the problems are even greater if there is no partner to share the responsibilities and work involved. There are various groups and organisations that will help and support the single parent, and the details are on page 307.

The single parent is often unable to afford to pay someone to care for the children while they are at work. Gingerbread is an association for one-parent families, with a national network of local self-help groups. In order for the single parent to go out to work there needs to be a child-care facility which operates for long enough hours and which takes full responsibility for the safety and whereabouts of the child. The Gingerbread group provides some child care for the under-fives, and after-school care. See page 307 for more information. Particular problems are experienced during school holidays. The Gingerbread group are able to offer help with established child-care facilities but they will also help you to set up your own in your area with other single parents. See page 307 for more information.

RÔLE-SWAPPING

Keith and Pam Leggett decided that Keith would look after the home and Pam would continue with her career. Keith describes the rôle of the househusband.

The decision to swap rôles was by no means an easy one. It involves a long-term commitment; both parties must be absolutely clear in their mind exactly what they are committing themselves, and each other, to. The wife is now the dominant partner in the relationship. She is the one who is seen to leave the house in the mornings. It is she who has to work late at the office, and who brings home the wages. She expects her husband to have a decent meal waiting for her when she eventually arrives home. As for the husband at home, it is he who gets out of bed first. He cooks breakfast, deals with baby, cleans the house, cooks lunch, and of course does the shopping. It all appears, at face value, to be perfectly straightforward. It all started on 15 December 1977. I had been working as a store detective for the previous two years. I was becoming disillusioned with my so-called prospects within this particular company. Pam, my wife, at that time worked as a health visitor. On returning to work she was also caring for Oliver, our first child, who was born in June. She would take him with her in the car while she did her rounds. At first, during the early weeks, all went well. But gradually life became more difficult. It was winter, and quite often circumstances would prevent her from taking him with her. This of course meant that I would have to alter my day off, which would sometimes prove to be difficult, to say the least. We had often discussed rôle reversal, and now it seemed a very good idea. I left my job instantly following a row over wages, which were pitifully low considering the responsibility, and there began a whole new career, unpaid but, as was proven later, a wealth of experience.

I have always related well to children, having several nephews and nieces, and I had also worked in a children's home for two years. The rôle of a father at home came easily for me. Learning to feed, wash and dress this little monster became a test for my patience, and taught me to control my temper. Already I could feel myself changing, becoming gentler. There were many funny and trying experiences. One day when I had just changed his pants he found the pot plants, and with absolute delight grabbed handfuls of earth and rubbed it into his romper suit. So off to the bedroom for another change and a ticking-off. I then deposited this yobbo of fourteen months on to the lounge carpet. It took just a couple of minutes to collect the soiled clothes and feed them into the washing machine. When I returned to the lounge his lordship was emptying the contents of the coal-bucket. However, instances such as these make one realise why wives often seem to develop headaches! I know that I did. That was just one child.

In November 1979, Emily arrived. The following summer we moved to a 1930s three-bedroomed detached house that was dirty and in need of some improvement. Trying to carry out the house improvements, caring for two scallywags and holding down a job at a hospital at night meant working three twelve-hour shifts on the Friday, Saturday and Sunday nights. Monday morning I would rush home to relieve Pam of the children, who were by then washed and dressed, having had breakfast, and take Oliver to the local school with Emily in tow. Home again for a quick breakfast, then take Emily to play school. Then rush back home in our ageing Citroën. By 9.50 a.m. I was in bed and hopefully asleep. At 11.15 a.m. I was awake preparing to collect Emily. I kept up this routine for two years. The months just flew past. In the summer I would snatch a couple of hours' sleep and then join the family down on the beach for a romp in the sand. At that time I used to feel far too tired to worry about doing the housework. During the week I felt like a zombie, but would still take the children to the park and walk the dog.

At the end of 1983 I left my job at the hospital. One of the patients asked me if I would be prepared to care for her in my own home for an agreed sum. After some considerable thought, we converted the dining-room into a bedroom, and in July the lady moved in with us. She is now ninety-three and very much part of the family.

On summing up, I don't think that I would have coped so well without Pam's unfailing support. Likewise she without mine. Having adjusted to home life, I now work full-time from home and can easily handle the family affairs. Both children enjoy a full and happy life. They are both equally fond of their mother and me. So being in my company far more often than their mother's has made no difference at all.

There are three things a child needs to make him or her a useful and happy member of the family and society: love, time and discipline. Not necessarily in that order, but lots of it.

KEITH LEGGETT

From my point of view the only extras that I would add would be: the occasional almost jealous feelings of the fact that I was not there to witness the developmental progress of the children; for example, Keith was there when Oliver first successfully used the pot and I wasn't!

Little things like I always noticed that when Keith dressed the children the colours clashed. I always made sure that I was there for the children's school functions, doctor's appointments, clinic check-ups and so on.

As far as my career development, I did not feel that I wanted to progress at as fast a rate as a man would have done, when the children were young. I turned down one job because I did not want the extra travel and time away when the children were small. This has made my career development slow.

I think that Keith gave the children much more of his time, being at home, than I think that I would have done, as I feel that women are more concerned generally about housework and this often comes first.

PAM LEGGETT

PREGNANCY AND WORKING

Many women these days work through their pregnancy and some go back to work a few weeks after the birth of their child. If you plan to work through your pregnancy, check with the doctor caring for you that there is no risk to your health in the work that you do. If there is a risk to your health or to that of the baby, talk to your employer and establish if it is possible to change your work routine and eliminate the risks.

Early in your pregnancy you need to discuss maternity rights and benefits with the personnel department or your employer. For details of maternity rights and benefits, see page 283. If you are planning to return after the birth of your baby, you will need to discuss maternity leave: see page 285 for details.

During your pregnancy try not to get overtired. If you do feel tired or unwell when you are at work, talk to the nurse, supervisor or a union representative. It may be possible to arrange for you to lie down or put your feet up for a while during your lunch-break.

Make sure that your posture is good. When standing try not to lean back. Stand up straight with your feet slightly apart. When you are sitting try not to slouch: put a cushion in the small of your back and sit up straight. It is important how you lift things when you are pregnant. Hold whatever you are lifting close to your body and lift by straightening your legs, so that they do the work and not your back.

What you eat is vital to your own health and to that of your baby. If you are unable to get a well-balanced nourishing meal at work, take a packed lunch with you. Have a good breakfast before you leave for work. If you are feeling nauseated or actually being sick in the mornings, leave more time to get up slowly. If you still feel sick by the time you arrive at work, ask if you can sit down for a while. Most people are very willing to help you in any way that they can; there is, however, a small minority that are intolerant and believe that if you are unable to pull your weight you shouldn't be at work. But don't let this stop you from asking for help.

When you get home try not to overdo things; if you can afford to, get some help in the house. Go for a short walk when you get home; it will help you to unwind and relax and keep you fit.

STRESS AT WORK

In Chapter 8 I have outlined the physical and psychological reactions to stress and the causes. One of the major causes of stress is generated by the working environment for both men and women. Some people are more prone to stress than others. Doctors have named two categories of people in relation to stress. Type 'A' are people who are probably industrious, aggressive and enjoy a challenge. Type 'B' are more easy-going; they are relaxed, calm and accept crises philosophically. Most people are a mixture of these two categories, exhibiting a mixture of both behaviours.

Signs of stress:

- You feel guilty when relaxing, feel you should always be on the go.
- You lie awake at night worrying about tomorrow.
- You are tense, your neck feels all tight and knotted.
- You are impatient or irritable and tend to interrupt when others are talking.
- You feel that you have a lot on your mind and have difficulty concentrating.
- You are smoking or drinking more than usual and you eat in a hurry.
- Life seems full of crises, and you are always having arguments.
- You have difficulty making decisions.
- You feel frustrated when people don't do what you want them to do.
- You frequently experience a butterfly stomach, dry mouth, sweaty palms and a thumping heart.

If this is how you feel, you are probably stressed.

I was working as a salesman in a team with two other people. We all got on very well indeed. I enjoyed work, although at times it was fairly stressful. My two colleagues left within a very short space of time of each other and were replaced by two young men who had very different values and attitudes.

All the time I felt I was competing against them. They were not interested in anyone else but themselves and their individual success. Deals were snatched from under my nose. The boss was giving me more and more responsibility because I was the only one left with experience of the firm. I was taking more and more work home and still not meeting the deadlines that he had set.

I couldn't talk to these two young men, because I didn't trust them. I was not going to hand over any of my work as I was sure that they would gain some kind of advantage. It got to the stage where I couldn't sleep. I was irritable, having rows at home with my wife and family. I was gaining weight because I couldn't stop eating. I had given up smoking two years previously and fortunately managed not to return to the habit. Unfortunately I was not so careful about alcohol and was drinking heavily. The whole time I felt that I was racing against time and getting nowhere, rather like a hamster running round and round in a wheel.

Then came the crunch. I was driving to work one morning; there had been an accident, and I was stuck in the traffic jam and I was getting in a terrible state about being late for a very important meeting. Suddenly I got the most dreadful pain in my chest; it was so severe that I could hardly breathe. I opened the car window, but it made no difference, so in an effort to get more air I got out of the car and apparently collapsed in the road. The next thing I remember is being in hospital, where I was told that I had had a heart attack. I was lucky it was only a small one.

My body had forced me to stop. I had to take a good long hard look at my lifestyle and admit that I was killing myself. In the weeks that it took me to recover I was supported by the hospital staff, my doctor and family.

I am now back at work and able to take a more sensible attitude to what I will and will not do. I set sensible deadlines, delegate more of my work and give myself more time to relax and enjoy life. I attend a stress clinic if I feel that life is speeding up again and find that talking about my problems reduces the stress. I have also taken up yoga and find that this is very beneficial. I go for long walks with my wife; I enjoy her company again and I am told that I am much easier to live with. I still have the occasional drink but I make sure that it is when I am relaxed and enjoying myself.

There must be thousands of people living their lives in the same way that I was before my heart attack. My advice to them is to stop, take a good look at what you are doing to yourself and your family. Seek professional help and advice before it is too late and remember no job is worth the ultimate sacrifice of your life.

SIMON WOODS

Simon was a classic type 'A' person and he has managed to modify his behaviour to become more of a type 'B' person. But it took a very dramatic event in his life to make him change.

What Causes Stress at Work?

Some of the sources of stress at work are directly related to the job, poor physical working conditions and time pressures. The workload may be too heavy, too light, too variable, too difficult or complex. There may be rôle ambiguity or conflict, a lack of identification or guidance about the job, people who are over-promoted or under-promoted, a lack of job security, the threat of dismissal or demotion, a poor relationship with the boss or subordinates or colleagues, difficulty delegating responsibility. Perhaps there are family problems or crises in your personal life as well.

What can be done to relieve stress at work?

■ Start by making a list of all the things that cause you stress. Include everything from the traffic jam, the late train, people that you work with, the amount of work you have to do. Make your list and learn to recognise situations that cause your stress. Recognise what is happening to you.

■ Remember your stress situation and when the traffic builds up, instead of becoming all tense, make a concerted effort to relax. Give your arms and neck a stretch, smile at someone in the car near you.

■ When you feel you are in a situation that may lead to stress, take some slow deep breaths. Breathe in deeply and exhale slowly.

■ Take some exercise; it has a very relaxing effect. Gentle jogging, cycling, swimming, whatever you enjoy. This exercise will help you to release all the pent-up energy and help you to sleep well at night. You could, like Simon, take up yoga or some other form of relaxation therapy.

■ If you are smoking and drinking more than usual, try to cut down. If you use either smoking or drinking as a way of unwinding, remember the effect is only temporary and there are more effective ways of doing something positive about your stress level.

■ Stop trying to do more than one thing at once. Plan ahead and take the tasks in order of priority. Make another list and tick off the tasks as they are achieved. Instead of rushing to get everything done at once and probably badly, you will be surprised at the time you really do have to get things done well, leading to a feeling of satisfaction in a job well done.

■ If you are the sort of person who talks at people, try to listen to what they say and have a conversation with them.

■ When you go to lunch or eat your packed lunch, forget about the work that you need to do, relax, enjoy your lunch, go for a walk afterwards, and you will be able to work more effectively having had a proper break.

■ If you are having problems with personalities at work, either talk to them about the conflicts or discuss it with your boss. If your partner is a good listener, talk to him or her about the conflict. Don't bottle up feelings of anger and frustration; you will only destroy yourself.

LOSING YOUR JOB

If you lose your job, whether you have been dismissed or made redundant, it leaves a feeling of worthlessness and dejection. When it is the breadwinner of the family there are the inevitable worries about supporting the family, outstanding bills, the mortgage repayment and all the other outgoing expenses associated with living. There is also the overwhelming feeling of failure both as a person and as the breadwinner. So often the person is made redundant or loses his job through no fault of his own; it is simply that the firm concerned can no longer afford to employ him. Even today the provision of material things and money is thought of as the prerogative of the man, the head of the family.

Pamela Brown's husband Malcolm was made redundant, and she describes the effect that it had on their lives and that of their two children.

A few years ago my husband was made redundant. The thought that he would use the redundancy money to start his own business was fairly attractive. However, it was not enough, so we thought of a bank loan to make up the difference. The bank manager persuaded us to take a much larger loan than we wanted, and when the business failed of course we couldn't pay it back. This worried my husband as he is not business-minded.

Then he got influenza, and I came home to find him crying, and the children were very frightened. He said that he had been feeling 'odd' for a few days and couldn't describe his feelings at the time, except that they were terrible.

I asked my parents to look after the children for a few days and phoned the family doctor, who gave us an immediate appointment. He prescribed some anti-depressants and sleeping tablets for my husband. The doctor explained that the pills might have to be changed as it was rather a 'hit and miss' affair as to what the right tablets should be. My husband used to sit and stare into space all day, and when we talked we had the same conversation over and over again. I found that I had to get out of the house and talk to other people just to unwind.

The pills started to work after about three weeks, and he gradually improved. He was very emotional for about six months, and then he got offered a job; at this stage he was still only 99 per cent recovered. He is still rather emotional about some things and doesn't talk about his 'illness'.

While he was ill we found that if anyone visited us he would rally round very well. The doctor explained that this problem could well recur at any time as there was a history of this kind of illness in his family. However, he now has a job and we are all right at the moment.

PAMELA AND MALCOLM BROWN

I have talked to so many women who have had to live and cope with the problems associated with their partner either losing their job or a business. Many of them had been made redundant, and the redundancy money was invested in a small business which unfortunately failed. Over a period of time their partner seemed to withdraw into himself, unwilling and unable to discuss the problems. They seemed to go through very similar stages rather like that of bereavement or grief, these stages not necessarily being in this order.

There is a stage of numbness, a feeling that this is not really happening to them, followed by feelings of denial. It is during this stage that the wife or partner needs to be alert to what is going on.

What to Do

It is important to take action and avoid the situation becoming worse. If there is no money coming in, try to persuade your partner to claim unemployment benefit. See page 309 for more information. This is sometimes very difficult as your partner may feel that he can manage and does not need this kind of help. He is proud and capable, and may see this as the ultimate humiliation and an admission of failure. Even so, try to discuss the problems and possible solutions with him.

It is quite possible that bills will not be opened, or just left unpaid. This may include the electricity, gas, telephone and other essential services, and the first indication that they have not been paid is when an official arrives to disconnect the supply. It is advisable to keep a track of these accounts and, if you are unable to pay them, either visit or write to the service concerned and explain the situation. More often than not, they will spread the bills over a longer period of time and give you time to pay. If your partner does not want you to become involved and hides these outstanding accounts, you could go and see the people concerned and ask to see the accounts for yourself.

Letters from the bank indicating a very serious financial problem may also go unopened or be ignored; this is often because your partner feels overwhelmed by the problem and unable to do anything constructive about it. So the existence of the problem is ignored, with a hope that it will go away. If all the accounts are in his name, it may be difficult to find out what is going on. Asking him directly if there is a problem may well be denied, so again you may have to make an appointment to see the bank manager and explain the situation. You will have to be very diplomatic in how you handle this as your partner may well see it as an unnecessary interference on your behalf.

If you own your house but have an outstanding mortgage and this is not paid, ultimately you could lose your home. Sometimes the first indication that this is happening is a court order from the company that loaned the money, demanding repayment of the mortgage in full. Again, this could be avoided by informing the company of the problem, and it is possible that they will also defer payments for a specified time; they cannot do this if they have not been informed. So make an appointment and check on the situation.

During this period of denial it is important to try to talk to your partner and to sort out the problems; ignoring them will only lead to greater problems and more heartache. Many women feel that they shouldn't interfere and are frightened to intervene in any way because when they do it generates a very hostile response. It is difficult, but you need to consider yourself, and if you have children you have got to do something for their sake. If you are not working but are able to get a job yourself, you may well have to do so, in which case discuss the problem with your partner and suggest that this might be a temporary solution to the problem until he is able to work again.

As Pamela described, all this may well lead to your partner suffering from depression, which renders the person concerned even less capable of doing anything practical about the situation. To seek urgent medical advice is very important; there is a need for outside help to ensure that you all survive this crisis. Tranquillisers and sleeping pills are often offered as help, but do make sure that they are only taken for a short period of time with regular visits to the doctor to discuss problems and progress. See also Chapter 9. Talking to someone outside the family, like your doctor, is therapeutic in itself. A problem aired and discussed with someone nearly always seems less overwhelming.

Watch for signs of depression such as withdrawal, difficulty sleeping, crying, unexplained headaches, lack of appetite or greatly increased appetite, irritability, smoking or drinking heavily, restlessness and take action. See also Chapter 8. Be aware that severe depression and an overwhelming feeling of failure may lead to feelings of self-destruction and suicide.

Hopefully there will be acceptance and the person will feel able to start again, to look for employment, or to restart the business. If it looks as though finding employment is going to be difficult, voluntary work will ensure that self-respect is maintained and something useful is accomplished.

CASE-STUDY: UNEMPLOYED

I was made redundant when the factory that I had worked in closed in 1985. I was forty-five years old, married, and had four children all at school. The feeling of being useless, unwanted and thrown on the scrap-heap was overwhelming, and reinforced by the people at the unemployment office who felt that there was very little hope that I would get another job. I had no trade, no skill, and had been employed as a factory worker since I left school at fifteen. There was nothing that I could do, and I was too old to start again. I had no capital behind me and therefore no prospects.

I signed on at the Social Security, and we had enough money to survive. I wanted to work, but was told that at my age there was not a lot they could offer. My wife had a part-time job cleaning, so when she left home in the morning I was left to wash up the breakfast things and tidy the house.

At first I spent hours watching television or just doing nothing. There was no point in my doing odd jobs for extra money, because it would have been taken off my benefit. I lost interest in everything around me; there seemed little point in doing anything. My mates went to the pub in the evening; but I couldn't go with them, because I couldn't afford to buy them a drink.

This cycle of self-destruction probably would have gone on and on if it hadn't been for our next-door neighbour. She is an old lady; I should think that she is about eighty years old. She has lived next door to us for years, and we always passed the time of day but nothing more. That winter we had a particularly heavy fall of snow, and I was clearing our front path. I noticed that her path was blocked with snow and ice, and I asked her if she would like me to clear it for her. She was very grateful and asked me in for a cup of tea. I had never been inside her house before, and it was in a bit of a state; it certainly needed a coat of paint. I got to know her quite well and often helped her with odd jobs around the house. One day I suggested to her that I would decorate the house for her if she bought the paint. We agreed, and I really enjoyed helping her.

She used to go to the village hall to the Over-Sixties Club, and she told me that they were always in need of young people to help, particularly when they went on outings. Being called a 'young person' was enough to persuade me to make contact. The man from Age Concern was delighted and asked me to help with all sorts of projects, repairs, organising entertainments and outings. I enjoyed being with the elderly and felt that I was doing something to help other people.

Since then I have been involved in all sorts of voluntary work. It may not be a paid job, but it keeps me busy and has given me back my self-respect.

PAUL HAYWOOD

There are so many people like Paul who are not able to get a job. This can make you feel so very useless and can have a severe and detrimental effect on self-esteem and also on physical and mental well-being. Voluntary work can be very rewarding, not financially but in making the individual feel that he is doing something that is worthwhile and will benefit others. Often they work with people much worse off than themselves, which helps to put their own problems into perspective. The other advantage is that the work is unpaid and does not affect any Social Security payments.

Voluntary groups and organisations are always in need of people to help them and the Citizen's Advice Bureau will be able to give you more information, or ask at your local library for a list of names and addresses. To reach this stage your partner will need a great deal of support from you and advice from people who specialise in helping others to find employment. There are courses if a change of occupation is indicated, help in starting a new business and information on a great variety of jobs, their availability and suitability. See page 368 for more details.

Also on page 370 I have listed your rights concerning employment, dismissal, unfair dismissal, industrial tribunal, redundancy, redundancy pay, terms and conditions of employment, and discrimination. There is also information on the types of training available, setting up your own business, and the addresses of organisations and publications that might help.

Fifty Years Old and Redundancy

Malcolm Brown was in his thirties when he was made redundant, and the difficulties of finding another job should certainly not be under-estimated. Finding another job when you are middle-aged can be even more difficult. You may be made to feel, by employers and other people, that you are too old to start again. This attitude is very shattering to the self-confidence and it is important to remember that this is not necess-arily true. Middle-aged people are at the peak of their experience and skill, but employers still seem to give priority to the young.

There are a range of services to help you get another job. This may involve retraining in modern up-to-date skills, taking a refresher course and looking for opportunities to work on community projects. For more details, see page 368.

With a little imagination and courage it is quite possible to make a job for yourself. Think about a service that you could offer for which people would pay: for example, dressmaking, hedge-cutting, gardening, accountancy, house-sitting, decorating or caring for someone who is sick or disabled. Maybe it is time for you to start a small business, particularly if you have been given some redundancy money. Examine the pros and cons very carefully. Draw up a list of your abilities, your strengths and weaknesses, examine the strengths list and establish if you could develop a business using these skills. Taking a business course could help you to develop skills that would enable you to be more competent. There are even courses that will teach you how to set up and run a small business. See page 368 for details. Visit your local college of further education and find out what courses are on offer; the library and the job centre will also give you information.

Look around your local area and see what services are required; perhaps you could develop the necessary skills and fill a hole in the market. If you are not particularly interested in earning money, find out about the voluntary services. Who needs help? What can you do to help them? Skills and talents that you take for granted and perhaps do not feel are very important could be invaluable to others. For the address of the Volunteer Bureau, see page 372. There is also a scheme called Voluntary Service Overseas, and they welcome mature skilled people who are willing and able to give up two years of their life to work in under-developed countries. See page 372 for the address.

The other question to ask yourself is: Do you really need or indeed want to work? Over the years you may well have had little time for leisure activities owing to the pressure of work. There may be hobbies and interests that you would like to pursue and develop. There may be courses at your local adult education centre that would enhance your interests or help you to find new ones. You are never too old to learn, but most people remember learning at school as being tedious and dull and are put off by past experience from taking an academic course. It really is very stimulating to explore a subject; it is not just about gaining a qualification but also the satisfaction gained from the act of learning and acquiring new knowledge. You could do this through a correspondence course or if you prefer the company and stimulation of other people, then join a class. There are also residential short courses if you feel like getting away to study.

These days more employers are offering early retirement. Before making any decisions it is important to seek advice from the personnel manager at work or your trade union about the effects of early retirement on your pension. He or she may be able to recommend a pre-retirement course. Planning for retirement is discussed in detail in Chapter 5.

THE DISABLED AND EMPLOYMENT

In Chapter 6 I talked to people who have come to terms with and overcome problems resulting from a variety of handicaps. Many of them have found a great deal of satisfaction from employment, some by helping other people who have similar problems to their own and others who are employed in business and many other careers. As the handicapped child grows into an adult he or she may well have a desire to find satisfying employment. Some mentally handicapped people, although they may be unable to read or write, and may suffer from additional handicaps like epilepsy or speech defects, are quite capable of working in a full-time job. Unfortunately, this is not always recognised by employers, and many mentally handicapped people find it impossible to get work.

In 1975 the Royal Society for Mentally Handicapped Children and Adults (Mencap) launched the Pathway Employment Service which introduces employers to mentally handicapped people and allows them to take them on as employees, without cost, for a probationary term before fully committing themselves. This scheme gives mentally handicapped people an opportunity to work, thus giving them a chance to grow in self-respect and independence by making a success of full-time employment. For more details, see page 373.

Whether your child is mentally or physically handicapped, the preparation for work in the outside world begins while he or she is still at school. Just as with the able-bodied young person (see earlier in this chapter), preparation and a sensible assessment of their capabilities are essential.

Talk to the teachers at school and establish his or her strengths and weaknesses, discuss further training and suitable employment. Talk about the future with the young person and establish his or her ambitions and come to a realistic decision about employment. For the physically handicapped it may be possible to undertake a course of study at home through a correspondence course. Alternatively many colleges now take disabled students providing that they have suitable access and facilities. There are also residential specialised colleges for handicapped students. There is a directory of residential colleges for handicapped students, a directory for school leavers giving information on further education, training and employment, and there is also financial help in the form of grants and allowances. See page 373 for details.

Having cared for a handicapped child for many years, if further training or employment means that he or she will have to leave home you may find the inevitable separation very difficult. Cutting loose the emotional ties and allowing independence is just as important for the handicapped as for the able-bodied. For help and advice about further training and employment for the mentally handicapped, see page 373.

For the newly disabled or impaired it may be that the previous employment is no longer suitable and you will need advice on retraining, suitable job opportunities, employment rehabilitation, how to get special aids for your employment and financial help for fares to work. See page 373 for the addresses of organisations that will help.

CHAPTER TWELVE

Victims of Crime, Violence and Accidents

VICTIMS OF CRIME AND VIOLENCE

Crime is a problem that affects us all, whether we are the victim or not. Some of us may be fortunate enough never to have experienced violence at first hand, but we have all read about it in the newspapers and seen it reported on the television. The fear that this engenders for ourselves and our families is very real indeed. The fact that it might happen to us is probably always in the back of our mind, and yet when it does happen it is always unexpected and disrupts the victim's life.

It was five o'clock on a Friday afternoon. I was baking and ran out of flour, so I thought that if I hurried I would just get to the shop on the corner before it closed. I grabbed my purse and hurried to the shop. There were plenty of people about, and it was broad daylight. Suddenly I was attacked from behind. Someone put their arm around my throat and pulled me backwards. The strength with which I was thrown to the ground took me completely by surprise. I was thrown to the ground with tremendous force.

I can remember very clearly that my attacker was a young man who smelt of stale cigarette smoke and strong body odour. He shouted at me, telling me to give him the purse. I was so frightened that I didn't respond, so he kicked me in the face; there was blood all over my face, so much that I couldn't see what was happening. He snatched the purse from my hand and then kicked me continuously in the chest and the stomach. All I could feel was the searing pain in my head and body. Then he ran off. No one came to my rescue during the attack despite the fact that I must have screamed for help.

When he had gone several people came over and helped me. Someone must have called the police and an ambulance. The police went with me to the hospital; they were very kind, but persistent in their questioning. They kept asking me if I could describe my attacker, but I couldn't remember what he looked like.

At the hospital they stitched up the wound over my eye and a large gash in my head. I had several broken ribs and sustained bruising to my body. They kept me in for three days until they were sure that physically I was all right.

My husband came to take me home. At home the police called and asked me to describe the man who attacked me, but I was still unable to give them a clear picture of what he looked like. It all happened so quickly I just didn't take anything in.

The thing that frightened me most was that my attacker might know me and where I lived and, as I had told the police, he might come back for revenge. From that day my life changed completely. I was frightened to be left on my own and even more frightened to go out without my husband. I had become a prisoner in my own home. This one episode could have ruined my whole life if I hadn't found the address and 'phone number of an organisation called the National Association of Victims Support Schemes in a magazine that I was reading while I was waiting to see the doctor.

When I got home I contacted them and I was visited by one of their volunteer visitors. With his help and support I have been able to pick up the pieces and start again. My only regret is that I did not find out about this group earlier. I had spent several long months of fear. At night when I closed my eyes I relived the attack. I was nervous and jumpy all the time with a constant fear that it would happen again. I still have moments when I relive the attack, but I feel more able to cope with their support.

DEBBIE WHITE

(Debbie has used an assumed name as she does not want to be identified)

Crimes of violence like this leave an emotional scar for a very long time after the physical wounds have healed. It is important for the victims to get help as soon as possible after an attack. The Victims Support Schemes have been set up to help people who are the victims of violence. Some people contact the scheme directly, while others are referred by the police shortly after the crime has been reported. The service is free and confidential: for more information, see page 374.

To prevent this type of crime there are a few simple precautions to take:

- If you are carrying money, make sure that it is in a purse or a wallet out of sight. Don't keep a wallet in a back trouser pocket.
- If you have just cashed a cheque in a bank, make sure that you have put the money safely out of sight before leaving the building.
- Don't carry more money than you need and always keep your cheque book and card separate. If you are carrying a handbag, keep it close to your body.
- If someone does make a grab for your handbag, remember you are more important. Protect yourself first: let go of the bag and, if there is a chance that someone will hear, shout as loudly as you can to try to attract help.
- Don't attach your name or address to your keys. If you lose them or they are snatched with your handbag, someone could easily use them to get into your home. For the same reason, do not keep anything in your handbag that could identify your address.
- There are very effective personal alarms that when set off let out a very loud and piercing noise that is enough to make any attacker run off and leave you alone.

Individual crimes of violence against women and young people attract a great deal of publicity, and this causes a great many of them to worry about their safety when they are alone. According to the police, the chances of becoming a victim of a serious crime are in fact very low. However, you will feel much safer if you take a few simple precautions whether you are at home, in your car, on public transport or in the street. The following advice was contributed by the Dorset police.

WOMEN AT HOME ON THEIR OWN

To help you feel safer in your own home, fit proper locks on doors and windows; simple night-latches are far too easy to open without a key. Fit security deadlocks on all external doors – either mortice deadlocks that fit into the door itself or rim deadlocks that fit on the back of the door. Proper locks needn't be that expensive; for about £50 you can buy a great deal of security. On the back doors fit key-operated mortice security bolts. These are relatively cheap and easy to fit.

When you are at home keep external doors locked. Draw your curtains after dark and, if you can afford it, have a telephone extension in your bedroom. Another piece of good advice is to make sure that your front door is on open view and not hidden by trees or bushes, and that the area is well lit with a bright light.

When you move into a new home change all the front and back door-locks; other people may still have keys that fit. Never forget to use the locks.

Fit a security door-chain or a door-limiter and a viewer to the front door. When someone calls always remember to use them. Make sure that you check the identity of the caller. If in doubt, call the company concerned and check the identity of the person before you let him in. Anyone from one of the public services will carry an identity card, and he is required to show it. If you are still doubtful, ask him to call back and make sure that you have a neighbour or friend with you when he returns.

Make sure that only your surname and initials are displayed on doorplates and in the telephone directory, so there is no indication that you are a woman living on her own.

If you put your house on the market, ask the estate agent to show any prospective buyers around. Don't show people around if the estate agent has not informed you that they are expected or if you are on your own.

When answering the telephone don't give your number. If the caller claims to have a wrong number, ask him or her to repeat the number required. Never reveal any information about yourself to a stranger and do not say that you are alone in the house. If you receive abusive or obscene telephone calls, put the receiver down immediately. Don't say anything: an emotional reaction is just what this type of caller wants. If the calls continue, inform the police and the operator. Keep a record of the date and time and content of each call as this may help the police to trace the caller and put a stop to the calls.

YOUNG PEOPLE AND WOMEN GOING OUT AT NIGHT

If you are going out at night on your own, keep an eye open for potential problems. Keep alert and don't daydream while walking along. Avoid short cuts through dimly lit, deserted areas and try to walk in the centre of the pavement, keep away from bushes and dark buildings. Walk on the side of the road that is facing oncoming traffic, then you will be able to see a car approaching and not be surprised by one that creeps up behind you. You will also be clearly seen in the headlights of other drivers. Carry a torch. Never hitch-hike or accept a lift from a stranger, whether it is day or night. If a car does approach you, or you are threatened, scream and run away in the opposite direction. By doing this you will gain valuable seconds and make it more difficult for the driver to follow you. If you are able make a mental note of the number and a description of the car, it will help the police trace the car and the driver.

If you know that you are going to be out late at night, arrange for a reliable lift home or book a taxi well in advance. Before getting into a taxi make sure that it is a genuine taxi; there will be a taxi licence displayed, and most taxis have an illuminated sign on the car.

As mentioned above, get a personal alarm and carry it with you at all times; make sure that it is easily accessible, not in the bottom of your handbag. Don't be afraid to use it. If you think that you are being followed by someone on foot, try crossing the street; if the person behind you also crosses the street, try crossing again several times. If you are still suspicious, run to the busiest place you can find. Joggers, cyclists and other people who enjoy outdoor activities can be especially vulnerable. So take sensible precautions by keeping to well-lit routes where there are plenty of people about. Choose the route in advance but vary it and the timing of the activity so that your behaviour is not predictable.

BABYSITTING

Many young people and women enjoy babysitting; it is a very satisfactory way of earning some extra money. Always make sure that you have a contact number for the child's parents, so that you can reach them in the case of an emergency. If anyone calls, don't let them in, and ask anyone who telephones to phone back and don't let them know that you are on your own. Keep a list of emergency numbers in case of problems. Don't agree to babysit unless arrangements have been made for you to be taken home. There is one other very important point that I always make to anyone who looks after my children and that is: in the case of a fire, get everyone out of the house, call the fire brigade and then contact us. The only valuable things in the house are the people.

TRAVELLING

Young people or women travelling on their own should avoid standing at isolated bus-stops and when on a bus always sit on the lower deck near the driver or conductor. On a train avoid empty compartments, sit in the part of the train that has the open style of seating where there are several people. Place yourself within easy reach of the communication cord. If someone pesters you, complain as soon as possible to the driver, conductor or guard.

In Your Car

When driving at night try to keep to main well-lit roads. Plan your route in advance and make sure that you have enough money and petrol to get you there and back and some change in case you need to make a phone call. Keep your car doors locked when you are driving, particularly the passenger door. If you stop at traffic-lights, it would only take a few seconds for someone to jump in beside you.

Don't give hitch-hikers or strangers a lift. If you see someone you think needs help, don't leave your car until you are 100 per cent sure that it is a genuine emergency. If in doubt, drive on to the nearest telephone and contact the police. If you think that you are being followed, don't stop – drive to the nearest police station or somewhere with lots of people so that you can get help. If you are driving along and another car swerves in front of you, forcing you to stop, stay in your car, doors locked, reverse quickly and then drive on to the nearest police station.

Park in well-lit areas where there are lots of people about, and look carefully around before you leave your car. Never leave valuables in the car. If you must leave something of value, lock it in the boot. When you return to the car have your keys ready in your hand, quickly check inside the car and in particular the back seat before getting in. At night avoid multi-storey carparks if you can. If you have to park there, take extra care when leaving and returning to your car. If you see someone hanging about near your car, wait until they have gone; it may just be a coincidence. If they are intent on staying near your car, go and find either a policeman or someone that you know to escort you to your car.

On Returning Home

If someone has driven you home, ask them to wait until you are safely inside. Get your key out before you approach the door, which you have left well lit. If, when you get home, you think that your home has been broken into, don't go in or call out. Go to a neighbour's house and call the police immediately. Wait there until the police arrive.

BURGLARY

There are more than 900,000 burglaries in Britain each year. That is, one in every twenty-five homes. Until you have been burgled, it is difficult to imagine just how unpleasant it is. Your personal things are rifled, your most valuable possessions are stolen, your peace of mind shattered.

We had been away on holiday to Spain and returned sun-tanned and happy only to discover that our house had been burgled. The place had been turned upside down, drawers emptied on to the floor, precious china ornaments had been smashed, the settee, chairs and mattresses had been slashed with a knife, and our treasured possessions stolen.

We felt as if our home had been violated by some unknown person. We called the police, who told us not to touch anything, so we sat amongst the mess waiting for the police to arrive. They appeared about half an hour later, examined everything, searched for fingerprints and other evidence. They asked the neighbours if they had heard or seen anything, but they hadn't. They weren't very hopeful that the thieves would be caught or our possessions recovered.

We were asked to make a list of everything that had been taken. You think that you know exactly what you have in your own home, but you don't. The main items like the television, the video, my wife's jewellery, our pension-books, savings-books and other valuables were obviously missing, and we listed all of them. But over the following months we discovered all sorts of things were missing, that we had forgotten about. For example, my father had given me a silver cigarette-case which had sat in a drawer for years, and I had forgotten all about it until it came up in conversation with my sister nearly a year later. When the weather got colder my wife decided to wear a sweater that she had, and that was missing along with several other items of clothing.

They could see that we were both frightened and confused, and suggested that we contact someone from the Victims Support Scheme; they gave us the telephone number, and I phoned them straight away. The police also suggested that a crime prevention officer should come and see us, to help us make our home more secure.

After they had gone we started to clear up. My wife destroyed all her underwear; she felt that it had been soiled and she could never wear any of it again. The person from the Victims Support Scheme was very helpful; she helped us to organise the repairs to the window where the thieves had got in, with claims to the insurance company, to replace our pension-books, and to notify the post office and the building society where we deposited our savings. She gave us time to talk about how we felt and said that if the case went to court she would come with us if we needed support.

The crime prevention officer called the next day; he reassured us that the average burglar is more interested in the sort of house that he can break into easily and quickly. They don't like locked windows and doors with security locks and are soon discouraged by houses that they can't get into easily. He also suggested that we marked any of our valuables that we had left, and anything new that we bought to replace what had been stolen, with a special security marker that can only be read under an ultraviolet light. We were to mark items with our postcode and house number on a hidden surface. He also suggested that we made a list of everything of value that we owned. To write down a description of the article or photograph it. Apparently every year hundreds of thousands of pounds' worth of lost or stolen property is recovered and not returned to its rightful owner because it cannot be identified.

Well, we did all this; it certainly kept us busy, and the house felt more secure. I only wish that we had taken more care to protect our property and prevented it from happening. It is a very hard lesson to learn.

HENRY AND DULCIE WESTON

In the event of a burglary, do not touch anything, leave everything exactly as it is. The police investigator is often helped by seeing exactly how the burglar behaved in your house, and in any case you might destroy valuable scientific clues. Call the police at once. While you are waiting for them to arrive, try to establish what is missing. Your chances of getting back any stolen property are increased if you can describe it exactly, with model and serial numbers of cameras, radios, video-recorders and so on. Make a note of these details when you acquire the item and keep the details in a safe place. If your property is marked, that is even better. If the police find fingerprints, they will need to take yours as well for comparison. Your fingerprints will be destroyed at the conclusion of the case.

As soon as possible, inform your insurance company of the burglary, and they will advise you on how to make a claim. Many people, in particular women, find this a very harrowing experience. The anxiety can far outweigh the value of the damage or theft. It can be very comforting to talk to someone from a Victims Support Scheme. Check if there is one which operates in your area. These trained volunteers offer a wealth of experience and advice which is usually of great moral and practical support to the victim of the crime. The police should be able to arrange the necessary contact with a local group.

I asked the police for advice on how to keep your home secure when you go away on holiday. They provided me with this very useful checklist and suggested that you read the list well in advance of your holiday, so that you could plan ahead. Then tick off the items just before you go away.

- Lock all doors and windows.
- Put all your tools away, then lock the garage or shed. If you have to leave a ladder out, padlock it to a secure fixture.
- Don't lock internal doors and desks. This only means more damage if someone breaks in.
- Cancel deliveries of milk, newspapers, etc.
- Deposit small valuable items, like jewellery, at the bank.
- Using an invisible marking pen, mark all remaining valuable items with your postcode and house number or the first two letters of the house name. Then, if they are stolen and subsequently recovered, the police can identify and return them to you.
- Don't draw your blinds and curtains. Curtains and blinds drawn during the day attract the thief. An automatic time-switch to switch on and off a light in a downstairs room is a good investment.
- Arrange for pets to be properly looked after.
- Turn off gas and water supplies. Turn off electricity unless you need it for a time-switch or freezer.
- Cut the lawns before you go.
- And, finally, don't forget to make sure your house and its contents are adequately insured.

You could also ask a neighbour to keep an eye on the house and to report anything suspicious to the police. Also ask him to remove any circulars or anything else that might advertise your absence. If he is a really good neighbour and you are away for a few weeks, he might even be persuaded to cut the grass. Remember to offer to do the same for him when he is away. Tell the police that you are away and also whether your neighbour has a spare key.

You don't have to be away for any length of time in order for a thief to get in and burgle your home. If windows are left open or unlocked, a key is left under the mat, the front, back or patio door is left unlocked or has a poor-fitting lock, or the latch to the front door can be reached through the letter-box, it only takes a few minutes for the thief to break in and enter. All these situations are an invitation to the thief who wants to get into your house, help himself to your valuables and get out as quickly as possible. So make sure that your home is secure. Fit locks to windows and, if you have louvre windows, get the glass slats glued in with epoxy resin adhesive, because the glass slats can be lifted out. Fit patio doors with top and bottom locks. Windows with locks are very difficult to force, and breaking glass is very noisy, particularly if the whole window needs to be smashed in order for the burglar to climb through on to a heap of broken glass. Fit mortice locks or rim locks to doors. If you feel that you are particularly at risk, it might be advisable to fit a burglar alarm. See page 374 for details.

If you are going out at night or during the day, shut and lock all doors and windows, especially the window in the lavatory or bathroom as there is nearly always a handy and substantial pipe to climb up just below it. Lock garages and sheds. Don't leave keys in secret hiding-places. When you are out at night, draw the curtains and leave a light on in a downstairs room and the radio playing. Before going to bed at night, check everything is locked. If you hear noises downstairs, or if you suspect someone is trying to break in, telephone the police. Do not tackle the burglar yourself.

VANDALISM

Vandalism is the defacing or destruction of property, and more often than not this is done by children. All around us are the results of vandalism. The smashed telephone-boxes, the broken windows in the bus shelter or empty houses. Vandalism is not just unsightly or causing inconvenience; sometimes it causes injury or may even endanger life. In the event of an accident a telephone call to the ambulance and the police is vital. If the telephone has been smashed and is unusable, the inevitable delay before finding a telephone that works could put the injured person's life in danger.

If you are a parent, you have a responsibility to know where your children are and to encourage them to occupy their time in constructive ways rather than roaming the streets and vandalising property. Do you know where your children are right now? Who they are with? What they are doing? Vandals are someone's children.

If you are not a parent, you can still help by doing something about vandalism. Next time you see someone vandalising property, call the police and tell them. You do not have to give your name and address if you prefer not to.

CHILDREN IN DANGER FROM STRANGERS

Children are at risk from so many aspects of life. The very process of growing up can lead a child into areas of danger such as the road, the railway, the river and many other dangerous places. One of the greatest dangers to a child is the friendly stranger who offers the child a sweet or a lift in his car. Children have always been at risk from evil-minded or sick individuals. Unfortunately children are trusting, which makes them so very vulnerable.

Whenever a child goes missing, our hearts go out to the parents in their anguish; we all hope that the child will be found safe and well. The cold chilling reality is often that the child is found dead, having been sexually assaulted. The parents and family of the child are left to grieve and the inevitable and perpetual distress caused by imagining what the child may have suffered before dying. Some children are found confused and distressed, having been sexually assaulted and then left by their attacker miles from home. The child is scarred with the memories of what was done to him or her, the parents and family left striving to rebuild a shattered life. For others there is no news; nothing is ever heard of the child again, leaving behind parents who fear that their child is dead, but as long as there is no body they hope that their child will be found alive.

Children are often abducted very close to their home, while playing nearby or running an errand. To prevent this happening parents have to make every effort to protect their children from these people. The police visit schools and talk to the children about the dangers posed by strangers. Teachers and parents need to reinforce the advice that is given by telling the child that there are rules about strangers that should never be broken. The advice from the police is to tell your child:

- Never go with anyone that you don't know.
- Even if it's someone you know, don't go with them without asking Mum or Dad first. Then make sure you get home at the time you are told.
- Never get into a stranger's car or go anywhere with a stranger.
- Never take sweets or money from a stranger.
- Always tell Mum where you are going as she needs to know where to start looking for you if something goes wrong.
- If a stranger approaches you, tell your parents, a teacher, a police officer, a lady or someone you know. Don't keep it to yourself because you don't want to appear silly.
- Don't play outside after dark and don't play in lonely places.

Parents can also do something to reduce the risk to their child:

- Know where your children are at all times, who they are with and what time they will be home.
- Children may find it difficult to tell you of something that has happened. Encourage them to talk and take time to listen.
- Seek help from the police, doctor, social worker or someone you can talk to, at an early stage. No one will mind. Anything you say will be dealt with calmly and in the strictest confidence.
- Have a secret codeword known only to the family, which can be used on the odd occasion when you are forced to send a stranger to collect your child from school or from the park. Instruct your child not to go with the person unless the codeword is used.

The above advice comes from the Dorset police in conjunction with the Thames Valley Police Liaison Department.

Never use the police as a threat or a punishment if your child is naughty. Encourage your child to see the policeman as someone who will help him if he is in trouble, and who is kind to children.

RAPE

Rape is being forced by a man to have sex with him. Children as young as six months and women as old as ninety have been raped. The law states that rape is 'the unlawful carnal knowledge of a female by force or fraud against her will'. 'Carnal knowledge' means penetration of the labia (outer lips) by the penis to any degree; full penetration and ejaculation need not take place in order to prove rape (*Harris's Criminal Law*, Sweet & Maxwell, 1973).

Rape or sexual assault can involve intimidation with threats or weapons, beating, choking, knifing, sexual and mental humiliation, urination, defecation or spitting on the victim, forced oral sex, multiple rape by one or more assailants, injury to the genitals – i.e., bottles, sticks and so on pushed up the vagina.

A woman's life can be totally disrupted by being raped, and many women suffer in silence because they have been humiliated, frightened, and find it impossible to talk about.

When I was eighteen years old, I was on my way to college. I was very excited at the prospect of starting my life as a student. Walking across the park, I was attacked and raped. Fortunately I was not too badly hurt physically, but emotionally I was destroyed. After threatening that he would come back and do it again if I told anyone, he ran off. I managed to get home and despite the threats I did tell my mother, who phoned the police.

The indignity of what followed added to my distress, but I know that it was necessary. I was examined by a doctor who did all she could to be gentle and kind; my clothes were taken away; and then I had to tell a policewoman exactly what had happened and describe my attacker. My mother stayed with me all the time and was very strong and supportive. She managed to contact my father, who came to the police station. He was very angry; I had never seen him like that before. He shouted at the police and blamed them for what had happened.

When we eventually got home I had a very hot bath and tried to wash what had happened to me away, but I couldn't. I felt so dirty. Then I seemed to go to pieces. I couldn't stop crying and shaking, so my mother called our doctor and he gave me some pills to help me sleep. I was so frightened that the man would find out that I had been to the police and would come back and get me, I was sure that he knew where I lived. My father said that if he found out who it was he would kill him before the police caught him. I seemed to have caused so much upset in our family, I felt that in some way I must have been to blame.

The police eventually caught the man, after he had raped another girl who was only fourteen. I then had to identify him. I didn't want to do this as I was scared of him seeing me, but the identification was done so that he couldn't see me. When the case came to court I had to relive the whole thing again; the questions were awful, and at times I was convinced that they thought that I was lying.

The man was sent to prison for three years. He just stood there staring at me, and I was sure that he was planning to find me when he got out.

I don't think that I shall ever get over this, although I was lucky I didn't get pregnant, but the effect on my life has been very damaging. My parents have been wonderful; they have helped me through some very bad times. I suppose not everyone has the support that I have had. We moved house soon after the trial, tried to put this behind us, to forget and to start again. I have been at college for two years now. I have made lots of friends but I cannot form any sort of a relationship with a man; I just don't trust them.

This young lady prefers to remain anonymous in case she should be recognised.

What Should You Do if You Have Been Raped?

Anyone who has been raped is under no legal obligation to report it to the police, but it should be remembered that the attacker is more than likely to do it again and your evidence might put him safely behind bars. Rape Crisis Centres have been set up all over the country, and you can telephone them and ask for advice and support: see page 375 for the telephone numbers. If you decide to report it to the police, the Rape Crisis Centre offers this advice:

■ Report the rape to the police as soon as possible. Delay may go against your case.
■ If at all possible, tell someone what has happened as soon as you can; a witness to your distress and early complaint will help.
■ Do not wash, tidy yourself or change your clothing; you may destroy valuable medical evidence.
■ Do not take any alcohol or drugs.
■ Call a friend or call the Rape Crisis Centre, so that someone can give you support during police and medical procedures.
■ Take a change of warm clothing with you; the police may keep some of your original clothing for tests and evidence.

■ Making notes about the rape may help you when you give your statement, but don't worry if you can't do this. Important things to remember are the sequence of events, details, and what was said.

Whether or not you report the rape to the police, it is important to talk to someone about what has happened. If you decide not to go to the police, seek medical advice, so that you can be checked for sexually transmitted diseases, possible injury and pregnancy.

The police procedure will mean that you will be at the police station for several hours, during which time:

■ You will be asked to give a statement that will be written down by a police officer. Make sure that you read the statement carefully and make changes if necessary before you sign it. You can ask for a woman police officer to take your statement.
■ You will be asked intimate questions by the police. There is no reason why you should talk to any officer other than the one in charge of your case.
■ You will be examined by a doctor, both externally and internally. This is to collect medical evidence of rape or sexual assault. You can ask that this examination is carried out by your own family doctor or a woman doctor.
■ You may be asked to look at mug shots, accompany the police to the scene of the crime or identify your assailant.
■ You can ask for your name not to be read out in court.
■ If you feel that you are not being well treated, ask to see the police officer in charge of the station.

It is sensible to think about what you would do if you were physically attacked. The first thing to do is to make as much noise as you can: shout, scream, use a personal alarm. Could you fight back? Effective ways of inflicting pain so that your attacker releases you are getting your fingers and fingernails in his eyes, chopping or punching his eyes, mouth and ears, biting, kicking him in the knees and shins, pulling your knee up sharply into his groin. A woman who is being attacked has every right to defend herself with reasonable force. An umbrella, hairspray or car keys can be used against an attacker – make sure that they are easily accessible. Take a course in self-defence, learn and practise how to defend yourself. For more information, contact your local library, education authority or sports centre.

The law in the United Kingdom does not allow you to carry anything that can be described as an offensive weapon. This includes any items that have been specially adapted such as a sharpened comb or a knife or a gun.

Once you are free, run. It is often more effective to shout 'Fire' rather than 'Help' to attract attention and get help; it is more likely to get a reaction.

If you are unable to get free, or your attacker has a gun or a knife, it may be better not to resist and at least stay alive. Try to stay calm, talk quietly and carefully, remind him that you are a human being. Don't excite him further by answering his questions about how you are feeling. If you have to answer, reply with factual answers such as 'You are hurting my back'.

Concentrate on what he looks like, any unusual features, his clothing, an accent or speech pattern, a smell on his clothing like petrol. Try to think about something definite and routine or plan how you will notify the police when you get free. Try not to show pain and weakness as this may encourage him to become more violent.

Women's groups and Rape Crisis Centres are really very helpful because they have experience of dealing with many victims. They understand the varied reactions and feelings that women have after being raped. They will counsel, offer advice and comfort you. They will seek legal advice on your behalf and help you cope with this crisis in your life. These groups agree that the most beneficial emotion to express after rape is anger and the least and most destructive is guilt; they will help you to come to terms with these feelings.

CHILD ABUSE

There are three types of child abuse: sexual abuse, physical abuse and neglect. Most of the sexual offences are between adult men and girls. The Incest Crisis Line defines incest as 'any overt sexual act made against a child, by someone in parental control of that child at that time'. By that they mean anything from a french kiss or indecent exposure to full intercourse, by anyone that the child has been taught to trust. The effects of a betrayal of that trust should never be underestimated. The majority of cases that they deal with are of father-and-daughter incest, but they work with all sides of any situation when they are requested to. For more information about Incest Crisis Line, see page 375.

Sexual abuse is emotionally damaging to the child, and the child may complain of frequent headaches, stomach complaints, skin disorders or anxieties such as desperate clinging, bed-wetting, nightmares, or school work may be affected. What is sexual assault, and what should a child do about it? Sexual assault is being touched by someone or made to do something to another person in a way that you don't like. Men who sexually assault or abuse children may be strangers or part of the family, like fathers, uncles, brothers, grandfathers, or stepfathers. They may also be teachers, social workers, friends, babysitters or neighbours. Nobody, not even a parent, has the right to do anything sexual to you that you do not understand or want. It is always all right to want it to stop. Anything that makes you feel frightened, such as the person touching you with his hands, rubbing against you with his body or kissing you in a way that you don't like and frightens you, is wrong.

If you are asked to take off your clothes, even if you are told that it is a game or a punishment, and it makes you afraid, it is wrong. You may not fully understand what is going on but it may scare you so much that you cannot forget it. If you feel ill or sore after being sexually assaulted, you need to see a doctor. Sometimes the most difficult thing to do is to tell someone else what is happening. So think of all the people that you know and trust and tell one of them what has been happening.

The person you tell can help you stop this happening. They may tell the person that is sexually assaulting you to stop or they may tell the police or the Social Services. Sometimes they do not do anything about it, or they may not believe you, but this does not mean that it is not happening to you, or that you are wrong to talk about it and want it stopped. If the person you told was someone in the family and they have not done anything about it, tell your teacher at school. There is also a telephone number for you to call and an address for you to write to, on page 375, and they will help you.

Physical Abuse

Physical abuse is when a baby or a child is physically beaten, or thrown across a room, swung around by an arm or a leg, thrown against a wall, tortured such as being burned with cigarettes, bitten or shaken.

Neglect

Neglect comes in two forms, physical and mental, and denies the child concerned food, warmth, shelter and love. Physical neglect occurs when a baby or child is left unwashed, his nappies left unchanged, or he is starved of food. Mental neglect is when parents deprive their child of love and affection, ignore the child and show no interest in his emotional or intellectual development.

What Can Be Done to Help These Children?

Sexual Abuse
- If a child tells you that he or she is being abused, listen to what the child is saying. Give the child time to explain what is happening in his or her own words.
- Reassure the child that you believe what he or she has told you. Children very rarely lie about sexual assault; if you appear to disbelieve him or her, you will only contribute to the damage caused by the assault.
- Don't blame the child for what has happened.
- Instruct the child to tell you immediately if the offender attempts sexual assault again.
- Reassure the child that he or she is safe.
- Respond to questions and feelings that the child expresses about the assault with a calm matter-of-fact attitude but do not pressure the child to talk about it.
- Respect the child's privacy by not telling a lot of people or letting other people question him or her.
- Get some help and advice. Talk to your family doctor or phone one of the crisis lines: see page 375.
- If you are the child's parent:
  Try to continue with a normal routine at home, the usual activities, bed-times and rules.
  Inform brothers and sisters that something has happened to the child, but that he or she is safe now and will be all right. Do not discuss the details of the assault but make sure that your other children are given enough information to protect themselves from the offender.
  Talk about your feelings with someone that you trust. Do not discuss the situation repeatedly in front of your child or children.

Not all children are able to tell parents that they have been assaulted. Changes in behaviour may be a signal that something has happened:

- a child who is reluctant to go to a particular place or be with a particular person
- a child who shows an unusual interest in the genitals of other people or of animals. He or she may try to express affection in inappropriate ways such as 'french kissing' or fondling a parent's genitals.
- a child who refuses to change in front of others in situations such as physical education or swimming classes
- a child who isolates himself
- a child who fears bathrooms, showers, closed doors
- a child who has a sudden marked loss or increase in appetite
- a child who suddenly develops lots of new fears, and needs more reassurance than in the past
- a child who is afraid to go home after school or continually runs away from home
- a child whose artwork involves sexually explicit parts of the body or sexually abusive details

These are very general indicators that the child may be troubled, though not necessarily about sexual assault. The child may have some of these problems or none at all. It is the combination, frequency and duration of indicators that will alert you to a problem. Try to notice all changes in usual behaviour.

Physical Violence or Non-Accidental Injury

Teachers, friends and health professionals should look for the following signs:

- bruising on the face and around the mouth; multiple bruising of different ages as indicated by the colour-changes – for example, bruises that are turning yellow or brown colour; finger-mark bruises and human bite marks
- bleeding from the mouth of a baby as the result of a teat being thrust into the mouth; gum or teeth injury from direct blows
- cigarette burns, leaving a discreet small circular lesion
- in school, a child unwilling to undress in front of staff or other children, for fear that the signs of a beating or bruising may be seen
- a child afraid to go home after school or continually running away from home
- visible injury that cannot be explained
- plausible explanations to an injury which does not fit the case
- a child who is unhappy, miserable and unusually withdrawn

If you are a parent who is afraid that you will physically abuse your child, or you have already done so and are frightened that you will do it again, you can contact Parents Anonymous, who have a twenty-four-hour telephone service. You can remain anonymous and, if you need them, social workers and doctors are available: see page 375 for details.

Neglect

The National Society for the Prevention of Cruelty to Children recommend that the general public, teachers and health professionals watch for, and report to them, the following signs of child neglect:

- children left on their own indoors
- children wandering the streets
- children who are regularly left in charge of younger brothers and sisters
- children who are unusually withdrawn and miserable
- children who are unusually aggressive
- children who are desperate for affection
- children who are dirty, smelly or look underfed
- children who have serious difficulties at school

If you suspect that a child is being abused or neglected, contact the NSPCC and talk to someone about your fears and suspicions. See page 375 for the telephone number.

Another aspect of the problem of child abuse is when parents who do not abuse their children are frightened to take a child to hospital in case they are accused of doing so, with the result that the child is taken away.

My son had fallen down stairs and banged his head; the result was an enormous bruise on his head. He is the sort of child that is always falling over and always has a bruise or scratch or cut somewhere on his body. In the past he has managed to fall off a swing and broken his arm, he has sprained his ankle several times, he knocked his baby front teeth out when he fell off his bike. You just never know what he will do next.

There has been so much in the papers and on the television about parents taking their child to a hospital, and then being accused of battering their child, that really I was afraid to take him to the hospital.

MRS K. RYAN

This type of head injury could have developed into a very serious condition overnight and the child should have been seen by a doctor. But I can understand Mrs Ryan's concern, so I talked to a social worker about these feelings of anxiety amongst parents. She felt that any child taken to the family doctor with an injury such as a broken bone or a knock on the head would be viewed by the doctor, who would know the family background, as a patient who simply had an accident; that he would bear in mind the family background and wouldn't be pointing an accusing finger at the parents. So, in the case of an accident where the child's life is not in immediate danger, if you are worried about being accused of child abuse, seek medical advice from your family doctor and if necessary he will refer you to the hospital.

WIFE ABUSE

In the United Kingdom it is estimated that within one in every hundred marriages the woman suffers severe violence. Battering is often linked with sexual violence and rape but may also involve attempted strangulation, suffocation, kicking, punching, beating, the use of weapons, or even pouring boiling water over her. Battering is not only physical but also includes mental torture and humiliation.

Men who batter women do not come from any specific class or background; they include the rich and the poor, the educated and the uneducated. It is a problem that has been going on for centuries. Women who are fortunate enough to be married to a man who does not resort to physical violence sometimes find it difficult to understand why a woman who is repeatedly battered by her husband stays with him. It is not always as easy as it sounds, just to get up and leave your husband and your home, particularly if you have young children and are dependent on your husband for money to survive. Where would the woman and her children go? A woman who is battered often has had her self-esteem literally beaten out of her. She may be made to feel that in some way she deserves to be beaten. Many women feel too ashamed to tell anyone what is going on, so they just put up with it. If a woman calls the police, she may fear and she will probably get more violence after they have left.

The next contributor has stated that she wishes to remain anonymous for her own and her children's safety.

*

How would you feel if a violent attacker had the key to your front door? I am a survivor of domestic violence, who lived with this fear for ten years. Many women continue to do so unless they are prepared to do something about it. Why don't they? The psychological aspects that bind one person to another are complex. As often as not, the man will be sorry and ashamed, and promise that it will never happen again, but invariably it does. Forever waiting for the next blow confused and blinded me until I didn't know which way to turn. This kind of torture destroyed my self-esteem, trust and confidence.

What could I do? It takes a great deal of courage to admit that you are a victim of domestic violence, not only because it is an admission of failure but also because it will probably start a chain of events which will require even more courage and stamina.

Long before I had even considered getting a divorce, a friend advised me to write a 'diary of events' just in case I should ever need to recall the dates and details of violent incidents to a solicitor or court. Looking back, I realise the only way that I dealt with the problem was to operate some form of selective amnesia. I realised when I eventually saw a solicitor how much I had chosen to forget which was in fact of vital importance.

Apart from this, the most crucial thing that I was persuaded to do was see my family doctor. Even if there are no visible signs of attack, it is important to record the incident and/or the injuries, however minor, as this may be needed for housing and legal evidence later.

At that time I was totally unaware that such places as Women's Refuge existed. But I was lucky and had friends and family that I could escape to for safety and support. Not everyone is so fortunate, and now I would unquestionably suggest to anyone who suffers mental or physical abuse from their partners to contact their nearest Women's Refuge or Refuge Support Group. They will provide information about a place of safety where you can go for just a night, a few days or longer if necessary. They are trained to offer a 'listening ear', and advice on legal, financial and housing rights. Each individual case is different. Their telephone numbers are available from the Samaritans, Citizen's Advice Bureaux, police or Social Services.

Three years ago my ex-husband was granted access to my children, now aged nine and eleven, to be co-ordinated by Court Welfare. He was totally unable to accept the finality and reality of the divorce, and his persistent obsession with me and the desire for revenge has led him on a campaign of terror against me, my children, family and friends. He is an alcoholic and even when sober has shown no respect for the law.

He has repeatedly been committed to prison for breaching 'anti-molestation' injunctions, molesting the children and making 'death threats' on the phone.

His pattern of behaviour continues to be unpredictable and aggressive. Despite three attempted suicides, he is described by the medical profession as 'bad' not 'mad'.

I have asked that it be put on record that I think my children are at risk when alone with him, and agreed to supervised access, but he refuses this, and Court Welfare say they don't have the 'manpower' to implement this. So it has been disregarded, which to me assumes my ex-husband's demands are more important than the children's emotional or physical welfare.

Where does that leave the children? Court Welfare say he has right of access unless he causes actual bodily harm. In other words I must wait for something serious to happen, and in the mean time ignore any psychological damage he may cause. I find this unacceptable.

Various professionals who are connected with the children – their headmaster, parish priest, health visitor and community police officer – have all suggested it would be a good idea to have some sort of joint 'case conference' to discuss the best solution. I agree, but, again, this option has been disregarded by Court Welfare.

It is an ongoing situation, and our safety has always been dependent on the local police force. Again, I have been lucky to have an understanding community police officer who has supported me throughout. He has never minimised how dangerous my ex-husband could be, or ignored any call for help; he has actively encouraged me to summon the police at the slightest breach of the injunctions.

The long build-up of psychological and physical abuse leaves you emotionally paralysed, and my first concern was and must always be the children; in order to care for them there has to be someone who is willing to acknowledge my needs, and let me talk about my life and future. It is important for the community at large to respond to each individual woman's needs with serious and sympathetic support.

My problems are by no means over. I owe my new-found self-esteem and confidence to my family and friends, the children's well-being to their caring teachers and health visitor, and our safety to the police.

Because I feel so strongly about the need for refuges and support groups I have become involved in setting up a sanctuary in my area for abused women, so that they can come in safety with or without their children, to rest, recover and think with the support of other sympathetic women.

Hopefully some will survive as I have done.

Sometimes the only answer is to leave home, and refuges, safe houses or shelters have been set up all over the country to meet this need. A refuge is a house where any woman, whether married or not, who has been ill-treated by a man can live with her children in safety. There are now a hundred refuges in England, and women can stay in a refuge for as long as they need to. Many women are frightened that the man will track them down if they go to a refuge that is too near to their home, but it is possible to go to a refuge as far away or as near as you want. For information on how to get in touch with a refuge, see page 376.

Not all women want to leave their home; they just need someone to talk to who will understand and give them some help and advice. Women's Aid are able to listen to your problems, and give information and advice about legal, financial and housing rights. See page 376 for the address.

If you decide not to return home, you will need to think about leaving the refuge and getting a permanent home. For your rights as a homeless person contact the Citizens' Advice Bureau – address and telephone number in the local telephone directory.

The courts do have the power to grant orders designed to protect a woman from a violent man, either to exclude him from her home or to prevent further assaults on herself or her children. The courts can also give the police powers to arrest the violent man who breaks the court order. In practice these court orders are not always easy to get, and having got one may not make any difference to the man's behaviour.

VICTIMS OF ACCIDENTS

Every day thousands of people suffer injury. For some it means death, for others permanent disablement and for others prolonged painful recovery. Injury is the largest single cause of death before middle age, the largest single cause of temporary and permanent disablement at any age. Injury is no respecter of persons; we are all at risk: on the roads, in the home, in industry, in school, on the playing-fields. And the toll of civil and other violence is an important cause of injury in all age groups. It is, sadly, also responsible for untold misery and hardship amongst those who suffer the consequences of injury for the rest of their lives.

It was leap year, 29 February 1964, when the car accident happened. I was living and working just outside Norwich pending my marriage in September of that year. One important factor at that particular time was my being a foreigner, Norwegian, which in itself was no problem under normal circumstances. My parents and family, apart from my sister, were all living in Norway. My sister had married an Englishman and was living in a small town called Dereham about fourteen miles from Norwich. They had one daughter, but the tragedy was that my sister suffered from mental instability. Thus, the practical help and support that followed came from my fiancé's parents and family. It was only years later that I came to understand the full extent and impact that the accident had in shaping my whole future.

David was driving me back to work that particular February evening; the weather was bleak with patchy fog and black ice. It was a familiar road, and without question he was driving too fast for the weather conditions. Unable to negotiate a sharp bend, the Mini skidded and ended up in a ditch on the wrong side of the road. Our luck was that no other vehicles were coming the other way. The impact was so great that the windscreen flew outwards, the doors were jammed and the car was in fact a complete write-off. I had sustained fractures of my left tibia and fibula just below the knee and a deep wound at the same site where my leg had made contact with the tuning-button of the radio. David had a broken pelvis and a dislocation of his hip. These were the facts of the crash.

When it came to leaving hospital it was not possible to return immediately to my job and I had nowhere to live. It was decided therefore that, still greatly incapacitated and just able to handle a pair of crutches, I move in with my fiancé's parents. A lovely home and they were so kind; they felt responsible for me, I suppose. I was there until mid-July when I returned to Norway to get ready for the wedding.

The injury was such that I had a full plaster from hip to foot with just the toes showing, and needing help even to get dressed; the most embarrassing thing was going to the loo and being unable to pull my pants on and off. Gradually and with difficulty all this became a matter of course, an acceptance of what needed to be done.

In this period of time I felt totally isolated and alone, not because I was on my own – being surrounded with people in fact – but there was no one really to talk to about what had happened and the intense mental effect which the accident had had on me. Continuing fear and apprehension of car travel, deep concern and apprehension about the state of my leg and what it would be like when the plaster was removed, and continuing concern for the whole of the unenviable circumstances in which I found myself filled this time when I had plenty of time to think. I had had doubts about marrying David before the accident; now I felt trapped. Had the accident not happened, I am certain the marriage would not have taken place. Communication between us was bad, the accident never spoken of in any depth, and thus resentment started to build up. This was even worse when he returned home from hospital and we were together under his parents' roof like total strangers.

Again the desperate need to communicate what I felt and thought was paramount in my mind, but who was there to turn to? No one.

When the plaster came off, my leg was very swollen, the wound below the knee was infected and the leg misshapen. The knee was out of line, causing my leg to bow slightly, and the leg was shorter than my right leg. During all this time the pain and discomfort was unrelenting, but now it became secondary because I had to learn to walk again, to get all the muscles working with the help of physio-therapy. It was towards the end of August when I eventually managed to throw away my walking-stick.

The appearance of my leg was of great concern as well as the weakness of the knee, which on so many occasions locked and I had to manipulate it back to normal. Not a major consequence perhaps, but even now after twenty-four years the dull ache and always having to watch what I do is a constant reminder of an unnecessary accident and a marriage which would not otherwise have taken place and which inevitably failed after eight years. How could I have avoided this? How could I have said to David's parents 'Thanks and good-bye'? Our future home was being built. Could I have said, 'Stop the wedding preparations taking place in Norway – Sorry, it's all off'?

My mental reaction looking down at my leg was of continuing anguish and concern. I felt so ugly and had gained a considerable amount of weight as a consequence of all the inactivity during these months and also not really caring. Later, when arriving back in Norway and meeting my parents, the look of disbelief at this stranger, as I expected it would, added to a growing insecurity and a total lack of confidence. Their easy-going extroverted daughter had changed into a withdrawn insecure person. I was twenty-one years old.

Who could have told me and helped me to come to terms with the accident and all its implications and consequences? Who could I turn to? The decisions and responsibility are entirely mine in the end. I was at a crossroads in my life and I took the wrong turning. In retrospect, had I had guidance and help from someone on the outside, someone with sympathy, advice and good sense, who would just have listened to the spoken word which in itself is such a great help in putting thoughts into perspective, would I then have stopped and taken another and happier road?

This case-history was given to me by John MacNae who is a consultant of an accident and emergency department in a large hospital. As a result of caring for so many injured people he has developed a special support group to meet the needs of people who have been involved in accidents and sustained injuries that inevitably changed their lives. The foundation was formed in 1973, and the common bond which brought these people together was the recognition of the endemic and escalating tragedy of accidental and non-accidental injury, both nationally and internationally, and the need to meet the complex and special problems which result for the individual and the community. For more information about the Friends of the Injured, see page 376.

So the end of this chapter concludes the book. A book that is full of the true stories of people who have suffered some kind of crisis in their lives, the sort of catastrophes that most of us have only dreamed about in our worst nightmares. It could have been a very sad book, and I have to say that many of the case-studies have moved me to tears, but the overwhelming and constant theme throughout the book is the ability of all these people to survive the most appalling catastrophes. They are all survivors, they have lived through crises that have changed their lives completely, but in a strange way these traumatic events have made them stronger and left them with a feeling that their experiences should not be wasted but, rather, used to help others.

This is a positive book full of hope and aspirations for the future. No matter what crises life throws at you, there is someone who has experienced the same problems; someone who really knows how you feel because they have been there. They are willing to help by sharing their experiences with you, and the main objective of this book was to make the task of finding the appropriate help much easier. Within the covers of this book there is someone somewhere who can help you through whatever crisis you are struggling with at the moment, and with a positive approach and sound sensible advice they will help you to become a survivor.

Help Directory

Many of these addresses are in London, but this is only the main contact-point. If you get in touch with these people, they will give you the address of a group which is nearer your home.

CHAPTER 1: PREGNANCY, CHILDBIRTH AND SUB-FERTILITY

Maternity Benefits

Free Dental Treatment

You have a right to free NHS dental treatment while you are pregnant, provided you were pregnant at the start of the treatment, and for a year after your baby's birth. Tell your dentist that you are pregnant, and you won't have to pay. Get leaflet D11, *NHS Dental Treatment*, for more information.

Free Prescriptions

You have a right to free NHS prescriptions while you are pregnant and for a year after your baby's birth. Ask your doctor or midwife for form FW8 as soon as you are sure that you are pregnant, or at any time until your baby is born. When you are getting a prescription for your baby or for any other child who is under sixteen, fill in the back of the prescription form; then you don't have to pay. If you didn't apply for free prescriptions while you were pregnant, and your baby was born less than a year ago, fill in form A in leaflet P11, *NHS Prescriptions*.

For Mothers at Work

Statutory Maternity Pay (SMP) is a weekly payment which has replaced both the maternity allowance from the DHSS and maternity pay from employers. It is paid by employers for up to eighteen weeks. You do not have to intend to return to work to get it.

You are usually entitled to get SMP if all the following apply:

(a) You have been employed by the same employer for at least six months into the qualifying week, which is fifteen weeks before the week in which the baby is due: the twenty-sixth week of your pregnancy. If your employer dismissed you because of your pregnancy, see below.

(b) On average you earn enough to pay Class 1 National Insurance (NI) contributions. (If you pay reduced-rate NI contributions, you may still be entitled.)

You will not normally qualify for SMP if you do not work at least into the qualifying week. But if you were dismissed from your job earlier than this because it would have been dangerous for you to continue to do the job as an expectant mother – i.e., a job such as a radiographer – you may be treated as satisfying the conditions for SMP.

You may be treated as satisfying the conditions if you were 'fairly dismissed' before the qualifying week. Dismissal by reason of your pregnancy might be fair if your condition made it impossible for you to do your job adequately or where it would be against the law for you to do that particular job while you were pregnant, and your employer could not offer you a suitable alternative job. Discuss this with your employer. If there are difficulties, consult your Social Security office.

SMP can be paid up to eighteen weeks. Payment will be made for a 'core period' of thirteen weeks, starting with the sixth week before your baby is due. You can usually choose when to take the remaining five weeks. You can take it all before or after the 'core period', or some before and some after. SMP can't be paid for any week or part of a week you work.

How Much?

SMP is a weekly payment, but your employer will usually pay you at the time you would have received your normal wages. There are two rates of SMP. If you have been in the same employment for at least two years, or part-time for five years for at least eight hours a week, you can get a higher rate of SMP, which is 90 per cent of your normal wages for the first six weeks of your SMP.

After that you will get the lower rate, which is £32.85 (correct at the time of writing), for the remainder of your SMP period. If you have been in the same employment for between twenty-six weeks and two years, you will get the lower rate throughout the SMP period. You may have to pay tax and National Insurance contributions on SMP.

How to Get SMP

- Tell your employer that you intend to stop work because of your pregnancy.
- Do this at least three weeks before the date you actually stop work because of your pregnancy.
- Once you are twenty-six weeks pregnant ask your doctor for a maternity certificate (Mat B1), indicating when your baby is due, and give it to your employer. You can't be given this certificate earlier, and you can't be given more than one. Your employer will normally keep this certificate.

If you intend to go back to work after the baby is born: three weeks before you stop work tell your employer in writing that you will be stopping work, the week that the baby is expected, and state your intention to return to work. Your employer must pay you for time off while you keep appointments for antenatal care.

For full details of SMP, get leaflet NI 17A, *Maternity Benefits*. If you can't get SMP, you may be able to get Maternity Allowance from the DHSS.

For Mothers Who Can't Get SMP: The Maternity Allowance

If you can't get SMP, but you have recently given up your job, or changed jobs, or have recently been self-employed, you may be able to get up to eighteen weeks' Maternity Allowance from the DHSS.

To qualify for the new Maternity Allowance you must have paid standard-rate NI contributions for at least twenty-six of the fifty-two weeks ending with the fifteenth week before the week in which your baby is due.

The payment period for Maternity Allowance starts eleven weeks before your baby is due, but if you are still employed at that time your Maternity Allowance may start later. Payment will normally be made for a 'core period' of thirteen weeks, beginning six weeks before your baby is due, but it is up to you to decide when to take the remaining five weeks. You can take some before and some after, or all before or all after. But you cannot get the allowance for any week in which you are working.

Maternity Allowance is £30.05 a week (April 1987 rates).

How to Claim

Fill in form MA1, which you can get from your Social Security office or antenatal clinic. Send the form to your Social Security office after you are twenty-six weeks pregnant. Make sure that you also send your maternity certificate Mat B1, which you get from your midwife or doctor.

If your employer has refused to pay you SMP, he or she should issue you with a form SMP1, which you should send with your claim for Maternity Allowance. Don't delay in sending in your application, or you may lose some of your allowance. For full details, see leaflet NI 17A, *Maternity Benefits*.

If you are already off work and getting Statutory Sick Pay (SSP), this will stop when you change to SMP or Maternity Allowance, but you still have to tell your employer three weeks before you stop work because of your pregnancy.

For Mothers Who Need Extra Cash: Social Fund

If you find it hard to make ends meet, you may be able to get a Social Fund Maternity Payment to help pay for things for your new baby. A Social Fund Maternity Payment may be made if you or your partner is getting Income Support or Family Credit.

If you are adopting a baby, you can apply for a payment if the baby is not more than twelve months old when you apply. You can apply at any time from when you adopt up to three months later.

How Much?

At the time of writing, the payment is £80 for each baby expected or born. But the total amount will be reduced by any savings over £500 that you or your partner or any dependent children who live with you have.

Write to your Social Security office for a claim form. You can apply until your baby is three months old. You will need to send in your antenatal clinic card instead of your maternity certificate as proof that your baby is due.

After the Birth of Your Baby

You must register your baby within six weeks of the birth (three weeks if you live in Scotland). If you haven't chosen a name by then, they can be added in the next twelve months. Your midwife will tell you where the register office for your district is. The registrar will give you your baby's birth certificate and form FP58 (EC58 if you live in Scotland) on which you apply for your baby's NHS card. Your baby will need an NHS card so he or she can be registered with a GP. Complete the form FP58 and send it to your family doctor, who will send it to your Family Practitioner Committee; this committee will then send you an NHS card with your baby's number on it.

If you apply for benefits after your baby is born, you will need a maternity certificate (form Mat 1) from your doctor or midwife, and your baby's birth certificate. For Maternity Allowance you should always send in your maternity certificate. For Child Benefit you must use the birth certificate.

If Your Baby Is Stillborn

If your baby is born dead after the twenty-eighth week of pregnancy, your entitlement to these benefits does not change: free prescriptions and free dental treatment, Social Fund Maternity Payment and Statutory Maternity Pay (SMP). The doctor or midwife will give you a certificate of stillbirth which you should give to the registrar. If no doctor or midwife was present at the birth, ask the registrar for form 35, fill it in and give it back to the registrar. The registrar will give you a certificate of burial.

Child Benefit

This is a tax-free cash benefit paid for each of your children, whatever your income. At the time of writing this is £7.25 a week for each child. To claim, either write to the Social Security office or call in and collect an application form. Fill in the form and send it off with your baby's birth certificate in the envelope supplied, which does not need a stamp. For more details on Child Benefit, see leaflet CH1, *Child Benefit.*

One-Parent Benefit

If you are a single parent, you can claim One-Parent Benefit at the same time as Child Benefit. One-Parent Benefit is a tax-free cash benefit payable for your first child only: at the time of writing, £4.70 a week. To claim, get an application form and leaflet (CH11, *One-Parent Benefit*) from your Social Security office. Fill it in and send it off in the envelope provided, which does not need a stamp. For more information, see leaflet FB27, *Bringing Up Children.*

Home Responsibilities Protection (HRP)

This will protect your right to Retirement Pension as long as you are getting Child Benefit for a child under sixteen. You can't get HRP if you keep the reduced liability for National Insurance which some married women still have. You do not have to apply for HRP. You will get it automatically until your Child Benefit stops or your youngest child reaches sixteen. For more information, see leaflet NP27, *Looking After Someone at Home? How to Protect Your Pension.*

For other benefits associated with the family and low incomes, see the information in this help directory included in the section for Chapter 4.

Miscarriage

MISCARRIAGE ASSOCIATION,
18 Stoneybrook Close,
West Bretton,
Wakefield,
West Yorkshire WF4 4TP.
Tel. 092 485 515.
Aims to provide information and support for women and their families during and after miscarriage. This is a registered charity, manned by a group of caring women who give their time and services voluntarily. Support groups throughout the country.

Publications: a quarterly newsletter; basic information pack, 50p (information about the Association, pre-conception care, causes of miscarriage, book list, emotional aspects of miscarriage).

Leaflets: *What Every Best Friend Should Know* (5p); *D & C* (5p); *Hydatidiform Mole* (5p); *Be Fit and Healthy before You Start a Baby* by Dr B. Pickard (35p); *The Cervical Stitch (What It's Like)* (£2.25p); sample newsletter (£1). All prices include postage and packaging.

Unwanted Pregnancy – Abortion

BROOK ADVISORY CENTRES,
233 Tottenham Court Road,
London W1 9AE.
Tel. 01-580 2991 (appointments), 01-323 1522 (information).
The objects of the Brook Advisory Centres are the prevention and mitigation of the suffering caused by unwanted pregnancy by educating young persons in matters of sex and contraception and developing among them a sense of responsibility in regard to sexual behaviour. They will also give advice, assist and refer women for abortion.

PREGNANCY ADVISORY SERVICE,
11–13, Charlotte Street,
London W1P 1HD.
Tel. 01-637 8962.

PAS is a non-profit-making charity offering women considering abortion sympathetic advice and medical help. PAS has worked to develop counselling, has pioneered day-care abortion procedures and morning-after contraception. All PAS services are personal and confidential. Costs £25 for consultation; £140 for abortion under fourteen weeks; £170, fourteen to eighteen weeks; £255, eighteen to twenty-two weeks. Loan scheme available for women with financial problems.

FAMILY PLANNING ASSOCIATION,
St Andrews House,
27–35 Mortimer Street,
London W1N 7RJ.
Tel. 01-636 7866.
Clinics are run through the NHS, but you do not need a GP referral.

Giving Birth the Way You Want

ACTIVE BIRTH CENTRE,
55 Dartmouth Park Road,
London NW5 1SL.
Tel. 01-267 3006.
Aims to restore balance between 'natural' birth and medical technology. Runs antenatal exercise classes based on natural birth positions and yoga; they encourage self-help and personal responsibility.

Publications: *Active Birth* by Janet Balaskas (Allen & Unwin, 1983), £3.95 + 75p p&p; *The Active Birth Partner's Handbook* by Janet Balaskas (Sidgwick & Jackson, 1986), £4.95 + 75p p&p; *New Life* by Janet and Arthur Balaskas (Sidgwick & Jackson, 1983), £8.95 + £1 p&p; *Health Rights Handbook for Maternity Care* by Beverley Beech and Roz Claxton £1 + 40p p&p; *Birth Rights* by Sally Inch (Hutchinson), £6.95 + £1 p&p; *Baby Relax* by Peter Walker (Allen & Unwin, 1986), £5.95 + 75p p&p; *Birth at Home* by Sheila Kitzinger (Oxford University Press, 1980), £2.95 + 75p p&p; *Home Birth Handbook* by Viki Junor and Marianne Monaco (Souvenir Press, 1984), £4.95 + 75p p&p; *Active Birth Manifesto* by Janet and Arthur Balaskas (Allen & Unwin, 1983), 50p + 20p p&p. All the above available from Active Birth Centre.

Cassette: Active Birth Exercise Cassette, *Shape Up for Motherhood*, with Janet Balaskas, £6.99 + 75p p&p.

Films: On Betamax or VHS video systems, *Active Birth* with Janet Balaskas; to rent or purchase, contact Keith Madders 0372741237. On

16 mm film, *Birth in the Squatting Position*, £20 rental from the Active
Birth Centre.
  Please make cheques payable to Active Birth Sales.

MATERNITY ALLIANCE,
59–61 Camden High Street,
London NW1 7JL.
Tel. 01-388 6337.
Provides information on many maternity issues including pre-con-
ceptual health, employment benefit rights.

THE SOCIETY TO SUPPORT HOME CONFINEMENT,
17 Laburnham Avenue,
Durham City,
Durham DL13 3HA.
Tel. 0388 528044.
Advice and help to women who want to have their baby at home and are
having difficulties. Publishes information sheets and leaflets. Please send
stamped addressed envelope.

THE NATIONAL CHILDBIRTH TRUST,
9 Queensborough Terrace,
London W2 3TB.
Tel. 01-221 3833.
Aims to help women have their babies happily and without fear, and to
prepare young families for the experience of childbirth and parenthood.
Local groups all over the country which run antenatal classes, post-natal
support groups and breast-feeding counsellors. Publications on all
aspects of antenatal care, breast-feeding and so on.

Premature (Small-for-Dates) Babies

EARLYBIRTH ASSOCIATION,
Barbara Newton,
16 Warnham Rise,
Hollingbury,
Brighton,
East Sussex BN1 8DF.
Tel. 0273 559634.
Support group of mothers of premature babies offers non-medical
advice and help.

NIPPERS (National Information for Parents of Prematures: Education, Resources and Support),
c/o The Sam Segal Perinatal Research Unit,
St Mary's Hospital,
Praed Street,
London W2 1NY.
Tel. 01-725 1487.
National co-ordinating committee to help parents to find resources and support if their babies are premature or require admission to a special care baby unit.

Death of a Baby at Birth

STILLBIRTH AND NEONATAL DEATH SOCIETY (SANDS),
28 Portland Place,
London W1N 3DE.
Tel. 01-436 5881.
Offers a service through local groups all over the country, giving advice and long-term support of newly bereaved parents whose babies died after twenty-two weeks of pregnancy and within a month of birth.

Publications: pack of information leaflets £1.25p; sample newsletter £1; *Saying Goodbye to Your Baby* 95p; *Hospital Chaplains and SANDS: Report on a Joint Workshop*; *After Stillbirth and Neonatal Death – What Happens Next* £2.50p; pack of five companion leaflets for parents £2.50p.

THE COMPASSIONATE FRIENDS (CHILD DEATHS),
Gill Hodder,
6 Denmark Street,
Bristol BS1 5DQ.
Tel. 0272 292778.

See also information in section for Chapter 10.

THE TWINS AND MULTIPLE BIRTH ASSOCIATION – Bereavement Support Groups (TAMBA),
54 Broad Lane,
Hampton, Middlesex TW12 3BG.
Established to help parents who have suffered the loss of a newborn twin. Because they have a second baby, their loss is often under-estimated, and parents may feel inhibited about showing their grief.

Also supports parents who have lost both twins either as newborn babies or as miscarriage.

Sub-Fertility (Infertility), Artificial Insemination, Test-Tube Babies

BRITISH PREGNANCY ADVISORY SERVICE (BPAS),
Austy Manor,
Wootton Wawen,
Solihull,
West Midlands B95 6DA.
Tel. 05642 3225.
Also:
7 Belgrave Road,
London SW1V 1QB.
Tel. 01-222 0985.
Charitable organisation offering counselling and practical help and treatment about pregnancy, including pregnancy testing, abortion, contraception, infertility, psychosexual problems, problem pregnancies, and sterilisations both male and female.

CHILD,
'Farthings',
Gaunt Road,
Pawlett,
Near Bridgwater,
Somerset TA6 4SF.
Tel. 0278 683595.
Self-help group for couples with infertility problems. Offers information, advice, support and especially a caring, understanding, listening ear through a twenty-four-hour answering service, a quarterly newsletter, a series of fact sheets on infertility subjects and free medical advice.

INFERTILITY ADVISORY CENTRE,
144 Harley Street,
London W1N 1AH.
Tel. 01-486 0090.
Also at London Bridge Hospital,
Tel. 01-407 3100,
and Devonshire Hospital,
Tel. 01-486 7131.

A wide range of diagnostic tests available, also artificial insemination, fertility drugs and in-vitro fertilisation. Couples seen together; family doctor kept informed of the progress. Fees about £15 per consultation.

NATIONAL ASSOCIATION FOR THE CHILDLESS,
318 Summer Lane,
Birmingham B19 3RL.
Tel. 021-359 4887.
If you are struggling to found your family, the NAC is here to help you. It exists to give you advice about your fertility problems, about your feelings and worries during treatment, about coping with things if everything fails.

Publications and fact sheets: *Miscarriage* 50p; *Endometriosis* 50p; *Drugs Used in Infertility* 50p; *Male Infertility* 50p; *Blocked Tubes and Microsurgery* 50p; *Artificial Insemination by Husband* 50p; *Artificial Insemination by Donor* 60p; *Infertility Tests* 50p; *Test-Tube Babies* 60p; *Mucus Hostility in Infertility* 50p; *Ectopic Pregnancy* 50p; *Ovulatory Disorders* 50p; *Unexplained Infertility* 50p.

Booklets available from NAC: *Infertility* by Dr Andrew Stanway £5.40; *So You Want to Have a Baby* by Serono 60p; *Adopting a Child* by the British Agencies for Adoption £2.30.

Prices include postage and packaging.

Adoption and Fostering

DR BARNARDO'S,
Tanner's Lane,
Barkingside,
Essex IG6 1QC.
Tel. 01-550 8822.
Barnardo's Homefinding Project (01-551 0011) finds families and single parents who, after preparation, foster (long term) and/or adopt children needing permanent homes from Barnardo preparation units. Most of these children are over eight years old and/or physically or mentally handicapped.

FOSTERFACTS,
34 John Adam Street,
London WC2N 6HW.
Information about fostering children up to eighteen years old, including handicapped children. Service for those living within a fifty-mile

radius of London. Leaflets explaining what fostering of various kinds involves.

NATIONAL ADOPTION SOCIETY,
Hooper Cottage,
Kimberley Road,
London NW6 7SG.
Tel. 01-624 3411.
Arranges adoptions.

NATIONAL FOSTER CARE ASSOCIATION,
Francis House,
Francis Street,
London SW1P 1DE.
Tel. 01-828 6266/7.
Advice and information on all aspects of fostering; provides training materials, local support groups throughout the country.

NATIONAL ORGANISATION FOR COUNSELLING ADOPTEES AND THEIR PARENTS (NORCAP),
3 New High Street,
Headington,
Oxford OX3 5AJ.
Tel. 0865 750554 (Monday, Wednesday, Friday, 10 a.m.–4 p.m.).
A support group, providing sympathetic understanding, support and guidance, for adult adopted people and both their adoptive and birth parents, from someone who has had similar experiences. Aims to establish a national computerised register of adoptees and birth families to facilitate the exchange of medical, social and other non-identifying information.
    Publications: *Where to Find Adoption Records* £9; *Searching for Family Connections*; *Shared Experiences* £3. (Available through NORCAP.)

PARENT TO PARENT INFORMATION ON ADOPTION SERVICES,
Lower Boddington,
Daventry,
Northamptonshire NN11 6YB.
Tel. Byfield (0327) 60295.
Aims to help potential adopters by passing on information about how and where to apply, and to provide support, advice and encouragement for prospective and existing adopters, and long-term foster parents. They

have experience of adoption of tiny healthy infants through to teenagers and handicapped children, of all ages and many different racial origins.

CHAPTER 2: BABIES AND YOUNG CHILDREN

For financial support for single parents or families with financial difficulties, see Chapter 4: Single Parents.

Post-Natal Depression

ASSOCIATION FOR POST-NATAL ILLNESS,
7 Gowan Avenue,
London SW6.
Tel. 01-731 4867.
Runs a network of volunteers throughout the United Kingdom to advise and support women suffering from post-natal depression.

At Home with a Baby

MEET-A-MUM ASSOCIATION (MAMA),
c/o Kate Goodyer,
3 Woodside Avenue,
South Norwood,
London SE25 5DW.
Tel. 01-654 3137.
Self-help organisation for new mothers and those with young children who may feel tired, lonely, isolated and/or depressed after the birth of a child. Groups all over the United Kingdom where mothers can get together for social events, support and advice.

MOTHER'S UNION,
Mary Sumner House,
24 Tufton Street,
London SW1P 3RB.
Tel. 01-222 5533.
Organised by the Church of England. Will help mothers who are under stress. Phone-in service.

Babies That Cry a Lot and Don't Sleep

BM Cry-sis Support Group,
London WC1N 3XX.
Tel. 01-404 5011.
The aims are to support, emotionally, the parents of babies who cry
excessively and/or sleep poorly, causing great disruption and concern to
their parents. All members are parents themselves who have been
through this experience and fully understand how frustrating and
depressing a constantly crying baby can be. There is a national network
of volunteers who support parents but do not offer medical advice.

   Publications: *Crying Baby – How to Cope* by Pat Gray, £3.50 + 40p
p&p, available from Cry-sis, Kingscote, Furneaux Pelham, Herts SG9
OLC. *Tel. Brent Pelham 371; Sleepless Children* by Dr David Haslam
(Futura), £1.95.

Breast-Feeding Problems

Association of Breast-Feeding Mothers,
131 Mayow Road,
London SE26 4HZ.
Tel. 01-778 4769 (recorded message).
Counsellors available to discuss all aspects of breast-feeding and parent-
ing. Monthly newsletter in English, Spanish, Urdu, Gujerati, Bengali,
Punjabi, Greek and Turkish.

La Lèche League of Great Britain,
Box BM 3424,
London WC1 6XX.
Tel. 01-883 7801.
Help, advice and support from women who have successfully breast-fed
their own babies.

National Childbirth Trust,
9 Queensborough Terrace,
London W2 3TB.
Tel. 01-221 3833.
Breast-feeding counsellors.

Twins

TWINS AND MULTIPLE BIRTHS ASSOCIATION,
292 Valley Road,
Lillington,
Leamington Spa,
Warwickshire CV32 7UE.
Aims to give encouragement and support to parents of twins, triplets or more, to advance the education of the public about the incidence and effects of multiple births, to promote greater appreciation within the medical profession of the problems of multiple births, to increase public awareness of the special needs of twins and their families, to produce and disseminate helpful information and literature for parents of twins and more. They have Twins Clubs all over the country where parents can meet.

Booklets costing £1 each plus postage: *Guide for Mothers with Twins* by Judi Linney and members from Working Twins Clubs, for mothers expecting twins; *Supertwins Guide* by Kathy Topping, a book for parents of triplets, quads or more.

Leaflets (all cost 30p plus a large stamped addressed envelope): *Multiple Birth Fact Sheet; So You Are Expecting Twins; The Arrival of Twins; Bottle Feeding Twins; Breast Feeding Twins; Choosing Prams and Pushchairs for Twins; Coping with Sleepless Children; Toilet Training; Play; Safe Travel with Twins in the Car; Starting School: Together or Apart; Parent/Teacher Co-operation to Help Twins at School; Twins Language Development; Loss of Your Twins; Double Tragedy – Loss of Your Twin Babies; Siblings of Twins; Twins, Triplets and Higher Multiples in Special Care Baby Units.* Personal Experiences: *The Father of Twins; Caesarean with an Epidural – Twin Delivery; Three under 15 months; Identical Twins; Experience of a Mother with Triplets; Experience of a Mother with Quads; The Cot Death of a Twin Baby; Getting the Best Out of Grandparents; Combined Breast and Bottle Feeding.*

Books: *The Nature and Nurture of Twins* by Dr Elizabeth Bryan (Ballière Tindall, 1983), £9.95 postage free; *Twins in the Family* by Dr Elizabeth Bryan (Constable, 1984), £5.95 postage free; *Twins: From Conception to Five Years* by Avril Clegg and Anne Woollett (Century Publishing, 1983), £5.95 postage free; *The Twins Handbook* by Elizabeth Friedrich and Cherry Rowland (Robson Books, 1983), hardback £8.95, paperback £4.95, both postage free; *All about Twins* by Dr

Gillian Leigh (Routledge & Kegan Paul, 1983), £4.95 postage free; *Multiple Births – Preparation – Birth – Management* by Judi Linney (Wiley, 1983), £5.45 postage free; *Twins: A Survival Guide for Parents* by Carola Zentner (Macdonald, 1984), £2.50 postage free; *More Than One* by Di Macdonald (I. Henry, 1982), £5.95 + postage and packing; *The Twin Book* by Honor Walters and Alan Hopgood (Worlds Work, 1983), £5.95 postage free; *The Ten Twins* by Maureen Bryan (Australian, 1982), £1.95 postage free; *How Twins Grow Up* by Mary Rosambeau (Bodley Head, 1987), £10.95 postage free.

Booklets, leaflets and occasional papers from:
Beverly M. Harris,
35 St Michael's Close,
Madeley,
Telford,
Shropshire TF7 5SD.

Books available from:
Mrs Liz Pannell,
31 Denton Close,
Redhill,
Surrey RH1 5LB.

Please make cheques or postal orders payable to Twins and Multiple Births Association.

Recommended books for babies and toddlers: *Ourselves and Our Children* by the Boston Women's Health Collective (Penguin,); *Child Care and the Growth of Love* by John Bowlby (Penguin, 1970); *Living with a Toddler* by Brenda Crowe (Unwin Paperbacks, 1982); *Book of Childcare* by Dr Hugh Jolly (Allen and Unwin, 1985); *Baby and Child* by Penelope Leach (Penguin, 1980); *The Breast-Feeding Book* by Marie Messenger (Frances Lincoln, 1982); *Your Baby: Complete Book of Baby Care from Conception to Three Years* by Miriam Stoppard (Hamlyn, 1987); *The Baby and Child Book* by Drs Andrew and Penny Stanway (Routledge, 1976); *Your Growing Child* by Dr Miriam Stoppard (Octopus, 1983); *The Pre-School Book* by Brenda Thompson (Unwin Paperbacks, 1980); *The Macmillan Guide to Home Nursing* by Diana Hastings (Macmillan, 1986); *Early Days – You and Your Baby* (Disabled Living Foundation, 1973); *Guide to Pregnancy and Parenthood for Women on their Own* by Patricia Ashdown-Sharp (Penguin, 1975).

CHAPTER 3: SCHOOLCHILDREN AND ADOLESCENCE

For maternity and child benefit details, see information section for Chapter 1, and for single parents or families on low incomes Chapter 4, in the Help Directory.

Going Back to Work when You Have a Young Baby

Childminders
NATIONAL CHILDMINDING ASSOCIATION,
8 Masons Hill,
Bromley,
Kent BR2 9EY.
Tel. 01-464 6164.
This is a national organisation which offers information and support to anyone involved in childminding or child care in general. They have a very informative leaflet called *I Need a Childminder* which is specifically for parents looking for day care for their child. Send a stamped addressed envelope to the above address. Membership form and other publications on request.
For the list of registered childminders in your area and the cost per day or week, contact your local Social Services department.

Day Nurseries
Apply through your local Social Services.

Private Day Nurseries
Your local library will have a list.

Nannies
If you need a nanny, you will find that they advertise in two main magazines: *Nursery World* and *The Lady*. You could also contact:

NORLAND NURSERY TRAINING COLLEGE,
Denford Park,
Hungerford,
Berks RG17 OPQ.
Tel. 0488 82252.

PRINCESS CHRISTIAN COLLEGE,
26 Wilbraham Road,
Fallowfield,
Manchester M14 6JX.
Tel. 061-224 4560.

Nannies and au pairs can also be found through:

BRITISH EMPLOYMENT AGENCY,
Sussex House,
22 London Road,
Horsham,
Sussex RH1 2HA.
Tel. 0403 65571.

AU PAIR BUREAU (Piccadilly),
87 Regent Street,
London W1R 7HS.
Tel. 01-930 4757.

Starting School

Play Groups
PRE-SCHOOL PLAYGROUPS ASSOCIATION,
61–3 King's Cross Road,
London WC1X 9LL.
Tel. 01-833 0991.
This association was formed to encourage the formation of play groups
and mother-and-toddler groups for children under five.

Nursery Schools
These are run by the local education authority. Like all state schools they
are free. Private nursery schools are fee-paying, and the local education authority or the library will have a list of these and the fees charged.

Dyslexia

BRITISH DYSLEXIA ASSOCIATION,
Church Lane,
Peppard,
Oxfordshire RG9 5JN.

Tel. 04917 699.
This is the address of the co-ordinating office. They do not give advice to individuals but will refer you to your nearest Dyslexia Association where you will receive advice, support and therapy. Produces parents', teachers' and medical information sheets and leaflets. Publications list.

DEFINING DYSLEXIA,
132 High Street,
Ruislip,
Middlesex HA4 8LL.
Tel. 01-868 6810/01-950 1033.
Help for parents of dyslexic children. Self-help advisory service (in your home if necessary).

DYSLEXIA INSTITUTE,
133 Gresham Road,
Staines,
Middlesex TW18 2AJ.
Tel. 81 59498.
The institute provides informed advice for parents and teachers; expert examination of difficulties; specialist training and teaching; research. Teaching, assessment and training centres throughout the country.

HELEN ARKELL DYSLEXIA CENTRE,
14 Crondace Road,
London SW6 4BB.
Tel. 01-736 0748.
Also:
Frensham,
Farnham,
Surrey GU10 3BW.
Tel. 025125 2400.
Centre provides tuition for children and adults. Training courses for teachers. Only diagnosed dyslexics accepted for treatment. A forty-five-minute lesson costs £12. There is a subsidy fund for those with financial difficulties. Publishes a series of booklets suggesting practical ways of overcoming problems.

Problems with Reading, Writing and Arithmetic

If remedial teaching or advice is required, contact:

NATIONAL ASSOCIATION FOR REMEDIAL EDUCATION,
2 Lichfield Road,
Stafford ST17 4JX.
Tel. 0785-46872.

KIDS,
80 Waynflete Square,
London W10 6UD.
Tel. 01-969 2817.
For families with children with special needs. They work with the
parents and their handicapped child or a child with developmental and
learning problems. They develop suitable training programmes, give
information and advice. Offer counselling for parents and regular
meetings. They have a home-based learning service; developmental play
sessions; holiday play schemes for physically vulnerable and frail
children; training towards independence for adolescents with special
needs. Currently KIDS services are available in London at its centres in
Camden, Kensington and Chelsea, Hammersmith and Fulham.

Recommended Books for Parents to Help Their Children at Home

Learning the alphabet: *The Most Amazing Hide-and-Seek Alphabet Book* by Robert Crowther (Viking, 1978), ages 3–6; *B is for Bear* by Dick Bruna (Methuen, 1971), ages 3–6.

Counting: *The Very Hungry Caterpillar* by Eric Carle (Hamish Hamilton, 1970), ages 2–6; *Shapes/Numbers* (Watts), ages 6–8.

Learning to Read: *Best Word Book Ever* by Richard Scarry (Hamlyn), ages 4–6; *Bright and Early Beginners* (Collins), ages 4–6; Happy Families series by Allan Ahlberg (Puffin), ages 6–8; Ladybird Well-Loved Tales (Ladybird), ages 5–7; *Frog and Toad Tales* by Arnold Lobel (World's Work), ages 5–7.

Young children who read well: *The Enormous Crocodile* by Roald Dahl (Puffin), ages 6–9; *The Little Girl and the Tiny Doll* by Edward and Aingelda Ardizzone (Puffin), ages 6–9.

Writing practice: Ladybird Activity Books (Ladybird), ages 5–7; Ladybird also have a series of books to help you to teach your child reading, writing and counting; there is also a series of books called *The Ronald Ridout Scheme* written by Ronald Ridout, which help you to teach your child how to read, write and count. This is an excellent and inexpensive series published by Purnell.

Hyperactive Children

HYPERACTIVE CHILDREN'S SUPPORT GROUP,
59 Meadowside,
Angmering,
Littlehampton,
West Sussex BN16 4BW.
Help and support for hyperactive children and their families. Will refer you to a local group. Publishes booklet, *Help for Hyperactive Children,* which includes advice about diet, diet sheets and other information. Annual membership £5; members receive the booklet and a newsletter which is published three times a year.

Problems Including Truancy, Bullying, Stealing, etc.

ORGANISATION FOR PARENTS UNDER STRESS (OPUS),
106 Goldstone Road,
Whyteleafe,
Surrey CR3 OEB.
Tel. 01-645 0469. Linkline 01-645 0505.
How many times do you feel that your children are driving you round the bend? OPUS have groups all over the country, and there may well be one near you. There you will be able to share your worries and your distress. OPUS is a national organisation representing groups throughout the country who offer a telephone helpline service to parents experiencing problems with their children.

PARENTS ANONYMOUS LONDON,
6–9 Manor Gardens,
London N7 6LA.
Tel. 01-263 5672/01-263 8918. Twenty-four-hour service.
Completely confidential sympathetic advice and help for parents having problems with their children.

Adolescence

SAMARITANS,
17 Uxbridge Road,
Slough,
Berkshire SL1 1SN.

Tel. 0753 32713/4.
There are about 180 Samaritan branches in the United Kingdom and
Ireland, run by more than 20,000 volunteers. They offer a twenty-four-
hour confidential service for anyone. Many young people find talking to
the Samaritans very helpful indeed. The telephone number of your local
Samaritan office can be found in the telephone directory.

Cults

FAMILY ACTION INFORMATION AND RESCUE (FAIR),
BCM Box 3535,
PO Box 12,
London WC1N 3XX.
Tel. 01-539 3940.
FAIR is an organisation that will help distressed relatives and friends of
young adults who have joined various extremist religious cults. They
originally dealt solely with the 'Moonies', but have since broadened
their sphere of concern to over a hundred groups operating in the
United Kingdom.

CHAPTER 4: ADULT RELATIONSHIPS

Loneliness

NATIONAL COUNCIL FOR VOLUNTARY YOUTH SERVICES,
Wellington House,
29 Albion Street,
Leicester LE1 6GD.
Tel. 0533 554910.
Helps and educates young people to develop their physical, mental and
spiritual capacities.

NATIONAL FEDERATION OF EIGHTEEN PLUS GROUPS,
Nicholson House,
Old Court Road,
Newent,
Gloucestershire GL18 1AG.
Tel. 05831 821210.

Anyone between the ages of eighteen and thirty welcome to club activities which the members organise. Activities include debates, discussions, drama, rambling, bowling and dancing.

SAMARITANS,
17 Uxbridge Road,
Slough,
Berkshire SL1 1SN.
Tel. 0753 32713/4.
To contact them locally, look up the telephone number in the phonebook. Someone to talk to in confidence.

Adolescents and Sex

BROOK ADVISORY CENTRES,
233 Tottenham Court Road,
London W1 9AE.
Tel. 01-580 2991 (appointments), 01-323 1522 (information).
Confidential and sympathetic advice on contraception, pregnancy, abortion, emotional and sexual problems of the young. Also provide free supplies of contraceptives.

CONTRABOX LTD,
Perrotts Brook House,
Perrotts Brook
Cirencester
Gloucester GL7 7BS
Tel. 028-583475

LONDON YOUTH ADVISORY CENTRE,
26 Prince of Wales Road,
London NW5 3LG.
Tel. 01-267 4792/3.
Has trained medical and counselling staff to help young people between twelve and twenty-five and their parents with problems about personal relationships, school and family problems, decisions about contraception and sexual behaviour.

Recommended Books for Young People about Sex
B. H. Claesson, *Boy, Girl, Man, Woman* (Penguin, 1971); Jane Cousins, *Make It Happy* (Penguin, 1988); Peter Mayle, *Where Did I Come From?* (Macmillan, 1975); Clare Rayner, *The Body Book* (Piccolo, 1979).

End of a Relationship, Separation and Divorce

LONDON WOMEN'S AID,
52–4 Featherstone Street,
London EC1.
Tel. 01-251 6537 (twenty-four-hour answering service).
Provides temporary accommodation in refuges for women. Offers support and advice. Publishes excellent leaflet called *Divorce Your Right*, containing information on separation and divorce, maintenance, children, custody and care and legal aid (5p plus a stamped addressed envelope).

NATIONAL MARRIAGE GUIDANCE COUNCIL,
Herbert Gray College,
Little Church Street,
Rugby,
Warwickshire CV21 3AP.
Tel. 0788 73241.
Co-ordinates activities of about 160 local marriage guidance councils that undertake counselling for people seeking help in a relationship, heterosexual, married or homosexual. Some counsellors are trained to help with psychosexual problems.

NATIONAL COUNCIL FOR THE DIVORCED AND SEPARATED,
13 High Street,
Little Shelford,
Cambridge,
CB2 5ES.
Tel. 01-300 4669 (day), 01-254 2080 (evening), 01-223 1007 (evening).
Promotes the interests and welfare of all persons whose marriages have ended in divorce or separation. Activities through 150 branches throughout the United Kingdom. Counselling centres offering advice on legal, financial, property and Social Services matters. Has a postal advisory service.

Sexual Problems

BRITISH ASSOCIATION FOR COUNSELLING,
37a Sheep Street,
Rugby,
Warwickshire CV21 3BX.
Tel. 0788 78328/9.

Able to give information, counselling and help to people with psychosexual problems.

Brook Advisory Centres, see above.

Family Planning Association,
St Andrews House,
27/35 Mortimer Street,
London W1N 7RJ.
Tel. 01-636 7866.
Not only offers family planning advice but at separate clinics also offers sessions on sexual difficulties. Some clinics may require you to be referred by your family doctor.

Health Education Council,
78 New Oxford Street,
London WC1A 1AH.
Tel. 01-631 0930.
Provides free information leaflets on a very wide range of topics including health and human relationships.

Institute of Marital Studies,
Tavistock Centre,
Belsize Lane,
London NW3 5BA.
Tel. 01-435 7111.
Provides a professional therapeutic service to people who are experiencing difficulty with their marriage and sexual problems. Fees are income-related (£1 per £1,000 joint income per session, negotiable).

Marriage Guidance Councils, see above.

Single-Parent Families

Gingerbread,
35 Wellington Street,
London WC2E 7BN.
Tel. 01-240 0953.
Over 300 self-help groups for one-parent families throughout the United Kingdom. Offers social opportunities for adults and children plus practical advice and information.

Publications (all prices include postage and packing): *The Ginger-bread Handbook* £2.50 (£1.50 to Gingerbread groups); *Giving Advice* £3 (£2 to Gingerbread groups); *Starting a Crèche* £2.50 (£1.50 to Gingerbread groups); current annual report £1; Gingerbread's social policy statement 50p; *Ginger* magazine, quarterly; welfare publications on all aspects of the Social Security system (prices range from 10p to 25p + p&p).

HOLIDAY CARE SERVICE,
2 Old Bank Chambers,
Station Road,
Horley,
Surrey RH6 9HW.
Tel. 02937 74535.
Free service offers the elderly disabled, single parents and those on low income details of appropriate holidays, sources of financial help.

NATIONAL COUNCIL FOR ONE-PARENT FAMILIES,
255 Kentish Town Road,
London NW5 2LX.
Tel. 01-267 1361.
Offers free and confidential advice and help to single parents, and single pregnant women, concerning the law, welfare, benefits, housing, day care and emotional problems.

ONE-PARENT FAMILY HOLIDAYS,
25 Fore Street,
Praze,
Camborne,
Cornwall TR14 OJX.
Tel. 0209 831274.
Organises holidays for one-parent families in the United Kingdom and abroad. Send stamped addressed envelope for brochure with suggested holiday.

SINGLEHANDED LTD,
Thorne House,
Hankham Place,
Stone Cross,
Pevensey,
East Sussex BN24 5ER.
Tel. 0323 767507.

Introduces one-parent families to each other, in order to help them share problems and develop friendships. Also arranges holidays. Fee for a year's membership £35.

SINGLE PARENTS SUPPORT GROUP,
Holly Lodge,
14 Commercial Road,
Lower Parkstone,
Poole,
Dorset BH14 OJW.
Tel. Poole 675100 ext. 2686.
A self-help group, gets together for coffee, chats, outings and making new friends.

SINGLE PARENT LINKS AND SPECIAL HOLIDAYS (SPLASH),
Empire House,
Clarence Street,
Swindon,
Wiltshire SN1 2JF.
Tel. 0793 613220.
Help in organising holidays for one-parent families. Also children-only holidays ages eight to fourteen. Plus a holiday saving scheme.

FAMILIES NEED FATHERS,
BM Families,
London WC1N 3XX.
Tel. 01-852 7123.
A national society primarily concerned with the problems of maintaining a child's relationship with both parents during and following separation and divorce. Provides advice, support and group counselling to parents of both sexes who do not have custody of their children. About thirty-five branches throughout the country. Walk-in-Talk-in sessions in Conway Hall, Red Lion Square, London WC1, 7.30–9.30 p.m. first and third Friday of each month.

Social Security for the Single Parent or the Family on a Low Income

Family Credit
This is a benefit for working people who are employed or self-employed

and who have at least one child. It can be paid to people who are single parents, married or living with someone as if they are married to them.

Who May Be Able to Get Family Credit?

Family Credit can help people who are working for twenty-four hours a week or more, support at least one child who normally lives with them and have savings that are worth no more than £6,000. If someone who claims Family Credit has a partner, who they are married to, or who they live with as if they were married to them, their partner's savings are counted as well. If people cannot get Family Credit because they are working for less than twenty-four hours a week, they may be able to get a benefit called Income Support instead; see below.

How Family Credit Is Worked Out

Three main things are looked at when Family Credit is worked out:

(1) An amount of money that depends on the number of children in the family and how old the children are. Single persons will not get less Family Credit than a couple just because they are bringing up children on their own.

(2) The money that is coming in each week. This includes how much the adults and the children have coming in regularly, from work and things like Social Security benefits. Child Benefit, One-Parent Benefit and Housing Benefit are not counted.

(3) How much the adults and the children have, in things like savings accounts.

Savings of less than £3,000 will not affect Family Credit.

Savings between £3,000 and £6,000 will make a difference. Each £250 or part of £250 will be treated as if it was bringing in £1 a week.

If a child has more than £3,000 savings, no allowance will be added on to Family Credit for that child. Otherwise a child's savings will not be counted.

People who have more than £6,000 of savings will not get any Family Credit.

How Much Family Credit Can People Get?

The exact amount each person can get will be worked out by the Family Credit Unit in Blackpool after they apply. These examples give some idea of how much people may be able to get. They only give a rough idea. Those who think that they may be able to get Family Credit should send in a claim form.

People will normally get the same amount of Family Credit for twenty-six weeks. But Family Credit may be paid for more weeks or fewer weeks during the first twelve months of the new scheme, which commenced in April 1988. Family Credit is tax-free.

Example 1: A single parent with one child under eleven
Money coming in each week   about £70
Family Credit they may be able to get   about £25

Example 2: A couple with two children aged four and six
Money coming in each week   about £90
Family Credit they may be able to get   about £17

Example 3: A couple with four children aged seven, twelve, fourteen and sixteen
Money coming in each week   about £110
Family Credit they may be able to get   about £34

How Is Family Credit Paid?
It is paid in two ways: either directly into a bank account or building society account (this is called payment by credit transfer; the money is paid into the account every four weeks); or by order book that can be cashed every week at a post office.

Other Help People Can Get while They Are Getting Family Credit
Anyone receiving Family Credit will not have to pay for any of the following, for themselves or for their partner or their children: NHS prescriptions; NHS dental treatment; travel to hospital for NHS treatment. They will also get help with the cost of glasses. Some people may also be able to get:

■ help with paying for where they live. People who pay rent or rates may be entitled to help from their local council called Housing Benefit.
■ help from the Social Fund if they have a new baby, funeral expenses or other exceptional expenses. See Social Fund below.

How to Claim Family Benefit
Complete the claim form FC1. This is available from post offices and Social Security offices and will include information about Family Credit as well.
In two-parent families, the woman should normally claim.

More information about Family Credit and other benefits can be found in leaflets FB4, *Help While You Are Working*; FB27, *Bringing Up Children*; and for a detailed explanation of Family Credit get leaflet N1261, *A Guide to Family Credit*.

Income Support

This is a benefit to help people who do not have enough money to live on. It replaced Supplementary Benefit in April 1988. Income Support is intended to meet regular weekly needs. People may be able to get help with exceptional expenses which are difficult for them to pay from their regular income from the Social Fund. More information about Social Fund below.

Who May Be Able to Get Help from Income Support?

People who do not have enough money to live on, and who are unemployed, or sixty or over, or bringing up children on their own, or too sick or disabled to work, or only able to work part-time, or staying at home to look after a disabled relative.

People can get help from Income Support even if they have savings of up to £6,000. If someone who claims Income Support has a partner, who they are married to or who they live with as if married to them, their partner's savings are counted as well. If the savings are worth up to £3,000, it will not make any difference to the Income Support they can get. Savings between £3,000 and £6,000 will make a difference. Each £250 or part of £250 will be treated as if it was bringing in £1 a week. If a child has more than £3,000 savings, no allowance will be added on to Income Support for that child. Otherwise a child's savings will not be counted.

Income Support cannot normally help people who work for twenty-four hours or more a week, or who have a partner who works for twenty-four hours or more a week. Some people may still be able to get Income Support even if they are working for twenty-four hours or more a week. These are people who work at home as a childminder or are so disabled that they cannot earn much money.

If people are earning money, it can make a difference to their Income Support. The first £5 a week of a person's earnings will not be counted. The first £5 a week of their partner's earnings will also not be counted. For some people £15 of their earnings will not be counted if they are lone parents or getting a Disability Premium or doing special jobs such as part-time firefighter or auxiliary coastguard or a couple under sixty who have been out of work and getting Supplementary Benefit or Income Support for two years or more.

If people cannot get Income Support because they are working for twenty-four hours or more a week, they may be able to get a benefit called Family Credit instead; see above.

How Much Income Support Can People Get?

There are fixed amounts that the law says people in different circumstances need to live on. These fixed amounts are set out at the end of this section. The amount of Income Support a person can get depends mainly on how much the law says they need to live on, and how much money they already have coming from things like Social Security benefits and part-time work. Savings worth more than £3,000 will also make a difference.

There are different systems for working out how much Income Support people can get while living in board and lodgings, hostels, residential care and nursing homes. Local Social Security offices will be able to give more information about this.

How to Claim

People usually claim Income Support by filling in a claim form. Unemployed people should go to their local Unemployment Benefit office and ask for the form B1. People who are not unemployed can get a form SB1 from a post office. When they send in this form they will be sent a claim form to fill in. Or they could get in touch with their local Social Security office and ask them for an Income Support claim form. Some people may be able to have an interview instead of filling in a claim form.

Choosing Who Claims Income Support

If both partners in a couple might be entitled to Income Support, either one of them can claim benefit. If one of the couple can't work because of illness, they may get more Income Support after twenty-eight weeks if the person who is ill claims. People should claim as soon as they think they might be entitled to Income Support. If they delay claiming they could lose money.

How Income Support Is Paid

People who are unemployed are usually paid Income Support by girocheque at the end of each two-week period of the claim. The giros are usually sent out by the Unemployment Benefit office and they can normally be cashed at a post office. Other people are usually paid by an order book that can be cashed every week at a post office.

Help with the Cost of Housing

Rent and rates: If someone gets Income Support, they will be able to get Housing Benefit from their local council, to help them pay their rent and rates. But they will have to pay part of their rates themselves and their water charges. Extra money for any ground rent that has to be paid can also be added on to Income Support.

Mortgages and home loans: Income Support can also help pay the interest on mortgages or home loans. The amount will depend on the person's age.

People under sixty: If both the person getting Income Support and their partner are under sixty, an amount will be added to cover half the interest that they have to pay for the first sixteen weeks after they start getting Income Support. After this sixteen weeks, an amount to cover all the interest will normally be added on.

People sixty or over: If either the person getting Income Support or their partner is sixty or over, an amount to cover the interest will normally be added on.

Other Help You Can Get while Getting Income Support

People who get Income Support do not have to pay for any of these things for themselves or for their partners or for their children: NHS prescriptions, NHS dental treatment, travel to hospital for NHS treatment. They will also get help with the cost of glasses. They may also be able to get help from the Social Fund if they have a new baby, funeral expenses or other exceptional expenses.

More Information

For more information about Income Support and other benefits, get leaflets: FB6, *Retiring?*; FB9, *Unemployed?*; FB23, *Young People's Guide to Social Security*; FB27, *Bringing Up Children?*; or FB28, *Sick or Disabled?* For a detailed explanation of Income Support, get leaflet SB20, *A Guide to Income Support.* All these leaflets are available from Social Security offices. The phone-numbers and addresses are in the phone-book. Look under 'Social Security' or 'Health and Social Security'.

Some of these leaflets will also be available in post offices. For advice or help with Social Security, use Freeline Social Security 0800-666 555.

Allowances and Premiums

Allowances: There are different weekly allowances for the people described here. They will get all the allowances that they qualify for (amounts correct at time of writing: April 1988).

Single people (per week)

16–17 years old	£19.40
18–24 years old	£26.05
25 and over	£33.40

Couples (per week)

Both under 18	£38.40
With at least one of the couple over 18	£51.45

For each child in the family (per week)

Under 11	£10.75
11–15 years old	£16.10
16–17 years old and doing a full-time course that is not above A level or OND standard	£19.40
18 years old and doing a full-time course that is not above A level or OND standard	£26.00

Premiums

(Amounts correct at time of writing: April 1988) Premiums are extra weekly amounts for people with special needs. If a person qualifies for more than one premium, they will normally only get the premium that gives the most money. But Family Premium, Disabled Child's Premium and Severe Disability Premium can be paid as well as any other premiums that people qualify for.

For people with children (per week)

If they have at least one child, they qualify for Family Premium	£6.15
If they have a child who is getting Attendance Allowance or Mobility Allowance or who is registered blind, they qualify for the Disabled Child's Premium	£6.15

	Single	Couple
If they are bringing up one or more children on their own, they qualify for the Lone Parent Premium	£3.70	

For long-term sick or disabled people (per week)

	Single	Couple
If a person or their partner is getting certain benefits because they are disabled or cannot work, such as Invalidity Benefit, Severe Disablement Allowance, Mobility Allowance, or Attendance Allowance, they qualify for the Disability Premium	£13.05	£18.60
If a person or their partner is registered blind, they qualify for the Disability Premium	£13.05	£18.60
If a person is sick and cannot work and has been sending in doctor's statements about this for at least twenty-eight weeks, they qualify for the Disability Premium	£13.05	£18.60
If a person is living alone (or with another person who is getting Attendance Allowance) and gets Attendance Allowance, and no one is getting Invalid Care Allowance for looking after them, they qualify for the Severe Disability Premium	£24.75	£24.75
or the Higher Pensioner Premium or if both qualify		£49.50

For people aged sixty or over (per week)

	Single	Couple
If a person or their partner is 60–79 years old, they qualify for the Pensioner Premium	£10.65	£16.25
If a person or their partner is 60–79 years old and getting Attendance Allowance, Invalidity Benefit, Severe Disablement Allowance, or is registered blind, they qualify for the Higher Pension Premium	£13.05	£18.60
If a person or their partner is 80 or over, they qualify for the Higher Pensioner Premium	£13.05	£18.60

The Social Fund

The following information is only about Social Fund payments. Maternity benefits are explained in the information section for Chapter 1. Funeral payments are described in the information section for Chapter 10.

The Social Fund is a scheme to help people with exceptional expenses which are difficult for them to pay from their regular income. There are three types of discretionary payment: Budgeting Loans, Crisis Loans and Community Care Grants. There is a limited amount of money available for these payments. When they look at an application, Social Fund officers have to look at the needs of all the people who apply for help and decide which needs can be met from the money available.

Budgeting Loans are for people getting Income Support. They are to help them pay for something that they need but that they cannot afford at the time they need it. Savings worth over £500 will make a big difference to Budgeting Loans.

Budgeting Loans have to be paid back. The loan is usually paid back by taking money from the person's Social Security benefit each week. If the person stops getting benefit, perhaps because he starts work, he will still have to pay back the money.

Can anyone who is getting Income Support get a Budgeting Loan? The person applying for the Budgeting Loan, or their partner, must have been getting Income Support for each of the last twenty-six weeks without a break. One break of fourteen days or less does not matter. Their partner is the person who they are married to or someone who they live with as if they were married to them.

People cannot get a Budgeting Loan if they or their partner are involved in a trade dispute. And the Social Fund officer must be sure that the person can afford to pay the money back.

To apply, complete form SF300, *Grants and Loans from the Social Fund;* these forms are available from Social Security offices.

Crisis Loans are to help people pay for things they need urgently because of an emergency or because of a disaster.

Who may be able to get a Crisis Loan? Anyone may be able to get a Crisis Loan. They are not just for people who are getting Income Support or some other Social Security benefit. But you can only get a Crisis Loan if there is no other way of preventing a serious risk to your health or safety or your family's health or safety. For example, someone might get a Crisis Loan to pay for their immediate needs if they are burgled and they have no money or savings.

Crisis Loans have to be paid back. If the person is getting Social Security benefits, the loan may be paid back by taking the money from the benefit each week. If the person isn't getting Social Security benefits, the loan will still have to be paid back.

To apply, get in touch with the nearest Social Security office. The phone number and the address are in the phone-book under 'Social Security' or 'Health and Social Security'. The person will then have an interview.

Community Care Grants are for people getting Income Support or who expect to get Income Support when they move into the community.

They are to help them return to the community rather than having to be in care – for example, in a hospital, nursing home, old people's home or residential care home; or return to the community from places like hostels for the homeless, detention centres or local authority care for young people; or stay in the community rather than having to be in care; or cope with very difficult problems in their family such as disability, long-term illness or family breakdown; or pay for fares to visit someone who is ill or for another urgent reason. Savings worth over £500 will make a difference to Community Care Grants.

If someone gets Income Support, they will not have to pay back the Community Care Grant. If someone does not get Income Support when they move into the community, they will have to pay the grant back.

To apply, complete form SF300, *Grants and Loans from the Social Fund*. These are available from Social Security offices.

Grants and loans from the Social Fund are paid by girocheque from the Social Security office. For more information about the Social Fund and other benefits, get: FB8, *Babies and Benefits;* FB27, *Bringing Up Children;* FB28, *Sick or Disabled?;* FB29, *Help When Someone Dies.* For a detailed explanation of the Social Fund, get leaflet SB16, *A Guide to the Social Fund.* All these leaflets are available from Social Security offices. The phone numbers and addresses are in the phone-book under 'Social Security' or 'Health and Social Security'. Some of these leaflets will also be available in post offices. For advice or help with Social Security, use Freeline Social Security 0800-666 555. Free telephone enquiry service.

Housing Benefit

This is a government scheme to help people on low incomes pay their rent and rates. It is run by local councils. Housing Benefit can be paid to people who are working or do not work; pay rent to a council or to a private landlord; own their own home. People do not have to be getting other Social Security benefits to get Housing Benefit.

Full-time students can claim Housing Benefit like other people during summer vacation. They may also be able to claim Housing Benefit at other times of the year if they are not living in a hall of residence or other accommodation that is rented from a college or university which they attend.

What does Housing Benefit cover? It can cover some or all of the rent and up to 80 per cent of the rates that someone has to pay to live in their own home. Housing Benefit does not give help with mortgage repayments, but home-owners may still be able to get help with their rates.

Rent can include some service charges for things like children's play areas, cleaning shared areas and/or lifts. Housing Benefit cannot normally help with the cost of buying a home, the cost of fuel for heating, lighting and cooking, the cost of meals that are included in the rent, water charges, some service charges for things like personal laundry and household cleaning, ground rent (feu duty in Scotland) and service charges for homes if the lease was originally for more than twenty-one years, or the rates for business premises.

Most people who get Income Support are automatically entitled to Housing Benefit if they pay rent or rates. People living in board and lodgings, hostels, residential care or nursing homes cannot get Housing Benefit as well as Income Support. This is because Income Support pays for their board and lodging. If someone stops getting Income Support, they may still be entitled to Housing Benefit. But they will need to make a new claim so that the council can check their new circumstances.

How much Housing Benefit will a person get? The amount of Housing Benefit depends on:

■ the amount of rent and rates.
■ the number of people living in the same place. Generally if the person claiming Housing Benefit has a partner who he is married to, or who he lives with as if he were married to her, or has dependent children, his Housing Benefit will be increased. But if there are grown-up children, elderly parents, boarders or sub-tenants their Housing Benefit will normally be reduced.
■ the amount that the law says people need in different circumstances to live on. These are fixed amounts called allowances and premiums. They are set out at the end of the section above on Income Support.
■ the amount of money coming in from things like Social Security benefits or maintenance payments. Money from some Social Security benefits, such as Mobility Allowance and Attendance Allowance, is not counted.
■ money coming in from work. The first £5 a week of a person's earnings will not be counted, or £10 a week if they have a partner. For some people £15 of their earnings will not be counted if they are lone parents, or getting the Disability Premium, or doing special jobs such as part-time firefighter or auxiliary coastguard. If they have a partner, both their incomes are added together before the £15 is ignored. Savings worth less than £3,000 do not affect Housing Benefit. Savings between £3,000 and £6,000 will make a difference to the amount of Housing Benefit. Each £250 or part of £250 will be treated as if it was bringing in £1 a week. If the savings are worth more than £6,000, they

will not be able to get any Housing Benefit at all. If a child has more than £3,000 savings, no allowances will be added on to Housing Benefit for that child. Otherwise a child's savings will not be counted.

How is Housing Benefit paid? There are two main ways:

- For rent or rates paid to the council, by reducing the amount that has to be paid. If Housing Benefit is paid this way, the person who is entitled to Housing Benefit will not actually receive any money.
- For rent or rates paid to someone else such as a housing association or private landlord, normally by paying money to the person who is entitled to Housing Benefit. The money may be paid by cheque or cash, or paid directly into an account.

How to claim: People who claim Income Support will get a form to fill in for claiming Housing Benefit. This form is NHB1. It should be filled in and sent to the Social Security office with the Income Support claim form. The Social Security office will pass it on to the local council to deal with.

People who are not claiming Income Support will need to get a form from their local council. If a person is already getting Income Support and becomes responsible for paying rent or rates, he should claim Housing Benefit from his local council.

More information about Housing Benefit can be found in leaflet RR1, *Help with Housing Costs*. For a detailed explanation of Housing Benefit, get leaflet RR2, *A Guide to Housing Benefit*. These leaflets are available from your local Social Security office and post offices. For advice or help with Social Security, use Freeline Social Security 0800-666 555 (free telephone enquiry service).

If you need more information, get in touch with your local council; ask in your library about who to contact. Or go to the Citizen's Advice Bureau.

Transvestism, Trans-sexualism, Gays and Lesbians

ALBANY TRUST COUNSELLING,
24 Chester Square,
London SW1W 9HS.
Tel. 01-730 5871.
A voluntary organisation and specialising in sexual/psychological counselling. They deal with marital relationship problems. They also have a

very wide range of clients from transvestites, trans-sexuals, to gay
people, to abused and depressed people. Counsellors all hold recognised
professional qualifications.

BEAUMONT SOCIETY,
BM Box 3084,
London WC1N 3XX.
The Beaumont Society was formed to relieve the mental and emotional
stress of all persons who are in any manner affected by Gender
Dysphoria related to transvestism or trans-sexualism or both, and to
protect the good mental and physical health of all such persons.
Voluntary nationwide self-help society. Free information to all
enquirers; social meetings provide opportunities for new transvestites
to meet those with experience. Also:

WOMEN OF THE BEAUMONT SOCIETY,
BM WOBS,
London WC1N 3XX.

GEMMA,
BM Box 5700,
London WC1N 3XX.
Gemma is a group of lesbians with or without disabilities, founded in
1976 to lessen the isolation of disabled lesbians of all ages. They also aim
to make the lesbian/gay community and society generally more aware of
their needs for a social life relevant to them and hence their rights
regarding access and information. In 1981 they produced the first
Disabled Gays Access Guide, and in subsequent years two further
guides, one national and one (with GLC funding) for London. All these,
thanks to the Royal National Institute for the Blind, were also available
in braille. In addition to befriending and information work they can
provide speakers for gay and non-gay groups in the London area.

LONDON LESBIAN AND GAY SWITCHBOARD,
BM Switchboard,
London WC1N 3XX.
Tel. 01-837 7325.
Twenty-four-hour information and help for lesbians and gay men. Will
also refer those recently bereaved to the Gay Bereavement Group; men
who are new to London to the Befriending Group; and mature gay men
and women to Pink Wrinkle.

PARENTS' ENQUIRY,
Mrs Rose Robertson,
16 Honley Road,
Catford,
London SE6 2HZ.
Tel. 01-698 1815.
Counselling for homosexual teenagers and their families. Will approach parents on behalf of gay sons/daughters. Advice and pen-pal service.

SELF HELP ASSOCIATION FOR TRANS-SEXUALS (SHAFT),
106 Barton Avenue,
Keyhm,
Plymouth PL2 1NZ.
Information on medical, professional and counselling help for trans-sexuals and those who think they may be. Friendship and help for the person concerned and families. Members throughout the country.

CHAPTER 5: THE MIDDLE AND LATER YEARS

The Menopause

THE MENOPAUSE COLLECTIVE,
c/o Women's Health Information Centre (WHIC),
52 Featherstone Street,
London EC1Y 8RT.
Tel. 01-251 6580.
WHIC is an information and resource centre for women's health issues. They are a women's organisation independent of the National Health Service. They work with and act as a resource for individual women in health groups, self-help groups, community groups, trade unions, and other women's groups. Their goals are to make information available to women on women's health and to support self-help groups. They have a library of articles, books, pamphlets and leaflets from a wide variety of sources. All women are welcome to use the library, which covers a broad range of women's health issues. Women are invited to come and see the literature or to write or phone with requests for information.

Recommended Reading

Mary Anderson, *The Menopause* (Faber & Faber, 1983); Wendy

Cooper, *No Change* (Arrow, 1983); Dr Barbara Evans, *Life Change: A Guide to the Menopause, Its Effect and Treatment* (Pan, 1988); Rosetha Reitz, *Menopause: A Positive Approach* (Allen & Unwin, 1985); Dr Miriam Stoppard, *Every Woman's Lifeguide* (Macdonald, 1985).

Fifty Years Old

MID-LIFE CENTRE,
318 Summer Lane,
Birmingham B19 3RL.
Tel. 021-359 3563.
Studies the subject of mid-life (thirty-five to fifty-five) and lobbies for understanding of mid-life issues and problems. Offers personal advice on pre-retirement, changing lifestyles, divorce, career change, menopause and mental approach. Publishes *Mid-Life Review*.

Planning for Retirement

EMPLOYMENT FELLOWSHIP,
'Willowthorpe',
High Street,
Stanstead Abbotts,
Near Ware,
Hertfordshire SG12 8AS.
Tel. 0920 870158.
Runs retirement workshops and centres, plus activity groups and employment bureaux to help people who are retired or elderly to find employment. Also initiates neighbourhood community care schemes to help the elderly frail and housebound.

MID-LIFE CENTRE, see above.

PRE-RETIREMENT ASSOCIATION,
19 Undine Street,
London SW17 8PP.
Tel. 01-767 3225.
Provides help and guidance on retirement planning, including psychological approach, employment concerns, finance, housing, health, leisure activities. Free information and advice service for members and pre-retirement courses. Special retirement-planning holidays. Publishes

Choice magazine £1 monthly from your newsagent or from: Choice Publications Ltd, 12 Bedford Row, London WC1R 4DU. *Tel. 01-404 4320.* Also has extensive book-list and library.

RETIRED EXECUTIVES ACTION CLEARING HOUSE (REACH),
89 Southwark Street,
London SE1 OHD.
Tel. 01-928 0452.
Free employment service (payment of expenses only), putting retired executives in touch with charitable organisations who need their skills.

SUCCESS AFTER SIXTY,
40–1 Old Bond Street,
London W1X 3AF.
Tel. 01-629 0672.
Employment agency for retired and redundant people (London area only) registers over-fifties. Can give advice on how earnings will affect pensions. Fees charged to employers. Mainly office staff.

Living on a Pension

Who Can Get State Retirement Pension?
- people who have reached state pension age (sixty for a woman, sixty-five for a man) and who have retired, or who can be treated as retired, from their regular job.
- people who have paid (or been credited with) enough National Insurance (NI) contributions.

Your retirement pension is made up of:
- *Basic Pension.* Your NI contributions. If you haven't paid or been credited with enough contributions over your working life to get a full Basic Pension, you may get a reduced one. You may be able to pay some arrears of contributions to increase your Basic Pension. Ask your Social Security office about this.
- *Additional Pension.* This is the earnings-related part of your Retirement Pension. The amount you get depends on your earnings since April 1978 on which you paid NI contributions.
- *Graduated Pension.* This depends on the amount of Graduated NI contributions paid between April 1961 and April 1975, when this pension scheme was in operation.

Other additions:
■ You can get an Invalidity Addition if you had an Invalidity Allowance shortly before you reached pension age. But if you are due Additional Pension and/or guaranteed minimum pension see below under Occupational Pension; the total of these will be deducted from your Invalidity Addition.
■ An Age Addition is paid to everyone aged eighty or over.

Extra pension for dependants – you can get extra pension for one of the following:
■ your wife, unless she already gets a Basic Pension (or some other benefit) of at least the amount of the extra pension;
■ or husband, provided you are entitled to an increase of Sickness, Unemployment or Invalidity Benefit for him immediately before you qualify for your pension;
■ or a woman who looks after a child or children for whom you are entitled (or treated as entitled) to Child Benefit;
■ and for a child or children for whom you are entitled (or treated as entitled) to Child Benefit;
■ but you cannot be paid extra pension for an adult dependant (as above) who is earning more or getting an occupational pension of more than a set amount each week.

If you get a reduced Basic Pension, these extra amounts, apart from the one for children, will also be reduced.

How Much?
At the time of writing (April 1988), £41.15 per claimant plus £24.75 per spouse. Dependants £8.40 per child under eighteen.

How to Claim Retirement Pension:
Your local Social Security office will send you a claim form about four months before you reach pension age. If you haven't received one three months before you reach pension age, ask at your local Social Security office. Be sure to go to the National Insurance part of the office. Complete the form and return it to the Social Security office. If you are not sure when you are going to retire, fill in as much of the form as you can and send it back. Make sure that you inform the Social Security office as soon as you know the date on which you are retiring.

If you are a woman aged sixty-five or over, or a man aged seventy or over, you can get your pension whether you have retired or not. However, you still need to claim it. You can do this for up to four months before you reach sixty-five (woman) or seventy (man). Ask at your Social Security office for a form. You must claim separately for any of the following:

■ your wife (but she must normally claim for herself if she is applying for a pension based on your contributions)
■ or your husband
■ or a woman caring for your children
■ and your children

Don't delay claiming or you may lose benefit.
The date of retirement that you put on your claim form should be one of the following:

■ The day after you give up your regular job, if you are still working when you reach pension age.
■ or the day you reach pension age, if you have already given up your regular job.
■ or the date from which you wish to be treated as retired, if you are carrying on working but not earning enough to affect your pension.

It may be best to make your date of retirement a pension pay-day.

How and When It Is Paid

Either at the end of every four weeks or every thirteen weeks directly into a bank or building society account, or weekly by a book of orders which you can cash at a post office of your choice. If you choose to be paid by order book, your pension will be paid from the first pension pay-day of your retirement. This is usually a Monday, but in some cases may be a Thursday. Pension pay-day for widows is usually a Tuesday.

Early Retirement

If you retire before the state pension age, you need to consider the following points:

■ You will not be able to get your state Retirement Pension until you reach state pension age.
■ To get Unemployment Benefit you must be available for, and capable of, work with an employer and satisfy all other conditions for payment of benefit. Get leaflet NI12, *Unemployment Benefit.*
■ Voluntary early retirement may stop you getting Unemployment Benefit for up to thirteen weeks, even if you are willing to consider

suitable job opportunities, but if you intend to claim Unemployment Benefit you should say so on the first day you are unemployed.

If you are sixty or over and getting an occupational pension, your Unemployment Benefit may be reduced. Get leaflet NI230, *Unemployment Benefit and Your Occupational Pension*. You may be able to claim Income Support: see page 312. If you have retired early because you were made redundant, your redundancy payment may take your savings over the amount beyond which Income Support is paid.

■ Once you have retired, for whatever reason, you will no longer pay National Insurance contributions, unless you start work again before you are of pension age. But you may need to pay voluntary contributions to safeguard your right to a full state pension. Check with your Social Security office. If you are a man of sixty or over, you will automatically be credited with NI contributions (instead of having to pay voluntary contributions) for the tax year containing your sixtieth birthday and the next four years. To qualify, you must be living in Great Britain for at least twenty-six weeks in each tax year after you have retired. Voluntary contributions are valid for only a limited range of Social Security benefits, including state Retirement Pension. Get leaflet NI42, *National Insurance Voluntary Contributions*, from your local Social Security office.

If You Put Off or Cancel Your Retirement

You can put off your retirement to beyond state pension age, or you can cancel your retirement and temporarily give up your pension if you want to return to work. By putting off or cancelling your retirement you can earn extra pension when you finally retire or when you reach age sixty-five (woman) or seventy (man). And you can only cancel your retirement once. Get leaflet NI92, *Earning Extra Pension by Cancelling Your Retirement*, from your Social Security office.

If you work for an employer, you do not have to pay any more NI contributions. But your employer must continue paying his contributions in the normal way.

When you send back your claim form, your Social Security office will automatically send you a 'Certificate of Age Exception' to give to your employer so that he knows you don't have to pay NI contributions.

If you are self-employed, you do not have to pay any more Class 2 NI contributions. You should return your contribution card, if you have one, to your Social Security office. You do not have to pay Class 4 contributions for any tax year after the one in which you reached pension age, but you may have to pay Class 4 contributions during the first year of retirement. Get leaflet NI41, *National Insurance Guide for Self-Employed People*, and NP18, *Class 4 National Insurance Contributions*.

How Other Benefits May Affect Your Pension

Some benefits may reduce your Basic Pension, though they have no effect on your Additional Pension or Graduated Pension. Any extra pension you get for a dependant may also be reduced if they get another benefit. If someone is claiming extra benefit for you as a dependant, it will be reduced by the amount of your Basic Pension. Check with your Social Security office.

How Earnings Affect Your Pension

If you are a woman aged sixty-five, or a man under seventy, you can earn up to £75 a week before it affects any of the following: Basic Pension, Invalidity Addition, extra pension for your spouse, children, or a woman caring for your children. Your pension can also be affected in certain circumstances by the earnings or occupational pension of your spouse or partner. But your earnings do not affect either the Additional Pension or the Graduated Pension. Get leaflet NP32, *Your Retirement Pension*, from your Social Security office.

Married Women

A married woman can qualify for a pension in either of two ways. First, if you have paid enough standard (full-rate) NI contributions, you can get a Basic Pension in the same way as a single woman or man. Second, you can get a Basic Pension based on your husband's contributions if he is getting a pension, you are over sixty and you can be treated as having retired.

Normally, you can only get the higher of these pensions. But if the pension based on your own contributions is less than the maximum that a married woman can get on her husband's contributions you can combine the two up to that maximum. Get leaflet NP32B, *Retirement Benefits for Married Women*, from your Social Security office.

Widows

If you were widowed before the age of sixty, when you reach sixty you can do one of the following:

- claim a Retirement Pension if you have retired from regular work;
- or continue to get any NI Widow's Benefit that you are entitled to until you retire or reach sixty-five;

■ or put off drawing your Retirement Pension, carry on working and give up any NI Widow's Benefit you are getting. You can then get extra pension when you eventually reach sixty-five.

Whichever you choose, you can change your mind any time up until you are sixty-five.

If you are widowed after sixty, generally you can get a Retirement Pension based on your late husband's contributions, whether you have retired or not.

You may be able to get Widow's Benefit instead. This depends on whether you or your husband (or both of you) were getting a Retirement Pension when he died, and on whether you have any children. Get leaflet NP32A, *Your Retirement Pension If You Are Widowed or Divorced.*

Widowers

If you were widowed before the age of sixty-five, and if you are not entitled to a full Basic Pension, your wife's contributions may be taken into account to give you a better pension. If you were incapable of work when your wife died, or became so within thirteen weeks of being widowed, you may be able to get Invalidity Pension based on your wife's contributions. Get leaflet NI16A, *Invalidity Benefit.*

If you were widowed after the age of sixty-five, and if you are not entitled to a full Basic Pension and your wife was under sixty when she died, her contributions may be taken into account to give you a better pension. If your wife was over sixty, you may be able to get a retirement pension based on her contributions plus one based on your contributions, up to the maximum a single person can get. Get leaflet NP32A, *Your Retirement Pension If You Are Widowed or Divorced.*

Divorced People

If you are not entitled to a full Basic Pension, your former wife or husband's contributions may be taken into account to give a better pension. You do not have to wait until your former wife or husband retires. Get leaflet NP32A, *Your Retirement Pension If You Are Widowed or Divorced.*

Over-Eighty Pension

If you are eighty or over, you may get a non-contributory Retirement Pension if you do not get a Basic Pension, or get only a reduced one, and you (or your husband or former husband) satisfy certain residence conditions. Get leaflet NI184, *Over 80 Pension.* Claim form is included.

Going Into Hospital

Your pension will be reduced after eight weeks if you go into hospital for in-patient treatment on the NHS. However, if you are living in a local authority residential home or similar place before going into hospital, your pension will be reduced immediately.

If you have already been in hospital for NHS treatment for more than eight weeks, when you become due for state Retirement Pension your pension will be reduced immediately. Any extra pension you get for a dependant may also be reduced if he or she goes into hospital. Get leaflet NI9, *Going into Hospital?*

Going Abroad

You can usually get your pension paid anywhere abroad. If you go abroad for less than three months, you can let your pension build up and cash the orders when you get back. But you can't cash an order over three months old. If you go abroad for more than three months, you can get your pension paid to you abroad.

If you are living abroad when pension rates go up for pensioners living in the United Kingdom, you will get the increased rate if you are living in a European Community country, or a country outside the European Community with which the United Kingdom has a reciprocal agreement and which allows you to get the increased rate. If you live in a country outside the European Community which doesn't have a special arrangement with the United Kingdom, your pension will stay the same as when you left this country. Tell your Social Security office in plenty of time before you go, so they can make the necessary arrangements. Get leaflet NI38, *Social Security Abroad,* or write to: DHSS, Overseas Branch, Newcastle upon Tyne NE98 1YX.

Your Occupational Pension

If you were a member of your employer's occupational pension scheme, you were probably contracted out of the Additional Pension (earnings-related) part of the state scheme. If so, your state pension will not include the Additional Pension part of the scheme. But your employer's scheme must by law provide a Guaranteed Minimum Pension (GMP) to replace the additional pension. You have a legal right to information about your pension scheme. You will be given basic information about the scheme and have a right to ask for, and be given, copies of its legal and financial documentation. (You may be asked to pay for copies of the legal documentation.) You also have the right to ask for and be given statements of the pension amounts and entitlements you have built up in a scheme and of the rights and choices you have in deciding how to use them to your best advantage. If you need more information about your employer's scheme, you should ask the manager of the scheme.

How Your Occupational Pension May Affect Your State Pension

If your occupational pension includes a Guaranteed Minimum Pension (GMP) because you have been contracted out, the amount of that GMP is taken into account when working out the earnings-related part of your Retirement Pension – the Additional Pension (see above). When you retire an Additional Pension is worked out as if you had not been contracted out and the amount produced compared with your GMP. If the GMP is more than, or the same as, the Additional Pension, your Retirement Pension will not include any Additional Pension. If the GMP is less than the Additional Pension, the difference is added to your Retirement Pension. Although GMP may remain at the same level, your Additional Pension will be looked at each year to ensure it is protected against inflation. If the Additional Pension is increased, it will again be compared with your GMP in the same way. Get leaflet NP32, *Your Retirement Pension*, from your Social Security office.

If you were self-employed, your occupational pension, if any, will be paid by a policy or policies you will have arranged for this purpose with one or more insurance or pension companies. If you need information about your scheme, you should ask the appropriate department of the insurance or pension company concerned. If your pension is made up from several policies, you should ask the agent or broker who made the arrangements.

Income Tax

Most of the amounts which make up your Retirement Pension are treated as your income for tax purposes and should be included on any tax return. If you want to know more, ask your local tax office or tax enquiry-point.

Other Help

Supplementary Pension, see Income Support, page 312.
Extra Help: Rent and Rates, see page 318, Income Support.
Help with heating costs, see page 319, Income Support.
Christmas Bonus: You get a tax-free bonus with your pension shortly before Christmas each year. The amount is announced in advance and is also shown in leaflet NI196, *Social Security Benefit Rates and Earnings Rules*. Only one payment can be made per person, but you may get an extra bonus if you are entitled to an increase for your spouse, and both of you are over pension age by the end of the week in which the bonus is

paid. The bonus is usually paid automatically with your pension payment. But if you think you have a right to it and haven't got it by the end of December ask at your Social Security office. There is a time-limit for paying the bonus, so do not delay.

Free prescriptions: Just fill in the back of the prescription before you give it to the chemist.

Free NHS dental treatment, vouchers for glasses and hospital fares: You can get these if you are getting Income Support, or have a low income. Get leaflets D11, *NHS Dental Treatment*; G11, *NHS Vouchers for Glasses*; H11, *Fares to Hospital*.

Services for the Elderly

Ask at your local council's Social Services department or your local Citizen's Advice Bureau for information about home helps, Meals on Wheels, day centres and social clubs, special transport schemes and residential homes.

Reduced Fares

British Rail: You can buy a senior citizen's railcard if you are sixty or over. This allows you to travel at reduced cost on many train journeys. The railcard lasts for one year and can be bought at most stations.

Bus and Underground: Some local transport services offer free or reduced travel on buses or the Underground. Ask your local bus service or London Regional Transport for details.

The Elderly

Living with an elderly relative/helping the elderly person to stay in their own home.

AGE CONCERN,
Bernard Sunley House,
60 Pitcairn Road,
Mitcham,
Surrey CR4 3LL.
Tel. 01-640 5431.
Advice, information. Will advise and support elderly bereaved. Local telephone numbers and addresses in the phone-book.

Publications: *Your Rights for Pensioners* by Age Concern (1987 edn), 90p; *Know Your Medicines* by Pat Blair, Age Concern, £3.75; *Survival Guide for Widows* by Age Concern, £3.50; *Gardening in Retirement* by Age Concern, £1.95; *In Touch with Cataracts* by Margaret Ford, £1 from Age Concern.

ASSOCIATION OF CARERS,
First Floor, 21–3 New Road,
Chatham,
Kent ME4 4QJ.
Tel. 0634 813981.
Self-help groups for people caring for the disabled and/or elderly who are dependent relatives. Give advice, counselling, information on welfare rights. Publishes *Help at Hand.*

BRITISH PENSIONERS AND TRADE UNION ACTION ASSOCIATION,
Norman Dodds House,
315 Bexley Road,
Erith,
Kent DA8 3EX.
Tel. 0474 61802.
Will help the elderly with social insurance problems, benefits, housing and so on. Offers counselling, representation at tribunals. Has 300 branches all over the country.

COUNSEL AND CARE FOR THE ELDERLY,
131 Middlesex Street,
London E1 7JF.
Tel. 01-621 1624 (10.30 a.m.–4.00 p.m., Monday–Friday).
Helps people of pensionable age by providing a free advisory service on all matters of concern. May be able to assist with the cost of nursing care in pensioner's own home.

DISTRESSED GENTLEFOLK'S AID ASSOCIATION,
Vicarage Gate House,
Vicarage Gate,
London W8 4AQ.
Tel. 01-229 9341.
Allowances and grants for gentlefolk in distress: for example, the elderly, single parents. Thirteen nursing homes and residential homes for people in need.

FRIENDS OF THE ELDERLY AND GENTLEFOLK'S HELP,
42 Ebury Street,
London SW1 OLZ.
Tel. 01-730 8263.
Help for the elderly with winter warmth and makes regular allowances to people who wish to stay in their own homes. Residential and nursing homes for men and women mainly from professional backgrounds.

HELP THE AGED,
16–17 St James's Walk,
London EC1R OBE.
Tel. 01-253 0253.
Provides information and advice, organises 'Good Neighbour' schemes. Provides advice and funding for Housing Associations and Housing Trusts, day centres, work centres and mobile chiropody units. Publishes newspaper *Yours* for the aged and other publications.

HOLIDAY CARE SERVICE,
2 Old Bank Chambers,
Station Road,
Horley,
Surrey RH6 9HW.
Tel. 02937 74535.
Free service advises the elderly on details of appropriate holidays, including accommodation, transport, package holidays, sources of financial help.

NATIONAL COUNCIL FOR CARERS AND THEIR ELDERLY DEPENDANTS,
9 Chilworth Mews,
London W2 3RG.
Tel. 01-262 1451/2.
Free information and guidance for those looking after the elderly and/or infirm on benefits, holidays, help and relief. Forty branches throughout the country.

Housing/Accommodation

CARE SEARCH,
United Response,
1 Thorpe Close,
Portobello Green,

London W10 5XL.
Tel. 01-960 5666/7.
Have lists and details of every type of residential care for the elderly in the country stored on computer. Search fee £5. Will provide a list of places suitable for the person you are trying to place.

SALVATION ARMY,
280 Mare Street,
London E8 1HE.
Tel. 01-985 1181.
Homes for the aged.

CHAPTER 6: THE DISABLED AND THE HANDICAPPED

Mental and Physical Handicaps

General Help

AGE-CARE LTD,
Renray Group,
King Street,
Middlewich,
Cheshire CW10 9LG.
Tel. 060 684 3717.
Specialises in equipment, aids and adaptations for the aged and disabled.

DISABLEMENT INFORMATION ADVICE LINE (DIAL),
DIAL House,
117 High Street,
Clay Cross,
Near Chesterfield,
Derbyshire S45 9DZ.
Tel. 0246 864498.
Central information bank of disablement information advice lines, a network of specialised services catering for disabled people, their carers and the caring profession. Publishes *New Beginnings* and *Mobility Aids.*

DISABLED LIVING FOUNDATION,
380–4 Harrow Road,
London W9 2HU.
Tel. 01-289 6111.
Information service particularly about incontinence, clothing, aids and
equipment.

DISABLEMENT INCOME GROUP,
Attlee House,
28 Commercial Street,
London E1 6RL.
Tel. 01-247 2128/6877.
Advisory service on benefits, services, etc.

FAMILY FUND,
PO Box 50,
York YO1 1UY.
Helps families caring for children who are very severely handicapped.

GREATER LONDON ASSOCIATION FOR DISABLED PEOPLE (GLAD),
336 Brixton Road,
London SW9 7AA.
Tel. 01-274 0107.
Information service for the disabled in London. Publishes *GLAD*
quarterly magazine, four issues price £3. Publications list on request.

REHABILITATION ENGINEERING MOVEMENT ADVISORY PANEL
(REMAP),
25 Mortimer Street,
London W1N 8AB.
Tel. 01-637 5400.
Panels of engineers, therapists and doctors who will provide engineering
solutions to many problems of disability. Also offer support, friend-
ship, advice and help with employment for people who are disabled.

ROYAL ASSOCIATION FOR DISABILITY AND REHABILITATION
(RADAR),
25 Mortimer Street,
London W1N 8AB.
Tel. 01-637 5400.
Advice, information about access, holidays, housing and mobility. Welfare
advice and help, and skills and disability training. Publishes information
leaflets.

ROYAL SOCIETY FOR MENTALLY HANDICAPPED CHILDREN AND
ADULTS,
MENCAP National Centre,
123 Golden Lane,
London EC1Y ORT.
Tel. 01-253 9433.
Offers practical help, advice, support and information for the mentally
handicapped and their families. Helps with welfare problems, legal counselling, holidays, Gateway clubs. Operates Pathway Employment Service,
permanent employment for mentally handicapped people. Also acquires
property which is converted into individual homes for the mentally
handicapped.

THE SPASTICS SOCIETY,
12 Park Crescent,
London W1N 3EQ.
Tel. 01-636 5020.

FAMILY SERVICES AND ASSESSMENT CENTRE,
16 Fitzroy Square,
London W1P 5HQ.
Tel. 01-387 9571.
Provides counselling, advice, information and grants to those with
cerebral palsy. Two hundred local groups all over the country. Also
runs schools, residential centres, hostels, short-term family care units,
hotels, integrated housing, sheltered workshops and work centres.
  Recommended reading: *Handling the Young Cerebral Palsied
Child at Home* by Nancie R. Finnie (Heinemann, 1974); *Help Starts
Here – for Parents of a Handicapped Child* by National Children's
Bureau, 8 Wakley Street, Islington, London EC1V 7QE, Tel. 01-278
9441; *Let Me Speak* by Dorothy M. Jeffree and Roy McConkey,
Human Horizons series (Condor Books, 1976); *Let Me Play* by
Dorothy M. Jeffree, Roy McConkey and Simon Hewson, Human
Horizons series (Souvenir Press, 1985); *Play Helps – Toys and Activities
for Handicapped Children* by Roma Lear (Heinemann, 1986); *You and
Your Handicapped Child* by Ann Purser (Allen & Unwin, 1981);
literature from Toy Libraries Association, Seabrook House, Wyllyotts
Manor, Darkes Lane, Potters Bar, Herts EN6 2HL; *Teaching the
Handicapped Child to Dress* (Friends of the Centre for Spastic Children, 1972); *Feeding Can Be Fun* by Mary Ryan (Spastics Society,
1981); *The Handicapped Child* by Bowley and Gardner (Livingstone,
1900); *Helping the Handicapped Child*, No. 2, *At School,* by R.

Gulliford (National Foundation for Educational Research); *Learning to Cope* by Edward Whelan and Barbara Speake, Human Horizons series (Souvenir Press, 1979); *Deaf-blind Baby: A Programme for Care* by Peggy Freeman (Heinemann, 1985); *Incontinence* by Dorothy Mandelstam (Heinemann Health Books for the Disabled Living Foundation, 346 Kensington High Street, London W14 8NS).

Financial

INVALIDS AT HOME,
23 Farm Avenue,
London NW2 2BJ.
Tel. 01-452 2074.
Helps invalids to leave hospital and live at home. Grants for equipment and other needs at request of social workers.

CITIZEN'S ADVICE BUREAUX, local addresses and telephone numbers in the telephone directory. Offers free advice on family and personal matters, social security, health and medical, housing, consumer complaints, etc.

Transport and Travel

JOINT COMMITTEE ON MOBILITY FOR THE DISABLED,
14 Birch Way,
Warlingham,
Surrey CR3 9DA.
Tel. 08832 2801.
To improve the indoor and outdoor mobility of physically disabled people.

DIAL-A-RIDE,
Federation of London Dial-a-Rides.
Tel. 01-482 2325.

LONDON REGIONAL TRANSPORT UNIT FOR DISABLED PASSENGERS,
Tel. 01-222 5600, ext. 3299.
A public transport service for people with disabilities who cannot use buses or Tube trains. Fares similar to bus fares, travel in minibuses adapted to take wheelchairs.

DISABLED DRIVERS' ASSOCIATION,
Drake House,
18 Creekside,
London SE8 3DZ.
Tel. 01-692 7141.
Self-help organisation. Helps the disabled towards independence through information on conversion of vehicles, etc. They also advise on welfare rights, etc.

DISABLED DRIVERS MOTOR CLUB,
1a Dudley Gardens,
London W13 9LU.
Tel. 01-840 1515.
Deals with cross-Channel ferry concessions, acts as agents for RAC.

Help for Specific Handicaps

Autism

NATIONAL AUTISTIC SOCIETY,
276 Willesden Lane,
London NW2 5RB.
Tel. 01-451 3844.
Advisory and information service for parents. Runs schools and adult centres.

Brain-Injured Children

BRITISH INSTITUTE FOR BRAIN-INJURED CHILDREN,
Knowle Hall,
Knowle,
Bridgwater,
Somerset TA7 8PJ.
Tel. 0278 684060.
Programmes of stimulation therapy to help child with mental handicap, autism, dyslexia, Down's syndrome, cerebral palsy, etc.

TADWORTH COURT CHILDREN'S HOSPITAL,
Tadworth,
Surrey KT20 5RU.
Tel. 073 73 57171.

Provides treatment for chronically sick, handicapped and terminally ill children. Nursing and physiotherapy staff have considerable experience in treating children with cystic fibrosis and chest problems. Provides short-term care for children, from birth to sixteen years, with degenerative conditions, giving parents a break. Holiday Unit from May to September enabling handicapped children to have a holiday. Rehabilitation Unit for children with head injuries, individual programmes developed to maximise the child's recovery. Also St Margaret's School at Tadworth Court for profoundly multi-handicapped children from eight to sixteen.

Cystic Fibrosis

CYSTIC FIBROSIS RESEARCH TRUST,
Alexandra House,
5 Blyth Road,
Bromley,
Kent BR1 3RS.
Tel. 01 464 7211/2.
Three hundred branches and groups all over the country offering mutual support and advice.

TADWORTH COURT CHILDREN'S HOSPITAL, as above.

Down's Syndrome

DOWN'S CHILDREN ASSOCIATION,
3rd Floor, Horne's Premises,
4 Oxford Street,
London W1N 9SL.
Tel. 01-580 0511 (twenty-four-hour helpline).
Support and information for parents. Self-help branches and groups all over the country.

NATIONAL CENTRE FOR DOWN'S SYNDROME,
9 Westbourne Road,
Edgbaston,
Birmingham B15 5TN.
Tel. 021-454 3126.
Carries out assessments and studies.

Haemophilia

HAEMOPHILIA SOCIETY,
c/o PO Box 9,

16 Trinity Street,
London SE1 1DE.
Tel. 01-407 1010.
Practical advice and friendship. Financial aid for cases of hardship.

Huntington's Chorea

COMBAT,
Association to Combat Huntington's Chorea,
34a Station Road,
Hinckley,
Leicester LE10 1AP.
Tel. 0455 615558.
Family counselling service.

Multiple Sclerosis

ACTION FOR RESEARCH INTO MULTIPLE SCLEROSIS (ARMS),
4a Chapel Hill,
Stansted,
Essex CM24 8AG.
Tel. 0279 815553.
Self-help groups of people who have MS or are related to someone with it. Therapy centres.

Publications: *Why a Diet Rich in Essential Fatty Acid?* (ARMS research), £1.50; *Multiple Sclerosis* by Judy Graham (Thorsons, 1985), £5.50; *Multiple Sclerosis Simple Exercises* by Gill Robinson (ARMS, 1980), £3.50. Plus many other very useful publications including diet books, cassettes and a magazine. Send to ARMS for a list of publications.

MULTIPLE SCLEROSIS SOCIETY,
25 Effie Road,
Fulham,
London SW6 1EE.
Tel. 01-736 6267.
With 360 branches all over the country. They are run voluntarily, many by people with MS, their families and friends who see that the members are visited regularly and get all the aids and benefits to which they are entitled. They also raise money to contribute to the cost of central research.

Publications: *Living with Multiple Sclerosis* by Elizabeth Forsythe (Faber & Faber, 1988), £2.95; *Multiple Sclerosis: A Personal Exploration* by Alexandra Burnfield (Souvenir Press, 1985), £5.95 plus 65p p&p;

Learning to Live with Multiple Sclerosis by R. Dowe, R. Povey and G. Whitley (MS Society), £2.55 including p&p.

Muscular Dystrophy

MUSCULAR DYSTROPHY GROUP OF GREAT BRITAIN AND NORTHERN IRELAND,
Nattrass House,
35 Macaulay Road,
London SW4 OQP.
Tel. 01-720 8055.
Groups all over the country provide a link between sufferers and their families.

Phenylketonuria

NATIONAL SOCIETY FOR PHENYLKETONURIA AND ALLIED DISORDERS LTD,
Worth Cottage,
Lower Scholes,
Pickels Hill,
Keighley,
West Yorkshire BD22 ORR.
Tel. 0535 44865.
Support groups throughout the country.

Rheumatism and Arthritis

ARTHRITIS CARE,
6 Grosvenor Crescent,
London SW1X 7ER.
Tel. 01-235 0902/0905.
Support, help and information on all aspects of having and coping with arthritis, such as aids, suitable holiday centres and welfare services.

THE ARTHRITIS AND RHEUMATISM COUNCIL,
41 Eagle Street,
London WC1R 4AR.
Tel. 01-405 8572.
With 1,070 local support branches. Offers advice, information.

Spina Bifida and Hydrocephalus

ASSOCIATION FOR SPINA BIFIDA AND HYDROCEPHALUS (ASBAH),
22 Upper Woburn Place,
London WC1H OEP.
Tel. 01-388 1382.

Ninety support groups all over the country offering mutual support. Advice, practical and financial help available, care home for children and independence training courses.

Publications: *Your Child with Spina Bifida* by J. Lorber, 60p; *Your Child with Hydrocephalus* by J. Lorber, 60p; *Nursery Years* by Simon Haskell and M. Paull, 60p; *Little Joe: A Grandmother's Story*, 40p; *Sex and Spina Bifida*, £1.75.

Spinal Injuries

SPINAL INJURIES ASSOCIATION,
76 St James's Lane,
London N10 3DF.
Tel. 01-444 2121.
Link scheme where somebody who has a spinal injury will befriend and visit a newly injured person. Runs two narrow boats for self-catering holidays. Personal injury claim service.

Strokes

VOLUNTARY STROKE SCHEME,
Manor Farm,
Appleton,
Abingdon,
Oxfordshire.
Tel. 0865 862 954.
Volunteers visit patients' homes to stimulate brain activity. Run clubs, outings, etc. About seventy groups all over the country.

The Deaf, the Blind, and the Deaf and Blind

THE BRITISH CENTRE FOR DEAFENED PEOPLE,
19 Hartfield Road,
Eastbourne,
East Sussex BN21 2AR.
Tel. 0323 638230.
Offers professional assistance when an adult suffers irreversible hearing-loss which is severe or total. Individually tailored residential rehabilitation courses for the deafened person and their family.

THE ROYAL NATIONAL INSTITUTE FOR THE DEAF,
105 Gower Street,
London WC1E 6AH.
Tel. 01-387 8033.

Publication list including books written by deaf people: *Hearing Impairment: A Guide for People with Auditory Handicaps and Those Concerned with Their Care and Rehabilitation* by K. Lysons (Woodhead-Faulkner, 1984); *How to Cope with Hearing Loss* by K. Lysons (Granada, 1980); *Deafness in the Adult: What Hearing Loss Means and What Can Be Done to Help* by W. Brinson (Thorsons, 1986); and many other publications. Send to the above address for a complete list. Books may be bought or borrowed from their library.

THE NATIONAL FEDERATION OF THE BLIND,
Unity House,
Smyth Street,
Westgate,
Wakefield WF1 1ER.
Tel. 0924 377012.
Self-help organisations concerned with all matters relating to the blind. Advice and information. Membership £3 per year. Publishes quarterly magazine.

NATIONAL DEAF-BLIND HELPERS LEAGUE,
18 Rainbow Court,
Paston Ridings,
Peterborough PE4 6UP.
Tel. 0733 73511.
Organises social functions, clubs, etc. Helps to get deaf-blind people in contact with each other. Provides material help for holidays, equipment and sickness. Short-stay holiday facilities at the League centre. Personal friends for individual deaf-blind people.

Social Security Benefits for the Sick and the Disabled

Statutory Sick Pay (SSP)

If you work for an employer and earn enough to pay Class 1 National Insurance (NI) contributions (including married women's reduced-rate contributions), you will usually get Statutory Sick Pay (SSP) from your employer when you are off sick. You can get SSP for up to twenty-eight weeks in a spell of sickness (spells with eight weeks or less between them count as one spell). You can get SSP only if you are off sick for four days or more in a row.

If you are still sick after twenty-eight weeks of SSP, you can claim Invalidity Benefit. If your employer's obligation to pay you SSP ends before twenty-eight weeks, you can claim Sickness Benefit. In both cases, your employer will give you a form to make your claim. SSP is £47.20 or £32.85 per week depending on earnings (April 1987 rate). Claim by telling your employer you are sick, and he will arrange for SSP to be paid to you. For more details, see NI224, *Statutory Sick Pay – Check Your Rights.*

Sickness Benefit

If you are incapable of work and cannot get SSP from your employer, you may be able to get Sickness Benefit. You can also get it if you are self-employed or unemployed. You can get Sickness Benefit only if you are off sick for four days or more in a row. You have to have paid enough NI contributions. Married women and widows who pay reduced-rate NI contributions cannot get Sickness Benefit unless they are claiming because of an accident at work or an industrial disease; see below.

You can get Sickness Benefit for up to twenty-eight weeks. You may be allowed to do some work while you are getting Sickness Benefit if you earn less than £26.00 per week (April 1987 rates) and you do the work under medical supervision (for example, in hospital) or to improve your health.

You must ask your Social Security office if the work is allowed before you start work. Benefit is £30.05 per week (April 1987 rates) if you are under pension age. If you are over pension age, you can get £37.85 per week.

If you are employed and do not get SSP, or your SSP runs out, get a claim form from your employer (form SSP1E or SSP1T). Otherwise get form SC1 from the Social Security office, doctor's surgery or hospital. More information from leaflet NI16, *Sickness Benefit.*

If You Go Into Hospital

Most Social Security benefits are paid to help with your ordinary needs at home, or for special needs, or for disablement. When you, or your partner or child are in hospital some of these needs are met by the NHS, as your benefit may go down or stop. But if you are paying the whole cost of accommodation and non-medical services in hospital your Social Security benefits are not affected (except for Invalid Care Allowance: see below).

Always tell your Social Security office at once if you or your partner or child go into hospital and let them know the date that you (or they) come out as soon as the hospital tells you. The Social Security office can then make sure that you get the right amount of benefit. Also tell the Social Security office if you (or your partner or child) are allowed home, even if only for a few days. The full rate of benefit can be paid for a person at home, even if it goes down while he or she is in hospital. For more information, see leaflet NI9, *Going into Hospital?*

If You Become Ill while You Are Pregnant

You may be able to get SSP or Sickness Benefit but you cannot if you are already getting either Statutory Maternity Pay or Maternity Allowance. See also page 283 and get leaflet FB8, *Babies and Benefits.*

If You Have Been Sick for Six Months (Invalidity Benefit)

If you cannot work after twenty-eight weeks when your Sickness Benefit or SSP ends, you can claim Invalidity Benefit. If you first become sick before you are fifty-five (women) or sixty (men), you can get Invalidity Allowance as well. You may also get extra pension based on your earnings since 1978. You cannot get Invalidity Allowance in full as well as extra pension.

You may be allowed to do some work while you are getting benefit if you earn less than £26 a week (April 1987 rates) and you do the work under medical supervision (for example, in hospital) or to improve your health. Ask your Social Security office if the work is allowed before you start work. Invalidity Benefit is £39.50 a week (April 1987 rates).

If you are employed and you do not get SSP or your SSP runs out, get a claim form SSP1E or SSP1T from your employer or get SC1 from your Social Security office, doctor's surgery or hospital. More details in leaflet NI16A, *Invalidity Benefit.*

Severe Disablement Allowance

If you have been incapable of work for twenty-eight weeks or more, and cannot get Sickness Benefit or Invalidity Benefit because you have not paid enough NI contributions, you may be able to get Severe Disablement Allowance (SDA). You can claim SDA if you are between sixteen and sixty if you are a woman, sixty-five if you are a man. It is tax-free. It is not means-tested.

If you first become incapable of work after your twentieth birthday, you can only get SDA if you are at least 80 per cent disabled. If you are under nineteen and still at school or college, you may still be able to get SDA if you have less than twenty-one hours a week of supervised study. But any time spent in education that would be unsuitable for someone of the same age and sex who does not have a disability does not count (e.g., learning to do things that other people your age can easily do, like getting dressed or going shopping).

If you are a woman over sixty or a man over sixty-five, you can get SDA only if you had a right to SDA on the day before your sixtieth or sixty-fifth birthday. SDA is £23.75 a week (April 1987 rates). To claim use the form in leaflet NI252, *Severe Disability Allowance*, which also contains more information.

Mobility Allowance

If you are aged between five and sixty-six, and unable to walk or virtually unable to walk, you can claim Mobility Allowance. If you qualify for Mobility Allowance before you reach sixty-five, you can go on getting it until you are seventy-five. You can get Mobility Allowance whatever other money you have coming in and even if you are getting other benefits including Income Support. Mobility Allowance is £22.10 a week (April 1987 rates). Use the form in leaflet NI211, *Mobility Allowance;* this also includes further details.

Attendance Allowance

If you need a lot of help from another person because you are mentally or physically disabled, you can claim Attendance Allowance. This is a weekly cash benefit paid to you and not to the person looking after you. You can get Attendance Allowance even if there is not anyone to look after you. Attendance Allowance is tax-free, and it can normally be paid in full on top of other Social Security benefits. You do not need to have paid NI contributions to get it. There are two rates, depending on whether you need to be looked after all day or all night, or both. Attendance Allowance is £31.60 or £21.10 a week (April 1987 rates). Claim on the form in the leaflet NI205, *Attendance Allowance*, where you will also find more details. If you would like this money paid directly into your bank or building society account, also get leaflet NI251, *Attendance Allowance – Payment Direct into Bank or Building Society Accounts.*

Injured by Crime

If you are injured as a result of a crime of violence, you can claim Criminal Injuries Compensation. You can also get it if you were injured while trying (or helping) police to prevent a crime or arrest a suspected criminal. If you are a victim of violence within your family, you are also covered. The amount you get depends on how much pain or suffering you are caused by the injury and on any loss of earnings or any out-of-pocket expenses. You will not qualify if all these items are worked out to add up to less than £400 for violence outside your family, or £500 for violence within your family. For more information, see leaflet *Crimes of*

Violence – a Guide to the Compensation Scheme, available from: Criminal Injuries Compensation Board, Whittington House, 19–30 Alfred Place, Chenies Street, London WC1E 7EJ. Tel. 01-636 9501.

Vaccine Damage

If you have been severely disabled as a result of vaccination, you can get a one-off tax-free payment of £20,000 (for claims since June 1985). Write to: Vaccine Damage Payment Unit, DHSS, Norcross, Blackpool FY5 3TA. More information in leaflet HB3, *Payment for People Severely Disabled by Vaccine.*

Industrial Injuries Disablement Benefit

If you become disabled as a result of an accident at work, you may be entitled to Industrial Injuries Disablement Benefit. You may also get it if you become disabled as a result of one of the industrial diseases known to be a risk in your job. You can get Industrial Injuries Benefit even if you continue to work or return to work. How much you get depends on how badly disabled you are. Loss of all sight or all hearing, or loss of both hands, normally counts as 100 per cent disablement, and you will get the maximum amount of benefit. The full rate of pension is £64.50 a week (April 1987 rates). Leaflet NI6, *Industrial Injuries Disablement Benefit*, tells you what form to use in the B1100 series; for more details, see NI6, *Industrial Injuries Benefit*, and NI2 if you have an industrial disease.

Industrial Injury Compensation

If you were injured at work through the fault of your employer, your employer should pay you compensation. The amount that you can get depends on how badly you are injured or disabled. Your employer has to display a certificate of insurance covering liability for this compensation. For more information, ask a solicitor or your trade union. The secretary of the local Law Society will give you an introduction to a solicitor; see the Law List in libraries to find the address of the local secretary. Citizen's Advice Bureaux also keep a list of solicitors.

War Disablement Pension

If you are disabled because of service in the armed forces between 1914 and 1921 or at any time since 3 September 1939, you can get War Disablement Pension. You can also claim if you were a merchant seaman who got a war injury or a civilian who was disabled because of the Second World War. How much you get depends on how badly you are disabled. You get a pension if your disablement is 20 per cent or more.

You get a lump sum if it is 19 per cent or less. The full pension is £64.50 a week (April 1987 rates). Claim by writing to: War Pensions Branch, DHSS, North Fylde Central Office, Norcross, Blackpool FY5 3TA. For more information, see general leaflet FB16, *Sick or Injured through Service in the Armed Forces;* also MPL153, *Help for the War Disabled;* and MPL154, *Rates of War Pensions and Allowances.*

Mobility Supplement

If you are a war pensioner and have difficulty walking because of your war disablement, you can get Mobility Supplement. You cannot get Mobility Supplement if you are already getting Mobility Allowance; see above. Mobility Supplement is £24.55 a week (April 1987 rates). Claim using leaflet MPL153, *Help for the War Disabled;* there is also more information in this leaflet.

Invalid Care Allowance

If you spend at least thirty-five hours a week looking after someone who gets Attendance Allowance or Constant Attendance Allowance under the Industrial Injuries or War Pensions schemes, you may be able to get Invalid Care Allowance. You can claim if you are between sixteen and sixty if you are a woman, sixty-five if you are a man. The allowance is £23.75 a week (April 1987 rates). Claim using the form in leaflet NI212, *Invalid Care Allowance;* there is also more information in this leaflet.

Other Cash Help

Income Support, see page 312.
Help with heating costs, see leaflet SB17, *Help with Heating Costs,* and Income Support, page 312.
Help with fares to hospital, leaflet H11, *Fares to Hospital.*
Help with rent and rates, see Housing Benefit, page 318.
NHS prescriptions: the following have the right to free NHS prescriptions: children under sixteen, women over sixty, men over sixty-five, war service pensioners (for items for their accepted disablement), people on Income Support or Housing Benefit or Family Credit, pregnant women or women who have had a baby within the last twelve months, people with illnesses needing a lot of medicines (such as epilepsy, Addison's disease, diabetes insipidus, diabetes mellitus). The full list of illnesses and the claim form are in leaflet P11, *NHS Prescriptions.*

Prescription Season Tickets

If you need prescriptions often but cannot get them free, you can buy a pre-payment certificate to cover four months or twelve months. This

will save you money if you need more than five items in four months or
more than fifteen items in twelve months. To claim get FP95 (EC95 in
Scotland) from a Social Security office, post office, chemist or NHS
Family Practitioner Committee (Health Board in Scotland); for more
information, see leaflet P11, *NHS Prescriptions*.

NHS Dental Treatment

People on Income Support, Housing Benefit, Family Credit get free
NHS dental treatment; ask your dentist for form F1D.

Help with the Cost of Glasses

NHS sight-tests are free for everyone. If you need new glasses and
qualify for help, you will be given a voucher to help pay for them. You
get a voucher automatically if you are a child under sixteen (or aged
under nineteen and still in full-time education) or in a family that gets
Income Support and Family Credit or free milk and vitamins on income
grounds, or free prescriptions on income grounds. If you qualify, tick
the box on the sight-test form; otherwise ask your optician for form F1.
For more details, see leaflet G11, *NHS Vouchers for Glasses*.

Services for Disabled People

See leaflets HB1, *Help for Handicapped People*, and HB2, *Equipment
for Disabled People*.
All leaflets are free of charge and available from your Social Security
office listed in the telephone directory under 'Social Security' or 'Health
and Social Security'. If you are unable to pick these up, write to: Leaflets
Unit, PO Box 21, Stanmore, Middlesex HA7 1AY.

CHAPTER 7: COPING WITH ILLNESS

Babies, Children and Adults in Hospital

Books for children going into hospital: *The Check Up*, Helen
Oxenbury (Walker, 1983); a humorous approach to a hospital check up.
Linda Goes to Hospital, Barry Wade (A & C Black, 1981); *Going to*

Hospital – Starter Facts (Macdonald Education, 1980); *Going Into Hospital*, Jean Althea (Dinosaur, 1986).

Complaints

Make your complaint in hospital to the ward sister. If you complain after leaving the hospital, do so in writing to the manager of the hospital or the District General Manager. If you are not satisfied with the result, complain in writing to the Community Health Council (address in the telephone-book). The next stage if there is no action is to write to: The Health Service Commissioner (Ombudsman), Church House, Great Street, London SW1. Tel. 01-212 7676.

If you have suffered a medical accident, i.e., wrong diagnosis or treatment, you will get help and support from: Action for the Victims of Medical Accidents (AVMA), 24 Southwark Street, London SE1 1TY. Tel. 01-403 4744.

Changing Your General Practitioner (GP)

If you have moved house, sign part A on your medical card, give it to the doctor in the new area that you live in. He will sign it and send it to the Family Practitioner Committee (FPC), who will send you a new one. The address is on your medical card. If you change GP for any other reason, you can ask your doctor to release you by signing part B of your card, which you must complete. Then take the card to the new doctor, who must sign part A and send it to the FPC. Or if you would rather not see your doctor you can send it directly to the FPC and tell them that you no longer wish to be on Dr X's list. They will return it with a slip which allows you to transfer not sooner than two weeks and not more than six weeks after they receive it. You then complete part 1 of the slip and take it to your new doctor, who must sign and send your card to the FPC for replacement. If you have lost your card, you will have to ask for an application form, which you will send with your letter of transfer. Complaints about your family doctor should be sent in writing to the FPC.

PARENTS LIFELINE,
Station House,
73d Stapleton Hall Road,
London N4 3QF.
Tel. 01-263 2265 (twenty-four-hour Crisis Line).

Offers support for parents whose children are critically ill in hospital. Volunteers are experienced and offer basic counselling skills and support, will meet parents on Intensive Care Units. Local contacts outside London.

Long-Term Illnesses

Asthma

ASTHMA SOCIETY AND FRIENDS OF THE ASTHMA RESEARCH COUNCIL,
300 Upper Street,
Islington,
London N1 2XX.
Tel. 01-226 2260.
Provides support for sufferers and their families. Ninety branches throughout the country. Publishes many useful pamphlets.

Acquired Immune Deficiency Syndrome (AIDS)

TERRENCE HIGGINS TRUST,
BM AIDS,
London WC1N 3XX.
Tel. 01-833 2971 (Monday–Friday 7 p.m.–10 p.m.; Saturday–Sunday 3 p.m.–10 p.m.).
Offers help and counselling to those with AIDS, their family and friends. Information about safe sex and blood tests.

WORLD ASSOCIATION OF PEOPLE WITH AIDS,
BM AIDS,
London WC1N 3XX.
Tel. 01-831 0330.
Aims to improve the quality of life of people with AIDS. Publishes *Living with AIDS*, a book for the newly diagnosed.

Back Trouble

BACK PAIN ASSOCIATION,
31–3 Park Road,
Teddington,

Middlesex TW11 OAB.
Tel. 01-977 5474/5.

Cancer

CARE (CANCER AFTER-CARE AND REHABILITATION SOCIETY),
Lodge Cottage,
Church Lane,
Timsbury,
Bath BA3 1LF.
Tel. 0761 70731.
Local support groups offer moral support and advice to cancer patients
and their families, visiting, financial help and information about hospice
care and welfare rights.

CANCER LINK,
46a Pentonville Road,
London N1 9HF.
Tel. 01-833 2451.
Information service and support groups. About 250 groups to support
the patient and their family.

CANCER RELIEF MACMILLAN FUND,
Anchor House,
15–19 Britten Street,
London SW3 3TY.
Tel. 01-351 7811.
Support, advice and help, including financial.

MASTECTOMY ASSOCIATION OF GREAT BRITAIN,
26 Harrison Street,
King's Cross,
London WC1H 8JG.
Tel. 01-837 0908.
Practical information before and after the removal of a breast.

WOMEN'S NATIONAL CANCER CONTROL CAMPAIGN,
1 South Audley Street,
London W1Y 5DQ.
Tel. 01-499 7532/3/4.
Encourages the prevention and early detection of cancer.
Recommended reading *Coping with Cancer* by Rachel Clyne (Thor-
sons, 1986); *Cancer: A Guide for Patients and Their Families* by Chris

and Sue Williams (Wiley, 1986); *Guide to Cancer* by Pat Young (Churchill Livingstone, 1986).

Chest and Heart Problems

BRITISH HEART FOUNDATION,
102 Gloucester Place,
London W1H 4DH.
Tel. 01-935 0185.
Publishes useful leaflets on all aspects of prevention and help with chest and heart problems.

CHEST HEART AND STROKE ASSOCIATION,
Tavistock House North,
Tavistock Square,
London WC1H 9JE.
Tel. 01-387 3012.
Helps sufferers and runs a programme of rehabilitation, counselling and welfare services.

Crohn's Disease and Ulcerative Colitis

CROHN'S IN CHILDHOOD RESEARCH APPEAL (CICRA),
48 Ewell Downs Road,
Ewell,
Epsom,
Surrey KT17 3BN.
Tel. 01-393 4403.
Self-help group for parents of children suffering from Crohn's disease or ulcerative colitis.

COELIAC SOCIETY OF THE UNITED KINGDOM,
PO Box 220,
High Wycombe,
Buckinghamshire HP11 2HY.
Tel. 0494 37278.
Seventy groups offering help, information and advice.

Colostomy

COLOSTOMY WELFARE GROUP,
38–9 Eccleston Square,
London SW1V 1PB.
Tel. 01-828 5175.

People who have had colostomy operations offer advice, support by phone or will visit.

Diabetes

BRITISH DIABETIC ASSOCIATION,
10 Queen Anne Street,
London W1M OBD.
Tel. 01-323 1531.
Help for diabetics of all ages. Publishes magazine every two months, free to members; numerous publications on all aspects of diabetes including children's books such as *I Have Diabetes*, 95p, and diet and recipe books such as *Better Cookery for Diabetics* by Jill Metcalfe, £2.95. Send for publication list.

Eczema

NATIONAL ECZEMA SOCIETY,
Tavistock House North,
Tavistock Square,
London WC1H 9SR.
Tel. 01-388 4097.
Offers support to sufferers and their families.

Epilepsy

NATIONAL SOCIETY FOR EPILEPSY,
Chalfont Centre for Epilepsy,
Chalfont St Peter,
Gerrards Cross,
Buckinghamshire SL9 ORJ.
Tel. 02407 3991.
Offers advice and help for people with epilepsy plus a residential and assessment unit for 400 people. Send for publication list.
Recommended reading: *Epilepsy: The Facts* by A. Hopkins (Oxford University Press, 1981); *The Epilepsy Handbook* by S. McGovern (Sheldon Press, 1982).

Ileostomy

ILEOSTOMY ASSOCIATION OF GREAT BRITAIN AND IRELAND,
Amblehurst House,
Chobham,
Woking,

Surrey GU24 8PZ.
Tel. 09905 8277 (twenty-four-hour answering service).
Support for those who have undergone or are about to undergo an
ileostomy operation. Advice and information. Home and hospital
visiting service available.

Kidney Disorders

THE BRITISH KIDNEY PATIENT ASSOCIATION,
Bordon,
Hampshire GU35 9JP.
Tel. 04203 2021/2.
Provides information on dialysis, transplantation, kidney donation and
all aspects of renal failure. Welfare information and financial aid to many
kidney patients. Three dialysis holiday centres in France, Majorca and
Sussex.
Recommended reading: *Timbo: A Struggle for Survival* by Elizabeth
Ward (New English Library, 1988), £2.95. The author of this very
moving book is the mother of Timothy, known to his family and friends
as Timbo.

Laryngectomy

NATIONAL ASSOCIATION OF LARYNGECTOMY CLUBS (NALC),
4th Floor,
39 Eccleston Square,
London SW1V 1PB.
Tel. 01-834 2857.

Leukaemia

LEUKAEMIA CARE SOCIETY,
PO Box 82,
Exeter,
Devon EX2 5DP.
Tel. 0392 218514.
Helps patients and their families, offers moral support, companionship
and hospital visits. Some financial assistance and eleven holiday
caravans.

Migraine

MIGRAINE TRUST,
45 Great Ormond Street,

London WC1N 3HD.
Tel. 01-278 2676.
Information, help and counselling. Support groups throughout the country.

Parkinson's Disease

PARKINSON'S DISEASE SOCIETY OF THE UNITED KINGDOM LTD,
36 Portland Place,
London W1N 3DG.
Tel. 01-323 1174.
List of contact addresses for support. Information leaflets and newsletter.

Psoriasis

PSORIASIS ASSOCIATION,
7 Milton Street,
Northampton NN2 7JG.
Tel. 0604 711129.
Self-help. Provides personal contact.

CHAPTER 8: MENTAL ILLNESS

Anxiety

BE NOT ANXIOUS,
33 Broadview Avenue,
Rainham,
Kent ME8 9DB.
Tel. 0634 34262 (1 p.m.–5 p.m.).
Counselling service by phone, letter or cassette for those with anxiety states or agoraphobia.

Phobias

ACTION ON PHOBIAS,
8 The Avenue,
Eastbourne,

Sussex BN21 3YA.
Tel. 03215 3227.
Provides tapes on relaxation, basic and advanced stress control, and all
kinds of phobias.

LIFESKILLS LTD,
3 Brighton Road,
London N2 8JU.
Tel. 01-346 9646.
Provides tape cassettes and books; training course in phobias, anxiety
states, over-eating, examination stress, smoking, insomnia and interper-
sonal problems.

OPEN DOOR ASSOCIATION,
c/o 447 Pensby Road,
Heswall,
Wirral,
Merseyside L61 9PQ.
Help for people suffering from anxiety, agoraphobia and other phobias.
Cassettes and books.

PHOBIC ACTION,
Greater London House,
547–51 High Road,
Leystone,
London E11 4PR.
Tel. 01-558 6012.
Community support for phobias and anxiety states. Home visiting: *Tel.*
01-554 0711 and *01-594 5386.*

PHOBIC TRUST,
25a The Grove,
Coulsdon,
Surrey CR3 2BH.
Tel. 01-660 0332.
Links small self-help groups throughout the country.

Depression

DEPRESSIVES ANONYMOUS,
36 Chestnut Avenue,
Beverley,

North Humberside HU17 9QU.
Tel. 0482-860619
Self-help for depressives.

DEPRESSIVES ASSOCIATED,
PO Box 5,
Castletown,
Portland,
Dorset DT5 1BQ.
Information, help and encouragement for people with depression and their families.

Schizophrenia

NATIONAL SCHIZOPHRENIA FELLOWSHIP,
78–9 Victoria Road,
Surbiton,
Surrey KT6 4NS.
Tel. 01-390 3651/2/3.
National network of support groups.

Anorexia Nervosa and Bulimia Nervosa

ANOREXIC AID,
The Priory Centre,
11 Priory Road,
High Wycombe,
Buckinghamshire HP13 6SL.
Self-help groups for those suffering from anorexia nervosa or bulimia nervosa. Send stamped addressed envelope for local contact and information.

ANOREXICS ANONYMOUS,
45a Castelnau,
Barnes,
London SW13 9RT.
Tel. 01-748 3994.
Counselling and advice for those suffering from anorexia nervosa, bulimia nervosa and other eating disorders.

ANOREXICS FAMILY AID,
Sackville Place,
44 Magdalen Street,
Norwich NR3 1JE.
Tel. 0603 619090.
Self-help groups all over the country to help those suffering from anorexia nervosa and bulimia nervosa and their families.

BANISH (BULIMIA AND ANOREXIA NERVOSA INTERMEDIATE SELF-HELP),
27 Lawrence Avenue,
Lytham St Annes,
Lancashire FY8 3LG.
Tel. 0253 726829.
Support groups in Lancashire, information sheets posted to other areas.

Stress

ORGANISATION FOR PARENTS UNDER STRESS (OPUS),
106 Godstone Road,
Whyteleaf,
Surrey CR3 OEB.
Tel. 01-645 0469.
Will give contact-numbers of groups all over the country for parents under stress.

SAMARITANS,
17 Uxbridge Road,
Slough,
Berkshire SL1 1SN.
Tel. 0753 32713/4.
Twenty-four-hour confidential service for people who are in despair, in distress or in need of someone to talk to. Telephone numbers of local contacts in the phone-book.

General Care

BRITISH HERBAL MEDICINE ASSOCIATION,
3 Amberwood House,
Walkford,
Christchurch,

Dorset BH23 5RT.
Tel. 0202 431901.
Able to refer people to local qualified herbal practitioners.

BRITISH HOLISTIC MEDICAL ASSOCIATION,
179 Gloucester Place,
London NW1 6DX.
Tel. 01-262 5299.
List of medically qualified practitioners of holistic medicine.

BRITISH HOMOEOPATHIC ASSOCIATION,
27a Devonshire Street,
London W1N 1RJ.
Tel. 01-935 2163.
Referral service for medically qualified homoeopathic doctors (Britain
and abroad).

BRITISH HYPNOTHERAPY ASSOCIATION,
67 Upper Berkeley Street,
London W1H 7DH.
Tel. 01-723 4443.
Details of nearest registered practitioners, their qualifications and fees.

BRITISH MEDICAL ACUPUNCTURE SOCIETY,
67–9 Chancery Lane,
London WC2 1AF.
Membership list available so that people can be referred to qualified
acupuncturists via their own GP.

BRITISH OSTEOPATHIC ASSOCIATION,
8–10 Boston Place,
London NW1 6QH.
Tel. 01-262 5250/1128.
Publishes a directory of medically qualified practitioners.

MIND (NATIONAL ASSOCIATION FOR MENTAL HEALTH),
22 Harley Street,
London W1N 2ED.
Tel. 01-637 0741.
Help and support for the mentally disabled and their families; 200 local
groups.

PHILADELPHIA ASSOCIATION,
14 Peto Place,
London NW1 4DT.
Tel. 01-486 9012.
Places of refuge, individual and group psychology for people in mental
distress.

PSYCHIATRIC REHABILITATION ASSOCIATION,
The Groupwork Centre,
21a Kingsland High Street,
London E8 2JS.
Tel. 01-254 9753 (twenty-four-hour answering service).
Encouragement and support for ex-psychiatric patients, providing day
and residential care, and social activities.

Senile Dementia

AGE CONCERN,
128 Great Victoria Street,
60 Pitcairn Road,
Mitcham,
Surrey CR4 3LL.
Tel. 01-640 5431.

ALZHEIMER'S DISEASE SOCIETY,
3rd Floor,
Bank Building,
Fulham Broadway,
London SW6 1EP.
Tel. 01-381 3177.
Assists with the problems of pre-senile and senile dementia and sup-
ports families. Over sixty-five branches throughout the country. See
also financial help from the DHSS, pages 312, 320 and 344, for all aspects
of mental ill-health.

CHAPTER 9: ADDICTION TO DRUGS, ALCOHOL AND TOBACCO

Drugs

FAMILIES ANONYMOUS UK,
88 Caledonian Road,
London N1 9DN.
Tel. 01-278 8805 (twenty-four-hour answering service).
A chain of self-help groups; parents who will help you.

NARCOTICS ANONYMOUS,
PO Box 246,
London SW10 ODP.
Tel. 01-351 6794/01-351 6066 (12 noon–8 p.m.).

RELEASE,
169 Commercial Street,
London E1 6BW.
*Tel. 01-377 5905 (10 a.m.–6 p.m., Monday–Friday), 01-603 8654
(twenty-four-hour emergency service).*

RE-SOLV,
St Mary's Chambers,
19 Station Road,
Stone,
Morden,
Surrey SM4 5DX.
Tel. 0785 817885/0785 46097.
Help and advice for all problems arising out of solvent abuse.

TURNING POINT,
3rd Floor,
CAP House,
9–12 Long Lane,
London EC1A 9HA.
Tel. 01-606 3947.
Rehabilitation for people with alcohol- or drug-related problems.

THE TEACHERS ADVISORY COUNCIL ON ALCOHOL AND DRUG
EDUCATION,
2 Mount Street,
Manchester 2.
Send for publications on alcohol and drug abuse.

Recommended Reading

Drug Misuse: A Basic Briefing (DM3), available from Dept DM, DHSS
Leaflets Unit, PO Box 21, Stanmore, Middlesex HA7 1AY. *What to Do
about Glue Sniffing*, available from your local Health Education Unit
(see in the phone-book under 'Health Authority'), or from Solvent
Abuse, Dept M50, 13–39 Standard Road, London NW10.

For further information and publications, contact: ISDD (Institute for
the Study of Drug Dependence), 1–4 Hatton Place, London EC1N 8ND.

Where to Get Help Locally

Ask your family doctor, or talk to a teacher, social worker, probation
officer or Citizen's Advice Bureau. They may be able to put you in
touch with a drug-counselling agency or other local help. If not,
contact: SCODA (Standing Conference on Drug Abuse), 1–4 Hatton
Place, London EC1N 8ND. *Tel. 01-430 2341.*

Alcohol

ALCOHOLICS ANONYMOUS,
General Service Office,
PO Box 1,
Stonebow House,
Stonebow,
York YO1 2NJ.
Tel. 0904 644026 (9 a.m.–5 p.m.). In Greater London: *Tel. 01-834 8202
(10 a.m.–10 p.m., and answering service).*
More than 2000 groups throughout the country.

ACCEPT (ADDICTIONS COMMUNITY CENTRES FOR EDUCATION,
PREVENTION, TREATMENT AND RESEARCH),
ACCEPT Clinic,
200 Seagrave Road,
London SW6 1RQ.
Tel. 01-381 3155/2112.

Counselling service and treatment centres for people with alcohol problems or suffering from tranquilliser misuse and their families.

AL-ANON FAMILY GROUPS,
61 Great Dover Street,
London SE1 4YF.
Tel. 01-403 0888 (twenty-four-hour service).
Help for relatives and close friends of problem drinkers; 800 groups all over the country.

Smoking

ASH (ACTION ON SMOKING AND HEALTH),
5–11 Mortimer Street,
London W1N 7RH.
Tel. 01-637 9843/6.
Help on how to give up smoking.

HEALTH EDUCATION COUNCIL,
78 New Oxford Street,
London WC1A 1AH.
Send for leaflets on how to give up smoking and many other health education leaflets.

Tranquillisers

CADETT,
22 Lansdown Road,
London W11 3LL.
Tel. 01-727 9447.
Counselling for soft-drug dependency, including tranquillisers, also family support, bereavement, alcohol and depression.

TRANX UK LTD (NATIONAL TRANQUILLISER ADVISORY COUNCIL),
25a Masons Avenue,
Wealdstone,
Harrow,
Middlesex HA3 5AH.
Tel. 01-427 2065/01-427 2827 (twenty-four-hour answering services).
Advice and support for users of tranquillisers. Self-help groups to help you give up your tranquillisers.

CHAPTER 10: DYING – THE LAST CHAPTER OF LIFE

Dying

MACMILLAN NURSES: Contact through your family doctor, community nurses or hospital doctors.

MARIE CURIE MEMORIAL FOUNDATION,
28 Belgrave Square,
London SW1X 8QG.
Tel. 01-235 3325.
Advisory or counselling service for cancer patients and relatives, provides day and night service run by community nurses for patients in their homes and runs welfare grant scheme.

ST CHRISTOPHER'S HOSPICE,
51–9 Lawrie Park Road,
Sydenham,
London SE26 6DZ.
Tel. 01-778 9252.
Can provide full information about hospice and home-care teams in the United Kingdom.

Bereavement

THE COMPASSIONATE FRIENDS,
6 Denmark Street,
Bristol BS1 5DQ.
Tel. 0272 292778.
An international organisation of bereaved parents offering friendship and understanding to other bereaved parents.

CRUSE,
126 Sheen Road,
Richmond,
Surrey TW9 1UR.
Tel. 01-940 4818 or 9047.
Provides a national service of bereavement counselling, advice and information, and social contact.

NATIONAL ASSOCIATION FOR WIDOWS,
c/o Stafford and District Voluntary Centre,
Chell Road,
Stafford ST16 2QA.
Tel. 0785 45465.
Advice and support group for widows.

FOUNDATION FOR THE STUDY OF INFANT DEATH,
15 Belgrave Street,
London SW1X 8PS.
Tel. 01-235 1721.
Advice and counselling for newly bereaved parents, particularly after a cot death.

Recommended Reading
L. Burton (ed),*Care of the Child Facing Death* (Routledge & Kegan Paul, 1974). Consumer Association, *What to Do when Someone Dies, Wills and Probate* (Hodder, 1986). I. Crichton, *The Art of Dying* (Peter Owen, 1976). J. Hinton, *Dying* (Penguin, 1967). C. Murray Parkes, *Bereavement* (Tavistock Press/Penguin, 1972).

Help from Social Security with Funeral Expenses
You or your spouse may get help from the Social Fund to help pay for a funeral if either of you is responsible for arranging the funeral. It depends whether you or your spouse get Income Support or Housing Benefit, and the amount of your savings and the cost of the funeral. The amount may be recovered from the estate of the person who has died. If you wish to claim, ask your Social Security Office for form SF200; and for more details see leaflet FB29, *Help When Someone Dies*, or D49, *What to Do after a Death*. See also page 312, Income Support, Housing Benefit, and page 335, Sick and Disabled.

Suicide

SAMARITANS,
17 Uxbridge Road,
Slough,
Berkshire SL1 1SN.
Tel. 0735 32713/4.
Offer twenty-four-hour service for people who feel suicidal.

CHAPTER 11: WORK

Careers Advice

Local careers services provide advice on training and employment opportunities, particularly for younger people. The address of your local careers office is in the phone-book under the Local Education Authority or Careers Service.

MANPOWER SERVICES COMMISSION: Look in the phone-book under Manpower Services Commission.

DEPARTMENT OF TRADE AND INDUSTRY,
1 Victoria Street,
London SW1H OET.
Tel. 01-215 5544.

INDUSTRY DEPARTMENT FOR SCOTLAND,
Alhambra House,
45 Waterloo Street,
Glasgow G2 6AT.
Tel. 041-2482855.
Assistance for business.

LOCAL ENTERPRISE AGENCIES: For your nearest agency, contact Business in the Community: *Tel. 01-235 3716,* or in Scotland *Tel. 031-5569761.*
These agencies can offer a wide range of advice and support to small businesses and those setting up in business.

EMPLOYMENT MEASURES UNITS:

Midlands
2 Duchess Place,
Hagley Road,
Birmingham B16 8NS.
Tel. 021-4557111;

North-East
Condercum House,
171 West Road,
Newcastle upon Tyne NE15 6PL.
Tel. 091-2722294;

North-West
Sunley Building,
Piccadilly Plaza,
Manchester M60 7JS.
Tel. 061-8329111;

South-East
Hanway House,
27 Red Lion Square,
London WC1R 4NH.
Tel. 01-405 8454;

Scotland
Pentland House,
47 Robb's Loan,
Edinburgh EH14 1UE.
Tel. 031-4438731;

Wales and South-West
1st Floor Government Buildings,
Block 4, St Agnes Road,
Gabalfa,
Cardiff CF4 3UF.
Tel. 0222-693131.

These offices will give advice and information on the New Worker's
Scheme, the Job Release Scheme and the Job Splitting Scheme.

Local Job Centres can be found in the telephone directory. Ask at the
Job Centre for leaflet *Action for Jobs,* which includes employment,
training and enterprise programmes of the Department of Employment
and Manpower Services Commission. Plenty of helpful advice for the
able-bodied and the disabled.

Recommended reading: Jobhunting Kit, Manpower Services Commission, COIC Information Centre, Room W1101, Moorfoot, Shef-
field S1 4BR. Sections on job-hunting, preparation and presentation at
job interviews.

Single Parents Working

NATIONAL COUNCIL FOR ONE PARENT FAMILIES,
255 Kentish Town Road,
London NW5 2LX.
Tel. 01-267 1361.
Publications on lone parenthood, policies for one-parent families,
welfare and legal rights for lone parents; reading-lists including topics
such as children in one-parent families, divorce, health, lone fathers,
schoolgirl mothers, single mothers and illegitimacy, and many others.
Send to the above address for the Council's leaflet of publications called
In Print.

Unemployment Benefit

If you have recently left school, you probably won't be able to get Unemployment Benefit because it's a National Insurance benefit and you probably won't have paid enough or any National Insurance contributions Class 1. If in doubt, ask at your unemployment office. To get Unemployment Benefit you must be willing and available to take up any suitable full-time work or an approved training scheme such as Youth Training Scheme (YTS). Unemployment Benefit is £31.45 a week (April 1987 rates).

How to Claim

If you are under eighteen and think that you may be entitled to Unemployment Benefit, take your P45 form and your NI number card to your careers office. (You will only have a P45 form if you have worked for an employer before. It is the form your employer gives you when you leave, and shows how much tax and National Insurance you have paid.) If you are eighteen or over, take them to the Unemployment Benefit office on the first day you are unemployed. For more information, see leaflet FB9, *Unemployed?*, and NI12, *Unemployment Benefit*.

If you have not got a job and do not have enough money to live on, you may be able to get Income Support; see page 312.

If you do voluntary or part-time work, your rights to various benefits and pensions may be affected. For information about Social Security benefits and pensions, and on your liability to pay NI contributions, get leaflet FB26, *Voluntary and Part-Time Workers*.

Debt

Debt: A Survival Guide, available from the Office of Fair Trading and the Central Office of Information.

Rights Concerning Employment

Dismissal: Provided you have worked for your employer for at least six months, you have the right to ask for a written statement of the reasons why you were dismissed. If your employer unreasonably refuses to provide a statement, or provides one which is inadequate and untrue, you can complain to an industrial tribunal.

Unfair Dismissal: Employees are protected against unjust dismissal by the unfair dismissal provisions of the legislation, but they must have worked for their employers for at least two years. If you think that you have been unfairly dismissed and have the necessary qualifying period of service, you may make a claim of unfair dismissal to an industrial tribunal. If your employer has made things so difficult for you at work that you had no choice but to resign, you may bring a claim of Constructive Unfair Dismissal to an industrial tribunal.

But there may be valid reasons for dismissal; your employer may have acted reasonably for any one of these reasons: inability to do the job; serious misconduct; another substantial reason, e.g., refusing to accept necessary changes in your job; redundancy; a statutory duty on either the employer or the employee which prevents the employment being continued.

Industrial Tribunal: You must apply within three months of your complaint happening (six months for redundancy). Do it as soon as possible.

If you are in a union, start there. They should be able to advise you. If you are not, go to the Citizen's Advice Bureau and ask for help. The Advisory Conciliation and Arbitration Service (ACAS) should also be able to help you. You will need a form (IT1) to apply to the tribunal. You can get that form from an Unemployment Benefit office or a job centre.

If the tribunal finds that you were unfairly dismissed, you may ask for either reinstatement, re-engagement or compensation. You may say which you want before or at the tribunal hearing. Do get help. It can be complicated. Help from:

EQUAL OPPORTUNITIES COMMISSION,
Overseas House,
Quay Street,
Manchester M3 3HN.
Tel. 061 833 9244.

COMMISSION FOR RACIAL EQUALITY,
Elliot House,
10–12 Allington Street,
London SW1E 5EH.
Tel. 01-828 7022.

LEGAL AID:
The Director,
Legal Aid,
Head Office,
Newspaper House,
8–16 Great New Street,
London EC4 3BN.
Tel. 01-353 7411.
Redundancy: Reasonable notice of redundancy is a right. Basically, you are entitled to as many weeks' notice as the number of years you have worked for a firm up to a maximum of twelve weeks.
Redundancy Pay: You won't get redundancy pay if you were sacked for any legitimate reason or for ill health; you have not worked for your present employer for at least sixteen hours per week for at least two years – or at least five years if you have only worked between eight and sixteen hours each week; you are a woman over sixty or a man over sixty-five; you work in one of the jobs that does not entitle you to redundancy pay.

Important: you may lose your redundancy pay if you are offered but refuse suitable alternative work; you leave without giving written notice; you leave for another job before you have been dismissed.

You will usually be able to get a redundancy payment from your employer if you are over eighteen and under sixty (sixty-five for a man) and had worked for your employer for at least two years since the age of eighteen. The amount of payment depends on your pay, age and length of service. Redundancy payments are not taxed if under £25,000. More information in leaflet NI231, *Made Redundant?*

Voluntary Work

VOLUNTEER CENTRE,
29 Lower Kings Road,
Berkhampsted,
Hertfordshire HP4 2AB.
Tel. 04427 73311.
Focal point for everything that concerns volunteers.

VOLUNTARY SERVICE OVERSEAS,
9 Belgrave Square,
London SW1X 8PW.
Tel. 01-235 5191.

To help Third World development by providing opportunities for skilled volunteers to work overseas.

Disabled and Handicapped Working

Information on facilities for further education from: Specialist Careers Officer for the Handicapped at Careers Office or Local Education Departments usually located in town hall or council offices.

THE SPASTICS SOCIETY,
Careers Office,
16 Fitzroy Square,
London W1P 5HQ.
Tel. 01-387 9571.

MENCAP PATHWAY EMPLOYMENT SERVICE,
169a City Road,
Cardiff CF2 3JB.
Tel. Cardiff 482072.

NETWORK FOR THE HANDICAPPED LTD (NETWORK),
16 Princeton Street,
London WC1R 4BB.
Tel. 01-831 8031/7740.
Offers legal advice, assistance and information to handicapped people and their families and represents them at tribunals where necessary.

Education Grants and Allowances for the Disabled

DIAL UK,
DIAL House,
117 High Street,
Clay Cross,
Near Chesterfield,
Derbyshire S45 9DZ.
Tel. 0246 864498.
Ask for advisory booklet by DIAL sponsored by Barclays called *16+ and What Now?*

CHAPTER 12: VICTIMS OF CRIME, VIOLENCE AND ACCIDENTS

Victims of Crime and Violence

NATIONAL ASSOCIATION OF VICTIMS SUPPORT SCHEMES,
17a Electric Lane,
Brixton,
London SW9 8LA.
Tel. 01-326 1084.
Offers practical information, advice and emotional support to people who have suffered as a result of crime. Local groups all over the country.

PARENTS OF MURDERED CHILDREN SUPPORT GROUP (part of the Compassionate Friends),
c/o Ann Robinson,
10 Eastern Avenue,
Prittlewell,
Southend-on-Sea,
Essex SS2 5QU.
Tel. 0702 68510.
This is a sub-group of the Compassionate Friends, who offer support and help to parents whose children have been murdered.

Burglary

Alarms:

THE NATIONAL SUPERVISORY COUNCIL FOR INTRUDER ALARMS,
St Ives House,
St Ives Road,
Maidenhead,
Berkshire SL6 1QS.
Tel. 0628 37512.
Conform to British Standards of installation. Send for a list of approved installers.

Rape

RAPE CRISIS CENTRE,
PO Box 69,
London WC1X 9NJ.
Tel. 01-278 3956 (office hours), 01-837 1600 (twenty-four-hour service).
Twenty-four-hour counselling, medical and legal help for women and
girls who have been raped or sexually abused. Service is free and
confidential. Groups all over the country.

Incest

INCEST CRISIS LINE,
32 Newbury Close,
Northolt,
Middlesex UB5 4JF.
*Tel. 01-422 5100/01-890 4732/01-302 0570/0702 584702/0965 31432
(mothers of abused children).*
Telephone helpline, advice, practical aid, guidance and assistance for the
victims of incest.

PARENTS ANONYMOUS LONDON,
6–9 Manor Gardens,
London N7 6LA.
Tel. 01-263 5672/01-263 8918 (twenty-four-hour service).
Confidential and sympathetic advice for parents who fear that they may
abuse their children. Doctors and social workers available if they are
needed.

NATIONAL SOCIETY FOR THE PREVENTION OF CRUELTY TO CHILDREN
(NSPCC),
67 Saffron Hill,
London EC1N 8RS.
Tel. 01-242 1626.
Twenty-four-hour service and practical help to parents who are under
stress and as a result physically or emotionally treat their children badly.
Prefer to keep families together and work towards this aim. Will treat
any information from family, friends or neighbours as confidential.

Battered Wives – Refuges

LONDON WOMEN'S AID,
52–4 Featherstone Street,
London EC1.
Tel. 01-251 6537 (twenty-four-hour answering service).

WOMEN'S AID FEDERATION LTD,
PO Box 391,
Bristol BS99 7WS.
Tel. 0272 420611.

WOMEN'S AID CENTRE,
116 Portland Street,
Manchester M1 4RP.
Tel. 061-236 6540 (10 a.m.–4 p.m., Monday–Friday).
Provides temporary accommodation in refuges for women and children
who have suffered physical, mental or sexual abuse. Also offers support
and advice to those women who are not willing to live in a refuge. With
120 groups all over the country.

Victims of Accident

FRIENDS OF THE INJURED,
The Trauma Foundation,
21 West Smithfield,
London EC1A 9HY.
With the guidance and support of the medical division, Friends of the
Injured will offer friendship, active assistance and advice to help injured
people to carry out ordinary everyday tasks or help resolve problems
which the injured person and/or his family are unable to cope with.